"An Ald Reht"

"An Ald Reht": Essays on Anglo-Saxon Law

By

Carole Hough

CAMBRIDGE SCHOLARS
PUBLISHING

"An Ald Reht": Essays on Anglo-Saxon Law,
by Carole Hough

This book first published 2014

Cambridge Scholars Publishing

12 Back Chapman Street, Newcastle upon Tyne, NE6 2XX, UK

British Library Cataloguing in Publication Data
A catalogue record for this book is available from the British Library

ISBN (10): 1-4438-5480-8, ISBN (13): 978-1-4438-5480-1

To my mother,
and to the memory of my father

CONTENTS

List of Plates

All plates can be found in the colour centrefold,
between Chapters 12 and 13.

List of Tables

PREFACE

These thirteen essays explore aspects of the legal system of Anglo-Saxon England, with a particular focus on the interpretation of individual laws and their implications for the position of women in society. They represent a programme of research carried out over the last two decades, building on each other to offer insights into the operation of English law from its beginnings in the sixth century through to its preservation in manuscripts dating from the tenth to early twelfth. As in many areas of Anglo-Saxon studies, the approach is inter-disciplinary, bringing together historical, linguistic and palaeographical evidence in order to advance our knowledge of this formative stage in the development of the English legislative tradition.

Part I is designed to outline major issues with regard to the promulgation, purpose and significance of the law-codes, and to provide a context for what follows. The first essay offers an introduction to the legal corpus, presenting an overview of the extant legislation from the Anglo-Saxon period alongside other types of legal documents such as charters and wills. The second essay discusses the relationship between secular and ecclesiastical law, and the third examines seventh-century legislation as evidence for the status of women in early Anglo-Saxon England. This essay draws substantially on revisionist interpretations of individual laws, presented in full in the eight essays comprising Part II. Finally, Part III focuses on manuscripts, arguing that the deployment of individual letter-forms, and of numerals as opposed to words, reflects the influence of different exemplars, and hence throws light on the relationships between different copies of the laws.

I have tried to avoid tampering too much with the original texts of the essays, since as Patrick Wormald has pointed out, 'Reprinted work that differs significantly from its original form sows bibliographical confusion'.[1] Nevertheless, it has been good to have an opportunity to make minor revisions and updatings, particularly to the references. Two important books that have been published since the majority of essays in Part II first appeared are Wormald's *The Making of English Law: King*

[1] P. Wormald, *Legal Culture in the Early Medieval West: Law as Text, Image and Experience* (London and Rio Grande, 1999), p. xvi.

Alfred to the Twelfth Century. volume I: Legislation and its Limits (Oxford: Blackwell, 1999), and Lisi Oliver's *The Beginnings of English Law* (Toronto: University of Toronto Press, 2002). Both will already be familiar to many readers of this book, and are recommended to others. An immensely useful resource is the Early English Laws website at http://www.earlyenglishlaws.ac.uk/, which includes much relevant information as well as images of manuscript folios written before 1225 containing law-codes.

Several of the essays, including the fourth, which is published here for the first time, were originally presented as conference papers, and I am grateful to the audiences for lively discussions and insightful comments. My debts to individual academic colleagues are too many to list, so I shall mention here only three: Christine Fell, who first inspired and supported my interest in Anglo-Saxon law; Patrick Wormald, who provided advice and encouragement over many years; and Daria Izdebska, who took on the task of preparing these essays for publication and whose meticulous standards are evidenced on every page of the resulting book. Any remaining errors are my sole responsibility.

Glasgow, November 2013

ACKNOWLEDGEMENTS

The essays reprinted here first appeared in the following places, and are reprinted by kind permission of the original publishers or copyright holders.

1. *A Companion to Anglo-Saxon Literature*, edited by Phillip Pulsiano and Elaine Treharne (Oxford: Blackwell, 2001), pp. 170–187.

2. *Anglo-Saxon Studies in Archaeology and History* 11 (2000), 133–141. Copyright (2000) School of Archaeology, Oxford University, and author.

3. *Nottingham Medieval Studies* 51 (2007), 207–230. University of Nottingham.

5. *Anglia: Zeitschrift für englische Philologie* 119.4 (2001), 554–578. Berlin and Boston: De Gruyter, http://www.degruyter.com/view/j/angl.

6. *Journal of English and Germanic Philology* 98.1 (1999), 1–16. Copyright 1999 by the Board of Trustees of the University of Illinois. Used with permission of the University of Illinois Press.

7. *Anglo-Saxon England* 23 (1994), 19–34. Cambridge University Press.

8. *Nottingham Medieval Studies* 37 (1993), 1–6. University of Nottingham.

9. *Neuphilologische Mitteilungen* 98.1 (1997), 43–51. Modern Language Society of Helsinki.

10. *Medium Ævum* 66.1 (1997), 1–27. Copyright Society for the Study of Medieval Language and Literature 1997.

11. *Nottingham Medieval Studies* 41 (1997), 1–12. University of Nottingham.

12. *Scriptorium* 55.1 (2001), 57–79. Bruxelles: Centre d'Etude des Manuscrits.

13. *Writing and Texts in Anglo-Saxon England*, ed. Alexander R. Rumble, Publications of the Manchester Centre for Anglo-Saxon Studies, 5 (Cambridge: D. S. Brewer, 2006) pp. 114–136. Reprinted by permission of Boydell & Brewer Ltd.

Plates 12.1–12.10 and 13.3–13.5 are reproduced by kind permission of Medway Archives and Local Studies Centre.

Plates 13.1 and 13.2 are reproduced by kind permission of the Master and Fellows of Corpus Christi College, Cambridge.

PART I:

LAW AND SOCIETY

1.

LEGAL AND DOCUMENTARY WRITINGS

First published 2001: *A Companion to Anglo-Saxon Literature*, ed. P. Pulsiano and E. Treharne (Oxford: Blackwell), 170–187.

1. Introduction

A substantial corpus of legal and documentary writings survives from Anglo-Saxon England in the form of law-codes, royal diplomas and writs, and non-royal charters such as leases, records of dispute settlements, memoranda and wills. Produced for different purposes and at different times and places, this heterogeneous body of material comprises a range of different types of evidence. The law-codes, issued by English kings from the seventh to the eleventh centuries, are essentially prescriptive, tabulating legal norms or aspirations which may or may not reflect actual contemporary practice. Diplomas, writs and other charters are more descriptive, illustrating various aspects of the working of the legal system as it applied in particular situations. Most evidence relating to criminal law is preserved in law-codes and records of dispute settlements, while civil matters such as land ownership and grants of privileges appear in diplomas, writs and leases. As regards social class, the law-codes make provision for all ranks of society from kings to slaves, whereas diplomas and writs deal primarily with the upper classes, as to a lesser extent do wills. Diplomas are characteristically written in Latin, laws, writs and wills in the vernacular; but not all are extant in their original form, and some survive only in much later copies or translations. Each of these major categories of source material presents its own difficulties, but each preserves important and unique insights into the structure of law and society during the Anglo-Saxon period.

2. Law-Codes

The earliest Anglo-Saxon legislation is represented by three law-codes produced in Kent during the seventh century and uniquely preserved in the twelfth-century *Textus Roffensis* manuscript (Medway Archive and Local Studies Centre, MS DRc/R1).[1] The first was issued by King Æthelberht (r. *c.* 580–616) following his conversion to Christianity, a legislative act inspired by the Roman mission under Augustine according to Bede's account in *Historia ecclesiastica* II.5:

> Qui inter cetera bona quae genti suae consulendo conferebat, etiam decreta illi iudiciorum iuxta exempla Romanorum cum consilio sapientium constituit; quae conscripta Anglorum sermone hactenus habentur et obseruantur ab ea. In quibus primitus posuit, qualiter id emendare deberet, qui aliquid rerum uel ecclesiae uel episcopi uel reliquorum ordinum furto auferret, uolens scilicet tuitionem eis, quos et quorum doctrinam susceperat, praestare.

> Among other benefits which he conferred upon the race under his care, he established with the advice of his counsellors a code of laws after the Roman manner. These are written in English and are still kept and observed by the people. Among these he set down first of all what restitution must be made by anyone who steals anything belonging to the church or the bishop or any other clergy; these laws were designed to give protection to those whose coming and whose teaching he had welcomed.[2]

The phrase *iuxta exempla Romanorum* 'after the Roman manner' has caused some problems since the extant code shows no signs of Roman influence; but it has been suggested that Bede was referring either to the Roman practice of written law, a cultural innovation introduced through the medium of the Church,[3] or to the Romano-Christian ideology responsible for establishing the king's role in maintaining law and order and enforcing religious standards.[4] Most recently, D. R. Howlett presents an analysis of the code as a ten-part structure 'presumably in imitation of the Decalogue', and argues that the arrangement of Æthelberht's laws

---

[1] *Textus Roffensis: Rochester Cathedral Library Manuscript A.3.5. Part I*, ed. P. H. Sawyer, Early English Manuscripts in Facsimile 7 (Copenhagen, 1957).

[2] *Bede's Ecclesiastical History of the English People*, ed. B. Colgrave and R. A. B. Mynors (Oxford, 1969), pp. 150–1.

[3] W. A. Chaney, 'Aethelberht's Code and the King's Number', *American Journal of Legal History* 6 (1962), 161–77, at 151.

[4] P. Wormald, '*Lex Scripta* and *Verbum Regis*: Legislation and Germanic Kingship, from Euric to Cnut', *Early Medieval Kingship*, ed. P. H. Sawyer and I. N. Wood (Leeds, 1977), pp. 105–38.

exhibits Biblical style attributable to the influence of the missionaries.[5] Apart from the first section, which deals with offences against the new religion, the code may have been based largely on earlier, oral legislation, issued for the first time in written form. The hierarchical structure, progressing in sequence through laws relating to the church, the king, *eorl* and *ceorl*, followed by a personal injury tariff and sections dealing with women, servants and slaves, suggests a codification of existing law rather than legislation in the initial stages of enactment, while close parallels with continental Germanic law testify to a common origin in an established legal tradition. An oral origin may also help to explain the lack of chapter numbers in the extant manuscript. Whereas later Anglo-Saxon law-codes are divided into numbered clauses in the *Textus Roffensis* as in other manuscript witnesses, the Kentish laws are written consecutively, with clause divisions indicated by the use of initials. This may reflect an original conception not as a written text but as a spoken utterance, where the visual clues provided by chapter numbers would be irrelevant.

A temporal link between the promulgation of the laws in written form and the arrival of the missionaries is supported not only by Bede's statement, but by references to the church in the opening sequence of clauses and by a rubric assigning the laws to the time of Augustine. Although the rubric is not original, having been added to the twelfth-century manuscript in a later hand, it may, as J. M. Wallace-Hadrill suggests, derive from a lost prologue similar to the preambles preceding other English and continental legislation, and would therefore suggest a *terminus ad quem* of 604 or 609, depending on alternative traditions of the date of Augustine's death.[6] The issue of the appropriate penalty for robbing a church, the topic of the opening section of Æthelberht's code, is raised in question 3 of the *Libellus responsionum*, a letter purportedly written by Gregory the Great in 601 in response to questions raised by Augustine,[7] and this is usually taken to indicate that the laws were then in the process of being drawn up. F. Liebermann therefore dated the code to *c.* 602/3.[8]

This dating was challenged by H. G. Richardson and G. O. Sayleson on the grounds that with the exception of the first article, the code shows no signs of Christian influence and could well pre-date the arrival of

---

[5] D. R. Howlett, *British Books in Biblical Style* (Dublin, 1997), pp. 257–62.

[6] J. M. Wallace-Hadrill, *Early Germanic Kingship in England and on the Continent* (Oxford, 1971), p. 39.

[7] *Historia ecclesiastica* I, 27.

[8] *Die Gesetze der Angelsachsen*, ed. F. Liebermann, 3 vols. (Halle. 1903–16) III, 2.

Augustine.[9] Dismissing the opening section as an interpolation and claiming that Æthelberht was never actually converted to Christianity, they proposed that the laws may have been issued earlier in his reign, belonging to the late sixth century rather than the early seventh. Their hypothesis is not widely accepted by present-day scholars, but the suggestion that the opening section may be spurious is regularly revived, most recently by Patrizia Lendinara.[10] Supporting evidence is generally adduced from stylistic differences between Æthelberht 1 and the rest of the code, and from the fact that theft from the Church is penalized more heavily than theft from the king, requiring higher amounts of compensation than are compatible with Gregory's instructions to Augustine in *Libellus responsionum* 3, where simple restitution alone is required. Neither point, however, stands up to scrutiny. First, provisions relating to compensation for the church and its officials cannot have been drawn up until after the arrival of the missionaries, so they would inevitably be written in a different style from laws that were already in existence orally. Second, excessive amounts of restitution to the church are a recurrent feature of early legislation. Ch. 6 of the second series of Alamannic laws, issued during the early eighth century, demands restitution of twenty-seven times the amount stolen from a church,[11] while ch. 1.3 of the mid-eighth-century Bavarian laws demands restitution of between nine and twenty-seven times.[12] In England, the early-eighth-century *Theodore Penitential* book 1, sect. 3.2, directs that money stolen from a church is to be repaid fourfold, from a layman twofold, again contravening Gregory's instructions.[13] Æthelberht's code is therefore far from exceptional in this respect. It should also be noted that although numbered as a single clause in modern editions, regulations regarding restitution to the church are set out in the manuscript as seven separate provisions, whose cumulative weight is less easy to set aside than an isolated edict. The fact that this section was already present in the copy of Æthelberht's laws available to Bede in the early eighth century further reduces the likelihood that it is not original.

---

[9] H. G. Richardson and G. O. Sayles, *Law and Legislation from Æthelberht to Magna Carta* (Edinburgh, 1966), pp. 1–9.

[10] P. Lendinara, 'The Kentish Laws', *The Anglo-Saxons from the Migration Period to the Eighth Century: An Ethnographic Perspective*, ed. J. Hines (Woodbridge, 1997), pp. 211–43, at p. 236.

[11] *Leges Alamannorum*, ed. K. A. Eckhardt, Monumenta Germaniae Historica, Legum sectio I: Leges nationum Germanicarum 5.1 (Hanover, 1966), 74.

[12] *Lex Baiwariorum*, ed. E. von Schwind, Monumenta Germaniae Historica, Legum sectio I: Leges nationum Germanicarum 5.2. (Hanover, 1926), 270–2.

[13] *Councils and Ecclesiastical Documents Relating to Great Britain and Ireland*, ed. A. W. Haddan and W. Stubbs, 3 vols. (Oxford, 1869–73) III, 179.

It may be helpful to approach the discrepancy between Æthelberht 1 and *Libellus responsionum* 3 from another angle. Rather than playing a part in the drafting of Æthelberht's laws, Gregory's ruling on theft may have been issued in response to the unacceptable provisions of the opening section, a possibility raised briefly by Wallace-Hadrill.[14] Recent work on the *Libellus* itself, addressing the issue of why Augustine asked the questions to which Gregory sends his considered answers, may support this view. In an important article on the implications of the *Libellus* for missionary activity in southern England, Rob Meens points out that Augustine is unlikely to have been unfamiliar with church doctrine on matters such as ritual purity, the topic of questions 8 and 9, and suggests that the questions were raised because of points of difference between the British and Roman Churches.[15] A similar explanation may underlie question 3 on theft from a church. It is equally unlikely that Augustine would have been unfamiliar with church doctrine concerning theft, so it seems reasonable to deduce that here too what he required was not information but authority. Whether this was also necessitated by a challenge from the British Church, or by an excess of enthusiasm on the part of the compilers of the opening section of Æthelberht's code, the logical conclusion is that the *Libellus* in fact post-dates the promulgation of this sequence of laws. I would therefore suggest that the code as a whole must have been issued before rather than after 601, the most likely dating parameters being *c.* 599–600.

The second series of Kentish laws represents the only legislation to survive in the joint names of two Anglo-Saxon kings: Hlothhere, who succeeded his brother Egbert (664–73) to reign from 673 or 674 to 685, and Egbert's son Eadric, who defeated his uncle in battle in February 685 but held the throne only until an invasion by Cædwalla of Wessex in the following year. It is uncertain whether the laws were actually issued jointly. Alternative possibilities are that Eadric may have reissued during his own reign laws previously drawn up by Hlothhere, or that the extant series was compiled later from laws originally issued separately by each king. However, since there is evidence to support a tradition of joint kingship in Kent,[16] it is perhaps most likely that Eadric was associated

[14] Wallace-Hadrill, *Early Germanic Kingship*, p. 40.

[15] R. Meens, 'A Background to Augustine's Mission to Anglo-Saxon England', *Anglo-Saxon England* 23 (1994), 5–17.

[16] B. A. E. Yorke, 'Joint Kingship in Kent *c.* 560 to 785', *Archæologia Cantiana* 99 (1983), 1–19; *Charters of St Augustine's Abbey Canterbury and Minster-in-Thanet*, ed. S. E. Kelly, Anglo-Saxon Charters 4 (Oxford, 1995), 195–203.

with his uncle for part of the latter's reign, and that the laws were issued during a period of amity between the two rulers.

It is clear from the preamble that the laws of Hlothhere and Eadric were intended not as a self-contained code but as a supplement to the existing body of Kentish legislation:

Hloþhære 7 Eadric Cantwara cyningas ecton þa ǽ, þa ðe heora aldoras ær geworhton, ðyssum domum þe hyr efter sægeþ.[17]	Hlothhere and Eadric, kings of the people of Kent, augmented the laws which their predecessors had made by these decrees which are stated hereafter.

Æthelberht's laws were therefore still in force. The new series is again largely concerned with financial compensation, providing fuller details of procedural matters than the earlier code. The opening sequence, dealing with manslaughter committed by an *esne* (chs. 1–4), follows almost directly on from clauses concerning the unfree towards the end of Æthelberht's code. A widow's right to custody of her children, briefly alluded to in Æthelberht 79,[18] is here reaffirmed with additional information on the age of majority and the role of the paternal kin (ch. 6). Information is provided on the value of the Kentish *wergild* (chs. 1 and 3), as well as on procedures for law-suits (chs. 5, 7–10) and on violations of a householder's *mund* (chs. 11–14). Introduced for the first time is a concern with trade, relating both to merchants and others visiting Kent, and to Kentish men buying goods in London (chs. 15–16).

Æthelberht's code was further supplemented by a third series of Kentish laws issued by King Wihtred (691–725) in 695. In contrast with the essentially secular legislation of Æthelberht and of Hlothhere and Eadric, the emphasis throughout Wihtred's code is on establishing Christian principles and strengthening the position of the church. The church is exempted from taxation and allocated a *mundbyrd* equal to that of the king (chs. 1 and 2). Illicit cohabitation is prohibited (chs. 3–6), penalties are established for working on the Sabbath or eating during a fast (chs. 9–11, 14–15), and for the first time, laws are issued forbidding heathen practices, that is, making offerings to devils (chs. 12 and 13). In chs. 16–24, the legal status of different ranks of the clergy is specified, and

---

[17] *Gesetze,* ed. Liebermann I, 9.

[18] C. Hough, 'The Early Kentish "Divorce Laws": a Reconsideration of Æthelberht, chs. 79 and 80', *Anglo-Saxon England* 23 (1994), 19–34, reprinted in this volume.

a communicant is allowed to swear an oath of greater value than a non-communicant.

The Kentish laws offer many difficulties of interpretation, partly because they represent a stage of the language for which little other evidence survives. Æthelberht's code comprises not only the beginning of legislative tradition in Anglo-Saxon England, but the earliest extant text in Old English. As Patrick Wormald demonstrates, its simplicity of syntax corresponds to a very primitive state of prose writing, with some 75 per cent of clauses representing simple conditionals.[19] A more sophisticated phraseology is found in the laws of Hlothhere and Eadric and of Wihtred, reflecting a developing prose style which offers little support for a recent suggestionthat the extant version of all three codes may represent a translation from an original Latin text.[20] Given, however, that the continental Germanic law-codes are in Latin, it remains uncertain why the vernacular was used in England. Wormald suggests the possibility that 'in England (as in Ireland) there was no one with the knowledge of Latin to bridge the gap between local custom and Latin vocabulary',[21] but as Susan Kelly points out, Theodore and/or Hadrian were resident in Kent at the time when the later seventh-century law-codes were produced.[22] The archaic vocabulary of all three codes, containing a high proportion of *hapax legomena*, presents a number of interpretational cruces, and these are exacerbated by the cryptic wording of the laws, which assume a pre-existing knowledge of the circumstances and tend to state baldly the amount of compensation due in a particular situation without specifying who is to pay it or to whom. This lack of clarity has led to much uncertainty concerning the application of individual laws, and is in part responsible for the current polarization of opinions concerning the position of women in early Anglo-Saxon England, with one group of scholars believing that women paid and received compensation on their own behalf, while another concludes that a male relative or guardian must have been responsible for all such transactions.

Roughly contemporary with Wihtred's legislation are the laws of the West Saxon King Ine (688–725/6), extant only as an appendix to the late-ninth-century *domboc* of Alfred the Great, but originally issued

[19] P. Wormald, '"Inter cetera bona ... genti suae": Law-Making and Peace-Keeping in the Earliest English Kingdoms', *Settimane di studio del Centro italiano di studi sull'alto medioevo* 42 (1995), 963–93, at 969–70.

[20] Lendinara, 'The Kentish Laws'.

[21] Wormald, '*Lex Scripta* and *Verbum Regis*', p. 115.

[22] S. Kelly, 'Anglo-Saxon Lay Society and the Written Word', *The Uses of Literacy in Early Mediaeval Europe*, ed. R. McKitterick (Cambridge, 1990), p. 57.

between 688 and 694. These are much less coherently structured than the Kentish codes, with several topics treated more than once; and it is possible, as Wormald suggests, that the extant compilation represents six individual sets of laws.[23] In this case, the dating evidence, based on a reference in the preamble to a bishop known to have died by 694 (Bishop Erconwald), would apply only to the first set (chs. 1–27), so that Ine's other laws may have been issued at any time up to the end of his reign in 725 or 726. It is uncertain to what extent they were edited by Alfred prior to inclusion with the composite *domboc*, but since a number of provisions are included which clash with Alfred's own,[24] there is a reasonable probability that Ine's laws have been reproduced in their entirety. A degree of co-operation between the kingdoms of Wessex and of Kent is reflected in a clause which appears in almost identical form in Ine 20 and Wihtred 28, stating that a stranger who leaves the road and neither shouts nor blows a horn may be killed with impunity on the assumption that he is a thief. Although sometimes taken as evidence of borrowing from one code to the other,[25] the fact that the clause is concerned with travellers, possibly from one kingdom to another, seems rather to reflect a reciprocal agreement between the two rulers.

No other regional law-codes have survived; and unless some of Ine's laws do indeed date from the latter part of his reign, no Anglo-Saxon legislation is extant from the eighth century or the first three-quarters of the ninth. From the late ninth century onwards, however, Anglo-Saxon kings became prolific legislators. The first national code was issued *c*. 887–93 by Alfred the Great, and survives in six manuscripts, the earliest being the mid-tenth-century Cambridge, Corpus Christi College 173. It is possible that, like Alfred's translation of Pope Gregory's *Cura pastoralis*, copies were distributed to various parts of his kingdom for consultation by the local authorities.[26] This would account for a number of references to the *domboc* in later codes, to which Simon Keynes draws attention.[27] Its practical value, none the less, must have been very limited. In all extant manuscripts, the combined laws of Alfred and Ine are prefaced by a lengthy translation of Mosaic law and are divided into 120 chapters to

[23] Wormald, '"Inter cetera bona …', 977–83.

[24] C. Hough, 'Alfred's *Domboc* and the Language of Rape: a Reconsideration of Alfred, ch. 11', *Medium Ævum* 66 (1997), 1–27, at 2–3, reprinted in this volume.

[25] Richardson and Sayles, *Law and Legislation*, p. 13.

[26] S. Keynes, 'Royal Government and the Written Word in Late Anglo-Saxon England', *The Uses of Literacy in Early Mediaeval Europe*, ed. R. McKitterick (Cambridge, 1990), pp. 226–57, at p. 232.

[27] *Ibid*. p. 233.

reflect, as Wormald argues, a symbolic unity between the Israelites and the Anglo-Saxons as the chosen races of God.[28] The chapter-divisions are illogical in terms of subject matter, and would have made it difficult to use the *domboc* for any practical purpose; but the symbolic value of 120 as the age of Moses the Lawgiver and as the number of members of the early Church evidently took precedence over functional considerations. There is in fact reason to believe that the Anglo-Saxon law-codes were not primarily intended for practical use. Not only are they highly selective and occasionally inconsistent, as with the discrepancies between the Alfred/Ine sections of the *domboc*, but there is little evidence that they were actually consulted in courts of law. Wormald points out that none of the Anglo-Saxon charters recording judicial decisions makes any reference to the written texts, [29] and Katherine O'Brien O'Keeffe draws attention to two documented cases where the written law was evidently not put into effect.[30] The law-codes do not represent legislation in the modern sense, but served a symbolic purpose, establishing the role of the king as law-giver. As Simon Keynes and Michael Lapidge comment in connection with Alfred's *domboc*, 'The act of law-making was a public display of a king's royal power, and provided an opportunity for him to express his political and ideological aspirations in legal form'.[31] It was a matter not simply of legislative content but of image-building.

The symbolic function of law-making helps to explain why so many Anglo-Saxon kings issued law-codes, even when they were essentially reiterating existing legislation. The extant body of Anglo-Saxon law is highly repetitive, with many clauses reproduced either exactly or in modified form in later codes, and it is likely that the preservation of early texts was often due to their potential use in the drafting of new laws. At least two series of laws were issued by Alfred's son Edward the Elder (*c.* 900–25), six by Alfred's grandson Æthelstan (*c.* 925–39), three by Edmund (*c.* 939–46), four by Edgar (*c.* 959–63), ten by Æthelred (*c.* 978–1014), and two by the Danish conqueror Cnut (*c.* 1020–3), many of whose laws, like those of his predecessor Æthelred, were drafted by Archbishop Wulfstan of York.[32] Not all represent royal codes as such,[33]

---

[28] Wormald, '*Lex Scripta* and *Verbum Regis*', p. 132.

[29] Wormald, '"Inter cetera bona ...', 122.

[30] K. O'Brien O'Keeffe, 'Body and Law in Late Anglo-Saxon England', *Anglo-Saxon England* 27 (1998), 209–32, at 228–9.

[31] S. Keynes and M. Lapidge, *Alfred the Great: Asser's 'Life of King Alfred' and Other Contemporary Sources* (London, 1983), p. 39.

[32] D. Whitelock, 'Wulfstan and the Laws of Cnut', *English Historical Review* 63 (1948), 433–52, reprinted in her *History, Law and Literature in 10th–11th Century*

and not all survive in their entirety. For instance, fragments only are extant of IX and X Æthelred, while III and IV Æthelstan, III Edmund, and IV Æthelred are preserved only in an early twelfth-century Latin translation of Anglo-Saxon law known as *Quadripartitus*, recently discussed in detail by Wormald.[34] Some codes have been lost altogether. These include treaties relating to the northern and eastern parts of England mentioned in II Edward 5.2, and laws issued to enforce the Christian religion by Æthelberht's grandson Eorcenberht (r. 640–64), now known only from a passing reference by Bede in *Historia ecclesiastica* III.8.

No legislation is extant from the kingdoms of Mercia or Northumbria, although Alfred claims in the Preface to his own law-code to have drawn on the laws of Offa of Mercia as well as those of Æthelberht of Kent and Ine of Wessex:

> 49.9. Ic ða Ælfred cyning þás togædere gegaderode 7 awritan het, monege þara þe ure foregengan heoldon, ða ðe me licodon; 7 manege þara þe me ne licodon ic áwearp mid minra witena geðeahte, 7 on oðre wisan bebead to healdanne. Forðam ic ne dorste geðristlæcan þara minra awuht fela on gewrit settan, forðam me wæs uncuð, hwæt þæs ðam lician wolde ðe æfter ús wæren. Ac ða ðe ic gemette awðer oððe on Ines dæge, mines mæges, oððe on Offan Mercna cyninges oððe on Æþelbryhtes, þe ærest fulluhte onfeng on Angelcynne, þa ðe me ryhtoste ðuhton, ic þa heron gegaderode, 7 þa oðre forlét.[35]

> I then, King Alfred, gathered these together and ordered to be written many that pleased me of those which our forefathers kept; and I rejected many of those that did not please me with the advice of my councillors, and ordered them to be kept in a different way. I did not dare presume to set in writing many at all of my own, because I did not know what would please those who should come after us. But I collected herein those that I found which seemed to me most just, either from the time of my kinsman Ine, or of Offa, king of the Mercians, or of Æthelberht, who first received baptism among the English, and I omitted the others.

England (London, 1981); D. Whitelock, 'Wulfstan's Authorship of Cnut's Laws', *English Historical Review* 70 (1955), 72–85, reprinted in her *History, Law and Literature in 10th–11th Century England*, (London, 1981).

[33] Keynes, 'Royal Government and the Written Word', pp. 235–42.

[34] P. Wormald, '"*Quadripartitus*"', in *Law and Government in Medieval England and Normandy: Essays in Honour of Sir James Holt*, ed. G. Garnett and J. Hudson (Cambridge, 1994), pp. 111–47.

[35] *Gesetze,* ed. Liebermann I, 46.

No trace of Offa's laws has survived, unless, as Wormald suggests, Alfred was referring not to a vernacular law-code but to an extant Latin capitulary of twenty canons dating from 786.[36] The capitulary was presented by papal legates to a synod held by Offa under their auspices, and has a number of points in common with some of Alfred's own laws. For instance, there are striking parallels between the treatment of marriage and inheritance in the fifteenth and sixteenth canons and in Alfred 8, one of three clauses in the *domboc* to contain Mercian vocabulary.[37] This in itself, however, seems to point to the existence of an intermediate text in the vernacular. Furthermore, Wormald's suggestion that Offa's laws may have taken a different form from 'a code in the mould of Æthelberht's, Ine's and Alfred's own'[38] may allow insufficient weight to the political value of such a code. Wormald himself has done much to demonstrate the prestige-value of early legislation as a reflection of 'the ideological aspirations of Germanic kingship';[39] and since both Kent and Wessex had already produced written legislation, it would be surprising if Mercia had not taken the opportunity to do the same. Although some at least of the Mercian laws mentioned in Alfred's Preface may have borne a close resemblance to the capitulary of 786, this does not preclude the existence of a separate law-code. Possibly the papal legates took existing legislation into consideration when drafting their canons for the Mercian people: alternatively, as Whitelock, Brett and Brooke suggest, the laws of Offa may well have been influenced by the legatine decrees.[40]

Apart from any of Offa's laws that may be represented in the 786 capitulary or in Alfred's *domboc*, the only records of either Mercian or Northumbrian legislation are preserved in short texts known as *Norðleoda Laga* 'Law of the North people' and *Mircna Laga* 'Law of the Mercians'. These form part of a group of unofficial texts concerned with social rank and *wergild* values, apparently compiled by Archbishop Wulfstan during the early eleventh century. In the same group are *Geþyncðo* 'Rank', *Að* 'Oath', and *Hadbot* 'Compensation for offences

[36] P. Wormald, 'In Search of King Offa's "Law-Code"', *People and Places in Northern Europe 500–1600: Essays in Honour of Peter Hayes Sawyer*, ed. I. Wood and N. Lund (Woodbridge, 1991), pp. 25–45. The capitulary is published in *Alcuini Epistolae*, ed. E. Dümmler, Monumenta Germaniae Historica, Epistolarum Karolini Aevi 2 (Frankfurt, 1895), no. 3.

[37] *Councils and Synods with other Documents Relating to the English Church: I. AD 871–1204*, ed. D. Whitelock, M. Brett and C. N. L. Brooke, 2 vols. (Oxford, 1981) I, 18.

[38] Wormald, 'In Search of', p. 43.

[39] Wormald, '*Lex Scripta* and *Verbum Regis*', p. 106.

[40] *Councils and Synods*, ed. Whitelock et al. I, 18.

against people in holy orders'. Marriage law is documented in another unofficial text known as *Be Wifmannes Beweddunge* 'On the betrothal of a woman', also generally dated to the late tenth or early eleventh century despite close parallels with a sequence of laws dealing with the marriage contract in the seventh-century code of Æthelberht. Both state that a payment is to be made by the prospective bridegroom (Æthelberht 77; *Wif* 2); both refer to the *morgengifu*, or property granted by the bridegroom to the bride (Æthelberht 81; *Wif* 3), both specify the amount of property to which the woman will be entitled if her husband dies first (Æthelberht 78; *Wif* 4); and both stipulate that the widow's inheritance rights are to be reduced on remarriage (Æthelberht 80; *Wif* 4). Comparison of the two texts would suggest that marriage law remained remarkably stable throughout the Anglo-Saxon period.

The same cannot be said of Anglo-Saxon law in general. In other respects, there are fundamental differences between the seventh-century law-codes and those of later kings. Crimes are increasingly regarded as offences against society rather than against individuals, leading to a change of emphasis from the compensation of victims to the punishment of offenders. The principle of straightforward financial redress which underlies much of Æthelberht's legislation is replaced by punitive fines, capital punishment and mutilation. Thus whereas the penalty for theft in Æthelberht's code ranges from twofold to twelvefold restitution depending on the status of thief and victim (chs. 1, 4, 9, 28, 90), the same offence under Wihtred is punishable by slavery or death (chs. 26–8), and under Ine by slavery, death or mutilation (chs. 7, 12, 37). By the time of King Alfred, anyone who stole from a church might lose his hand (ch. 6), while IV Æthelstan 6 provides for a thief to face death by drowning if a free person, and by stoning or burning if a slave. An effective illustration of changing attitudes is provided by the treatment of adultery in seventh- and eleventh-century law. According to Æthelberht 31, the adulterer has to pay a *wergild* (whether his own or that of the woman or her husband is unclear), and also to meet the financial costs of acquiring a second wife for the wronged husband. Under II Cnut 53, on the other hand, the guilty woman forfeits all her property to her husband, and loses her nose and ears.

3. Charters

Like the practice of written legislation, charters were introduced to England by the church during the seventh century. Characteristically written in Latin on a single sheet of parchment, their initial purpose was to record a grant of land or of privileges by the king to a religious house, and to act as the title-deed for the estate of 'bookland' thereby created. These royal grants are known as 'diplomas', a term which also includes confirmations of earlier grants by later kings. Gradually, however, charters came to be used for a wider range of purposes, including grants to laymen, records of dispute settlements, memoranda, and over a hundred extant leases, some of which are in the vernacular. The vernacular was also used for the boundary clauses of diplomas, identifying the extent of the estates granted and exchanged. These are of the first importance in the study of land use and administration, and often contain early forms of place-names otherwise recorded only in post-Conquest sources.

Out of *c.* 1,100 extant diplomas, about two hundred survive in their original single-sheet form, preserving crucial evidence for the study of Anglo-Saxon script and manuscript production. The rest comprise later copies, often entered into cartularies, and these can be difficult to distinguish from forgeries fabricated in support of a spurious claim to land or privileges, some of which may include genuine elements. Indeed, the authenticity even of single-sheet versions can only be verified through close study of palaeographic, linguistic and diplomatic features.[41] Scholarly opinion in respect of individual charters is summarized by P. H. Sawyer,[42] whose total of 1,539 entries (excluding bounds and lost or incomplete texts) includes not only the royal diplomas issued in Latin by Anglo-Saxon kings, but also the various other types of charters to be discussed below. A new edition of the entire corpus is currently in progress.[43] All will be cited by the number assigned to them in Sawyer's catalogue, abbreviated as S.

---

[41] P. Chaplais, 'Some Early Anglo-Saxon Diplomas on Single Sheets: Originals or Copies?', *Journal of the Society of Archivists* 3.7 (1968), 315–36, reprinted in *Prisca Munimenta*, ed. F. Ranger (London, 1973), pp. 63–87.

[42] *Anglo-Saxon Charters: An Annotated List and Bibliography*, ed. P. H. Sawyer, Royal Historical Society Guides and Handbooks 8 (London, 1968). A revised version is now available at http://www.esawyer.org.uk.

[43] *Charters of Rochester*, ed. A. Campbell, Anglo-Saxon Charters 1 (London, 1973); *Charters of Burton Abbey*, ed. P. H. Sawyer, Anglo-Saxon Charters 2 (London, 1979); *Charters of Sherborne*, ed. M. A. O'Donovan, Anglo-Saxon Charters 3 (Oxford, 1988); *Charters of St Augustine's Abbey Canterbury and Minster-in-Thanet*, ed. S. E. Kelly, Anglo-Saxon Charters 4 (Oxford, 1995); *Charters of Shaftesbury Abbey*, ed. S. E. Kelly, Anglo-Saxon Charters 5 (Oxford, 1996); *Charters of Selsey*, ed. S. E. Kelly, Anglo-Saxon Charters 6 (London, 1998); *Charters of Abingdon Abbey, Part 1*, ed. S. E. Kelly, Anglo-Saxon Charters 7 (Oxford, 2000); *Charters of Abingdon Abbey, Part 2*, ed. S. E. Kelly, Anglo-Saxon Charters 8 (Oxford, 2001); *Charters of the New Minster*, Winchester,

The date at which charters were first produced in England is uncertain. The earliest authentic examples date from the 670s, but display a variety of formulas which suggests that the charter tradition was already well established and beginning to diversify. It is fully possible that earlier documents may have been lost, and although circumstantial evidence points to Archbishop Theodore as the instigator, a case has also been made for Augustine.[44] It is even possible that the origins of the charter tradition are to be sought outside the Roman mission. As with the law-codes, the majority of early records are from the south of England, weighting the evidence in favour of a connection with the Italian church; but Wormald[45] argues for a more diverse origin, including both Frankish and Celtic influences, and this view may be supported by recent work highlighting the role of the Frankish and British churches in the conversion process.[46]

The structure of the royal diploma is heavily formulaic, characteristically beginning with an invocation, followed by a religious proem, the grant itself, a sanction, boundary-clause, dating-clause and witness-list. There are many variations from this norm, however, and distinctive groups of charters have been identified, such as the 'alliterative' type of the 940s and 950s, and the 'Dunstan B' type of the mid-tenth century. Characteristic features of the former include a rhythmical style with much alliteration,

---

ed. S. Miller, Anglo-Saxon Charters 9 (Oxford, 2001); *Charters of St Paul's, London*, ed. S. E. Kelly, Anglo-Saxon Charters 10 (Oxford, 2004); *Charters of Malmesbury Abbey*, ed. S. E. Kelly, Anglo-Saxon Charters 11 (Oxford, 2005); *Charters of St Albans*, ed. J. Crick, Anglo-Saxon Charters 12 (Oxford, 2007); *Charters of Bath and Wells*, ed. S. E. Kelly, Anglo-Saxon Charters 13 (Oxford, 2007); *Charters of Peterborough Abbey*, ed. S. E. Kelly, Anglo-Saxon Charters 14 (Oxford, 2009); *Charters of Glastonbury Abbey*, ed. S. E. Kelly, Anglo-Saxon Charters 15 (Oxford, 2012); *Charters of Northern Houses*, ed. D. A. Woodman, Anglo-Saxon Charters 16 (Oxford, 2012); *Charters of Christ Church Canterbury, Part 1*, ed. N. P. Brooks and S E Kelly, Anglo-Saxon Charters 17 (Oxford, 2013); *Charters of Christ Church Canterbury, Part 2*, ed. N. P. Brooks and S. E. Kelly, Anglo-Saxon Charters 18 (Oxford, 2013).

44 P. Chaplais, 'The Origin and Authenticity of the Royal Anglo-Saxon Diploma', *Journal of the Society of Archivists* 3 (1965), 48–61, reprinted in *Prisca Munimenta*, ed. F. Ranger (London, 1973), pp. 28–42; P. Chaplais, 'Who Introduced Charters into England? The Case for Augustine', *Journal of the Society of Archivists* 3 (1969), 526–42, reprinted in *Prisca Munimenta*, ed. F. Ranger (London, 1973), pp. 88–107.

45 P. Wormald, *Bede and the Conversion of England: the Charter Evidence*, Jarrow Lecture (1984), pp. 13–19.

46 Meens, 'A Background to Augustine's Mission'; I. Wood, 'The Mission of Augustine of Canterbury to the English', *Speculum* 69 (1994), 1–17.

the use of the third person rather than the first, and some unusual inclusions in the witness-lists. This group appears to be associated with Bishop Cenwald of Worcester, who appears in all examples with full witness-lists. The 'Dunstan B' charters, produced between about 951 and 975 and using a diplomatic protocol apparently developed by Abbot Dunstan for the Glastonbury scriptorium, begin with a dating-clause instead of an invocation or proem, and share a preference for particular formulas to introduce the boundary-clause and witness-list, and for the attestation.[47]

By the later Anglo-Saxon period, writs had also come into use. Generally much shorter than diplomas and written in the vernacular, these were sealed letters intended to be read out to the shire court or other official meeting, announcing changes in land ownership and the like. Some 120 writs survive, six of them in their original form. Characteristic features include an opening protocol which names the sender and the addressee(s) and contains a greeting. Although writs are extant only from the eleventh century, the occurrence of a similar protocol at the beginning of King Alfred's Preface to his translation of Pope Gregory's *Cura pastoralis* suggests that they were already current in England by the late ninth, and this is confirmed by a reference to an *ærendgewrit* in a passage interpolated by Alfred into his translation of St Augustine's *Soliloquia*.[48]

Up to the end of the ninth century, royal charters appear to have been drawn up at religious houses by ecclesiastical scribes acting on behalf of the beneficiaries. Thus Kentish charters were produced at Rochester and at Christ Church, Canterbury, and Mercian charters at Worcester. The situation during the tenth and eleventh centuries is less clear. There is evidence for some form of centralized production from the 930s and 940s, and much discussion has focused on the putative existence of a royal chancery. On the one hand, the case that charters continued to be produced in ecclesiastical scriptoria has been strongly made by Pierre Chaplais.[49] On the other hand, the view that a central agency attached to the king's household was responsible for the production of royal diplomas and writs

[47] S. Keynes, 'The "Dunstan B" Charters', *Anglo-Saxon England* 23 (1994), 165–93.

[48] F. E. Harmer, *Anglo-Saxon Writs* (Manchester, 1952), pp. 10–11.

[49] Chaplais, 'The Origin and Authenticity'; P. Chaplais, 'The Anglo-Saxon Chancery: From the Diploma to the Writ', *Journal of the Society of Archivists* 3 (1966), 160–76, reprinted in *Prisca Munimenta*, ed. F. Ranger (London, 1973), pp. 43–62; P. Chaplais, 'The Royal Anglo-Saxon "Chancery" of the Tenth Century Revisited', *Studies in Medieval History Presented to R. H. C. Davis,* ed. H. Mayr-Harting and R. I. Moore (London, 1985), pp. 41–51.

is developed by Keynes,[50] who also suggests that such an agency may already have been emerging in ninth-century Wessex.[51]

Charters shed additional light on various aspects of Anglo-Saxon law and society, supplementing the information preserved in the law-codes. Despite the non-survival of written legislation from the early kingdom of Mercia, for instance, charter evidence attests to the existence of an organised system of law and administration. In S 98, King Æthelbald of Mercia (r. 716–57) grants remission of the taxes due on two ships to Bishop Milred and the church of Worcester. This shows that a toll system was already in operation, although the earliest extant legislation on this subject dates from the late tenth century (IV Æthelred 2). Remission of the toll due on two ships is also granted to Abbess Sigeburga by King Eadberht of Kent *c.* 761 (S 29), while S 91 records a grant of half the toll due on a ship to Abbess Eadburga by King Æthelbald in 748. The earliest extant Anglo-Saxon diploma to refer to the public duties of bridge and fortress building is S 59 dating from 770, a grant of land by Uhtred, sub-king of the Hwicce, endorsed by King Offa of Mercia. Of particular interest is a grant of land by Offa to Worcester Cathedral between 793 and 796 (S 146), which details the amount of taxes that could be raised from the estate. As well as constituting 'the only surviving statement of the amount the king could draw from an estate as his farm',[52] this suggests that the position of the church was less strong in Mercia than in Kent, where according to Wihtred 1 it was exempted altogether from taxation.

A substantial minority of extant charters are issued or witnessed by women, providing eloquent testimony to the legal autonomy of women in Anglo-Saxon England.[53] The grantees of many early diplomas are also female, testifying to the position of women as rulers of religious communities during the seventh and eighth centuries; while later grants and leases to laywomen, either in their own right or in association with husbands or other relatives, illustrate the role of women as land-holders throughout the Anglo-Saxon period. Charter evidence also confirms that

---

[50] S. Keynes, *The Diplomas of King Æthelred 'The Unready' 978–1016: a Study in their Use as Historical Evidence* (Cambridge, 1980); S. Keynes, 'Regenbald the Chancellor (*sic*)', *Anglo-Norman Studies* 10 (1988), 185–222.

[51] S. Keynes, 'The West Saxon Charters of King Æthelwulf and his Sons', *English Historical Review* 109 (1994), 1109–49.

[52] *English Historical Documents c. 500–1042*, ed. D. Whitelock, 2nd ed. (London, 1979), p. 507.

[53] C. Hough, 'Women and the Law in Early Anglo-Saxon England' (unpubl. PhD dissertation, Univ. of Nottingham, 1993), pp. 174–203.

women were considered to be 'oath-worthy',[54] and indeed that they played a part in the administration of justice. As Frank Stenton points out, whereas the 'earliest unequivocal reference to the exercise of jurisdiction by a lord of lower rank than the king'[55] (i.e. the granting of *sacu* and *socn*) occurs in a charter of 956 in favour of the Archbishop of York (S 659), the second such grant three years later concerns the allocation of similar rights over Howden and eight dependent villages in south Yorkshire to a woman named Quen (S 681). This has obvious implications for the legal status of women during the mid-tenth century.

Charters also constitute a primary source of evidence for Anglo-Saxon case-law. Wormald identifies a corpus of 178 cases drawn from a variety of sources including charters, chronicles, saints' lives and Domesday Book.[56] Many contain details of legal procedure; and several instances of disputes which turned on the possession of diplomas or other forms of documentation are discussed by Wormald and Keynes.[57] This section will conclude with a brief examination of a case involving criminal law, in order to consider how far the course adopted corresponds to provisions within the law-codes.

The case is no. 27 in Wormald,[58] and is recorded in S 362, a grant to Æthelwulf of an estate at Wylye in Wiltshire by Edward the Elder. The grant includes a reference to an earlier forfeiture of the estate by Wulfhere and his wife, which resulted from Wulfhere's desertion under King Alfred:

> Ista vero prænominata tellus primitus fuit. præpeditus á quodam duce nomine Wulhere . et ejus uxore quando ille utrumque et suum dominum regem Ælfredum . et patriam ultra jusjurandum quam regi et suis omnibus optimatibus juraverat sine licentia dereliquit. Tunc etiam cum omnium juditio

> Truly this afore-named estate was originally forfeited by a certain ealdorman, Wulfhere by name, and his wife, when he deserted without permission both his lord King Alfred and his country in spite of the oath which he had sworn to the king and all his leading men. Then by the judgment of all the

[54] Hough, 'Alfred's *Domboc* and the Language of Rape', at 6–7.
[55] F. Stenton, *Anglo-Saxon England*, 3rd ed. (Oxford, 1971), p. 495.
[56] P. Wormald, 'A Handlist of Anglo-Saxon Lawsuits', *Anglo-Saxon England* 17 (1988), 247–81.
[57] P. Wormald, 'Charters, Law and the Settlement of Disputes in Anglo-Saxon England', *The Settlement of Disputes in Early Medieval Europe*, ed. W. Davies and P. Fouracre (Cambridge, 1986), pp. 149–68; Keynes, 'Royal Government', at 248–51.
[58] Wormald, 'A Handlist'.

sapientium Geuisorum et Mercensium . potestatem et hereditatem dereliquit agrorum.[59]

councillors of the Gewisse and of the Mercians he lost the control and inheritance of his lands.[60]

To some extent this is in line with the law-codes. Ine 51, which, as part of the composite *domboc* issued by King Alfred, was presumably in force at the time of Wulfhere's desertion, states that a nobleman was to forfeit his land for neglecting military service:

Gif gesiðcund mon landagende forsitte fierd, geselle CXX scill. 7 ðolie his landes; unlandagende LX scill.; cierlisc XXX scill. to fierdwite.[61]

If a man of *gesith* rank who owns land neglects military service, he is to pay 120 shillings and forfeit his land; one who does not own land, 60 shillings; one of *ceorl* rank, 30 shillings as a fine for neglecting military service.

Forfeiture continued to be the penalty for desertion throughout the later Anglo-Saxon period, appearing again in the eleventh-century laws of Cnut. II Cnut 77 reads as follows:

77. 7 se man, þe ætfleo fram his hlaforde oððe fram his geferan for his yrhþe, si hit on scipfyrde, si hit on Landfyrde, þolige ealles þæs þe he age 7 his agenes feores; 7 fo se hlaford to þam æhtan 7 to his lande, þe he him ær sealde.

77. And the man, who flees from his lord or from his companions because of his cowardice, whether it is on a naval or military expedition, is to forfeit all that he possesses and his own life; and the lord is to succeed to the possessions and to his land, which he had given him.

77,1. 7 gyf he bocland hæbbe, ga *þæt* þam cingce to handa.[62]

77,1. And if he has bookland, it is to pass into the king's hands.

---

59 *Cartularium Saxonicum*, ed. W. de G. Birch, 3 vols. and index (London, 1885–93) II, 243.

60 *English Historical Documents*, ed. Whitelock, p. 542.

61 *Gesetze,* ed. Liebermann I, 112.

62 *Ibid*. I, 364.

The reference to King Alfred in S 362 may suggest that Wulfhere deserted from an army under the personal command of the king. This situation is dealt with in VI Æthelred 35:

7 gif hwa of fyrde butan leafe gewende, þe cyning [sylf on] sy, plihte his are.[63]	And if anyone deserts an army where the king himself is present, he is to forfeit his property.

There is also another point to be considered. Wulfhere's crime was not simply that he deserted, but that he contravened his sworn oath to king and country. This topic is covered by the opening chapter of Alfred's code, which deals with the keeping of oaths and shows that in extreme instances, oath-breaking could result in the forfeiture of property. According to Alfred 1.4, an oath-breaker who refused to submit to punishment would be liable for such a penalty:

Gif hine mon togenedan scyle, 7 he elles nylle, gif hine mon gebinde, þolige his wæpna 7 his ierfes.[64]	If he will not submit unless force is used, and he is bound, he is to forfeit his weapons and his property.

Thus Wulfhere could have forfeited the estate at Wylye on either count.

There is, however, one aspect of this case that appears to be at odds with written legislation. This concerns the reference to Wulfhere's wife. According to S 362, the estate was forfeited by Wulfhere and his wife because of his desertion. The extent of his wife's involvement, if any, is quite unclear, and she is not even named in the charter. In general, the law-codes define precisely the limits of a married woman's liability. For instance, Wihtred 12 distinguishes between the case of a husband who secretly makes offerings to devils and one who does so in collaboration with his wife. In the first instance, the husband alone is to forfeit his possessions and his *healsfang*; in the second, both husband and wife are to forfeit their possessions and *healsfang*. Ine 7 stipulates that a woman is implicated in a theft perpetrated by her husband only if she knows about it; and Ine 57 specifically exonerates a married woman from responsibility for her husband's theft of cattle, allowing her to retain her third of the joint property if she declares on oath that she has not eaten the stolen meat. Similarly in VI Æthelstan 1, a married woman is allocated a third of the goods forfeited by a husband convicted of theft, provided she has not

[63] *Ibid.* I, 256.
[64] *Ibid.* I, 48.

acted as accessory to the crime. Here, on the other hand, Wulfhere's wife seems to have forfeited her share of an estate for a crime committed by her husband alone. In this respect, the scrupulous division of responsibility implied by the law-codes does not appear to have been carried out in practice.

4. Wills

The testamentary dispositions of nearly seventy Anglo-Saxon men and women are recorded in vernacular charters dating from the mid-ninth century onwards. The corpus is established by Lowe,[65] who identifies a total of sixty-four vernacular wills, about a third of them extant in single-sheet charters datable to the eleventh century or before, and the rest in post-Conquest copies. Forty-six are by men (including two kings – Alfred and Eadred), thirteen by women, and five in the joint names of husband and wife. Other wills have been lost, including that of King Æthelwulf of Wessex (839–58), referred to in the will of his son Alfred the Great; and several are known only from Latin translations or abstracts preserved in the *Historia Ramesiensis*, the *Liber Eliensis*, and the St Albans cartulary. In some instances, wills were made orally in the presence of witnesses, as with the dispositions of Æthelric, son of Æthelmund (S 1187), and these may not always have been committed to writing.[66]

The extant wills fall into two main categories: the bequest or *post obitum* gift, and the multi-gift will. Three types of *post obitum* bequest are represented: the *precaria oblata* (*traditio cum reservatione usufructus*), where the property was first given to the donee but was then reacquired for one or more lives; the *precaria remuneratoria* (*census pro investitura*), whereby the donor paid rent to the donee in acknowledgement of the latter's right to the property, and the *precaria data* (*traditio post obitum*), whereby the property continued to belong to the donor until death without payment of any fee. Multi-gift wills include a number of bequests, but seldom dispose of the testator's entire possessions. Although there are at least three accounts of death-bed wills,[67] the majority of dispositions

---

[65] K. A. Lowe, 'Lay Literacy in Anglo-Saxon England and the Development of the Chirograph', *Anglo-Saxon Manuscripts and their Heritage*, ed. P. Pulsiano and E. M. Treharne (Aldershot, 1998), pp. 161–204.

[66] *Anglo-Saxon Wills*, ed. D. Whitelock (Cambridge, 1930), pp. xvi–xviii.

[67] *The Will of Æthelgifu: a Tenth Century Anglo-Saxon Manuscript*, ed. D. Whitelock (Oxford, 1968), pp. 19–20.

appear to have been made while the testator was alive and well, and they could be added to, emended, and even revoked.[68]

Unlike diplomas, which functioned as title-deeds, wills were often produced in duplicate or triplicate so that copies could be held by the testator and principal beneficiaries. King Alfred, in revising his earlier testamentary dispositions, declares that he had entrusted copies to many witnesses and has now burned all that he could find:

Þonne hæfde ic ær on oðre wisan awriten ymbe min yrfe þa ic hæfde mare feoh 7 ma maga 7 hæfde monegum mannum þa gewritu oðfæst 7 on þas ylcan gewitnesse hy wæron awritene. Þonne hæbbe ic nu forbær'n'ed þa ealdan þe ic geahsian mihte. Gif hyra hwylc funden bið, ne forstent þæt naht, forþam ic wille þæt hit nu þus sy mid Godes fultume.[69]	Now I had made other arrangements in writing concerning my inheritance, when I had more money and more kinsmen, and had committed the documents to many men, with whose cognisance they had been drawn up. I have now burnt the old ones which I could hear of. If any of these is found, it shall be of no value, since these are the arrangements which I now desire should stand, with God's help.[70]

Some wills were produced as chirographs, documents copied in duplicate, triplicate or quadruplicate on a single sheet of parchment and cut into separate parts after the word CYROGRAPHVM had been written across the whole. Each of the interested parties could then retain a part. Lowe establishes a corpus of sixty-four pre-Conquest charters produced as chirographs, and comments that the device 'seem[s] to have been almost exclusively reserved for recording contracts between parties'.[71] Of these sixty-four examples, no fewer than twelve are vernacular wills, while the remainder are mostly leases, agreements, and records of dispute settlements.

---

[68] K. A. Lowe, 'The Nature and Effect of the Anglo-Saxon Vernacular Will', *Journal of Legal History* 19 (1998), 23–61, at 36–8.

[69] *Select English Historical Documents of the Ninth and Tenth Centuries*, ed. F. E. Harmer (Cambridge, 1914), p. 18.

[70] *Ibid.* p. 52.

[71] Lowe, 'Lay Literacy in Anglo-Saxon England', p. 171.

5. Concluding Remarks

Any study of Anglo-Saxon legal and documentary writings must bear in mind the intensely fragmentary and unbalanced nature of the surviving material. Early law-codes are extant from one area of the country only, and deal with a very limited range of topics. Records of case-law belong primarily to the reigns of Alfred, Edgar and Æthelred, with a preponderance of early records from Kent. Writs appear to have been in use by the late ninth century, but survive only from the eleventh, while the royal diplomas attested from the 670s onwards may represent either the beginning of the Anglo-Saxon charter tradition or the continuation of a practice inaugurated almost seventy years before. The majority of extant wills are preserved in the archives of Bury St Edmunds, Christ Church, Canterbury, and the Old and New Minsters, Winchester, suggesting heavy losses from other parts of the country. Certain areas of the law are unrepresented in any of the known sources, and it is not always clear whether the relevant evidence has been lost or never existed in written form. A case in point is suggested by the boundary clauses of diplomas and leases of land, over a thousand of which are extant. It is axiomatic that penalties must have been in place for interfering with the boundary markers establishing the legal perimeters of the estates, but no trace of legislation or case-law on this topic survives. Comparison with continental law-codes confirms that such penalties were customary under Germanic law. Ch. 55 of the Burgundian code issued by King Gundobad during the late fifth century is concerned with disputes over boundaries, stipulating in 55.6 that a freeman who moved or destroyed a boundary marker was to lose his hand, while a slave guilty of the same offence was to be killed.[72] According to chs. 236–41 of the laws issued by the Lombard King Rothair during the seventh century, a freeman would incur financial penalties for digging out boundary markers, cutting down marked trees, or making false marks on other trees, with mutilation or death as the corresponding punishment for a slave.[73] Ch.12 of the mid-eighth-century Bavarian laws also contains lengthy provisions relating to deliberate or accidental interference with boundary markers, and to disputes over boundary markers,[74]

---

[72] *Leges Burgundionum*, ed. L. R. de Salis, Monumenta Germaniae Historica, Legum Sectio I: Leges nationum Germanicarum 2.1 (Hanover, 1892), 90–1.

[73] *Leges Langobardorum* , ed. F. Bluhme, Monumenta Germaniae Historica, Leges 4 (Hanover, 1869), 59.

[74] *Lex Baiwariorum*, ed. von Schwind, 398–405.

as does book 10, ch. 3 of the Visigothic Code.[75] Similar regulations must have been in force in England to safeguard the integrity of estate boundaries, and it is highly unlikely that no disputes ever turned on such a point; but this is an area of jurisprudence for which documentary evidence is entirely lacking. It serves as a salutary reminder that despite the range and variety of the material discussed in this chapter, there are many aspects of Anglo-Saxon government and administration on which the sources are completely silent.

[75] *Leges Visigothorum*, ed. K. Zeumer, Monumenta Germaniae Historica, Legum Sectio I: Leges nationum Germanicarum 1 (Hanover, 1902), 396–9.

2.

Penitential Literature and Secular Law in Anglo-Saxon England

First published 2000: *Anglo-Saxon Studies in Archaeology and History* 11, 133–141.

A close relationship between penitential handbooks and secular law-codes in Anglo-Saxon England has long been recognised.[1] Not only do they contain similar types of material, providing catalogues of penalties for offences, but a number of clauses within the extant law-codes have traditionally been taken to acknowledge and to support the authority of the penitentials, indicating that church and state acted together in the suppression of sin and crime. The degree of influence between ecclesiastical and secular legislation, however, remains uncertain, as does the extent to which penitential discipline may have been incorporated into the legal system.[2] The purpose of this paper is to attempt to address these questions by examining references to the penitentials within secular law, and references to secular law within the penitentials. It is my contention that previous studies of the law-codes have not always distinguished carefully enough between general allusions to penance and specific references to the penitential handbooks, and that only the latter can be regarded as firm evidence that the penitentials themselves functioned as an integral part of the legal process.[3]

---

[1] A ground-breaking study was T. P. Oakley, *English Penitential Discipline and Anglo-Saxon Law in Their Joint Influence* (New York, 1923).

[2] Such uncertainties are not, of course, confined to Anglo-Saxon England: the relationship between penitential literature and continental law is also problematic. Important work in this area has been carried out by Raymund Kottje, who argues strongly that the penitentials and the law-codes relate to distinct spheres. See for instance his '*Busse oder strafe?* Zur *Iustitia* in den *Libri Paenitentiales*', *Settimane di studio del Centro italiano di studi sull'alto medioevo* 42 (1995), 443–74.

[3] All quotations from Anglo-Saxon law are taken from *Die Gesetze der Angelsachsen*, ed. F. Liebermann, 3 vols. (Halle, 1903–16). Quotations from the

It is difficult to establish the date at which references to penance begin to appear in Anglo-Saxon law. Oakley claims that they are to be found in the late-seventh-century Kentish laws of Wihtred:

> Special decrees or laws demanding penance for specific crimes ... appear in Kent as early as Wihtred, who provides excommunication, with penance, for fornication and also gives special oath-privileges to a communicant.[4]

This is, however, less than certain. The pertinent clauses are Wihtred, chs. 3 and 4:

3. Unrihthæmde mæn to rihtum life mid synna hreowe tofon oþþe of ciricean ganaman ascadene sien.	3. Men living in illicit cohabitation are to turn to a right life with repentance of sins, or to be excluded from the fellowship of the Church.
4. Æltheodige mæn, gif hio hiora hæmed rihtan nyllað, of lande mid hiora æhtum 7 mid synnum gewiten;	4. Foreigners, if they will not regularise their marriages, are to depart from the land with their goods and their sins.

---

three eighth-century penitential handbooks traditionally known as the *Theodore Penitential*, the *Egbert Penitential* and the *Bede Penitential* are from *Councils and Ecclesiastical Documents Relating to Great Britain and Ireland*, ed. A. W. Haddan and W. Stubbs, 3 vols. (Oxford, 1869–73). Quotations from the later handbooks traditionally known as the *Pseudo-Egbert Confessional* and the *Pseudo-Egbert Penitential* are from *Ancient Laws and Institutes of England*, ed. B. Thorpe, folio edition (London, 1840), although I do not necessarily follow Thorpe's punctuation. Quotations from the *Late Old English Handbook for the Use of a Confessor* are from R. Fowler, 'A Late Old English Handbook for the Use of a Confessor', *Anglia* 83 (1965), 1–34. The penitential handbooks are discussed in detail by A. J. Frantzen, 'The Tradition of Penitentials in Anglo-Saxon England', *Anglo-Saxon England* 11 (1983), 23–56, who prefers the term *Scrift boc* for the *Pseudo-Egbert Confessional*. See also T. Charles-Edwards, 'The Penitential of Theodore and the Iudicia Theodori', *Archbishop Theodore: Commemorative Studies on his Life and Influence*, ed. M. Lapidge, Cambridge Studies in Anglo-Saxon England 11 (Cambridge, 1995), pp. 141–74. A major study of Anglo-Saxon legislation is P. Wormald, *The Making of English Law: King Alfred to the Twelfth Century. volume I: Legislation and its Limits* (Oxford, 1999). For short accounts and additional references, see A. J. Frantzen, 'Confession and Penance' and 'Penitentials', and P. Wormald, 'Laws', in *The Blackwell Encyclopaedia of Anglo-Saxon England*, ed. M. Lapidge et al. (Oxford, 1999), p. 120, pp. 362–3 and pp. 279–80.

[4] Oakley, *English Penitential Discipline*, pp. 144–5.

4,1. swæse mæn in leodum ciriclicæs gemanan ungestrodyne þoligen.[5]	4,1. Our own men, in this people, are to forfeit the fellowship of the Church, without confiscating their goods.[6]

The influence of the Church is manifest here as elsewhere in Wihtred's law-code, but there is no indication that the phrase *mid synna hreowe* refers to penance. The law makes no mention of a confessor nor of prescribed penalties, and it should be noted that Wihtred's code predates the earliest known English penitential, the eighth-century *Theodore Penitential*. It is fully possible that the phrase *mid synna hreowe* refers to repentance in general rather than to penance in particular.

Frantzen too adduces Wihtred's laws as evidence that 'the early law codes treat ecclesiastical penance as an addition to secular penalties', citing, in addition to the clauses quoted above, regulations concerning the protection of church property and the enforcement of Sunday observance.[7] These topics, however, may be taken to indicate support for ecclesiastical authority without necessarily involving penitential discipline. Much depends on the interpretation of the phrase *7 boca dom* in Wihtred, ch. 5:

Gif ðæs geweorþe gesiþcundne mannan ofer þis gemot, þ*æt* he unriht hæmed genime ofer cyngæs bebod 7 biscopes 7 boca dom, se þæt gebete his dryhtne C scll' an ald reht.[8]	If after this meeting, any *gesith-born* man chooses to enter into an illicit union in spite of the command of the king and the bishop and the decree of the books, he is to pay to his lord 100 shillings according to ancient law.[9]

---

[5] *Gesetze*, ed. Liebermann I, 12.

[6] *English Historical Documents c.500–1042*, ed. D. Whitelock, 2nd ed. (London, 1979), p. 396.

[7] A. J. Frantzen, *The Literature of Penance in Anglo-Saxon England* (New Brunswick, 1983), p. 79. The same position is taken by E. N. Lert, 'Fault in the Law: the Influence of the Penitentials on the Anglo-Saxon Legal System', *Catholic Lawyer* 31 (1987), 264–76, at 274, but this cannot be regarded as a fully independent viewpoint since Lert relies heavily on the work of Frantzen and Oakley, repeatedly citing their studies rather than the primary texts. In his summary account on 'Confession and Penance' in *The Blackwell Encyclopaedia of Anglo-Saxon England*, Frantzen claims only that 'the interaction of penance and secular law is apparent as early as the laws of Alfred'.

[8] *Gesetze*, ed. Liebermann I, 12.

[9] *English Historical Documents*, ed. Whitelock, pp. 396–7.

Frantzen contends that '"books" here could mean the penitentials as well as ecclesiastical canons'.[10] Such a possibility, however, is not even considered by recent editors of the laws. Liebermann notes that the books in question are 'Kanonische Rechtsbücher, hier nicht nur Bibel;'[11] Attenborough repeats Schmid's suggestion that the relevant statutes may have been those laid down at the Council of Hertford;[12] and Whitelock glosses succinctly, 'books of ecclesiastical canons'.[13] Indeed, it seems to me that penitential handbooks would not quite fit the context here. The phrase *bōca dom* is parallel to *cyngæs bebod 7 biscopes*, and refers to laws that have been broken. The penitentials were lists of penalties rather than of rules: 'systematic manuals of penance containing long schedules, or tariffs, of specific penances for corresponding lists of sins'.[14] They would therefore be expected to figure, if at all, in the latter part of the sentence, in conjunction with the fine of one hundred shillings.

It would appear, then, that there are no conclusive references to penance in the law-codes of seventh-century England. Unfortunately no legislation survives from the eighth or early ninth centuries;[15] but Alfred's great *domboc* provides clear indications of ecclesiastical penalties operating in conjunction with secular law during his reign (871–899).

---

[10] Frantzen, *The Literature of Penance*, p. 79.

[11] *Gesetze*, ed. Liebermann III, 27.

[12] *The Laws of the Earliest English Kings*, ed. F. L. Attenborough (Cambridge, 1922), p. 180.

[13] *English Historical Documents*, ed. Whitelock, p. 397. The sources of canon law in England in the seventh and eighth centuries are discussed by M. Brett, 'Theodore and the Latin Canon Law', *Archbishop Theodore: Commemorative Studies on his Life and Influence*, ed. M. Lapidge, pp. 120–40.

[14] T. P. Oakley, 'The Penitentials as Sources for Mediaeval History', *Speculum* 15 (1940), 210–23, at 211.

[15] The amount of legislation lost from this period is uncertain, but appears to include a law-code issued by King Offa of Mercia which is referred to by both Alcuin and Alfred. However, Patrick Wormald argues that Offa's legislation need not have taken the form of a vernacular law-code such as those of Æthelberht and Ine, but may rather be identified with an extant Latin capitulary dating from 786 and comprising twenty canons on ecclesiastical subjects ('In Search of King Offa's "Law-Code"', *People and Places in Northern Europe 500–1600: Essays in Honour of Peter Hayes Sawyer*, ed. I. Wood and N. Lund (Woodbridge, 1991), pp. 25–45). Whether or not this suggestion is correct, the capitulary certainly represents the most important single source of information on early Mercian law. For further discussion, see C. Hough, 'Legal and Documentary Writings', *Introduction to Anglo-Saxon Literary Culture*, ed. P. Pulsiano and E. Treharne (Oxford, 2001), reprinted in this volume.

The relevant clauses are chs. 1,2, 1,8, 5,4 and 14, and are worth quoting in full. Alfred, ch. 1,2 reads as follows:

Gif he þonne þæs weddige þe him riht sie to gelæstanne 7 þæt aleoge, selle mid eaðmedum his wæpn 7 his æhta his freondum to gehealdanne 7 beo feowertig nihta on carcerne on cyninges tune, ðrowige ðær swa biscep him scrife, 7 his mægas hine feden, gif he self mete næbbe.[16]	If, however, he pledges what it is right for him to perform, and leaves it unfulfilled, let him with humility give his weapons and his possessions into his friends' keeping and be 40 days in prison at a king's estate; let him endure there what penance the bishop prescribes for him, and his kinsmen are to feed him if he has no food himself.[17]

The crucial phrase here is *ðrowige ðær swa biscep him scrife*, with the verb *scrifan* denoting the imposition of penance after confession. The punishment is thus twofold, involving both imprisonment and penance. So too an oath-breaker who absconds is liable to both financial and ecclesiastical penalties according to Alfred, ch. 1,8:

Gif þær ðonne oþer mennisc borg sie, bete þone borgbryce swa him ryht wisie, 7 ðone wedbryce swa him his scrift scrife.[18]	If, however, there is secular surety for him, he is to pay for the breach of surety as the law directs him, and for the breach of pledge as his confessor prescribes for him.[19]

There may be a deliberate balancing here of *borgbryce* and *wedbryce*, *ryht* and *scrift*, reflecting an attempt to bring together the two elements of secular and religious law.

Alfred, ch. 5,4 concerns the church's right of sanctuary, and reads as follows:

Eac cirican frið: gif hwelc mon cirican gesece for fara gylta hwylcum, þara ðe ær geypped	Further sanctuary of the church: if any man has recourse to the church on account of any crime

[16] *Gesetze*, ed. Liebermann I, 48.
[17] *English Historical Documents*, ed. Whitelock, p. 409.
[18] *Gesetze*, ed. Liebermann I, 48.
[19] *English Historical Documents*, ed. Whitelock, p. 409.

nære, 7 hine ðær on Godes naman geandette, sie hit healf forgifen.[20]	which has not been discovered, and there confesses himself in God's name, it is to be half remitted.[21]

This is more ambiguous, since the verb *geandettan* normally refers to confession rather than to penance. The Toronto *Dictionary of Old English* defines the primary meaning as 'to confess', with no implications of atonement unless accompanied by the verb *(ge)betan.*[22] Oakley deduces that 'criminals who sought sanctuary, and there confessed their offences to a priest, should have half of the secular composition remitted'.[23] Logically, however, there seems to be no reason for the mere act of confession to warrant remission of punishment, and so it must be concluded that in this context *geandettan* implies not only the act of confession but its sequel, the performance of prescribed penance. On this reading, it is submission to ecclesiastical discipline that reduces the secular penalty.

The verb *geandettan* occurs again in Alfred, ch. 14:

Gif mon sie dumb oððe déaf geboren, þæt he ne mæge synna onsecggan ne geandettan, bete se fæder his misdæda.[24]	If anyone is born dumb, or deaf, so that he cannot deny sins or confess them, the father is to pay compensation for his misdeeds.[25]

The type of atonement is not specified, but presumably refers to secular penalties. It would be logical for a deaf-mute's father to be responsible for compensating anyone injured by his actions, but ludicrous to undertake spiritual penance by proxy.

In sum, Alfred, chs. 5,4 and 14 provide evidence of religious terminology infiltrating secular law. Chs. 1,2 and 1,8 prescribe a combination of secular and ecclesiastical penalties, and ch. 5,4 allows a reduction of secular punishment provided that penance is undertaken. This reflects a high level of co-operation between secular and ecclesiastical authorities during the

[20] *Gesetze*, ed. Liebermann I, 52.
[21] *English Historical Documents*, ed. Whitelock, p. 410.
[22] Dictionary of Old English Project, *Dictionary of Old English A–G.* Version 2.0. CD-ROM, 2008 (hereafter DOE), s.v. *ge-andettan, ge-andettian.*
[23] T. P. Oakley, 'The Cooperation of Medieval Penance and Secular Law', *Speculum* 7 (1932), 515–24, at 517.
[24] *Gesetze*, ed. Liebermann I, 58.
[25] *English Historical Documents*, ed. Whitelock, p. 411.

late ninth century, and shows that the church played a major role in the administration of justice. It may not, however, reflect a correspondingly high level of dependence on the penitential handbooks. Alfred's code does not mention them as such. Penances are to be undertaken *swa biscep him scrife* 'as the bishop prescribes for him' (ch. 1,2), or *swa him his scrift scrife* 'as his confessor prescribes for him' (ch. 1,8). This need not imply recourse to the penitentials, for similar directions occur frequently within the handbooks themselves. For instance, the *Pseudo-Egbert Confessional*, ch. 12 directs that a deacon or a monk who begets a child is to fast stringently, *swa him bisceop oððe deman tæcan*[26] 'as the bishop or judges direct him'. The *Pseudo-Egbert Penitential* Book 2 ch. 16 directs that a woman who breaks her religious vows is to atone *swa hire scrift hire tæce*[27] 'as her confessor directs her', and the same phrase occurs at the end of the following canon concerning a girl who has not yet taken religious vows. Book 2 chs. 18 and 19 leave the penalty for marrying a close relative or a nun to *bisceopes dome*[28] 'the bishop's judgement'; and ch. 20 directs that a man or woman who marries more than twice is to do penance *swa hyra scrift him tæce 7 wissige*[29] 'as their confessor directs and guides them'. The *Late Old English Handbook for the Use of a Confessor* directs that a homicide is to fast for seven years, three on bread and water and the other four *swa his scrift him tæce*[30] 'as his confessor directs him'; while Section 4 concludes with the instructions that a person who has committed a wide range of sins is to atone deeply, *swa swa man him tæce*[31] 'as he is directed'. These phrases clearly refer to the discretion of the individual confessor rather than to the provisions of the penitential handbooks. Their occurrence in secular legislation may logically be taken to have a similar frame of reference.

References to penance become more common in law-codes dating from the tenth and eleventh centuries. II Æthelstan, ch. 26 supports the penitential system by refusing Christian burial to an oath-breaker unless penance has been carried out:

Ond se ðe manað swerige, 7 hit him on open worþe, ðæt he næfre eft aðwyrþe ne sy, ne	And he who swears a false oath, and it becomes known against him, is never afterwards to be

[26] *Ancient Laws*, ed. Thorpe, p. 349.
[27] *Ibid.* 370.
[28] *Ibid.* 370.
[29] *Ibid.* 371.
[30] Fowler, 'A Late Old English Handbook', at 21 lines 131–2.
[31] *Ibid.* at 26 line 303.

binnon nanum gehalgodum lictune ne licge, þeah he forðfore, buton he hæbbe ðæs biscopes gewitnesse, ðe he on his scriftscire sy, þæt he hit swa gebet hæbbe, swa him his scrift scrife.[32]	entitled to an oath, nor is he to be buried in a consecrated cemetery when he dies, unless he has the witness of the bishop in whose diocese he is that he has done penance for it as his confessor has prescribed for him.[33]

The following sub-clause specifies the procedure for ensuring that the penance is complied with:

26,1. 7 his scrift hit gecyþe þam biscope binnon XXX nihta, hweþer he to þære bote cirran wolde. Gif he swa ne dó, bete be þam þe se biscop him forgifan wille.[34]	26,1. And his confessor is to inform the bishop within 30 days whether he was willing to submit to that penance. If he does not do so, he is to pay in accordance with what the bishop will allow him.[35]

Similarly, I Edmund, ch. 3 forbids anyone guilty of bloodshed to enter the king's presence before undertaking penance:

Gif hwa Cristenes mannes blód ageote, ne cume he na on ðæs cyninges neawiste, ær he on dædbote ga, swa him biscop tæce 7 his scrift him wisige.[36]	If anyone sheds the blood of a Christian man, he shall not come anywhere near the king until he proceeds to do penance, as the bishop appoints for him or his confessor directs him.[37]

The following clause goes on to deny Christian burial to anyone who has seduced a nun or committed adultery, *buton he gebete*:

4. Se þe wið nunnan hæme, gehalgodre legerstowe ne sy he wyrðe – buton he gebete – þe ma þe manslage; *þæt* ilce we	4. He who has intercourse with a nun, unless he make amends, shall not be allowed burial in consecrated ground any more

[32] *Gesetze*, ed. Liebermann I, 164.
[33] *English Historical Documents*, ed. Whitelock, p. 422.
[34] *Gesetze*, ed. Liebermann I, 164.
[35] *English Historical Documents*, ed. Whitelock, p. 422.
[36] *Gesetze*, ed. Liebermann I, 184.
[37] *The Laws of the Kings of England from Edmund to Henry I*, ed. A. J. Robertson (Cambridge, 1925), p. 7.

cwædon be æwbrice.[38]	than a homicide. We have decreed the same with regard to adultery.[39]

It is not wholly clear whether *gebetan* in this context refers to financial or spiritual reparation. The verb appears elsewhere in the law-codes with either meaning,[40] and it may well be that both senses are included here. So too II Edmund, ch. 4 uses the term *bot* to refer both to the reparation due to the kin of a murder victim and to the penance exacted by the church:

Eac ic cyðe, þæt ic nelle socne habban to minu*m* hirede, ær he hæbbe godcunde bote underfangen 7 wið þa *mæg*ðer gebet on bote befangen 7 to ælcum rihte gebogen, swa biscop him tæce, ðe hit on his scyre sy.[41]	Further, I make it known that I will allow no resort to my court before he [the slayer] has undergone ecclesiastical penance and undertaken the prescribed compensation to the kindred, and submitted to every legal obligation, as the bishop, in whose diocese it is, instructs him.[42]

Another verb of payment, *agyldan*, is connected with penance in VI Æthelred, ch. 52:

7 á swa man bið mihtigra her nu for worulde oþþon þurh geþingða hearra on hade, swa sceal he deoppor synna gebetan 7 ælce misdæda deoror agyldan...[43]	And always the greater a man's position in this present life or the higher the privileges of his rank, the more fully shall he make amends for his sins, and the more dearly shall he pay for all misdeeds...[44]

[38] *Gesetze*, ed. Liebermann I, 184.
[39] *The Laws*, ed. Robertson, p. 7.
[40] DOE, s.v. *ge-bētan*.
[41] *Gesetze*, ed. Liebermann I, 188.
[42] *English Historical Documents*, ed. Whitelock, p. 428.
[43] *Gesetze*, ed. Liebermann I, 258.
[44] *The Laws*, ed. Robertson, p. 107.

Here again it is difficult to determine whether the frame of reference is spiritual reparation or monetary amendment to the king or church, and it may even be possible that no clear distinction is being made.[45]

Penance is inseparable from secular punishment in the laws drawn up by Archbishop Wulfstan for Kings Æthelred and Cnut.[46] Ch. 22 of V Æthelred, the first code in Wulfstan's distinctive prose style, reads:

7 æghwylc Cristen man do, swa hi*m* þearf is: gyme his Cristendomes georne 7 gewunige gelomlice to scrifte 7 únforwandodlice his synna gecyðe 7 geornlice bete, swa swa him man tæce.[47]	And every Christian man is to do what is needful for him; heed zealously his Christian duties, and form the habit of frequent confession, and freely confess his sins and willingly atone for them as he is directed.[48]

It is also clear from ch. 29 of the same code that penance was a legal requirement at this time:

7 gif ænig amánsumad man, butan hit friðbena sy, on þæs cynges neaweste ahwar gewunige, ær ðam þe he hæbbe godcunde bote georne gebogene, þon*ne* plihte he hi*m* sylfum 7 eallan his æhtan.[49]	And if any excommunicated man – unless it be a suppliant for protection – remain anywhere in the king's neighbourhood before he has submitted readily to ecclesiastical penance, it is to be at the peril of his life, and all his possessions.[50]

---

[45] See the discussion of commutations below. The different shades of literal and figurative meaning acquired by the verb *agyldan* are fully documented in DOE, s.v. *āgyldan*.

[46] Wulfstan's authorship of laws issued by Æthelred and Cnut was demonstrated by D. Whitelock, 'Wulfstan and the Laws of Cnut', *English Historical Review* 63 (1948), 433–52, and 'Wulfstan's Authorship of Cnut's Laws', *English Historical Review* 70 (1955), 72–85. Both articles are reprinted in her *History, Law and Literature in 10th-11th Century England* (London, 1981). A recent discussion is by M. K. Lawson, 'Archbishop Wulfstan and the Homiletic Element in the Laws of Æthelred II and Cnut', *English Historical Review* 107 (1992), 565–86, reprinted in *The Reign of Cnut: King of England, Denmark and Norway*, ed. A. R. Rumble (London, 1994), pp. 141–64. See also P. Wormald, 'Æthelred the Lawmaker', *Ethelred the Unready: Papers from the Military Conference*, ed. D. Hill, *British Archaeological Reports*, British Series 59 (1978), 47–80.

[47] *Gesetze*, ed. Liebermann I, 242. The clause is repeated in VI Æthelred, ch. 27.

[48] *English Historical Documents*, ed. Whitelock, p. 445.

[49] *Gesetze*, ed. Liebermann I, 244.

The principle is similar to that of II Edmund, ch. 4, in that there is no recourse under secular law until penance has been carried out.

Other references to penance in the later law-codes include VIII Æthelred, ch. 40 *for Gode betan*[51] 'make amends before God', X Æthelred, ch. 1, *ure misdæda georlice betan*[52] 'eagerly make amends for our misdeeds', and I Cnut, ch. 18,1 *æfre geswican 7 geornlice betan*[53] 'for ever desist and eagerly make amends'. Probably the clearest expression of co-operation between secular law and penance appears in II Cnut, ch. 38,2:

7 godcunde bote sece mann symle georne be boctæcinge, 7 woruldcunde bote sece man be woruldlage.[54]	And ecclesiastical amends are always to be diligently demanded according to the instruction in books [of penance] and secular amends according to the secular law.[55]

Here again we see the dual meaning of OE *bot*, on the one hand a spiritual atonement and on the other the rendering of a debt to society, the two ideas balancing each other in Wulfstan's stylized prose. There is also a direct reference to the penitentials themselves in the term *boctæcing*. It is, however, important to bear in mind that Wulfstan himself may have written one of the surviving penitential handbooks. The *Late Old English Handbook for the Use of a Confessor* survives in a number of eleventh-century manuscripts associated with Wulfstan, and the possibility that Wulfstan may have been the author is discussed by Fowler, who identifies a number of parallels with the codes drafted by him for Æthelred and Cnut.[56] The close relationship between the penitentials and secular

---

[50] *English Historical Documents*, ed. Whitelock, p. 446.

[51] *Gesetze*, ed. Liebermann I, 268.

[52] *Ibid.* I, 270.

[53] *Ibid.* I, 298.

[54] *Ibid.* I, 338.

[55] *English Historical Documents*, ed. Whitelock, p. 460.

[56] Fowler, 'A Late Old English Handbook', at 6–12. The suggestion that 'Wulfstan may have written parts of the text, and have had a hand in the compilation' is also made by Dorothy Whitelock (*Councils and Synods with other Documents Relating to the English Church*, 2 vols. (Oxford, 1964–81) I, 313, n.5), and is repeated by K. O'Brien O'Keeffe, 'Body and Law in Late Anglo-Saxon England', *Anglo-Saxon England* 27 (1998), 209–32, at 211 n.7. An alternative possibility preferred by Patrick Wormald (personal communication) is that the work may have been quoted or – at most – adapted by Wulfstan.

legislation in late Anglo-Saxon England may therefore be due to Wulfstan's involvement with both.

The majority of references to penance, in fact, occur in the laws drafted by Wulfstan during the early eleventh century. These may not be typical of the Anglo-Saxon period as a whole, although the paucity of other contemporary material makes it impossible to reach any certainty on this point. As Archbishop of York, Wulfstan was naturally keen to see ecclesiastical discipline enforced through secular law; and as advisor to both Æthelred and Cnut he was in a strong position to put this into effect. His legislation cannot necessarily be used as evidence for the penitential system in general.

In sum, the law-codes do not appear to incorporate penitential discipline until the late tenth century, when the practice may be attributed to the influence of Archbishop Wulfstan. However, evidence of co-operation between ecclesiastical and secular authorities may also be sought in the penitentials themselves. Just as the later Anglo-Saxon law-codes were used to reinforce the penitential canons, so too the penitentials contain clauses supporting secular law. In the *Pseudo-Egbert Penitential* Book 4 ch. 13, for instance, fasting is imposed in addition to the payment of compensation to the injured party:

Gif hwylc man reafige oðerne æt his dehter, bete wið þa frynd 7 fæste hyra ægðer I gear, Þodnes-dagum 7 Frige-dagum, on hlafe 7 on wætere, 7 þa oðre dagas brucon hyra metes buton flæsce, 7 nime hig syððan to riht-æwe gif þa frynd wyllað.[57]	If anyone robs another of his daughter, he is to compensate the friends and each of them is to fast for one year, Wednesdays and Fridays, on bread and water, and on the other days partake of food except for meat, and he is afterwards to take her as his lawful wife if the friends are willing.

In the *Theodore Penitential* Book 1 Section 3 ch. 3, the penance for theft is shortened if restitution is made:

Qui sepe furtum fecerit VII. annis penitentia ejus est, vel quo modo sacerdos judicaverit, id est, juxta quod conponi possit quibus nocuit. Et qui furtum	Whoever has often committed theft, seven years is his penance, or such a sentence as his priest shall determine, that is, according to what can be

[57] *Ancient Laws*, ed. Thorpe, p. 379.

> faciebat, penitentia ductus semper debet reconciliari ei quem offendebat, et restituere juxta quod ei nocuit: et multum breviavit penitentiam ejus. Si vero noluerit aut non potest, constitutum tempus penitentiæ manet per omnia.[58]

> arranged with those whom he has wronged. And he who used to steal, when he becomes penitent, ought always to be reconciled to him against whom he has offended and to make restitution according to the wrong he has done to him; and [in such case] he shall greatly shorten his penance. But if he refuses, or is unable, let him do penance scrupulously for the prescribed time.[59]

Similarly, Section 4 ch. 1 allows the penance for murder to be shortened on payment of the legal *wergild*:

> Si quis pro ultione propinqui hominem occiderit, peniteat sicut homicida, VII. vel X. annos. Si tamen reddere vult propinquis pecuniam æstimationis, levior erit penitentia, id est, dimidio spatii.[60]

> If one slays a man in revenge for a relative, he shall do penance as a murderer for seven or ten years. However, if he will render to the relatives the legal price, the penance shall be lighter, that is, [it shall be shortened] by half the time.[61]

The implications of this are difficult to assess. According to Oakley:

> it will be seen ... that the additional penance to be performed in case composition has not been paid may justly be regarded as a punishment for failing to satisfy or yield to the secular law; and that thus the Penitentials served as powerful means for reinforcing the somewhat weak secular authority.[62]

---

[58] *Councils and Ecclesiastical Documents*, ed. Haddan and Stubbs III, 179.
[59] J. T. McNeill and H. M. Gamer, *Medieval Handbooks of Penance* (New York, 1938), p. 187.
[60] *Councils and Ecclesiastical Documents*, ed. Haddan and Stubbs III, 180.
[61] McNeill and Gamer, *Medieval Handbooks of Penance*, p. 187.
[62] Oakley, *English Penitential Discipline*, p. 89.

Harding argues along similar lines:

> For its ideas, and also for much of its effectiveness, secular law relied on the Church.[63]

This may, however, be overstating the case. There is no reason to believe that Anglo-Saxon kings were incapable of exercising their authority, and a number of indications to the contrary.[64] Quite the opposite impression is given, for instance, by chs. 1 and 2 of the preamble to the so-called laws of Edward and Guthrum:[65]

1. Ðis ærest, *þæt* hig gecwædon, *þæt* hí ænne God lufian woldon 7 ælcne hæþendom georne aworpen.	1. In the first place they declared they would love one God, and zealously renounce all heathen practices.
2. 7 hig gesetton woruldlice stéora eac, for ðam þingu*m* þe hig wistan, *þæt* hig elles ne mihton manegum gesteoran, ne fela manna nolde to godcundre bote elles gebugan, swa hy sceolde; 7 þa woruldbote hig gesetton gemæne Criste 7 cynge, swa hwár swa man nolde godcunde bote gebugan mid	2. And they also fixed secular penalties because they knew that otherwise there would be many people whom they would not be able to control, and that otherwise many men would not be willing to submit as they ought to do, to the amends required by the church. And they fixed secular amends

---

[63] A. Harding, *The Law Courts of Medieval England* (London, 1973), p. 21.

[64] See for instance B. Yorke, *Kings and Kingdoms of Early Anglo-Saxon England* (London, 1990), p. 44, who comments of the early kingdom of Kent: 'The evidence of lawcodes, estates, proprietary religious houses, coinage and the pattern of royal succession all bear witness to a well-organized kingdom in which there was effective royal control.' Similarly, Campbell discusses 'evidence for a powerful and elaborate system of government in England' ('Observations on English Government from the Tenth to the Twelfth Century', *Transactions of the Royal Historical Society*, 5th series 25 (1975), 39–54, reprinted in *Essays in Anglo-Saxon History* (London, 1986), pp. 155–70, at p. 155); and Wormald identifies 'mounting indications of the sheer efficiency of government in Anglo-Saxon England' ('In Search of King Offa's "Law-Code"', at p. 25).

[65] D. Whitelock, 'Wulfstan and the So-called Laws of Edward and Guthrum', *English Historical Review* 56 (1941), 1–21, reprinted in her *History, Law and Literature in 10th–11th Century England*, demonstrates that this code does not date from the reign of Edward the Elder but was drawn up during the early eleventh century, probably by Archbishop Wulfstan.

rihte to bisceopa dihte.[66]

which should be divided between Christ and the king, wheresoever people would not legally submit to the amends required by the church and determined by the bishops.[67]

Far from being needed to support a 'weak secular authority', this sounds much more as though penitential discipline could only be enforced by means of secular law.

The influence of penitential literature on the secular law-codes is seen in other respects besides the mutual endorsement of penalties. During the later Anglo-Saxon period, principles underlying the penitential system began to be incorporated into secular legislation. One instance concerns the way in which penalties were assessed. A common theme in the handbooks is that the status of the offender was to be taken into consideration in assigning penances. As Payer comments, 'Youth, necessity, and force, for example, are mitigating circumstances, while superior ecclesiastical rank and connection with the sacred are aggravating circumstances'.[68] The principle is clearly set out in the *Bede Penitential* Section 9:

Hæc de qualitate hominum, sicut supra diximus, excerpsimus qualiter penitere vel judicare debeant, si pauper aut dives, si liber aut servus, si juvenis aut adulescens, si minus sapiens aut gnarus, si clericus aut monachus, si in gradu vel sine gradu.[69]

These things we have compiled, as we said above, concerning the condition of men, [showing] how they ought to do penance or to adjudge it: whether poor or rich, free or a slave; whether a boy or a youth; whether lacking in wisdom or learned; whether a cleric or a monk, whether in orders or without orders.[70]

During the late tenth and early eleventh centuries, this concept was carried over into the law-codes. Frantzen points out that the link between

[66] *Gesetze*, ed. Liebermann I, 128.
[67] *The Laws*, ed. Attenborough, p. 103.
[68] P. J. Payer, *Sex and the Penitentials: the Development of a Sexual Code 550–1150* (Toronto, 1984), p. 131.
[69] *Councils and Ecclesiastical Documents*, ed. Haddan and Stubbs III, 333.
[70] McNeill and Gamer, *Medieval Handbooks of Penance*, p. 235.

culpability and status in II Cnut, chs. 38,1 and 68,1 derives from the penitentials, as does the commutation of the death penalty in II Cnut 30,5:

> the man of higher rank must atone 'the deeper both to God and to men for wrongdoing'; the weak and sick must not be punished as severely as the strong and powerful. These statements echo the penitentials. So too does the substitution of mutilation for the death penalty: 'thus one can punish and at the same time preserve the soul'.[71]

Indeed, these ideas are already to be found in codes drafted previously by Archbishop Wulfstan for Æthelred. V Æthelred, ch. 3 condemns the death penalty for small offences;[72] and VI Æthelred, ch. 52 directs that both secular and ecclesiastical penalties should be assessed according to the rank and ability of the offender:

> 7 á swa man bið mihtigra her nu for worulde oþþon þurh geþingða hearra on hade, swa sceal he deoppor synna gebetan 7 ælce misdæda deoror agyldan, for þam þe se maga 7 se unmaga ne beoð ne gelice, ne ne magon na gelice byrþene ahebban, ne se unhala þe ma þa*m* halum gelice; 7 þy man sceal medmian 7 gescadlice toscadan, ge on godcundan scriftan ge on woroldcundan steoran, ylde 7 geogoþe, welan 7 wædle, hæle 7 unhæle, 7 hada gehwilcne.[73]

> And always the greater a man's position in this present life or the higher the privileges of his rank, the more fully shall he make amends for his sins, and the more dearly shall he pay for all misdeeds; for the strong and the weak are not alike nor can they bear a like burden, any more than the sick can be treated like the sound. And therefore, in forming a judgment, careful discrimination must be made between age and youth, wealth and poverty, health and sickness, and the various ranks of life, both in the amends imposed by the ecclesiastical authority and in the penalties inflicted by the secular law.[74]

This represents a radically different approach from that of the early law-codes, which tend to stipulate a flat rate of compensation according to the status of the injured party. Again it appears that links between secular

---

[71] Frantzen, *The Literature of Penance*, p. 147.

[72] *Gesetze*, ed. Liebermann I, 238.

[73] *Ibid.* I, 258.

[74] *The Laws*, ed. Robertson, p. 107.

law and the penitentials are generally restricted to the later Anglo-Saxon period.

The way in which the later law-codes distinguish between crimes committed deliberately or accidentally has also been attributed to penitential influence. Harding comments:

> Meetings of the witan were often secular assemblies and church synods combined, and we know that Bishop Wulfstan composed some of the great laws of King Cnut, introducing to 'secular judgments' the distinctions between degrees of liability for wrong-doing (according to whether for instance it was intentional or unintentional) which had been discovered in 'religious penances'.[75]

Harding cites II Cnut, ch. 68 in support of this statement, although the same theme occurs in VI Æthelred, ch. 52,1, drafted previously by Wulfstan.[76] However, a distinction between intentional and unintentional crimes is already present in earlier codes. Alfred, ch. 13, for instance, deals with the case of someone killed accidentally during tree-felling:

> Gif mon oðerne æt gemænan weorce óffelle ungewealdes, agife mon þa*m* mægum þæt treow, 7 hi hit hæbban ær XXX nihta of þa*m* lande, oððe him fó se to ðe ðone wudu age.[77]

> If at a common task a man unintentionally kills another [by letting a tree fall on him] the tree is to be given to the kinsmen, and they are to have it from that estate within 30 days, or else he who owns the wood is to have the right to it.[78]

So too Alfred, ch. 36, concerning impalement on a spear, differentiates carefully between degrees of liability according to the care taken by the spear-holder, and demands an additional fine if he is accused of deliberate intent:

> 36. Eac is fundon: gif mon hafað spere ofer eaxle, 7 hine mon on asnaseð, gielde þone wer butan wite.

> 36. Moreover, it is established: if anyone has a spear over his shoulder, and a man is transfixed on it, the wergild is to be paid without the fine.

---

[75] Harding, *The Law Courts of Medieval England*, pp. 20–1.

[76] *Gesetze*, ed. Liebermann I, 258.

[77] *Ibid.* I, 56.

[78] *English Historical Documents*, ed. Whitelock, p. 411.

36,1. Gif beforan eagum asnase, gielde þone wer; gif hine mon tio gewealdes on ðære dæde, getriowe hine be þam wite 7 mid ðy þæt wite afelle,	36,1. If he is transfixed before his eyes, he is to pay the wergild; if anyone accuses him of intention in this act, he is to clear himself in proportion to the fine, and by that [oath] do away with the fine,
36,2. gif se ord sie ufor þonne hindeweard sceaft. Gif hie sien bu gelic, ord 7 hindeweard sceaft, þæt sie butan pleo.[79]	36,2. if the point is higher than the butt end of the shaft. If they are both level, the point and the butt end, that is to be [considered] without risk.[80]

It is unlikely, however, that this type of distinction is attributable to penitential influence. A strikingly similar clause appears in fifth-century Burgundian law, indicating rather that Alfred's ruling in this respect derives from a common Germanic legal tradition. *Lex Burgundionum* ch. 18,2 reads as follows:

Lancea vero vel quodcumque genus armorum aut proiectum in terra aut fixum simpliciter fuerit et casu se ibidem homo aut animal impulerit, illum euius arma fuerit, nihil iubemus exsolvere, nisi forte sic arma sua in manu teneat, ut homini periculum possit inferre.[81]	In truth, if a lance or any kind of weapon shall have been thrown upon the ground or set there without intent to do harm, and if by accident a man or animal impales himself thereupon, we order that he to whom the weapon belongs shall pay nothing unless by chance he held the weapon in his own hands in such a manner that it could cause harm to a man.[82]

Liebermann also notes a parallel with Frisian law,[83] where *Lex Frisionum Add.* III ch. 69 reads as follows:

[79] *Gesetze*, ed. Liebermann I, 68–70.
[80] *English Historical Documents*, ed. Whitelock, p. 414.
[81] *Leges Burgundionum*, ed. L. R. de Salis, Monumenta Germaniae Historica, Legum Sectio I: Leges nationum Germanicarum 2.1(Hanover, 1892), pp. 56–7.
[82] K. F. Drew, *The Burgundian Code* (Philadelphia, 1949), p. 35.
[83] *Gesetze*, ed. Liebermann III, 58.

Si homo quislibet telum manu tenet, et ipsum casu quolibet inciderit super alium, extra voluntatem eius qui illud manu tenet, in simplo iuxta qualitatem vulneris componatur.[84]	If a man is holding a weapon in his hand, and someone else is accidentally injured by it, without the intention of the person holding it in his hand, simple compensation is to be paid as appropriate to the nature of the wound.

This is one aspect of the Anglo-Saxon legal system that cannot be laid at Wulfstan's door.

The influence of penitential literature on the development of the later law-codes is paralleled by the way in which money payments, a key feature of secular legislation throughout the Anglo-Saxon period, were incorporated into the penitential system in the form of commutations. This meant that penance could be remitted in return for donations to the Church or to charitable causes. Section 7 of the *Egbert Penitential* is concerned with women, dealing in the first four canons with sexual abstinence before and after childbirth and during the Lent before Easter, and in chs. 5-10 with other sexual matters, witchcraft, and infanticide. Ch. 4 allows the penance to be commuted into monetary payment:

Qui in quadragesima ante Pascha cognoscet mulierem suam, noluit abstinere, ante peniteat vel suum pretium reddat ad ecclesiam, vel pauperibus dividat aut XX. et sex solidos reddat.[85]	Anyone who has sexual relations with his wife during the Lent before Easter, and refuses to abstain, is to do penance or to pay the appropriate price to the church, or to distribute 26 solidi among the poor.

The *Pseudo-Egbert Confessional*, ch. 2 allows redemption of penance at the rate of a penny per day:

7 seðe scyle ane wucan on hlafe 7 on wætere dædbote don, singe he þreo hund sealma cneowigende oððe IIII hund 7 twentig butan cneowunge, eallswa hit her bufan gecweden	And anyone who should do penance for a week on bread and water, is to sing 300 psalms on his knees or 420 without kneeling, just as is stipulated above, and anyone who should

[84] *Lex Frisionum*, ed. K. A. Eckhardt and A. Eckhardt, Monumenta Germaniae Historica, Fontes Iuris Germanici Antiqui 12 (Hanover, 1982), p. 96.
[85] Haddan and Stubbs, *Councils and Ecclesiastical Documents*, III, 423.

is, 7 seðe scyle monoð dædbote don on hlafe 7 on wætere, synge he twelf hund mid cneowunga oððe butan cneowunge þusend 7 six hund 7 hundeahtatig, ... 7 seðe sealmas ne cunne ne fæstan ne mæge, gedæle he æghwylce dæge ænne penningc oððe peniges wyrð þearfendum mannum...[86]

do penance for a month on bread and water, is to sing 1,200 on his knees or 1,680 without kneeling, ... and anyone who does not know the psalms and is unable to fast, is to give a penny or the value of a penny every day to poor people...

The same rate is stipulated in the *Pseudo-Egbert Penitential* Book 4 ch. 61:

An dæges fæsten man mæg mid anum penige alysan, oððe mid twam hund sealmum...[87]

One day's fast can be redeemed with a penny, or with two hundred psalms...

In general the system favoured the rich. However, the *Pseudo-Egbert Penitential* Book 4 ch. 60 gives a sliding scale of commutations according to the rank of the offender:

gif he bið welig, sylle for xii monða fæstene xxx solidos, þæt is on ure geþeode xxx scillinga; gif hine to swa mycelum ne onhagige, þonne sylle he xx scillinga; gif hine þonne to swa mycelum ne onhagige, sylle x scillingas; gif hit þonne þearfigende mann beo þæt him to x ne onhagige, sylle iii scillingas...[88]

if he is wealthy, he is to pay 20 solidi for a fast of 12 months, that is 30 shillings among our people; if he is not able to afford as much, then he is to pay 20 shillings; if he still cannot afford as much, he is to pay 10 shillings; if it is a needy man who cannot afford 10, he is to pay 3 shillings...

This was clearly intended to redress the balance; but to a modern eye it still appears out of keeping with the principle of spiritual atonement.

Commutations first appear in penitentials from England and Ireland, and are believed to derive from the secular system of monetary compensation. The trend was difficult to check. Oakley comments:

---

[86] *Ancient Laws*, ed. Thorpe, p. 346.
[87] *Ibid.* p. 385.
[88] *Ibid.* p. 385.

> During the ninth century, the allowing of commutations and redemptions became so extensive that numerous reform councils protested against the lax extension of commutations by numerous arbitrary penitentials. Though these protests produced some results in encouraging the compiling and use of severer, more authoritative penitential codes, yet they were unable to suppress the growing use of commutations and the shortening of the periods of penance.[89]

Again, this does not suggest that ecclesiastical authority was particularly strong in comparison with secular discipline. Influences between the penitentials and the law-codes acted in both directions, and were not always mutually beneficial.

In conclusion, there is little evidence of a close link between the penitentials and secular law in early Anglo-Saxon England. Although there were some undoubted areas of influence, such as the introduction of money payments into penitential handbooks, and the infiltration of religious terminology into the codes issued by Anglo-Saxon kings, the two forms of legislation appear to have operated largely independently until at least the end of the ninth century. During the late tenth and early eleventh centuries, regulations concerning penance were incorporated into secular law, apparently due to the influence of Archbishop Wulfstan. Suggestions that penitential discipline was needed to uphold secular authority at any time during the Anglo-Saxon period are fallacious, and the evidence indicates rather that the penitential system derived support from secular law.[90]

---

[89] Oakley, *English Penitential Discipline*, pp. 52–3.

[90] I am grateful to Patrick Wormald for some helpful comments on an earlier version of this paper.

3.

WOMEN AND THE LAW IN SEVENTH-CENTURY ENGLAND

First published 2007: *Nottingham Medieval Studies* 51, 207–230.

1. Introduction

The law-codes issued by Anglo-Saxon kings during the seventh century contain a number of references to women.[1] As with many of the early laws, these are often cryptically expressed and subject to varying interpretations, so that they have been taken to support widely different views of the status of women in contemporary society. Within the last decade or so, however, close studies of individual laws have made it possible to establish new readings of several of the relevant clauses, with major implications for the understanding of this body of evidence as a whole. The purpose of this paper is to re-examine the legal position of women in early Anglo-Saxon England as reflected in the extant legislation.

Four series of laws survive from seventh-century England, issued by the Kentish kings Æthelberht I, Hlothhere and Eadric, and Wihtred, and the West Saxon king Ine. As well as emanating from two different kingdoms, they span almost a century of social and political change. Æthelberht's code was issued around the turn of the century in response to the conversion by Roman missionaries, but appears to incorporate earlier legislation which had circulated orally during the pre-Christian era.[2]

---

[1] Some of the research for this paper was carried out during a period of study leave funded by the Leverhulme Trust and the University of Glasgow from October 1999 to September 2000. I am very grateful to the directors of the Leverhulme Trust and to the University of Glasgow for their support. I am also grateful to the staff of the Medway Archives and Local Studies Centre for their help during my visits to use the *Textus Roffensis* manuscript, and to the Librarian of Corpus Christi College, Cambridge for providing me with a microfilm of MS 383.

[2] Æthelberht's code is traditionally dated to *c.* 602/603, following, *Die Gesetze der*

Aimed largely at limiting the opportunity for feud, his laws define appropriate levels of compensation for various kinds of injury to person or property. The focus is predominantly secular, with close parallels with continental Germanic legislation. Unlike its continental counterparts, however, Æthelberht's code is written in the vernacular. It comprises the earliest extant text in English, and since it also contains a number of *hapax legomena* that may already have been archaic when the laws were first issued in written form, the linguistic difficulties it presents are considerable.[3]

Although Æthelberht died in 616, his code appears to have remained in force for the rest of the seventh century and beyond. A description of his laws in Book 2, ch. 5 of Bede's *Ecclesiastical History of the English People*, completed in 731, states *quae conscripta Anglorum sermone hactenus habentur et obseruantur ab ea* 'These are written in English and are still kept and observed by the people';[4] while a reference to Æthelberht's code alongside those of Ine and of the Mercian king Offa in ch. 49,9 of the Preface to the laws of Alfred the Great suggests that it still had some currency during the late ninth century.[5] It was supplemented rather than superseded by the laws issued by Kings Hlothhere and Eadric between 673 and 686, as is made clear by a statement in the preamble that the two kings *ecton þa ǽ, þa ðe heora aldoras ær geworhton* 'augmented the laws which their predecessors had made'.[6] These too are secular, dealing largely with matters of compensation, and introducing for the first

---

Angelsachsen, ed. F. Liebermann, 3 vols. (Halle, 1903–16) III, 2. An earlier dating to *c.* 599–600 is suggested in C. Hough, 'Legal and Documentary Writings', *A Companion to Anglo-Saxon Literature*, ed. P. Pulsiano and E. Treharne (Oxford, 2001), pp. 170–87, at 170–3, reprinted in this volume.

[3] Patrizia Lendinara lists 45 *hapax legomena* within the Kentish laws; see 'The Kentish Laws', *The Anglo-Saxons from the Migration Period to the Eighth Century: An Ethnographic Perspective*, ed. J. Hines (Woodbridge, 1997), pp. 211–43, at 223–4.

[4] *Bede's Ecclesiastical History of the English People*, ed. B. Colgrave and R. A. B. Mynors (Oxford, 1969), 150–1.

[5] *Gesetze*, ed. Liebermann I, 46.

[6] *Gesetze*, ed. Liebermann I, 9. The phrasing of the preamble leaves it unclear whether the laws were issued separately by Hlothhere, who reigned from 673 or 674 to 685, and his nephew Eadric, who reigned from 685 to 686, or jointly during a period of joint kingship. Palaeographical evidence suggesting that the first four clauses may originally have circulated separately is discussed in C. Hough, 'Numbers in Manuscripts of Anglo-Saxon Law', *Writing and Texts in Anglo-Saxon England*, ed. A. R. Rumble (Cambridge, 2006), pp. 114–36, at 128–9, reprinted in this volume.

time regulations concerning trade. A much stronger emphasis on ecclesiastical law appears in the later seventh-century code of the Kentish king Wihtred, datable on internal evidence to 695, and thus almost contemporary with the laws issued by King Ine for the neighbouring kingdom of Wessex between 688 and 694.[7] Both are concerned with enforcing Christian principles and integrating ecclesiastical ranks within the secular hierarchy; and some collaboration between the two law-givers may be reflected in the similarity betweenWihtred 28 and Ine 20, each stating that a traveller who departs from the road without shouting or blowing a horn may be assumed to be a thief.[8]

Whereas in the earlier Kentish laws, redress is made directly to the victim, the king now plays a more prominent role in the receipt of fines for breaches of social order. Ine's code is the longer and more wide-ranging, dealing with a broad range of issues relating to the economy, the church, and criminal and civil justice. It is poorly organised, with some repetition and lack of coherence; and as it survives only as an appendix to the laws issued *c.* 887–893 by King Alfred the Great, it is uncertain how closely the extant text represents the seventh-century legislation either in its entirety or in its original form.[9] The Kentish laws, by contrast, are highly structured (particularly those of Æthelberht) and despite surviving in a single post-Conquest manuscript, contain many early features which inspire confidence in the extant copy.[10]

---

[7] Ine ruled Wessex from 688 to 725 or 726, while one of the advisers mentioned in the preamble to his laws is Bishop Erconwald, who had been succeeded by 694.

[8] An alternative view is that the clause may have been borrowed from one code to the other. However, Simon Keynes suggests plausibly that Wihtred and Ine 'entered into some kind of alliance which allowed the kingdoms to prosper independently of each other'; see 'England, 700–900', *The New Cambridge Medieval History Vol. II c. 700–900*, ed. R. McKitterick (Cambridge, 1995), pp. 18–42, at p. 26.

[9] H. G. Richardson and G. O. Sayles drew attention to a contrast in styles between different sections of the code 'so marked that the inference seems justified that there has been an amalgamation of two or more texts of different dates and perhaps of different origin'; *Law and Legislation from Æthelberht to Magna Carta* (Edinburgh, 1966), p. 15. Patrick Wormald suggests that the extant compilation may comprise six sets of laws originally issued separately. In this case, the dating parameters established by the reference to Erconwald need relate only to the first set, chs. 1–27; *Legal Culture in the Early Medieval West: Law as Text, Image and Experience* (London, 1999), pp. 188–92.

[10] This view is challenged by Lendinara, 'The Kentish Laws', but linguistic, palaeographic, and syntactic evidence all supports the integrity of the extant text. The linguistic evidence is discussed by L. Oliver, *The Beginnings of English Law* (Toronto, 2002), pp. 25–34, the palaeographic evidence by C. Hough,

The majority of references to women occur in the laws of Æthelberht and Ine, with one in each of the second and third Kentish codes.[11] The relevant clauses are reproduced below in a semi-diplomatic edition with facing translation.[12] Because of the sequential organisation of Æthelberht's laws, more is lost here than elsewhere by removing individual clauses from their immediate context within the code. This and other issues affecting interpretation will be discussed in Section 3.

'Palaeographical Evidence for the Compilation of the *Textus Roffensis*', *Scriptorium* 55 (2001), 57–79, reprinted in this volume, and the syntactic evidence by Wormald, *Legal Culture*, pp. 183–7.

[11] Not included here are Wihtred 3–6, which prescribe penalties for *unriht hæmed* 'unlawful union' without stating what this involves – presumably a marriage or other sexual relationship not consecrated by the church, or within the prohibited degrees of kinship. Although these and other provisions enforcing the new religion were clearly innovative, the phrase *an ald reht* 'according to ancient right' in Wihtred 5 appears to reflect an attempt to give them the authority of established custom.

[12] The Kentish laws have been freshly edited from the only surviving manuscript, the early-twelfth-century Medway Archive and Local Studies Centre, MS DRc/R1 (*Textus Roffensis*, henceforth *TR*). Ine's laws survive in three manuscripts: Cambridge, Corpus Christi College 173, dating from the second quarter of the tenth century, Cambridge, Corpus Christi College 383, dating from the late eleventh or early twelfth century, and *TR*. (There are also fragments in London, BL Cotton Otho B.xi, dating from the early eleventh century, and in London, BL Burney 277, dating from the late eleventh, and an early-twelfth-century translation into Latin in the collection known as *Quadripartitus*.) CCCC 173 is generally considered the most reliable, and has been used as the base text here, working mainly from the facsimile edition *The Parker Chronicle and Laws*, ed. R. Flower and H. Smith (London, 1941). Variant readings from the other two manuscripts are noted, with the exception of the interchangeable graphs *þ* and *ð*, numbers in written form as opposed to Roman numerals, and punctuation. Word division is presented in accordance with modern editorial principles, with manuscript punctuation (comprising the raised point) represented by modern punctuation. Capitalisation is retained. No punctuation has been added, and none omitted except for the points flanking Roman numerals. With the exception of the tironian sign *7* for *and* or *ond*, abbreviations are expanded in italics unless otherwise stated. The numbering system is that of the standard edition of the Anglo-Saxon laws by Liebermann, from which much useful information has also been derived. Whereas the Kentish laws are written continuously in the manuscript, those of Ine are divided into numbered chapters with disparate material grouped together in order to fit Alfred's overall scheme of a *domboc* comprising the symbolic number of 120 chapters. Only the material relevant to women has been included here.

2.i. Kentish laws relating to women

Æthelberht

10. Gif man wið cyninges mægdenman geligeþ L scillinga gebete.

If anyone lies with a virgin belonging to the king, he is to pay 50 shillings compensation.[13]

11. Gif hio grindende þeowa sio xxv scillinga gebete. Sio þridde xii scillingas.

If she is a grinding slave, he is to pay 25 shillings compensation. The third [class]: 12 shillings.

14. Gif wið eorles birele man geligeþ xii scilł[14] gebete.

If anyone lies with a nobleman's serving-maid,[15] he is to pay 12 shillings compensation.

16. Gif wið ceorles birelan man geligeþ vi scillingu*m* gebete. Aet þære oþere ðeowa'n'[16] L scætta. Aet þare þriddan xxx scætta.

If anyone lies with a freeman's serving-maid,[17] he is to pay 6 shillings compensation.[18] For a slave of the second [class], 50 *sceattas*. For one of the third [class], 30 *sceattas*.[19]

31. Gif fri man[20] wið fries mannes wif geligeþ, his

If a free man lies with the wife of a free man, he is to pay

---

[13] This is equivalent to the king's *mundbyrd* '(compensation for violating the) right of protection', as defined in Æthelberht 8.

[14] Here and elsewhere, the abbreviation *scilł* or *sclł* has been left unexpanded as it may represent the accusative plural (*scillingas*), genitive plural (*scillinga*), or dative plural (*scillingum*) form.

[15] Literally 'female cup-bearer'.

[16] The final letter of *ðeowa'n'* is an interlinear addition in a different ink.

[17] Literally 'female cup-bearer'.

[18] Again, this is equivalent to the freeman's *mundbyrd*, as defined in Æthelberht 15.

[19] OE *sceat* here refers to 'a weight of gold equivalent to one-twentieth of a shilling', and should not be confused with the later use of the term to refer to a silver coin (P. Grierson and M. Blackburn, *Medieval European Coinage I: The Early Middle Ages (5th–10th Centuries)* (Cambridge, 1986), 157).

[20] The manuscript reading *fri man* is often treated as a compound. Arguments that the collocation represents two separate words are presented in C. Hough, '*Freo man*: a note on word division', *Neophilologus* 75 (1991), 641–3, and also apply

wergelde abicge, 7 oðer wif his agenu*m* scætte begete, 7 ðæm oðrum æt ham[21] gebrenge.	his/her wergild,[22] and to obtain another woman at his own expense, and to bring her to the other at his home.
73. Gif fri wif locbore leswæs hwæt gedeþ xxx scłł gebete.	If a free woman in a position of responsibility commits any violence, she is to pay 30 shillings compensation.
74. Mægþbot[23] sy[24] swa friges mannes.	The compensation payable by an unmarried girl is to be the same as that payable by a free woman.[25]

---

to the combination *fri wif* in Æthelberht 73. Hence I treat *fri man* as an *ad hoc* combination 'free man' in contradistinction to the term *ceorl* 'freeman', which designates a specific class within society.

[21] The manuscript reading *þam* has been emended to *ham* by successive editors. Oliver, *The Beginnings*, p. 69, defends the manuscript reading by suggesting a connection with the idiom found in German as *bei ihm* and in French as *chez lui*, both meaning 'at his home'. However, the traditional emendation is supported by comparison with the reading *æt ham* in Æthelberht 77.

[22] The *wergild*, lit. 'man-payment', was the value placed on a person's life. Here it is grammatically ambiguous whose *wergild* is meant. Arguments that the reference is to the husband's *wergild* are put forward by T. J. Rivers in two articles: 'A Reevaluation of Aethelberht 31', *Zeitschrift der Savigny-Stiftung für Rechtsgeschichte, Germanistische Abteilung* 93 (1976), 315–8; and 'Adultery in Early Anglo-Saxon Society: Æthelberht 31 in Comparison with Continental Germanic Law', *Anglo-Saxon England* 20 (1991), 19–25. As he acknowledges, however, continental analogues all require the adulterer to pay the woman's *wergild*. Scholars who take the *wergild* here to be that of the woman include *Die Gesetze der Angelsachsen*, ed. R. Schmid, 2nd ed. (Leipzig, 1858), p. 5, and C. Fell, *Women in Anglo-Saxon England* (Oxford, 1984), p. 64. A further possibility is that the seducer may be required to pay his own *wergild*, the interpretation preferred by *Ancient Laws and Institutes of England*, ed. B. Thorpe, folio edition (London, 1840) and *Gesetze*, ed. Liebermann III, 9.

[23] Oliver, *The Beginnings*, p. 76, reads incorrectly 'a point added later in a different ink' after *Mægþbot*. Although this is the impression given when the manuscript is lying flat on the table, when the page is held up to the light it becomes clear that the supposed point is in fact part of the original letter *t*.

[24] According to Liebermann (*Gesetze* I, 7) the second letter of *sy* is over an erasure. I cannot see evidence of an erasure here, but this would be in accordance with the scribe's practice elsewhere (e.g. Æthelberht 76, Æthelberht 77, Æthelberht 83), and the spacing is sufficient for two letters between the first letter of *sy* and the following word.

5. Mund þare betstan widuwan eorlcundre L scillinga gebete. Ðare oþre xx scłł, ðare þriddan xii scłł. Þare feorðan vi scłł.	The right of protection of a widow of the highest class of nobility is to be compensated for at 50 shillings. That of one of the second class at 20 shillings, of one of the third class at 12 shillings. Of one of the fourth class, at 6 shillings.
76. Gif man widuwan unagne genimeþ ii gelde seo mund sy.[26]	If anyone takes a widow who is not his own [legal wife], [the penalty] is twice the value of the right of protection.[27]
77. Gif man[28] mægþ gebigeð ccapi geceapod sy,[29] gif hit unfacne is; gif hit þonne facne is, ef[30] þær æt ham gebrenge 7 him man his scæt agefe.	If anyone pays for a girl, the bargain is to stand, if there is no fraud; if however, there is fraud, she is to be taken back home, and he is to be given back his money.
78. Gif hio cwic bearn gebyreþ healfne scæt age, gif ceorl ær swylteþ.	If she bears a living child, she is to have half the goods, if the husband dies first.

[25] This interpretation of Æthelberht 73 and 74 is proposed in C. Hough, 'Two Kentish Laws Concerning Women: A New Reading of Æthelberht 73 and 74', *Anglia* 119 (2001), 554–78, reprinted in this volume. Æthelberht 73 was previously taken to refer either to sexual or to financial misconduct (the latter being proposed in C. Fell, 'A *friwif locbore* Revisited', *Anglo-Saxon England* 13 (1984), 157–65), while Æthelberht 74 was taken to mean that injuries to a young woman were to be compensated at the same rate as injuries to a free man.

[26] Second letter of *sy* over an erasure, with space for two letters.

[27] This interpretation of Æthelberht 75 and 76 is proposed in C. Hough, 'The Widow's *Mund* in Æthelberht 75 and 76', *Journal of English and Germanic Philology* 98 (1999), 1–16, reprinted in this volume. Both clauses were previously taken to deal with the abduction of widows occupying a subordinate position under the guardianship of their relatives.

[28] The original reading *mon* has been emended to *man*, one of a number of linguistic changes made by the scribe on folios 1–37 of the manuscript.

[29] Second letter of *sy* over an erasure, with space for two letters.

[30] Possibly an error for *eft*.

79. Gif mid bearnum bugan wille, healfne scæt age.	If she wishes to live with the children, she is to have half the goods.
80. Gif ceorl agan wile swa an bearn.	If she wishes to take [another] husband, [she is to have the same share] as a child.[31]
81. Gif hio bearn ne gebyreþ fæderingmagas fioh agan, 7 morgengyfe.	If she does not bear a child, the paternal relatives[32] are to have the property and the morning-gift.[33]
82. Gif man mægþman[34] nede genimeþ, ðam agende L scillinga, 7 eft æt þam agende, sinne willan ætgebicge.	If anyone takes a girl by force, [he is to pay] 50 shillings to her guardian, and afterwards buy the guardian's consent.
83. Gif hio oþrum mæn in sceat bewyddod sy[35] xx scillinga gebete.	If she is betrothed to another man at a [bride] price, he is to pay 20 shillings compensation.
84. Gif gængang[36] geweorðeþ xxxv scilł, 7 cyninge xv scillingas.	If she is assaulted on the road, 35 shillings, and 15 shillings to the king.[37]

[31] This interpretation of Æthelberht 79 and 80 is proposed in C. Hough, 'The Early Kentish "Divorce Laws": A Reconsideration of Æthelberht, chs. 79 and 80', *Anglo-Saxon England* 23 (1994), 19–34, reprinted in this volume. The two clauses were previously taken to refer to divorce, and treated as evidence of the independent status of divorced women in early Kentish society.

[32] It is not clear whether these are relatives of the widow or of her late husband.

[33] The 'morning-gift' comprised that part of the marriage settlement paid by husband to wife the morning after the wedding night.

[34] The original reading *mægþmon* has been emended to *mægþman* by the scribe.

[35] Second letter of *sy* over an erasure, with space for two letters.

[36] Last two letters of *gængang* written over an erasure. According to Oliver, *The Beginnings*, p. 78, 'Deformed *g* here looks like a later interpolation'. Although it is unlike the scribe's usual *g*, however, it is written in the same ink as the rest of the word. There are signs of scraping towards the bottom of the second *n*, where the minims are also closer together than is usual in this hand. It seems that the scribe initially wrote *gængan*, and on realising his error, emended the second *n* by making it narrower in order to fit in an extra letter. The unusual shape of the final *g* is consistent with the elongation of letters inserted as interlinear additions by the scribe on other folios of the manuscript.

85. Gif man mid esnes cwynan geligeþ be cwicum ceorle ii gebete.	If anyone lies with the wife of an unfree servant[38] during the husband's lifetime, he is to pay 2 [shillings] compensation.[39]

Hlothhere and Eadric

6. Gif ceorl acwyle be libbendum wife 7 bearne, riht is *þæt* hit *þæt* bearn medder folgige, 7 him man[40] an his fæderingmagum wilsumne berigean geselle[41] his feoh to healdenne, oþ þæt he x wintra sie.	If a freeman dies leaving a living wife and child, it is right that the child should go with the mother, and one of its father's relatives who is willing to act is to be appointed trustee to look after its property until it is ten years old.

[37] The interpretation of the nonce occurrence *gængang* as 'waylaying' is proposed in C. Hough, 'A Reappraisal of Æthelberht 84', *Nottingham Medieval Studies* 37 (1993), 1–6, reprinted in this volume. Æthelberht 84 was previously taken to refer either to the pregnancy or to the return of the girl abducted in Æthelberht 82 and 83. Whereas Hough, 'A Reappraisal', leaves open the possibility that Æthelberht 84 should be read independently of the two preceding clauses, evidence that they form a related group referring to an abduction involving an attack on the open road is discussed further in C. Hough, 'Alfred's *domboc* and the Language of Rape: A Reconsideration of Alfred, ch. 11', *Medium Ævum* 66 (1997), 1–17, at 15–16, reprinted in this volume.

[38] Æthelberht's code progresses in descending order through the social hierarchy, concluding with the slave in chs. 89–90. Chs. 85–88 deal with the *esne*, an unfree category just above the slave class.

[39] The phrase *ii gebete* in this clause has previously been taken to refer to the payment of two-fold compensation. The new interpretation presented here is discussed in Section 3.

[40] Again, the scribe originally wrote *mon* but emended it to *man*. *Gesetze*, ed. Liebermann I, 10, notes 'geändert *men*', but I can find no justification for this and suspect that it must be a misprint in Liebermann's generally impeccable edition.

[41] The manuscript reading is *gefelle*, a nonce occurrence with no obvious etymology. The traditional emendation to *geselle* may be supported by comparison with subsequent clauses, Hlothhere and Eadric 8 and 10, in each of which the verb *gesellan* is juxtaposed with *byrig(e)an* in the sense 'give surety'.

Wihtred

12. Gif ceorl buton wifes wisdome deoflum gelde, he sie ealra his æhtan scyldig, 7 healsfange; gif butwu deoflum geldaþ, sion hio[42] healsfange, scyldigo 7 ealra æhtan.

If a freeman makes offerings to devils without his wife's knowledge, he is to forfeit all his goods and his *healsfang*;[43] if both make offerings to devils, they are both to forfeit their *healsfang*, and all their goods.[44]

2.ii. West Saxon laws relating to women

Ine

7. Be stale

Concerning theft.

Gif[45] hwa stalie[46] swa his wíf[47] nyte 7 his bearn geselle[48] lx scilł. to wite; gif[49] he ðonne stalie[50] on gewitnesse[51] ealles his hiredes[52] gongen[53] hie[54] ealle on ðeowot[55] x wintre[56]

If anyone steals without the knowledge of his wife and child(ren),[59] he is to pay 60 shillings as a fine; if, however, he steals with the knowledge of all his household, they are all to

[42] The original reading *hie* has been emended to *hio* by the scribe.

[43] The *healsfang* was a proportion of the *wergild*, sometimes (perhaps always) amounting to one tenth.

[44] It is unclear whether *7* in this clause means 'and' or 'or'. If *æhtan* refers to everything owned by the guilty couple as opposed to their moveable goods, the meaning must be 'or', but there would seem to be little sense in such an alternative. Moreover, the preceding clause stipulates forfeiture of *healsfang* for working on a Sunday, and it seems logical for the more serious offence of making offerings to devils to attract an additional penalty.

[45] CCCC 383 *Gyf.*

[46] *TR* and CCCC 383 *stalige*.

[47] *TR* adds *hit* above the line.

[48] *TR gesylle*, with *y* over an erasure; CCCC 383 *gesylle*.

[49] CCCC 383 *gyf.*

[50] *TR stalige*.

[51] CCCC 383 *gewitnysse*.

[52] *TR hyredes*.

[53] *TR gán* followed by erasure of two or three letters; CCCC 383 *gangen*.

[54] *TR hy*, with *y* over an erasure; CCCC 383 *heo*.

[55] *TR ðeowet*, with second *e* over an erasure; CCCC 383 *ðeowet*.

[56] *TR wintra*, with *a* over an erasure.

cniht mæg bion[57] ðiefðe[58] gewita.

go into slavery. A ten-year-old boy can be an accessory to theft.

23. Be elðeodies[60] monnes[61] slege[62]

Concerning the killing of a foreigner.

Gif[63] mon[64] elðeodigne[65] ófslea se cyning[66] ah twædne[67] dǽl[68] weres þriddan dæl sunu oððe mægas.[69] Gif[70] he ðonne mægleas sie[71] healf[72] kyninge[73] healf[74] se gesið. Gif[75] hit ðonne abbod[76] sie[77] oððe abbodesse[78] dælen[79] on þa ilcan wisan wið þone[80] kyning.[81]

If a foreigner is killed, the king is to have two-thirds of the wergild, his son or relatives the third part. If he has no relatives, half [is to go to] the king, and the companion [is to have] half. If, however, it is an abbot or abbess, they are to share in the same way with the king.[82]

---

[59] It is grammatically ambiguous whether *bearn* means 'child' or 'children'.

[57] *TR beon*, written above the line; CCCC 383 *beon*.

[58] *TR ðyfðe*; CCCC 383 *þyfðe*.

[60] *TR ælþeodiges*, with *æ* and first *e* over an erasure; CCCC 383 *ælðeodiges*.

[61] CCCC 383 *mannes*.

[62] *TR* and CCCC 383 *slæge*.

[63] CCCC 383 *Gyf*.

[64] *TR man*, with *a* altered from *o* by the scribe.

[65] *TR ælðeodigne*; CCCC 383 *ælþeodigne mon*.

[66] CCCC 383 *cyng*.

[67] *TR* and CCCC 383 *twegen*.

[68] *TR* adds *as þæs* above the line; CCCC 383 *dælas þæs*.

[69] *TR* and CCCC 383 *magas*.

[70] CCCC 383 *Gyf*.

[71] *TR sy*, with *y* over an erasure; CCCC 383 *sy*.

[72] CCCC 383 *half*.

[73] *TR cyninge*; CCCC 383 *cyning*.

[74] CCCC 383 *half*.

[75] CCCC 383 *Gyf*.

[76] *TR* and CCCC 383 *abbud*.

[77] *TR sy*, with *y* over an erasure; CCCC 383 *sy*.

[78] *TR* and CCCC 383 *abbudisse*.

[79] *TR* and CCCC 383 *dælon*.

[80] CCCC 383 *ðonne*.

[81] *TR* and CCCC 383 *cyning*.

[82] The clause continues with regulations relating to various classes of Britons, which are not reproduced here.

31. Be þon[83] þe mon[84] wíf byccge[85] 7 þon*ne*[86] sio[87] gift tostande[88]

Concerning paying for a wife, and then the marriage not taking place.

Gif[89] mon[90] wíf gebyccge[91] 7 sio[92] gyft[93] forð ne cume agife[94] þæt feoh 7 forgielde[95] 7 gebete þam byrgean[96] swa his borgbryce[97] sie.[98]

If anyone pays for a wife and the marriage does not proceed, the payment is to be returned and as much again, and the surety is to be recompensed according to the value of the breach of his surety.

38. Be þon[99] ðe ryhtgesamhiwan[100] bearn hæbben[101] 7 þon*ne* se wer gewite[102]

Concerning a legally married couple having a child, and then the man dying.

Gif[103] ceorl[104] 7 his wif bearn hæbben gemæne 7 fere[105] se ceorl forð[106] hæbbe sio[107] modor[108] hire bearn 7 fede[109] agife[110] hire mon[111] vi scilł. to fostre, cu on sumera oxan on wintra;[112] healden[113] þa mægas[114] þone frumstol,[115] oððæt hit gewintred[116] sie.[117]

If a freeman and his wife have a child together and the husband dies, the mother is to have her child and bring it up; she is to be given 6 shillings towards its maintenance, a cow in summer, an ox in winter;[118] the relatives are to take charge of the family home until it is grown up.

---

[83] *TR þam* (written above line); CCCC 383 *þan̲*.
[84] *TR man*, with *a* altered from *o* by the scribe; CCCC 383 *man*.
[85] *TR* and CCCC 383 *bycge*.
[86] This word is not present in CCCC 383.
[87] *TR seo*, altered from *sio* by the scribe; CCCC 383 *seo*.
[88] *TR tostande*, with *a* altered from *o* by the scribe; CCCC 383 *wiðstande*.
[89] CCCC 383 *Gyf.*
[90] *TR man*, with *a* altered from *o* by the scribe.
[91] *TR* and CCCC 383 *bycge*.
[92] *TR seo*, with *eo* over an erasure; CCCC 383 *seo*.
[93] *TR gift*.
[94] CCCC 383 *agyfe*.
[95] *TR forgilde*; CCCC 383 *forgylde*.
[96] CCCC 383 *byrgean* altered to *borgean*, possibly by the same hand that writes *borgan* in the margin. The latter is dated to the sixteenth century by *Gesetze,* ed. Liebermann I, 102.
[97] *TR* and CCCC 383 *borhbryce*.
[98] *TR sy*, with *y* over an erasure; CCCC 383 *sy*.
[99] *TR ðam*, altered from *ðon* by the scribe; CCCC 383 *ðan̲*.

57. Be cierlisces[119] monnes[120] stale

Gif[121] ceorl[122] ceap forstilð[123] 7 bireð[124] into his ærne[125] 7 befehð þærinne mon[126] þon*ne* bið[127] se his dǽl synnig[128] butan[129] þa*m* wife anu*m* forðon[130] hio[131] sceal[132] hire ealdore[133] hieran[134] gif[135] hio[136] dear mid aðe gecyðan þ*æt* hio[137] þæs forstolenan ne onbite nime hire ðriddan sceat.[138]

Concerning theft by a man of *ceorl* class.

If a freeman steals cattle[139] and takes it into his house, where it is seized, then he is guilty for his part,[140] except his wife alone, because she must obey her lord: if she dares to declare on oath that she has not tasted what was stolen, she is to take her third share.

---

100 *TR rihtgesamhiwan*; CCCC 383 *rihtgesamhiwan*.
101 *TR habban*, with first *a* over an erasure; CCCC 383 *habban*.
102 *7 þonne se wer gewite* not present in CCCC 383.
103 CCCC 383 *Gyf.*
104 *TR ciorl.*
105 CCCC 383 *fære.*
106 *TR 7 se ciorl forðfære.*
107 *TR seo*, with *eo* over an erasure; CCCC 383 *seo*.
108 *TR moder*, with *e* over an erasure.
109 *TR* adds *7* above the line.
110 CCCC 383 *agyfe.*
111 *TR man hire*, with *a* altered from *o* by the scribe; CCCC 383 *hire man*.
112 CCCC 383 *wintran.*
113 *TR healden*, with second *e* over an erasure; CCCC 383 *healdan*.
114 *TR* and CCCC 383 *magas*.
115 Letters *um* are missing from CCCC 173 because of a hole in the parchment, but the reading *frumstol* is clear in both *TR* and CCCC 383.
116 CCCC 383 *gewintrod.*
117 *TR sy*, with *y* over an erasure; CCCC 383 *sy*.
118 This is generally taken to be an annual allowance. T. Rivers suggests that rather than the widow actually being provided with a cow and an ox, 'What this law may mean is that a cow was milked and an ox harnessed to furnish the family's subsistence at the yearly value of six shillings' ('Widows' Rights in Anglo-Saxon Law', *American Journal of Legal History* 19 (1975), 208–15, at 212). Comparison with Ine 26, however, where the maintenance of a foundling is set at six shillings for the first year, rising to twelve shillings for the second year and thirty shillings for the third, indicates that provision of the two animals in addition to six shillings per year is not excessive for the family of a *ceorl*.
119 *TR cirlisces*; CCCC 383 *cyrlisces*.
120 *TR mannes*, with *a* altered from *o* by the scribe; CCCC 383 *mannes*.
121 CCCC 383 *Gyf.*

[122] *TR ciorl.*
[123] *TR forsteleþ*; CCCC 383 *forstylð.*
[124] *TR byrð*; CCCC 383 *bereð.*
[125] *TR huse*, with *ærne* added above the line.
[126] *TR 7 hit man ðærinne befehð*, with *man* altered from *mon* by the scribe; CCCC 383 *7 befehþ ðærinne*, with *mann* added above the line and *hitt* below in a later hand.
[127] CCCC 383 has *biþ* as an interlinear addition in a later hand.
[128] *TR scyldig*; CCCC 383 reads *synnig* but has *scyldig* as an interlinear addition in a later hand.
[129] *TR butan*, with *a* altered from *o* by the scribe.
[130] CCCC 383 *forðan.*
[131] *TR heo*, with *e* over an erasure; CCCC 383 *heo.*
[132] CCCC 383 *sceol*, but the *o* shows signs of alteration.
[133] *TR hlaforde*; CCCC 383 *ealdre.*
[134] *TR hyran*, with *y* over an erasure; CCCC 383 *hyran.*
[135] CCCC 383 *gyf.*
[136] *TR heo*, with *e* over an erasure; CCCC 383 *heo.*
[137] *TR heo*, with *e* over an erasure; CCCC 383 '*h'eo*, with *h* added above the line in a later hand.
[138] *TR nime hire ðriddan gescead*, with *gescead* over an erasure; CCCC 383 *nime hire ðæne ðriddan dæl ðære æhta.*
[139] OE *ceap* also has a more general sense 'moveable property', and this is how it is understood here by *Ancient Laws*, ed. Thorpe, p. 60, and *Gesetze*, ed. Liebermann I, 115. However, the sense 'cattle' occurs in Ine 40, and is supported in Ine 57 by the allusion to eating the stolen goods. Moreover, the preceding clause deals with the procedure for returning an unsound beast after purchase, and it seems logical for a law on the purchase of cattle to be followed by a law on cattle-theft.
[140] An alternative translation given in *The Laws of the Earliest English Kings*, ed. F. L. Attenborough (Cambridge, 1922), p. 55, and followed by Fell, *Women in Anglo-Saxon England*, p. 59, is 'he shall forfeit his share [of the household property]'. This makes good sense, especially in view of the *TR* reading *scyldig*, a term found elsewhere in Ine's code with a sense of forfeiture or liability (e.g. Ine 5 *Gif hwa sie deaðes scyldig* 'If anyone is liable for the death penalty', Ine 6 *sie he scyldig ealles his ierfes* 'he is to forfeit all his property', Ine 28 *þonne bið he wites scyldig* 'then he is liable for the fine' (*Gesetze,* ed. Liebermann I, 90, 100)). However, while the semantic range of both *synnig* and *scyldig* includes the idea of guilt, only *scyldig* refers to forfeiture, and this suggests that they would be used interchangeably only in the former sense. A further difficulty is that this interpretation of Ine 57 would require the word *dæl* to be in either the genitive or instrumental case. So far as I have been able to ascertain from A. di P.Healey and R. L. Venezky, *A Microfiche Concordance to Old English* (Toronto, 1980), there are no occurrences of such a construction where *scyldig* is combined with an uninflected noun. I therefore prefer the translation 'guilty for his part' suggested in

63. Be gesiðcundes monnes[141] fære[142]

Concerning travelling by a man of *gesið* class.

Gif[143] gesiðcund mon[144] fare þon*ne* mot he habban his gerefan mid him 7 his smið 7 his cildfestran.

If a man of *gesið* class travels, then he may have with him his reeve and his smith and his children's nurse.

Ancient Laws, ed. Thorpe, p. 60, and followed by *English Historical Documents, c. 500–1042*, ed. D. Whitelock, 2nd ed. (London, 1979), p. 405.

141 *TR mannes*, with *a* altered from *o* by the scribe; CCCC 383 *mannes*.

142 CCCC 383 *fare*.

143 CCCC 383 *Gyf*.

144 *TR man*, with *a* altered from *o* by the scribe; CCCC 383 *man*.

3. Discussion

Despite the disparate nature of the laws represented above, some common themes emerge. A widow's right to custody of her children is affirmed in three of the four codes (Æthelberht 79, Hlothhere and Eadric 6, Ine 38), although it is unclear whether the appointment of trustees from within the extended family indicates that the mother was not legally competent to act in such a capacity, or reflects a potential conflict of interest between herself and the children.[1] The stipulation in Hlothhere and Eadric 6 that the trustee is to be chosen from the paternal relatives appears to support the latter interpretation, as does the possibility raised in Æthelberht 80 that the mother may remarry. It seems unlikely that she would have been incapable of handling her children's affairs as widows otherwise appear to enjoy a high degree of financial autonomy, inheriting half the joint property from a marriage resulting in children (Æthelberht 78) and receiving compensation for offences against their dependants (Æthelberht 75). The only other women whose right to receive such compensation is explicitly stated within the early laws are abbesses, who themselves may often have been widows (Ine 23).[2] It is, however, possible that other clauses where gender is not specified may be intended to include women. Fell points out that the term *agend* 'could be used of any person in charge of a community, man or woman in charge of an estate, abbess in charge of a monastery, with regard to any of the dependants, male or female, within that community'.[3] The person entitled to compensation for the abducted girl in Æthelberht 82 may therefore have been a female, rather than a male, relative. Similarly, since women no less than men could be of *ceorl* (free) or *eorl* (noble) class, compensation for sleeping with their female slaves may have been payable to either sex under the terms of Æthelberht 14 and Æthelberht 16.

---

[1] A further possibility suggested to me by an anonymous referee of this paper is that such arrangements may reflect the bilateral nature of Anglo-Saxon kinship and a desire to maintain or to assert the claims and responsibilities of both kins.

[2] There are problems with the interpretation of this clause, which make it unsafe to draw firm inferences from it (see C. Hough, 'A Reconsideration of Ine, ch.23', *Neuphilologische Mitteilungen* 98 (1997), 43–51, reprinted in this volume). The meaning of *gesið* is uncertain, and it is not clear why it should take the nominative case in apposition to a dative form *kyninge*. It makes little sense for the king's share of the *wergild* to be reduced if the dead man had no relatives, and the plural form of the verb *dœlen* is difficult to account for. It seems likely that the received text is corrupt.

[3] Fell, *Women in Anglo-Saxon England*, pp. 15–6.

A stark contrast is presented in Æthelberht's code between the inheritance rights of a widowed mother (Æthelberht 78) and of a childless widow (Æthelberht 81), with the latter receiving nothing. On this basis, it has been suggested that 'the paternal inheritance destined for widows was more a provision for the children than for the widows, since widows were not entitled to inherit from their late husbands if they had no children'.[4] However, this does not appear to be supported by Æthelberht 80, where the share of the property inherited by the widow is contrasted with the share due to each child. The explanation may lie elsewhere. Both continental Germanic and later Anglo-Saxon law distinguish for purposes of compensation between offences against women of child-bearing age and against those in earlier or later life, with the former receiving twice or even three times as much as a pre-pubertal or post-menopausal victim.[5] A similar tendency to value women according to their capacity for child-bearing may underlie seventh-century English inheritance law.[6]

This hypothesis is supported by another recurring theme to emerge from the above corpus: the definition of women in terms of marital status. Whereas the legal standing of an Anglo-Saxon male depended on social class, with no further distinction being drawn once majority had been reached at the age of ten years, other factors come into play in relation to women. With the exception of clauses relating to different classes of female slaves within Æthelberht's code (Æthelberht 10, 11, 14, 16) and to the children's nurse of Ine 63, most laws here relate specifically to the unmarried girl (Æthelberht 74, 77, 82, 83, 84, Ine 31), the married woman (Æthelberht 31, 85, Wihtred 12, Ine 7, 57), or the widow (Æthelberht 75, 76, 78, 79, 80, 81, Hlothhere and Eadric 6, Ine 38). This is sometimes taken to reflect the importance placed on virginity in Anglo-Saxon society: 'Their virginity, or lack of it, determines the type of protection they receive under the law'.[7] A majority of these laws, however, are not concerned with the protection due to women, but with their rights, responsibilities, and duties. Moreover, rather than a binary distinction

---

[4] Rivers, 'Widows' Rights', 212.

[5] This is discussed in C. Hough, 'A New Reading of Alfred, ch. 26', *Nottingham Medieval Studies* 41 (1997), 1–12, reprinted in this volume.

[6] A further possibility suggested to me by an anonymous referee of this paper is that the next stage of a family, and thus claims on inheritance, is established not at marriage, but at the point where children are born. It may be that only then does a wife become fully part of a new family, with claims on her husband's kin and inheritance.

[7] M. P. Richards and B. J. Stanfield, 'Concepts of Women in the Laws', *New Readings on Women in Old English Literature*, ed. H. Damico and A. H. Olsen (Bloomington, 1990), pp. 89–99, at p. 93.

between virgin and non-virgin, there is a three-fold distinction between the unmarried girl, the married woman, and the widow. In many instances, social class is also either stated or implied, with a direct correspondence between women and men,[8] but a woman's rights were crucially affected by whether she had a living husband, a dead husband, or no husband at all. The legal position is thus based on what might be termed the 'three ages of women': pre-marriage, marriage and post-marriage.

The marriage contract also features in both Kentish and West Saxon law, with financial restitution being required in the event that an agreed marriage does not take place (Æthelberht 77, Ine 31). In neither case is it entirely clear whether the defaulter is the bride or groom, but since the initial outlay is made by the latter in the form of a payment to the bride or her family, the provision appears to be for his money to be returned to him in the event that the girl fails to fulfil her side of the bargain. The term *facen* in Æthelberht 77 is used in Ine 56 with reference to blemished cattle, and this is usually taken to imply that the girl can be sent back home if, after the marriage, she turns out to be 'a piece of damaged goods'.[9] This can scarcely be the case in Ine 31, however, since the term used for the bride in all three manuscripts – both in the rubric and in the text itself – is not *mægþ* 'virgin', as in Æthelberht 77, but *wif*, the generic term for a (sexually active) adult woman. There may be a possibility that this refers to the woman's second marriage, a topic of recurring importance in both seventh-century and later Anglo-Saxon law. Here at least the *gyft* must refer to the wedding itself,[10] indicating that the problem lies in the failure

---

[8] For instance, the compensation allocated to three of the four classes of widows in Æthelberht 75 corresponds to the *mundbyrd* (compensation for violating the right of protection) of the king (Æthelberht 8), nobleman (inferred from Æthelberht 13), and freeman (Æthelberht 15) respectively. P. H. Sawyer, *From Roman Britain to Norman England*, 2nd ed. (London, 1998), p. 173, suggests that the compensation of 20 shillings due to the second class of widow may correspond to the *mundbyrd* of a further noble class within Kentish society. This suggestion is explored further in C. Hough, 'The Structure of English Society in the Seventh Century: A New Reading of Æthelberht 12', this volume.

[9] R. Hill, 'Marriage in Seventh-Century England', *Saints, Scholars and Heroes: Studies in Medieval Literature in Honour of Charles W. Jones*, ed. M. H. King and W. M. Stevens, 2 vols. (Collegeville, MN, 1979) I, 67–75, at 69. An alternative reading provided by *Ancient Laws*, ed. Thorpe, p. 9, is that the bride-price is initially paid in cattle or goods, and that these are to be returned if faulty.

[10] The use of the term *gift* to mean 'wedding' is analysed in detail by A. Fischer, *Engagement, Wedding, and Marriage in Old English* (Heidelberg, 1986), pp. 36–44, who demonstrates that it is a West Saxon word and includes 'both the more

of one or both parties to complete the contractual agreement. It is possible that the prospective husband may be at fault in neglecting to fulfil his financial obligations,[11] but more likely that if the wedding does not take place after he has paid the agreed bride-price, double the money is to be recompensed to him.[12] This interpretation not only makes good sense, but is paralleled in other Anglo-Saxon and continental sources. The *Theodore Penitential* II, 12.34 states that if a girl refuses to live with the man to whom she is betrothed, his money is to be repaid plus a third, although if he backs out of the agreement, he simply loses his money;[13] while under seventh-century Lombard law, Rothair's Edict 192 states that if the relatives of a betrothed girl connive at her marrying someone else, her original fiancé is entitled to payment of double the marriage portion.[14]

The verb used in both Æthelberht 77 and Ine 31 to refer to the payment made by the bridegroom is *gebicgan*, the etymon of PDE *buy*. This has sometimes been taken to indicate that the bride was treated as a chattel rather than as a party to the contractual agreement, becoming her husband's property through purchase.[15] As long ago as 1876, however, Young pointed out that the use of a single legal form both for sale and for marriage need not imply that they were of the same nature,[16] while in 1943 Mezger demonstrated that the original meaning in Germanic law was 'exchange', in the sense 'to make a marriage-agreement through exchange of a gift'.[17] Anthropological evidence too indicates that 'purchase of

---

abstract "entrance into wedlock" and the more concrete "marriage ceremony with attendant festivities"'.

[11] This is the interpretation presented by early editors such as Thorpe, *Ancient Laws*, p. 53, and Schmid, *Die Gesetze*, p. 35, as well as by E. Young, 'The Anglo-Saxon Family Law', *Essays in Anglo-Saxon Law*, ed. H. Adams (Boston, MA, 1876), pp. 121–82, at p. 169. So too *An Anglo-Saxon Dictionary based on the Manuscript Collections of the late Joseph* Bosworth, ed. T. N. Toller (Oxford, 1898), p. 475, translates: 'If a man buy a wife and the sum agreed upon be not forthcoming'.

[12] This is the interpretation preferred by later scholars such as *Gesetze*, ed. Liebermann I, 103; *The Laws*, ed. Attenborough, p. 47; *English Historical Documents*, ed. Whitelock, p. 402.

[13] *Councils and Ecclesiastical Documents Relating to Great Britain and Ireland*, ed. A. W. Haddan and W. Stubbs, 3 vols. (Oxford, 1869–73) III, 201.

[14] K. F. Drew, *The Lombard Laws* (Philadelphia, PA, 1973), p. 88.

[15] This is the view taken for instance by D. M. Stenton, *The English Woman in History* (London, 1957), p. 8; Hill, 'Marriage', 69; A. Klinck, 'Anglo-Saxon Women and the Law', *Journal of Medieval History* 8 (1982), 107–21, at 109.

[16] Young, 'The Anglo-Saxon Family Law', p. 164.

[17] F. Mezger, 'Did the Institution of Marriage by Purchase Exist in Old Germanic Law?', *Speculum* 18 (1943), 369–71.

the wife ... is not a legitimate interpretation of brideprice in primitive societies'.[18] It is of course fallacious to assume that Old English words have the same meaning as their modern derivatives, and Fell argues for an alternative interpretation of the verb *bicgan* in marriage contexts as 'to pay for'.[19] Part of the problem is that it is unclear whether the payment was made to the woman's family or to herself. Mezger argues that 'it belongs to the bride and serves as a financial security for her',[20] and the same view is expressed by Fell.[21] This was certainly the case later in Anglo-Saxon England,[22] and despite a lack of unequivocal evidence relating to the early period, there seems no reason to believe that a radical change has taken place.

It is significant that the 'marriage sequence' in Æthelberht 77–81 is directly followed by the 'abduction sequence' from Æthelberht 82–84, since it appears from the financial arrangements outlined in Æthelberht 82 that the liaison was expected to result in marriage. This has sometimes been treated as evidence of an older system of 'marriage by capture',[23] but it should be noted that the clause focuses on the payment of compensation, and that the perpetrator is still obliged to negotiate the terms of a formal marriage contract as outlined in chs. 77–81. Both points seem to me to support Colman's view that the position taken towards abduction in English as in continental law is that 'it is not lawful, but that lawful unions could result if certain conditions were met'.[24] Both here and in Æthelberht 31, there is a concern to ensure that the bridegroom was not able to obtain a wife cheaply by bypassing the proper legal channels. The two clauses have often been compared, and indeed it has been suggested that Æthelberht 31 is concerned with a form of legalised abduction, with the consent of all parties.[25] However, the latter clause contains no vocabulary

---

[18] L. Lancaster, 'Kinship in Anglo-Saxon Society', *British Journal of Sociology* 9 (1958), 230–50, 359–77, at 243.

[19] Fell, *Women in Anglo-Saxon England*, p. 16.

[20] Mezger, 'Did the Institution?', 369.

[21] Fell, *Women in Anglo-Saxon England*, p. 16.

[22] An overview of the evidence is provided by Fell, *Women in Anglo-Saxon England*, pp. 56–73.

[23] See for instance F. Pollock and F. W. Maitland, *The History of English Law before the time of Edward I*, 2 vols. (Cambridge, 1898) II, 365; D. Bethurum, 'Stylistic Features of Old English Laws', *Modern Language Review* 27 (1932), 263–79, at 271; M. C. Ross, 'Concubinage in Anglo-Saxon England', *Past and Present* 108 (1985), 3–34, at 3.

[24] R. V. Colman, 'The Abduction of Women in Barbaric Law', *Florilegium* 5 (1983), 62–75, at 64.

[25] See for instance Colman, 'The Abduction', 70, and Ross, 'Concubinage', 12.

relating to abduction or assault, and Æthelberht's code is in general so logically structured that two laws on a similar topic would be expected to be grouped together.[26] Fell suggests conversely that Æthelberht 82 and 83 may refer not to abduction but to sexual intercourse or rape;[27] but in such a case we should expect the verb *geligan* 'to lie with' rather than *geniman* 'to take'.

The relationship between Æthelberht 82 and Æthelberht 83 is not entirely clear, since the reduction of compensation from 50 to 20 shillings appears to be linked with aggravating rather than extenuating circumstances. In the belief that compensation should be increased rather than reduced if the girl had already been engaged to someone else, scholars from at least the nineteenth century have taken this to be an additional payment, perhaps made to the original fiancé to compensate him for his loss.[28] There may, however, be an alternative explanation. Under the terms of Æthelberht 82, the abductor makes a heavy payment in order to achieve his objective of marriage. There is no indication in Æthelberht 83 that this objective is still within reach. An engagement *in sceat* was a contractually binding arrangement, and modern scholarship may have been too ready to assume that it would be set aside. I should like to suggest that rather than stipulating a supplementary fine, Æthelberht 83 may present an alternative scenario to the preceding clause. If the girl is free to marry, the abductor pays 50 shillings in addition to the usual marriage price. If she is not free to marry, his payment is reduced to 20 shillings. Æthelberht 84 would then follow directly on from Æthelberht 83, dealing with a situation where the disappointed suitor makes a last-ditch attempt by assaulting the girl on the open road – possibly, as suggested by comparison with Frankish legislation which I have discussed elsewhere, actually on her way to be married.[29] In such a case,

---

[26] For instance, Æthelberht 73 and 74, concerning compensation for assaults carried out by women, immediately follow the 'personal injury tariff' in Æthelberht 33–72, defining the compensation payable for injuries to various parts of the body; and Æth 76, imposing a heavy penalty on anyone who attempts to coerce a widow into marriage without a proper contract, is directly followed by regulations concerning the marriage contract itself.

[27] C. Fell, 'An Appendix to Carole Hough's Article "A Reappraisal of Æthelberht 84"', *Nottingham Medieval Studies* 37 (1993), 7–8.

[28] Young, 'The Anglo-Saxon Family Law', p. 168. Colman, 'Abduction', 69, cites parallels from Lombardic and Visigothic law, and states categorically that '[i]n Aethelberht's laws 20 shillings compensation had to be paid to the jilted man'.

[29] *Pactus Legis Salicae*, ed. Eckhardt 13,14; Hough, 'Alfred's *domboc*', 15–16. A point in favour of the traditional interpretation of Æthelberht 83 is the fact that

compensation rises from 20 to 35 shillings, in addition to a fine of 15 shillings payable to the king.

A small point in favour of this interpretation is the tense of the verb *sy* in Æthelberht 83. This is a present subjunctive, indicating that the engagement is still current, as opposed to the past subjunctive *wære*, which would support the view that it had been superseded. It is slightly unfortunate that, as in Æthelberht 76, 77 and probably 74, the second letter of *sy* has been written over an erasure. Although it is not possible to recover the original reading, the spacing indicates that two letters have been erased, and comparison with the scribe's practice elsewhere suggests that this is a linguistic revision of *sie* to *sy*.[30]

Some of the interpretive problems associated with the early laws stem from the use of vocabulary which is rarely if at all attested elsewhere. The nonce occurrence *mægdenman* in Æthelberht 10 is usually taken to refer to a virgin by analogy with the attested terms *mægden* and *mædenman*. Although this fits into the context of sexual relations, however, it is difficult to reconcile with the lower penalties stipulated in Æthelberht 11 if the woman is a *grindende þeowa* 'grinding slave' or a *þridde* 'third class'. Presumably these too could have been virgins. Comparison with Æthelberht 11 suggests rather that the *mægdenman* was a particular type of slave, and one well up in the hierarchy. Compensation for sleeping with her is set at a very high rate: fifty shillings is equivalent to the king's *mundbyrd* 'right of protection' as established in Æthelberht 8. As it appears from Æthelberht 14 and Æthelberht 16 that the seduction of a *birele* 'cup-bearer' was also compensated by payment of the owner's *mundbyrd*,[31] Thorpe suggested that the *mægdenman* may have held a similar post.[32] Unfortunately, however, the interpretation of *birele* is itself problematic. Although the literal meaning is 'cup-bearer', the occurrences in the laws have sometimes been taken to support a wider

---

Pactus Legis Salicae, ed Eckhardt 13,13 specifies compensation to the girl's original fiancé.

[30] *Textus Roffensis: Rochester Cathedral Library Manuscript A.3.5. Part I*, ed. P. H. Sawyer, Early English Manuscripts in Facsimile 7 (Copenhagen, 1957), 14, comments: 'When on fo. 3 lines 16, 20, 21 the *y* of *sy* is written over an erasure, the original form was probably *sie*, cf. fo. 2v line 16 *Gif dynt sie*'. Æthelberht 83 appears on fol. 3v lines 5–7.

[31] The *mundbyrd* of an *eorl* is not explicitly stated in Æthelberht's code, but may be inferred from Æthelberht 13, which gives 12 shillings as the compensation for manslaughter on an *eorl*'s premises.

[32] *Ancient Laws*, ed. Thorpe, pp. 2–3. The possibility is also considered by *Gesetze*, ed. Liebermann III, 7.

application 'serving-maid'.[33] On the one hand, the high amount of compensation required in Æthelberht 14 and 16 suggests that this was an important and distinctive office; on the other, the internal logic of Æthelberht's code would seem to require the term to include all female slaves above the second and third class. By the same token, the *mægdenman* of Æthelberht 10 might be taken to cover all female slaves not included within the grinding or third class categories. The issue cannot finally be resolved.

Terminology relating to the free classes may also be ambiguous, and indeed there are differences of usage even within the four seventh-century codes. Æthelberht's laws use *man* as both a generic and a masculine term, beginning *Gif man* 'If anyone' even where the subject is clearly masculine, as in chs. 10, 76, 77, 82 and 85. This tends to obscure the fact that OE *man* also has a broader sense 'human being', as reflected in the final element of the terms *mægdenman* (Æthelberht 10) and *mægþman* (Æthelberht 82), and may be partly responsible for the translation of the last two words of Æthelberht 74 in previous editions as 'free man'. I have argued elsewhere that the sense is in fact 'free woman', referring back to the *fri wif* of the preceding clause.[34] The later seventh-century laws use *ceorl* rather than *man* in masculine contexts, as in Hlothhere and Eadric 6 and Wihtred 12: *Gif ceorl.* The difficulty here is that OE *ceorl* means both 'freeman', referring to a particular rank in society, and 'husband'. The two meanings are clearly differentiated in Æthelberht's code, where the reference is to social class in ch. 16 and to marriage in chs. 78, 80 and 85, but either seems appropriate in instances such as Hlothhere and Eadric 6, Wihtred 12, Ine 38 and Ine 57. It may indeed be possible that both meanings are implied, so that the choice of a single translation forces a false distinction. Discussing Wihtred 12 and the following clause, referring to the same crime committed by a slave, Charles-Edwards comments:

> Here *ceorl* means both 'husband' in relation to his wife and 'freeman' in relation to the slave. Just before this passage the laws have been using the word *friman* 'freeman'; they switch to *ceorl* in order to express the freeman's rôle as husband and head of the family.[35]

---

[33] *English Historical Documents*, ed. Whitelock, p. 392; Dictionary of Old English Project, *Dictionary of Old English A–G*. Version 2.0. CD-ROM, 2008, s.v. *byrle*.

[34] Hough, 'Two Kentish Laws'.

[35] T. M. Charles-Edwards, 'Kinship, Status and the Origins of the Hide', *Past and Present* 56 (1972), 3–33, at 10.

It seems to me that a similar argument may be applied to the use of the term *wif* in both Kentish and West Saxon law. While this is the generic term for a sexually active adult woman in contradistinction to the virgin, it often appears within the context of marriage, and is most commonly linked with the rank of free man or *ceorl*. Like a *ceorl*, however, a *wif* may be married or unmarried, and the collocation *fri wif* in Æthelberht 73 reflects the independent status of the woman in her own right. It may therefore be possible to suggest that as with *ceorl*, *wif* means both 'wife' in relation to her husband and 'free woman' in relation to servants.

This suggestion is supported by the use of a different term, *cwyne*, to denote the wife of a servant in Æthelberht 85. Although sometimes translated 'woman', apparently with the implication that this may be a more casual relationship,[36] marital status is suggested by the use of the word *ceorl* to refer to her husband,[37] and this is consistent with the positioning of the clause at the end of a sequence concerning marriage and abduction. Unfortunately, interpretation of Æthelberht 85 as a whole is less than straightforward. The phrase *be cwicum ceorle* may be a legal formula, as it reappears more than four centuries later in the laws of Cnut, where II Cnut 53 begins *Gif be cwicum ceorle wif hi be oðrum were forlicge* 'If during the lifetime of her husband a woman commits adultery with another man'.[38] Although not recorded elsewhere in the extant corpus of Old English, the Latin equivalent occurs in a similar context in continental law. *Pactus Legis Salicae* 15 refers to the penalty for abducting a wife *uiuo marito* 'during the lifetime of her husband',[39] and the same phrase occurs in *Capitula Legi Salicae Addita* V, 133[40] and *Lex Ribuaria* 39.[41] More problematic is the meaning of the following phrase *ii gebete*. All previous editors take this to refer to two-fold compensation. The standard translation is that of Whitelock: 'If anyone lies with the woman of a servant while her husband is alive, he is to pay a two-fold

[36] *The Laws*, ed. Attenborough, p. 15; *English Historical Documents*, ed. Whitelock, p. 393.

[37] The alternative meaning of *ceorl* to refer to social class is of course ruled out here as the clause is concerned with the much lower rank of *esne*.

[38] *Gesetze,* ed. Liebermann I, 348.

[39] *Pactus Legis Salicae*, ed. K. A. Eckhardt, Monumenta Germaniae Historica, Legum Sectio I: Leges nationum Germanicarum 4.1 (Hanover, 1962); *Leges Alamannorum*, ed. K. A. Eckhardt, Monumenta Germaniae Historica, Legum sectio I: Leges nationum Germanicarum 4.1 (Hanover, 1962), 70.

[40] *Pactus Legis Salicae*, ed. Eckhardt, 267.

[41] *Lex Ribvaria*, ed. F. Beyerle and R. Buchner, Monumenta Germaniae Historica, Legum Sectio I: Leges nationum Germanicarum 3.2 (Hanover, 1954), 91.

compensation'.[42] The problem here is that it is not clear what amount of compensation is to be doubled. Liebermann takes it to be the sum payable for a single woman;[43] although he also discusses the possibility that the penalty may be double the value of the *esne*.[44] Alternatively, it may refer to a situation where the proviso *be cwicum ceorle* does not apply. Whatever the explanation, Æthelberht's code contains no corresponding clause defining the simple compensation for this offence. If the reference is to the doubling of a penalty, we must assume that at least one clause has been lost from the extant text. A further difficulty is that all other laws dealing with sexual offences within this code specify compensation in terms of fixed sums of money. Multiples occur mostly in relation to theft, with reference to the value of the item stolen.[45] Æthelberht 85 is not only ambiguous, but anomalous.

It appears to have escaped notice in relation to Æthelberht 85 that elsewhere in the Kentish laws, a Roman numeral can stand alone to designate a number of shillings. In Hlothhere and Eadric 10, the Roman numeral *C* is used to refer to a penalty of 100 shillings: *gelde þonne C buton aðe* 'he is then to pay 100 [shillings] without an oath'.[46] Given the elliptical style of Æthelberht's laws, it may be worth considering the possibility that the Roman numeral *ii* in Æthelberht 85 refers similarly not to two-fold compensation, but to two shillings. Comparison with other clauses concerning sexual offences within the same code suggests that this is not an implausible sum. The closest analogy is provided by Æthelberht 16, dealing with the dependants of a freeman. Since an *esne* was lower in status than a freeman, it seems unlikely that the sums involved in Æthelberht 85 would exceed the scale of compensation established in Æthelberht 16. It may be as well to discount the penalty of six shillings for sleeping with a *birele*, in view of the possibility noted above that payment of a sum equivalent to the owner's *mundbyrd* may reflect a high status attached to this office. Parallels to Æthelberht 85 may rather be sought in the penalties for sleeping with the freeman's second and third class slaves, set at 50 *sceattas* (2½ shillings) and 30 *sceattas* (1½ shillings) respectively. Compensation for sleeping with a servant's wife might be expected to fall somewhere around this mark. It may well have been two shillings.

---

42 *English Historical Documents*, ed. Whitelock, p. 393.
43 *Gesetze,* ed. Liebermann I, 8.
44 *Gesetze,* ed. Liebermann III, 16.
45 An example is Æthelberht 90: *Gif þeo steleþ, II gelde gebete* 'If a slave steals, he is to pay two-fold compensation' (*Gesetze,* ed. Liebermann I, 8).
46 *Gesetze,* ed. Liebermann I, 10. The reading occurs on *TR* fol. 4v line 7.

Late-seventh-century legislation from both Kent and Wessex is concerned to protect the separate legal identity of the married woman, defining the limits of her implication within a crime committed by her husband while at the same time making clear her responsibility for her own actions (Wihtred 12, Ine 7, Ine 57). All three clauses show that husband and wife were separately accountable under the law. However, whereas Wihtred 12 and Ine 7 focus on the woman's knowledge of her husband's crime, treating her as an accessory if she was aware of what he was doing, Ine 57 makes allowance for her unwilling involvement *forðon hio sceal hire ealdore hieran* 'because she must obey her lord'. It is presumably this phrase that forms the basis of a recent claim that:

> The written sources, and in particular the seventh-century laws of the West Saxon Ine ... describe passive women whose position is defined in relation to their menfolk (Ine 57).[47]

This may be rather a sweeping statement to support by a reference to a single law, especially as the same clause also makes it clear that the woman was considered oath-worthy and was entitled to a third share of the joint property. This is the first statement in the extant laws of a woman's right to clear herself of suspicion by oath, and it indicates that she was able to act as a principal in her own affairs. Oath-giving was central to the Anglo-Saxon legal system: indeed, oaths are mentioned in no less than nineteen clauses within Ine's code alone. The majority of these are oaths of exculpation, allowing oaths to be used to refute charges covering a range of offences including forced entry (Ine 45), homicide (Ine 16, 35, 54), theft (Ine 17, 25, 28, 46, 53) and conspiracy (Ine 52). It is thus of the utmost significance that women were considered to be oath-worthy. Only thus could they defend themselves at law and play a full part in the juridical process.

The reference in Ine 57 to *hire ðriddan sceat* 'her third share' suggests that this was the established proportion of the property due to the wife in late-seventh-century Wessex.[48] Although there is no evidence for

---

[47] N. Stoodley, 'Burial Rites, Gender and the Creation of Kingdoms: the Evidence from Seventh-Century Wessex', *Anglo-Saxon Studies in Archaeology and History,* 10 (1999), 99–107, at 106.

[48] Rivers, 'Widows' Rights', 212 n.15, comments: 'It appears reasonable to conclude that from Ine's time (late seventh century), the wife's inheritance becomes standardized at one-third'. Later law-codes are largely silent on this point, however, while extant wills do not support the theory of a three-fold division. Although it is fully possible that this is because one of the purposes of a will is to

a similar division in Kent, it is at least clear from Wihtred 12 that husband and wife each had possessions of their own.

4. Conclusions

Overall, the extant legislation from early Anglo-Saxon England shows a concern with the rights and duties of women which suggests that they played a role within the legal system comparable with, though not always identical to, the role of men. The evidence needs to be carefully weighed. On the one hand, married women were subordinate to their husbands, at least in late seventh-century Wessex (Ine 57). On the other, they had discrete property rights (Ine 57), and were separately accountable under the law (Ine 7, Ine 57), a situation which also applied in contemporary Kent (Wihtred 12). Most importantly, they were legally competent, with the right to exculpate themselves on oath from a false accusation (Ine 57).

Unmarried girls and women were also responsible for their own actions, and liable to pay compensation for offences (Æth 73, 74). Marriage and other forms of sexual relations were closely regulated, featuring in nearly half the clauses mentioning women (Æthelberht 10, 11, 14, 16, 31, 76, 77, 82, 83, 84, 85, Ine 31). Widows and abbesses were entitled to receive compensation for offences against their dependants (Æthelberht 75, Ine 23), and the inheritance and custody rights of widowed mothers were particularly carefully protected (Æthelberht 78, 79, 80, Hlothhere and Eadric 6, Ine 38). The childless widow, at least in early seventh-century Kent, inherited nothing, and this may be seen in the general context of a tendency to value women according to their capacity for child-bearing in early Germanic law.

Many of these themes are taken up in later Anglo-Saxon legislation from the time of Alfred the Great onwards, when a wider range of documentary and other sources also becomes available. Others, however, disappear from sight, and it is often uncertain whether legislation issued by later law-givers represents a continuation of earlier custom or a departure from it. As evidence for the early period, the four seventh-century codes are unparalleled. They represent unique and invaluable source material for the position of English women at the beginning of recorded history.

specify something different from the default position, it would be unsafe to assume that the practice continued unchanged throughout the later Anglo-Saxon period.

PART II:

NEW READINGS OF ANGLO-SAXON LAW

4.

THE STRUCTURE OF ENGLISH SOCIETY IN THE SEVENTH CENTURY: A NEW READING OF ÆTHELBERHT 12[1]

1. Introduction

Three main classes of freemen are generally recognised from the law-codes issued by the Kentish kings Æthelberht, Hlothhere and Eadric, and Wihtred during the seventh century. Their legal standing is defined by the respective values of *wergild*, the price payable for manslaughter in order to avert the feud, and of *mundbyrd*, the price payable for violation of the right of protection over dependants. The early laws are, however, very cryptically expressed, using archaic vocabulary and elliptical phraseology which lead to many difficulties of interpretation. A number of such cruxes are discussed elsewhere in this volume, particularly in the rest of Part II. The purpose of the present essay is to re-examine a problematic clause from Æthelberht's code, and to suggest that it contains a reference to a fourth class of Kentish freeman.

2. *Wergild* and *mundbyrd*

At the head of Kentish society was of course the king, with a *mundbyrd* of 50 shillings. No *wergild* is specified for the king, possibly because of the incompleteness of the source material, but possibly because his life

---

[1] A version of this essay was presented at the Tenth Meeting of the International Society of Anglo-Saxonists in Helsinki, 6–11 August 2001. My thanks are due to the Leverhulme Foundation and the British Academy for assistance with funding, and to members of the audience for a lively and fruitful discussion. I am particularly grateful to Christine Fell, who sharpened my thinking in many ways, and to Richard Marsden, who incorporated the as yet unpublished interpretation within the edition of the text in his *The Cambridge Old English Reader* (Cambridge, 2004), p. 49.

was beyond price.[2] Below him was the *eorl* or nobleman, with a *wergild* of 300 shillings and a *mundbyrd* of 12 shillings, while the *ceorl* or ordinary freeman was entitled to a *wergild* of 100 shillings and a *mundbyrd* of 6 shillings. These values are not systematically set out in the extant codes, but can be pieced together from individual clauses.[3] The respective *mundbyrds* for king and *ceorl* are defined in Æthelberht 8 and 15:

8 Cyninges mundbyrd: L scillinga.	The [breach of the] king's protection, 50 shillings.
15 Ceorles mundbyrd: VI scillingas.	The [breach of a] *ceorl*'s protection: six shillings.

That of the king is mentioned again in Wihtred 2 in the context of integrating the Church within the existing social hierarchy:

2 Ciricean mundbyrd sie L scll' swa cinges.	The [breach of] the Church's protection is to be 50 shillings like the king's.

The *mundbyrd* of an *eorl* is evident from Æthelberht 13 and 14, which specify a payment of 12 shillings for different types of breaches of protection:

13 Gif on eorles tune man mannan ofslæhþ, XII scill' gebete.	If anyone kills a man in a nobleman's estate, he is to pay 12 shillings compensation.

---

[2] The latter view is taken by J. Hines, 'Units of Account in Gold and Silver in Seventh-century England: *Scillingas*, *Sceattas* and *Pæningas*', *Antiquaries Journal* 90 (2010), 153–73. Discussing the sum paid in compensation for the death of the West Saxon prince Mul by Wihtred of Kent in the 690s, he argues (at 161) that the payment 'cannot properly be described as a regular *wergild*: our sources imply there was no such thing for a king or prince (*cyning* or *æþeling*) at this date'.

[3] The numbering of individual clauses has no manuscript authority. For convenience of reference, I use the numbering system established by *Die Gesetze der Angelsachsen*, ed. F. Liebermann, 3 vols. (Halle, 1903–16), the edition from which all quotations from the laws are taken. Unless otherwise stated, translations are from *English Historical Documents c. 500–1042*, ed. D. Whitelock, 2nd ed. (London, 1979).

14 Gif wið eorles birele man geligeþ, XII scill' gebete.	If anyone lies with a nobleman's serving-woman, he is to pay 12 shillings compensation.

Although not identified explicitly with *mundbyrd*, the correspondence is clear from the parallel between Æthelberht 14 and Æthelberht 16, where the same offence results in payment of a sum equal to the *ceorl*'s *mundbyrd* of 6 shillings:

16 Gif wið ceorles birelan man geligeþ, VI scillingu*m* gebete; æt þære oþere ðeowan L scætta; æt þare þriddan XXX scætta.	If anyone lie with a *ceorl*'s serving-woman, he is to pay six shillings compensation; [if] with a slave-woman of the second [class], 50 *sceattas*; [if with one of] the third [class], 30 *sceattas*.

The *wergild* of an ordinary freeman is defined in Æthelberht 21:

21 Gif man mannan ofslæhð, medume leodgeld C scillinga gebete.	If anyone kills a man, he is to pay as an ordinary wergild 100 shillings.

It is mentioned again in Hlothhere and Eadric 3:

3 Gif mannes esne frigne mannan ofslæhð, þane þe sie hund scillinga gelde, se agend þone banan agefe 7 oþer manwyrð þær tó.	If a man's servant kills a freeman, who has a wergild of 100 shillings, the owner is to give up the slayer, and the value of another man in addition.

Finally, that of an *eorl* is alluded to within a sub-clause of Hlothhere and Eadric 1:

1 Gif mannes esne eorlcundne mannan ofslæhð, þane ðe sio þreom hundum scll' gylde, se agend þone banan agefe 7 do þær þrio manwyrð to.	If a man's servant kills a man of noble birth, who has a wergild of 300 shillings, the owner is to give up the slayer and pay in addition the value of three men.

It is clear from the incidental references in particular, as well as from the dispersal of information throughout the three codes, that the laws do not aim to set out in full the values associated with different classes of society. Instead, they assume a good deal of background knowledge no longer available to the present-day reader. The information outlined above from the extant texts cannot therefore be taken to be comprehensive.

3. Kent and Wessex

The three-fold division of Kentish society seems to contrast with the situation in the neighbouring kingdom of Wessex, where the laws issued by King Ine towards the end of the seventh century refer to four classes of freemen, with two strata of nobility above the *ceorl*:

70 Æt twyhyndum were mon sceal sellan to monbote XXX scill., æt VIhynd*um* LXXX scill., æt XIIhynd*um* CXX scill.	For a man of a two-hundred wergild there is to be paid a compensation to the lord of 30 shillings; for a man of a six-hundred wergild, 80 shillings; for a man of a twelve-hundred wergild, 120 shillings.

It appears from Ine 70 that a West Saxon *ceorl* was entitled to a *wergild* of 200 silver shillings, probably the equivalent of the Kentish *ceorl*'s *wergild* of 100 gold shillings.[4] In that case, the 600-shilling *wergild* also mentioned in Ine 70 would correspond directly to the 300-shilling *wergild* of a Kentish *eorl*. Above that, however, is a higher class of West Saxon nobility with a *wergild* of 1,200 shillings which has no apparent equivalent in Kentish law. This is sometimes taken to reflect differences between the administrative structures of the two kingdoms. For instance, Keynes comments that West Saxon law appears to have been 'exercised through a hierarchy of royal and local officials in a more advanced state of development' than in Kent, and he adduces the existence of a higher class of nobility as evidence that 'the separation of an aristocracy was more pronounced'.[5] Similarly, Faith states that 'in Kent there was a smaller gap between highest and lowest'.[6]

---

[4] S. Lyon, 'Some Problems in Interpreting Anglo-Saxon Coinage', *Anglo-Saxon England* 5 (1976), 173–224, at 178. The relationship between the monetary systems of the two kingdoms is complex, and has been much discussed. An important revisionist study is Hines, 'Units of Account'.

[5] S. Keynes, 'The Developing State', *The Making of England: Anglo-Saxon Art and Culture AD 600–900*, ed. L. Webster and J. Backhouse (London, 1991), pp. 38–9, at 39.

[6] R. Faith, 'Social Class', *The Blackwell Encyclopaedia of Anglo-Saxon England*, ed. M. Lapidge, J. Blair, S. Keynes and D. Scragg (Oxford, 1999), p. 424.

An alternative view, however, is that the Kentish codes simply do not mention the higher noble class. The extant laws are highly selective, and it is possible – indeed, likely – that not all social groups appear. Sawyer draws attention to evidence of 'an elaborate social hierarchy', as reflected in the three classes of slave-girls within a ceorl's household (Æthelberht 16 quoted above) and the three classes of semi-free læts (Æthelberht 26 quoted below),[7] and points out that Æthelberht 75 identifies four classes of widow, with the *mund* of the first, third and fourth classes corresponding to the *mundbyrd* of the king, *eorl* and *ceorl* respectively:[8]

75 Mund þare betstan widuwan eorlcundre L scillinga gebete.	The right of protection of a widow of the highest class of nobility is to be compensated for at 50 shillings;
75,1 Ðare oþre XX scll', ðare þriddan XII scll', þare feorðan VI scll'.	that of one of the second class, at 20 shillings; of one of the third class, at 12 shillings; of one of the fourth class, at 6 shillings.[9]

On this basis, he posits the existence of 'a noble class above the 300-shilling eorl', indicating that 'the difference between the higher nobility of Kent and Wessex may be unreal'.[10] The suggestion derives support from Wihtred 5, which makes it clear that a *gesiþcund mann* – as the *eorl* was now known – was expected to be responsible to a lord:

5 Gif ðæs geweorþe gesiþcundne mannan ofer þis gemot, *þæt* he unriht hæmed genime ofer cyngæs bebod 7 biscopes 7 boca dom, se þæt gebete his dryhtne	If after this meeting, any *gesith-born* man chooses to enter into an illicit union in spite of the command of the king and the bishop and the decree of the books, he is to pay to his lord

[7] The status of the *læt* mentioned in Æthelberht 26 is far from clear.

[8] P. H. Sawyer, *From Roman Britain to Norman England*, 2nd ed. (London, 1998), p. 173.

[9] The translation is from my article, 'The Widow's *Mund* in Æthelberht 75 and 76', *Journal of English and Germanic Philology* 98 (1999), 1–16, reprinted in this volume.

[10] Sawyer, *From Roman Britain to Norman England*, p. 173.

C scll' an ald reht.	100 shillings according to ancient law.[11]

The *gesiþcund mann* cannot therefore have ranked immediately below the king. An intermediate class is strongly indicated, and it may be worth looking again at the earliest Kentish code for potential traces of it.

4. The *cyninges fedesl*

Æthelberht's code is hierarchically arranged in descending order of social class. An opening section on the church (Æthelberht 1) is followed by laws relating to the king (Æthelberht 2–12), to noblemen (Æthelberht 13–14), to freemen (Æthelberht 15–25) and to lower orders (Æthelberht 26), and then by a section on enclosures (Æthelberht 27–32), a personal injury tariff (Æthelberht 33–72), a sequence on women (Æthelberht 73–84), and a final section on servants (Æthelberht 85–88) and slaves (Æthelberht 89–90).[12] This means that any reference to a higher class of nobility would be expected to occur towards the end of the laws relating to the king in Æthelberht 2–12, or at the beginning of those relating to the *eorl* in Æthelberht 13–14. It may therefore be significant that Æthelberht 12 introduces a new character, the *cyninges fedesl*, in conjunction with the very sum of 20 shillings predicted by Sawyer as the *mundbyrd* of the higher stratum of nobility. The clause reads as follows:

12 Cyninges fedesl XX scillinga forgelde.	The king's *fedesl* is to be paid for with 20 shillings.

---

[11] As has often been pointed out, the reference to 'ancient law' cannot be taken literally, since the clause is 'self-evidently innovatory' (P. Wormald, *The Making of English Law: King Alfred to the Twelfth Century. Volume I: Legislation and its Limits* (Oxford, 1999), p. 102). Instead, it reflects the importance placed on tradition within the Anglo-Saxon legal system.

[12] The structure is discussed and tabulated by P. Wormald, '"Inter cetera bona … genti suae": Law-Making and Peace-Keeping in the Earliest English Kingdoms', in his *Legal Culture in the Early Medieval West: Law as Text, Image and Experience* (London, 1999), pp. 179–99 (first published *Settimana di Studio del Centro Italiano di Studi sull' alto Medioevo* 42 (Spoleto, 1995), 963–96). Alternatively, Æthelberht 17–32 may be grouped together as a miscellany of (mainly violent) criminal activities, as towards the beginning of my article, 'Two Kentish laws concerning women: a new reading of Æthelberht 73 and 74', *Anglia* 119 (2001), 554–78, reprinted in this volume.

I wish to suggest that the *cyninges fedesl* is in fact the Kentish counterpart of the 1,200-shilling West Saxon nobleman.

It seems to me that there may be two reasons why this possibility has not previously been considered. The first is a tendency to assume that monetary values in the law-codes relate to *wergild*. This assumption underlies most previous discussions of Æthelberht 12, the difficulty being that a *wergild* of 20 shillings would be ridiculously low for any freeman. Æthelberht 26 shows that up to four times that amount was payable for killing even a *læt*, possibly a semi-free class between *ceorl* and slave:

26 Gif læt ofslæhð, þone selestan LXXX scll' forgelde; gif þane oþerne ofslæhð, LX scillingum forgelde; ðane þriddan XL scillin forgelden.	If [anyone] kills a *læt*, he is to pay for one of the highest class 80 shillings; if he kills one of the second class, he is to pay 60 shillings; if one of the third class, he is to pay 40 shillings.

Unlike West Saxon and later Kentish law, however, Æthelberht's code characteristically defines social class not in terms of *wergild* but of *mundbyrd*. As we have seen, *wergild* values are given for neither king nor *eorl*, and that of a *ceorl* is known only from the *medume leodgeld* of Æthelberht 21. It is *mundbyrd* values that are explicitly stated for both king and *ceorl* in Æthelberht 8 and 15, and which may be inferred for the *eorl* from Æthelberht 13 and 14. If a higher noble class were represented within Æthelberht's code, a reference to *mundbyrd* would therefore be more likely than a reference to *wergild*. This applies particularly to Æthelberht 12, sandwiched as it is between clauses relating to *mundbyrd*. With the exception of Æthelberht 9, chs. 8–16 of Æthelberht's code are exclusively concerned with *mundbyrd* values and with violations of *mundbyrd*, and in this context a similar interpretation of Æthelberht 12 appears to be required.

Oliver draws attention to the fact that the syntactic formulation of Æthelberht 12 precisely parallels that of the statement of the king's *mundbyrd* in Æthelberht 8.[13] This in turn forms the template for the *ceorl*'s *mundbyrd* as given in Æthelberht 15, and there is also a similarity to the phraseology of Hlothhere and Eadric 1 *þane ðe sio þreom hundum scll' gylde*, where the *wergild* of an *eorl* is finally made known. As in Æthelberht 12, the verb used here is *(for)geldan* rather than *(ge)betan*, and whereas the context of manslaughter in the later law identifies the sum

[13] L. Oliver, '*Cyninges fedesl*: The King's Feeding in Æthelberht, ch. 12', *Anglo-Saxon England* 27 (1998), 31–40, at 31.

in question as the *wergild* of an *eorlcund mann*, the emphasis on *mundbyrd* throughout Æthelberht's code establishes this as the more likely value to be associated with the *cyninges fedesl*.[14]

Previous studies of Æthelberht 12 have quite properly tended to focus on etymological issues, and the second reason why the clause has not hitherto been associated with the nobility is that the etymology of OE *fedesl* appears to imply low status. Attested elsewhere only in a metathesized form *fedels* or *foedils* (four times in glossaries defining Latin *altile* 'fattened animal / fowl, fatling',[15] and once in a tenth-century charter as the first element of a compound noun *fedelsswin* 'fattened pig'[16]), it is evidently related to the verb *fedan* 'to feed', and has often been linked with the *ceorlæs hlafæta* '*ceorl*'s loaf-eater' of Æthelberht 25:

25 Gif man ceorlæs hlafætan ofslæhð, VI scillingum gebete.	If anyone kills a *ceorl*'s dependant, he is to pay six shillings compensation.

This is how Liebermann understood the term, translating it as *Königskostgänger* 'king's boarder' and drawing attention to Hlothhere and Eadric 15,[17] which states that a householder is responsible for a guest who has been lodged and fed at his house for three days:

15 Gif man cuman feormæþ III niht an his agenum hame (cepeman oþþe oðerne þe sio ofer mearce cuman) 7 hine þon*ne* his mete fede, 7 he þon*ne* ænigum mæn yfel gedo, se man þane oðerne æt rihte gebrenge oþþe riht forewyrce.	If anyone harbours a stranger, a trader or any other man who has come across the frontier, for three nights in his own home, and then supplies him with his food, and he then does any injury to any man, the man is to bring the other to justice or to discharge the obligations for him.

[14] Oliver, '*Cyninges fedesl*', 32 n. 6, points out that Æthelberht 4 uses *forgylde* as the verb of restitution for theft, while Æthelberht 5 uses *gebete* as the verb of restitution for killing, so that the uses of the two terms are not consistently differentiated in Æthelberht's code.

[15] Dictionary of Old English Project, *Dictionary of Old English A–G*. Version 2.0. CD-ROM, 2008 (hereafter DOE), s.v. *fēdels*.

[16] DOE, s.v. *fēdels-swīn*.

[17] *Gesetze*, ed. Liebermann I, 4; III, 7.

An alternative interpretation 'wet nurse' has sometimes been preferred by association with the female slaves mentioned in the two preceding clauses, Æthelberht 10 and 11:

10 Gif man wið cyninges mægdenman geligeþ, L scillinga gebete.	If anyone lies with a maiden belonging to the king, he is to pay 50 shillings compensation.
11 Gif hio grindende þeowa sio, XXV scillinga gebete. Sio þridde: XII scillingas.	If it is a grinding slave, he is to pay 25 shillings compensation; [if a slave of] the third [class], 12 shillings.

However, these clearly comprise a self-contained sequence dealing with sexual relations, and there is no reason to believe the *fedesl* to be female.[18]

In an appendix to her discussion of the language of the Kentish laws, Lendinara translates *fedesl* in Æthelberht 12 as 'fattened animal', but does not offer an explanation for its occurrence in Æthelberht 12.[19] A similar interpretation is considered and dismissed in the most recent and detailed analysis of the clause by Oliver, who proposes instead a new reading 'food render'.[20] A problem is that neither would represent the kind of topic found elsewhere in Æthelberht's code, and in neither context does the sum of 20 shillings seem appropriate. References to food renders in other early sources are generally given in terms of goods considerably in excess of a monetary value of 20 shillings, and there is no suggestion that commutation to a financial payment would be possible. An example is Ine 70,1:

70,1 Æt X hidu*m* to fostre X fata hunies, CCC hlafa, XII ambra Wilisc ealað, XXX hluttres, tu eald hriðeru oððe X weðeras, X gees, XX henna, X	As a food-rent from 10 hides: 10 vats of honey, 300 loaves, 12 'ambers' of Welsh ale, 30 of clear ale, 2 full-grown cows, or 10 wethers, 10 geese, 20 hens,

[18] *Ancient Laws and Institutes of England*, ed. B. Thorpe, folio edition (London, 1840), took Æthelberht 12 to follow directly on from Æthelberht 10–11, dealing with the penalty for sexual relations with another of the king's dependants. This is not quite clear from his translation 'Let the king's 'fed-esl' be paid for with xx. Shillings' (p. 3), but his unpaginated index lists Æthelberht 12 under 'Adultery, Fornication, etc.'. This interpretation is not supported by modern scholarship.

[19] P. Lendinara, 'The Kentish Laws', *The Anglo-Saxons from the Migration Period to the Eighth Century: An Ethnographic Perspective*, ed. J. Hines (Woodbridge, 1997), pp. 211–30, at p. 225.

[20] Oliver, '*Cyninges fedesl*', 37–40.

cesas, amber fulne buteran, V leaxas, XX pundwæga foðres 7 hundteontig æla.	10 cheeses, an 'amber' full of butter, 5 salmon, 20 pounds of fodder and 100 eels.

The total value is impossible to calculate, but since the eye of a single cow is worth a shilling according to Ine 59, it must amount to a significant sum. Moreover, the amount of food render is closely tied to the size of estate, no indication of which is given in Æthelberht 12. Although Oliver's translation '[For] feeding of the king, let him pay 20 shillings' is closely echoed by Wormald,[21] it can at best be regarded as speculative.

Liebermann's translation *Königskostgänger* is semantically acceptable and receives cautious support from Whitelock.[22] However, it depends on an unproven link with Hlothhere and Eadric 15 (quoted above) for the implication that the *fedesl* is a temporary guest. As Oliver points out, the parallel between the two clauses is not close, since the purport of the later law is that a host was legally responsible for his guest's behaviour, while according to this reading of Æthelberht 12, the king would be entitled to reparation if his guest were harmed.[23] The parallel with the *ceorlæs hlafæta* of Æthelberht 25 suggests a permanent member of the household; but it need not follow that the reference is to a lowly dependant in both cases.

5. The *cyninges geneat*

Comparison with the term *geneat* in West Saxon law may be useful here. Deriving from the verb *neotan* 'to enjoy', and explained by Toller as 'one who enjoys with another, one who belongs to the household *or* following (*comitatus*) of a superior',[24] this too appears to imply low status, and is used in that sense in Ine 22:

22 Gif ðin geneat stalie 7 losie ðe, gif ðu hæbbe byrgean, mana þone þæs angyldes; gif he næbbe, gyld ðu þæt angylde, 7	If your *geneat* steals and escapes from you, if you have a surety, demand the compensation from him; if he has no surety, pay you

[21] L. Oliver, *The Beginnings of English Law* (Toronto, 2002), p. 65; P. Wormald, *The First Code of English Law* (Canterbury, 2005), p. 4.

[22] *English Historical Documents*, ed. Whitelock, p. 392 n. 1.

[23] Oliver, '*Cyninges fedesl*', 33.

[24] *An Anglo-Saxon Dictionary Based on the Manuscript Collections of the Late Joseph Bosworth*, ed. T. N. Toller (Oxford, 1898); *Supplement* (1921), s.v. *geneat* I. DOE does not include *geneat* under letter *G*, and publication of letter *N* is not yet in sight.

ne sie him no ðy ðingodre.	the compensation, and he is not to be any nearer a settlement on that account.

Nonetheless, the highest class of West Saxon nobility, with a potential *wergild* of 1,200 shillings, is described in Ine 19 as a *cyninges geneat*:

19 Cyninges geneat, gif his wer bið twelfhund scill., he mot swerian for syxtig hida, gif he bið huslgengea.	A king's *geneat*, if his wergild is 1200 shillings, may, if he is a communicant, swear for 60 hides.

The clause is preserved in four manuscripts, leaving little margin for error,[25] and indeed the application of *cyninges geneat* is confirmed by its only other extant occurrence in the context of a list of high-ranking nobles in the *Anglo-Saxon Chronicle* entry for 896:

Þær wearð ofslægen Lucumon cynges gerefa 7 Wulfheard Friesa 7 Æbbe Friesa 7 Æðelhere Friesa 7 Æðelferð cynges geneat, 7 ealra monna fresiscra 7 engliscra .lxii. 7 þara deniscena .cxx..[26]	There were killed Lucumon the king's reeve and Wulfheard the Frisian and Æbbe the Frisian and Æðelhere the Frisian and Æðelferð the king's *geneat*, and altogether 62 Frisians and Englishmen and 120 Danes.

There is some confusion concerning the status of the *cyninges geneat*, possibly stemming from a reluctance on the part of modern scholarship to accept that the term *geneat* could be used to refer to both high and low rank. Thus *A Thesaurus of Old English* categorizes *cyninges geneat* alongside *huscarl* under section 12.01.01.08.01 'a servant, attendant',[27] although both recorded instances militate against such an interpretation. An influential view is that of Chadwick, who suggested that the term may have been applied especially to junior members of the royal household. He commented:

---

[25] These are Cambridge, Corpus Christi College, 173; Cambridge, Corpus Christi College, 383; London, British Library, Burney 277; and Medway Archive and Local Studies Centre, MS DRc/R1 (*Textus Roffensis*). *Cyninges geneat* is the reading in all four manuscripts.

[26] *MS A*, ed. J. M. Bately, *The Anglo-Saxon Chronicle: a Collaborative Edition* 3 (Cambridge, 1986), pp. 60–1.

[27] J. Roberts and C. Kay with L. Grundy, *A Thesaurus of Old English*, 2 vols. (London, 1995).

> it is hardly possible that the king's *geneat* should have been superior to the king's thegn. If that had been the case we should certainly have heard of such persons more frequently.[28]

However, this argument may fail to consider the paucity of source material from the early period, and the possibility that the term *cyninges geneat*, like *cyninges fedesl*, was already going out of use. Discussing the Norfolk place-name Neatishead 'household of the *genēat*' in an area of early Anglian settlement containing many archaic formations, Sandred notes that 'The status of a *genēat* is likely to have been higher in the early Anglo-Saxon period than later'.[29] It is certainly clear from Ine 19 that not all *cyninges geneat*s would be entitled to the highest *wergild* of 1,200 shillings, but the fact remains that this is the only class explicitly mentioned in early West Saxon law in connection with such a *wergild*. Indeed, Hines takes the *cyninges geneat* of Ine 19 and the *eorlcund mann* of Hlothhere and Eadric 1 to be counterparts, representing the highest rank of nobleman in West Saxon and Kentish society.[30]

Like OE *gesið*, which is most commonly used in Ine's laws to refer to the noble class, OE *geneat* originally means 'companion, member of a household', and Whitelock comments that 'In its technical sense a *geneat* differs from a *gesith* in not normally being of the noble class'.[31] The combination with the word *cyninges* is therefore crucial in transforming the meaning from 'a member of a private person's household, a vassal', as in Ine 22, to 'a member of the king's household, a noble', as in Ine 19. I suggest that the same may apply to *fedesl* and related terms. In Æthelberht 25, the collocation with the word *ceorlæs* leaves no doubt that the *hlafæta* is of low status and little value. Equally, the combination with the word *cyninges* in Æthelberht 12 may provide a strong clue that the *fedesl* ranks second only to the king.

Finally, it remains to draw attention to linguistic similarities between OE *fedesl* and OE *geneat* which may support the interpretation proposed

---

[28] H. M. Chadwick, *Studies on Anglo-Saxon Institutions* (New York, 1963), p. 139.

[29] K. I. Sandred, 'From the King's Retainers to Unfree Peasants: Some Reflexes of Anglian Social-Class Groups in Norfolk Place-Names', *Nomina* 9 (1985), 21–30, at 23. Sandred derives Neatishead from an OE *geneates hired* 'the household of the geneat' (at 21), as against earlier interpretations of the first element as OE *neat* 'cattle' or a personal name OE *snæt*. Somewhat oddly, he translates the place-name as 'the vassal's household' in the entry for Neatishead in his *The Place-Names of Norfolk Part Two: The Hundreds of East and West Flegg, Happing and Tunstead*, English Place-Name Society 72 (Nottingham, 1996), pp. 173–4.

[30] Hines, 'Units of Account', 154–5.

[31] *English Historical Documents*, ed. Whitelock, p. 401 n. 1.

in this essay. The verbs *fedan* 'to feed' and *neotan* 'to enjoy' belong to the same general semantic range, and the derivatives *fedesl* and *geneat* may have developed along parallel lines. It is at least suggestive that whereas *fedesl* is attested in the sense 'fatted animal', *geneat* is related to OE *neat* 'animal, head of cattle'.[32] The Kentish laws contain a high proportion of *hapax legomena*, alongside other terms of limited occurrence, some of them restricted to the legal register.[33] It is therefore fully plausible that an alternative sense of *fedesl*, corresponding to another attested sense of *geneat*, may be represented in Æthelberht 12.

6. Conclusion

To sum up, I suggest that the *cyninges fedesl* mentioned in the earliest Kentish law-code represents a rank of nobility between king and *eorl* corresponding to the West Saxon *cyninges geneat*. This interpretation offers several advantages over previous readings of Æthelberht 12. Firstly, it restores the structural coherence of this section of the code, progressing from laws relating to the king, through the higher and lower nobility, to the ordinary freeman and those of inferior rank. Secondly, it makes better sense of the sum involved, 20 shillings being the amount predicted from other evidence as the *mundbyrd* of a higher noble class. Thirdly, it is contextually appropriate, since Æthelberht 12 appears within a sequence of clauses exclusively concerned with *mundbyrd* values and with violations of *mundbyrd*. Fourthly, it removes the apparent discrepancy between the social hierarchies of Kent and Wessex during the seventh century. If the argument that I have presented here is correct, it would appear that the organisational structures of the two kingdoms were more closely similar than has previously been recognised.

[32] T. F. Hoad, *The Concise Oxford Dictionary of English Etymology* (Oxford, 1986), p. 310, s.v. *neat*[1], derives *neat* 'animal' from the same Germanic root as *neotian* 'enjoy'.

[33] These are usefully set out by Lendinara, 'The Kentish Laws', pp. 223–4.

5.

Two Kentish Laws Concerning Women: A New Reading of Æthelberht 73 and 74

First published 2001: *Anglia* 119, 554–578.

The law-code issued by King Æthelberht of Kent towards the beginning of the seventh century falls into fairly clearly defined sections.[1] It begins with laws relating to the church, collectively designated ch. 1 by modern editors.[2] These are followed by laws relating to the king (chs. 2–12), to noblemen (chs. 13–14) and to freemen (chs. 15–16), with a miscellany of (mainly violent) criminal activities in chs. 17–32. Chs. 33–72 comprise a personal injury tariff of the kind found in other early Germanic codes, setting out the compensation payable for various kinds of insults and injuries ranging from hair-pulling, bruising and disfigurement to broken limbs and the loss of body-parts such as an ear, eye, tooth, penis, thumb, finger, foot, toe, finger-nail or toe-nail. Next comes a sequence concerning women (chs. 73–84), dealing with such topics as widows' rights, the

---

[1] This paper was written during a period of study leave funded by the Leverhulme Trust and the University of Glasgow from October 1999 to September 2000. I am very grateful to the directors of the Leverhulme Trust and to the University of Glasgow for their support. Some of the material has been presented to research seminars at the Universities of Glasgow and Manchester, and to the International Medieval Congress at the University of Leeds, and I am grateful to those present for their comments and encouragement.

[2] An exception is L. Oliver, *The Beginnings of English Law* (Tornto, 2002), pp. 60–1, where this section is numbered 1–7. Æthelberht's laws are not numbered in the only extant manuscript, the twelfth-century *Textus Roffensis* (Medway Archive and Local Studies Centre, MS DRc/R1, fols. 1–3v), although there is a clear system of rubrication whereby each clause begins with an initial. For ease of reference, clauses will be cited throughout this article by the enumeration used in *Die Gesetze der Angelsachsen*, ed. F. Liebermann, 3 vols. (Halle, 1903–16) I, 3–8. All quotations from the Anglo-Saxon laws are from this edition unless otherwise stated.

marriage contract, and penalties for abduction,[3] while ch. 85 leads into the final section on servants and slaves (chs. 85–90) by defining the compensation for adultery with an *esnes cwynan* 'servant's woman'. Since the only manuscript containing Æthelberht's laws dates from the early twelfth century, it is by no means certain that the code has survived in its entirety or in the original order. On the other hand, there is no compelling reason to doubt it. Unlike the later-seventh-century laws of King Ine of Wessex, which are so disorganized and repetitive that they have plausibly been taken to represent separate sets of laws issued at different times,[4] Æthelberht's code is tightly structured and systematic, so that the consensus of opinion is that it is probably complete as it stands. Wallace-Hadrill, for instance, describes it as 'a coherent and well-ordered document, such as might be expected from the entourage of Augustine',[5] Wormald agrees that the code is 'rather well organized',[6] and Howlett argues that the arrangement of the laws exhibits Biblical style.[7] There is thus a reasonable possibility that in the case of interpretive cruxes, context within the code may be relevant to explication.

The first two clauses in the women's sequence, chs. 73 and 74, are concerned with compensation (*bot*), and like many of the Kentish laws they are very cryptically expressed. Æthelberht 73 reads as follows:

> Gif fri wif locbore leswæs hwæt gedeþ, XXX scll' gebete.[8]

---

[3] For a discussion of individual clauses, see my articles on 'The Widow's *Mund* in Æthelberht 75 and 76', *Journal of English and Germanic Philology* 98 (1999), 1–16; 'The Early Kentish 'Divorce Laws': a Reconsideration of Æthelberht, chs. 79 and 80', *Anglo-Saxon England* 23 (1994): 19–34; and 'A Reappraisal of Æthelberht 84', *Nottingham Medieval Studies* 37 (1993), 1–6, all reprinted in this volume.

[4] P. Wormald, '"Inter cetera bona ... genti suae": Law-Making and Peace-Keeping in the Earliest English Kingdoms', *Settimane di studio del Centro italiano di studi sull'alto medioevo* 42 (1995), 963–93, at 977–83, reprinted in his *Legal Culture in the Early Medieval West: Law as Text, Image and Experience* (London, 1999), pp. 179–99.

[5] J. M. Wallace-Hadrill, *Early Germanic Kingship in England and on the Continent* (Oxford, 1971), p. 40.

[6] Wormald, '"Inter cetera bona…', 970.

[7] D. R. Howlett, *British Books in Biblical Style* (Dublin, 1997), pp. 257–62.

[8] *Gesetze,* ed. Liebermann I, 7. I depart from Liebermann's punctuation in treating the nonce occurrence *fri wif* as two separate words rather than as a compound. The two elements are separated by a small gap in the manuscript, and comparison with the more common *fri man*, where the first element is always inflected separately, suggests a combination of adjective plus noun. (Cf. Carole Hough, '*Freo man*: a Note on Word Division', *Neophilologus* 75 (1991), 641–3.)

Interpretation of this clause is disputed. Most editors and commentators have taken it to refer to misconduct by a long-haired female, the standard translation being that of Whitelock:

> If a freewoman, with long hair, commits any misconduct, she is to pay 30 shillings compensation.[9]

Although Fell made a strong case for understanding the nonce occurrence *locbore* as a reference not to long hair but to responsibility for keys,[10] the traditional interpretation has proved difficult to dislodge, and Lendinara still takes 'with long hair' to be the literal meaning whether or not there might be an additional sense 'who is in charge of the keys'.[11] Proponents of the 'long haired' theory are divided between those who take this to be a sign of free birth and those who associate it with virginity. Among the former is Whitelock, who adds a footnote to her translation explaining, 'This is generally taken to be a distinguishing feature of a free, as opposed to a bond, woman'.[12] Attenborough has a similar note – 'The usual interpretation is that the long hair denotes the freeborn woman as opposed to the slave'[13] – while Acworth paints a fetching if perhaps fanciful picture of the Anglo-Saxon bride:

> Long hair was the sign of freedom, and the bride who was single and of free birth wore her hair flowing, wreathed with a garland of white and purple flowers to signify virgin purity and the blood of Christ.[14]

The problem is that there is no other evidence for long hair as a symbol of free birth in Anglo-Saxon society.[15] Besides, such a reading would

---

[9] *English Historical Documents c. 500–1042*, ed. D. Whitelock, 2nd ed. (London, 1979), p. 393.

[10] C. Fell, 'A *friwif locbore* Revisited', *Anglo-Saxon England* 13 (1984), 157–65.

[11] P. Lendinara, 'The Kentish Laws', *The Anglo-Saxons from the Migration Period to the Eighth Century: An Ethnographic Perspective*, ed. J. Hines (Woodbridge, 1997), pp. 211–30, at p. 214 and p. 223. Since 'hair' and 'key' are discrete meanings of *loc*, it is difficult to follow Lendinara's train of thought here. Oliver, *The Beginnings of English Law*, p. 72, follows Fell's interpretation.

[12] *English Historical Documents*, ed. Whitelock, p. 393 n. 4.

[13] *The Laws of the Earliest English Kings*, ed. F. L. Attenborough (Cambridge, 1922), p. 178.

[14] E. Acworth, *The New Matriarchy* (London, 1965), p. 60. Acworth is here discussing tenth-century marriage customs, but it is unclear whence the information on long hair is derived unless from Æthelberht 73.

[15] The possibility that hair may have been 'commonly worn long by barbarians of rank' and in particular by chieftains, a custom preserved longest in the

make *locbore* synonymous with *fri wif*.[16] The alternative view that long hair denoted an unmarried girl was preferred by Liebermann and has recently been supported by Ausenda.[17] Despite the continental parallels adduced by both, however, this interpretation is ruled out here by the collocation with *wif*, the generic term in Old English for an adult woman. As Bremmer demonstrates, OE *wif* 'woman who is not a virgin' designates either a married woman or a widow;[18] and as Fell also observes, a clear distinction is made between the *fri wif* of Æthelberht 73 and the *mægþ* of the adjacent ch. 74.[19]

Attested meanings of OE *loc* include both 'a lock of hair' and 'a locked place, a locking mechanism', and Fell supports her translation of *locbore* as 'in charge of the keys' by analogy with the compound *cægbore* 'key-bearer'. She also discusses the different types of compound in *-bora*:

> Some compounds are literal, some metaphorical. *Bora* may be used of someone who actually carries an object, as it must in *cægbora*, *hornbora*, *sweordbora* etc. In the case of compounds like *mundbora* or *rædbora*, however, the implications of the second element can only be 'the one who has responsibility for'.[20]

There is a difficulty here in that a compound with a word for an object such as *loc* 'locking mechanism' would seem to belong to the first group, while Fell's suggestion that *locbore* refers 'to the responsibility for the locks rather than to the carrying of keys'[21] appears to place it in the second. Moreover, it may be doubted whether two directly analogous compounds such as *cægbore* and *locbore* would be understood in so very different ways. It may therefore be worth drawing attention to a further possibility. A third meaning of OE *loc* is 'a close, conclusion, settlement',[22]

Merovingian dynasty, is discussed by J. M. Wallace-Hadrill, *The Long-Haired Kings and Other Studies in Frankish History* (London, 1962), pp. 156–7, but is unlikely to be relevant here.

[16] To account for the synonymy, Thorpe suggested that *fri wif* might have originated as a marginal gloss of *locbore* (*Ancient Laws and Institutes of England*, ed. B. Thorpe, folio edition (London, 1840) I, 8), but this was a desperate suggestion which has not been accepted by later scholars.

[17] *Gesetze,* ed. Liebermann III, 13. Ausenda's comments are published in the discussion following Lendinara's paper 'The Kentish Laws', 233–4.

[18] R. H. Bremmer, 'Widows in Anglo-Saxon England', *Between Poverty and the Pyre: Moments in the History of Widowhood*, ed. J. Bremmer and L. van den Bosch (London and New York, 1995), pp. 58–88, at p. 59.

[19] Fell, 'A *friwif locbore*', 159.

[20] *Ibid.* 161.

[21] *Ibid.*

[22] *An Anglo-Saxon Dictionary Based on the Manuscript Collections of the Late*

a sense that appears particularly appropriate in a legal context and that fits into the pattern of compounds with terms such as *mund* 'protection' and *ræd* 'counsel'. S 1456, a record of a late-tenth- or early-eleventh-century lawsuit concerning land-ownership,[23] describes the negotiators of the settlement as *þises loces ærendracan* 'the negotiators of this settlement', and concludes with a list of witnesses: *Þonne is her seo gewitnes þe æt þisum loce wæs ...* 'And these are the witnesses who were present at this settlement ...'[24] The Peterborough Manuscript of the *Anglo-Saxon Chronicle* records under the annal for 1094: *Syððan eft hi togædere coman mid þam ilcan mannan þe ær þet loc makedon ...*[25] 'Afterwards they met again with the same people who had previously made the settlement ...' A compound based on this meaning of *loc* might refer to a woman who was legally competent – one who was 'oath-worthy', able to enter into an agreement or to be a party to a contract. As with Fell's interpretation, the reference would be to a woman of mature years in a position of responsibility.

The crux of the matter concerns the nature of the offence. Whitelock's translation quoted above leaves this as an open question, while other editors have assumed that since a woman was involved, the theme must be sexual misconduct. Liebermann went so far as to conclude that the fine was payable by the seducer to the woman's guardian:

> Wenn eine Freie, eine Lockenträgerin, etwas Unzüchtiges thut, büsse [ihr Schänder ihrem Vormunde] 30 Schll.[26]

Doris Stenton also follows this reading,[27] but there is no evidence to justify the introduction of these additional characters. Fell demonstrates, by analogy with other laws in Æthelberht's code, that the fine must have been paid by the woman herself,[28] and this agrees with Whitelock's translation as also

---

Joseph Bosworth, ed. T. N. Toller (Oxford, 1898), p. 645, s.v. *loc* II; *Supplement* (1921), p. 619, s.v. *loc* IV.

[23] In references to Anglo-Saxon charters, S = *Anglo-Saxon Charters: an Annotated List and Bibliography*, ed. P. H. Sawyer, Royal Historical Society Guides and Handbooks 8 (London, 1968). A revised version is now available at http://www.esawyer.org.uk.

[24] *Anglo-Saxon Charters*, ed. A. J. Robertson, 2nd ed. (Cambridge, 1956), no. 69, pp. 142–43.

[25] *The Peterborough Chronicle 1070–1154*, ed. C. Clark, 2nd ed. (Oxford, 1970), p. 21.

[26] *Gesetze,* ed. Liebermann I, 7.

[27] D. M. Stenton, *The English Woman in History* (London, 1957), p. 7.

[28] Fell, 'A *friwif locbore*', 158.

with that of Attenborough.[29] Interpretation of *leswæs hwæt* as a sexual offence depends, as Fell also demonstrates, on an unwarranted assumption that 'female misconduct must imply sexual behaviour',[30] and in view of her arguments it can safely be discounted. However, her own suggestion that the woman is guilty of a financial rather than a sexual crime falls far short of proof. OE *lysu*, represented here in the genitive singular form *leswæs*,[31] is of rare occurrence and uncertain meaning, attested elsewhere only in Æthelberht 3 and in the phrase *Lot sceal mid lyswe* in *Maxims I* line 187a.[32] Æthelberht 3 reads as follows, with the standard translation by Whitelock:

> Gif cyning æt mannes ham drincæþ, 7 ðær man lyswæs hwæt gedo, twibote gebete.[33]

> If the king is drinking at a man's home, and anyone commits any evil deed there, he is to pay two-fold compensation.[34]

Again, the type of offence is unspecified, and although the collocation with *lot* 'deceit, fraud, cheating' in *Maxims I*, together with etymological links with *leas* 'fraud' and *los* 'loss', leads Fell to suggest that some kind of theft or cheating may be indicated,[35] this is wholly uncertain.[36] In her usual acerbic way, she comments:

> It may seem less self-evident to others than it does to me that if the king was drinking *æt mannes ham* the householder, and perhaps even the king, was more likely to be worried about the financial than the sexual morality of his household, but it is very easy to see ways in which the king's presence might readily provoke various kinds of theft, cheating or bribery.[37]

---

[29] *The Laws*, ed. Attenborough, p. 15: 'If a freeborn woman, with long hair, misconducts herself, she shall pay 30 shillings as compensation'.

[30] Fell, 'A *friwif locbore*', 158.

[31] The unrounding and lowering of /y/ to /e/ and the back spelling <æ> for <e> are both characteristic of Kentish dialect. Cf. A. Campbell, *Old English Grammar* (Oxford, 1959), p. 122, §288.

[32] *The Exeter Anthology of Old English Poetry: an Edition of Exeter Dean and Chapter MS 3501*, ed. B. J. Muir, 2 vols. (Exeter, 1994) I, 258.

[33] *Gesetze*, ed. Liebermann I, 3.

[34] *English Historical Documents*, ed. Whitelock, p. 391.

[35] Fell, 'A *friwif locbore*', 162–4.

[36] It evidently does not convince Lendinara, for instance, who defines *lysu* as 'what is depraved' without mentioning Fell's suggestion (225).

[37] Fell, 'A *friwif locbore*', 164.

This may well be the case, but the evidence of the early laws themselves suggests that the crime considered to present the greatest threat to the king's security was neither sexual nor financial misconduct but violence. Æthelberht 5 stipulates a penalty of fifty shillings for manslaughter in a *cyninges tune*:

Gif in cyninges tune man mannan ofslea, L scill' gebete.[38]	If anyone kills a man in the king's estate, he is to pay 50 shillings compensation.[39]

Ine 6 imposes a still heavier penalty for fighting in the king's house:

Gif hwa gefeohte on cyninges huse, sie he scyldig ealles his ierfes, 7 sie on cyninges dome, hwæðer he lif age þe nage.[40]	If anyone fights in the king's house, he is to forfeit all his possessions, and it is to be at the king's judgment whether he is to keep his life or not.[41]

By the late ninth century, the mere drawing of a weapon in the king's hall might result in the death penalty. Ch. 7 of the laws issued by King Alfred the Great reads as follows:

Gif hwa in cyninges healle gefeohte oððe his wæpn gebrede, 7 hine mon gefó, sie ðæt on cyninges dome, swa deað swa lif, swa he him forgifan wille.	If anyone fights or draws his weapon in the king's hall, and he is captured, it is to be at the king's judgment, whether he will grant him death or life.
7,1. Gif he losige, 7 hine mon eft gefó, forgielde he hine self á be his weregilde, 7 ðone gylt gebete, swa wer swa wite, swa he gewyrht age.[42]	7,1. If he escapes, and is afterwards captured, he shall always pay for himself with his wergild, and compensate for the crime, with wergild as with fine, according to what he has done.[43]

38 *Gesetze,* ed. Liebermann I, 3.
39 *English Historical Documents*, ed. Whitelock, p. 391.
40 *Gesetze,* ed. Liebermann I, 90.
41 *English Historical Documents*, ed. Whitelock, p. 399.
42 *Gesetze,* ed. Liebermann I, 52 and 54.
43 *English Historical Documents*, ed. Whitelock, p. 410.

A similar theme occurs in continental legislation, where chs. 36–38 of the first series of Lombard laws, issued by King Rothari in 643, deal with breaches of the peace where the king is present:

36. Si quis intra palatium regis, ubi rex praesens est, scandalum penetrare praesumpserit, animae suae incurrat periculum, aut redimat anima sua, si optenere potuerit a rege.	36. He who dares to create a disturbance (scandalum) within the king's palace when the king is present shall lose his life unless he can redeem his life from the king.
37. Si quis liber homo in eadem civitatem ubi rex praesens est aut tunc invenitur esse, scandalum penetrare praesumpserit, id est si incitaverit et non percusserit, sit culpabiles solidos duodicem in palatium regis. Nam si perfecerit et percusserit, sit culpabiles in palatium regis solidos viginti et quattuor; excepto plagas aut feritas si fecerit, sicut subter adnexum est, conponat.	37. The freeman who creates a disturbance in that district (civitas) where the king is present, although he does not strike a blow, shall pay twelve solidi to the king's palace [i.e., the royal fisc]. But he who raises a disturbance and also strikes a blow, shall pay twenty-four solidi to the fisc. In addition, he shall pay composition for any wounds or injuries which he caused as provided below (Rothair 43–128).
38. Si servus in eadem civitatem, in qua rex tunc invenitur esse, scandalum incitaverit, sit culpabiles in palatio regis solidos sex. Et si percusserit, sit culpabilis in palatium solidos duodicem, excepto feritas aut conpositiones plagarum, sicut in hoc edictum legitur.[44]	38. The slave who creates a disturbance in a district where the king is present, shall pay six solidi to the royal fisc. And if he also strikes a blow, then he shall pay twelve solidi to the fisc in addition to paying composition for the wounds or injuries as provided in this code.[45]

It may be relevant that Æthelberht 3 follows directly on from a law concerning violence against people summoned to the king's presence. Æthelberht 2 reads as follows:

---

[44] *Leges Langobardorum*, ed. F. Bluhme, Monumenta Germaniae Historica, Leges 4 (Hannover, 1869), 19.

[45] K. F. Drew, *The Lombard Laws* (Philadelphia, PA, 1973), pp. 59–60.

Gif cyning his leode to him gehateþ, 7 heom mon þær yfel gedo, IIbóte 7 cyninge L scillinga.[46]	If the king calls his people to him, and anyone does them injury there, [he is to pay] a two-fold compensation and 50 shillings to the king.[47]

Since a two-fold compensation is also stipulated in ch. 3, the latter clause may logically be taken to reflect the other side of the coin, referring to violence against people being visited by the king. I therefore propose the following interpretation of Æthelberht 3:

Gif cyning æt mannes ham drincæþ, 7 ðær man lyswæs hwæt gedo, twibote gebete.	If the king is being entertained on someone's estate, and anyone commits an act of violence there, he is to pay two-fold compensation.[48]

The possibility that Æthelberht 73 may be concerned with assault is raised in a footnote by Hollis:

> Ethelbert, 73, however, offers one of the instances of a penalty specifying direct female responsibility, which, like the immediately adjacent legislation (Ethelbert, 32–74), may refer to injury inflicted by violence.[49]

Curiously, Hollis offers no support for this statement other than a reference to Fell's article, where violence is not mentioned. Such a reading would, however, be fully in keeping with continental legislation penalizing women for participating in violence. Under the Bavarian laws of *c.* 744–48, a free woman who chooses to fight like a man forfeits the double compensation that she would normally receive for personal injury. Section IV comprises a personal injury tariff relating to freemen, and following the usual schedule of compensations, IV,30 reads as follows:

---

[46] *Gesetze,* ed. Liebermann , 3.

[47] *English Historical Documents*, ed. Whitelock, p. 391.

[48] Dictionary of Old English Project, *Dictionary of Old English A–G.* Version 2.0. CD-ROM, 2008 (hereafter DOE), s.v. *drincan* A.2, identify a sense 'to be entertained' which is attested only here but is clearly required by the context. OE *hām* in early place-names refers to a village or estate, so the law probably applies to an offence committed during the course of a visit – possibly of several days' or weeks' duration – by the king and his retinue.

[49] S. Hollis, *Anglo-Saxon Women and the Church: Sharing a Common Fate* (Woodbridge, 1992), p. 63 n. 73.

De feminis vero eorum, si aliquid de istis actis contigerit, omnia dupliciter conponantur. Et quia femina cum arma defendere se nequiverit, duplicem conpositionem accipiat. Si autem pugnare voluerit per audaciam cordis sui sicut vir, non erit duplex conpositio eius, sed sicut fratres eius ita et ipsa recipiat.[50]	If any of these acts happens to the women of those freemen, let all be compensated for twofold. Since a woman cannot defend herself with weapons, let her obtain a double compensation. If, however, she wishes to fight through boldness of heart, just as a man does, her compensation will not be twofold.[51]

Ch. 378 of the first series of Lombard laws also stipulates that a woman injured while brawling is to forfeit the compensation to which she would otherwise be entitled:

378. Si mulier libera in scandalum cocurrerit, ubi viri litigant, si plagam aut feritam factam habuerit, aut forsitan inpincta fuerit aut occisa, adpretietur secundum nobilitatem suam, et sic conponatur, tamquam si in fratrem ipsius mulieris perpetratum fuisset; nam alia culpa pro iniuria sua, unde nongenti solidi iudicantur, non requiratur, eo quod ipsa ad litem cocurrit, quod inhonestum est mulieribus facere.[52]	378. If a free woman participates in a brawl (scandalum) where men are struggling, and if she inflicts some blow or injury and perhaps in turn is struck or killed, she shall be valued according to her rank and composition shall be paid for her as if the deed had been done to a brother of that woman. But the penalty for such injury, for which 900 solidi have been adjudged, shall not be required since she had participated in a struggle in a manner dishonorable for women.[53]

Ch. 141 of the later Lombard laws issued by King Liutprand in 734 shows that female violence could be a serious social problem. The issue is

---

[50] *Lex Baiwariorum*, ed. E. de Schwind, Monumenta Germaniae Historica, Legum Sectio I, 5.2 (Hanover, 1926), 335.

[51] T. J. Rivers, *Laws of the Alamans and Bavarians* (Pennsylvania, PA, 1977), p. 134. This is ch. 29 according to Rivers' numbering.

[52] *Leges Langobardorum*, ed. Bluhme, 88.

[53] Drew, *The Burgundian Code*, p. 127.

addressed in a long and complex clause, of which the opening section only is reproduced here:

> 141. III. Relatum est nobis, quod aliqui hominis perfidi et in malitia astuti, dum per se non presumpsessent mano forti aut violento ordinem intrare in vicum aut in casam alienam, timentes illam conpositionem que in antiquo edicto posita est, fecerunt collegere mulieres suas, quascumque habuerunt, liberas et ancillas, et miserunt eas super homines, qui minore habebant virtute, et adprehendentes hominis de ipso loco, et plagas fecerunt, et reliqua mala violento ordine plus crudeliter quam viri exercuerunt.[54]

> 141.III. It has been related to us that certain perfidious and evil-minded men, not presuming themselves to enter armed into a village or into the house of another man in a violent manner since they fear the composition which has been set up in an earlier law (Rothair 279, 280), gather together as many women as they have both free and bond, and set them upon weaker men. Seizing these men the women rain blows upon them and commit other evil deeds in a violent manner more cruelly than men might do.[55]

This clause and others in Lombard law are discussed by Balzaretti, who comments that 'Female violence clearly puzzled the law-makers as much as it has perplexed historians'.[56] The topic has not previously been identified in Anglo-Saxon law, although it does occur in the penitential handbooks. For instance, *A Late Old English Handbook for the Use of a Confessor* addresses violence towards a maidservant by her mistress:

> Gyf wif hire man swingð for hwilcu*m* liðru*m* andan, *and* heo on ðam bið dead, *and* heo beo unscildig, fæste swa ðeah iii gear *and* reowsige hire misdæda æfre.[57]

> If a woman beats her maidservant through some malicious spite, and she dies as a result, and she is innocent, [the mistress] is to fast for three years and always to repent her misdeeds.[58]

---

[54] *Leges Langobardorum*, ed. Bluhme,170–1.

[55] Drew, *The Burgundian Code*, pp. 208–9.

[56] R. Balzaretti, '"These are Things that Men Do, Not Women": The Social Regulation of Female Violence in Langobard Italy', *Violence and Society in the Early Medieval West*, ed. G. Halsall (Woodbridge, 1998), pp. 175–92, at p. 187. Balzaretti goes on to argue that legal constructs of violent men and non-violent women were a means by which women were subordinated in Langobard society.

[57] R. Fowler, 'A Late Old English Handbook for the Use of a Confessor', *Anglia* 83 (1965), 1–34, at 21, lines 154–6.

[58] Author's translation.

The corpus of Anglo-Saxon case-law also contains a number of possible references to violence by women. The corpus is defined by Wormald, whose case no. 58 (S 877) concerns a forfeiture by the widow and son of Wulfbald 'both for his crimes and for their slaying of their kinsman, Eadmær, the king's thegn, with his fifteen companions', while case no. 67 (S 1242) is described as 'Queen Ælfthryth challenged that she had used excessive force in settling no. 66'.[59] Both date from the late tenth century, as does case no.43 (S 1377), recording a forfeiture by a widow and her son for attempting to cause the death of Ælfsige:

7 þ land æt Ægeleswyrðe headde an wyduwe 7 hire sune ær forwyrt forþanþe hi drifon serne stacan on Ælsie Wulfstanes feder 7 þ werð æreafe ...	The estate at Ailsworth had been forfeited by a widow and her son, because they drove an iron pin into Ælfsige, Wulfstan's father, and it was discovered ...[60]

Although usually taken to refer to witchcraft on the assumption that the pin was actually driven into an effigy of Ælfsige,[61] the passage is fully capable of a literal interpretation, and may refer quite simply to a physical assault by the woman and her son.[62]

The fact that a fixed fine is stipulated in Æthelberht 73 also makes it more likely that the offence is one of violence than of financial dishonesty. Penalties for theft in this code are otherwise assessed in multiples of

---

[59] P. Wormald, 'A Handlist of Anglo-Saxon Lawsuits', *Anglo-Saxon England* 17 (1988), 247–81, at 263, reprinted in his *Legal Culture in the Early Medieval West* (1999), pp. 253–87.

[60] *Anglo-Saxon Charters*, ed. Robertson, no. 37, pp. 68–9.

[61] See for instance the discussion by A. Davies, 'Witches in Anglo-Saxon England: Five Case Histories', *Superstition and Popular Medicine in Anglo-Saxon England*, ed. D. G. Scragg (Manchester, 1989), pp. 41–56, at pp. 49–51. Davies notes, however, that the punishment meted out does not accord with contemporary law on witchcraft.

[62] Much depends on the interpretation of the phrase *7 man teh þ morð forð of hire inclifan* immediately following the passage quoted. Robertson's translation, 'and the deadly image was dragged out of her room', takes *morð* to refer to an effigy, but this meaning of the term is not attested elsewhere. Primary meanings of *morð* are 'death', 'that which causes death' and 'murder' (*An Anglo-Saxon Dictionary*, ed. Toller, p. 698, s.v. *morþ*), so the reference might alternatively be to the *serne stacan* 'iron bar' with which Wulfsige was attacked. As Robertson (*Anglo-Saxon Charters,* p. 324) notes, no other instances of 'pin-sticking magic' are on record from the Anglo-Saxon period although the offence is mentioned in penitential literature.

the amount stolen (e.g. chs. 1, 4, 9, 28, 90), while crimes involving sex or assault are compensated by payment of a fixed sum (e.g. chs. 5–6, 10–11, 13–14, 16–22, 24–26, 33–72), or under aggravated circumstances of double the usual sum (e.g. chs. 2–3, 85). Fell acknowledges that her interpretation 'is unsatisfactory in so far as we cannot tell the scale or the type of dishonesty that is being fined', but goes on to argue:

> Given the heavy nature of the fine we are entitled to think in terms of robbing the treasury rather than the store-cupboard. When, for example, the king was staying at any residence where he would be expected to fulfil his rôle as *sincbrytta*, someone would have to take charge of the 'treasure' for the length of his stay, and this may be the kind of situation for which the law was designed.[63]

As Fell admits, this is 'pure speculation'. Such a law might rather be expected to occur towards the beginning of the code alongside Æthelberht 3, and I myself do not envisage a visiting king handing over his treasury to the lady of the house. A fine of thirty shillings would, however, seem reasonable for assault. This is the amount specified elsewhere in Æthelberht's code for disabling a shoulder (ch. 38), causing injury serious enough to need medical treatment (ch. 62) or damaging the groin (ch. 63); and in comparison with fifty shillings for manslaughter on the king's premises (ch. 5), sleeping with the king's *mægdenman* (ch. 10) or abducting a girl (ch. 82), and with twenty for lending weapons later used for manslaughter (ch. 20), binding a free man (ch. 24) or breaking the skull (ch. 37), it is not implausible as a fine for violence inflicted by a woman.

To return to the semantic range of OE *lysu*, Fell writes as follows:

> The possibilities are three: first, that ... it did mean sexual depravity or could be used with that range; secondly, that it was a rather vague word which could be used of any range of criminal conduct,... thirdly, that it had a more precise meaning clear to the Anglo-Saxons if not necessarily to us.[64]

The second and third possibilities may not be mutually exclusive if it is accepted that a general term may take on a more precise meaning from the context in which it appears. Æthelberht 73 follows directly on from the personal injury tariff, and I suggest that this provides a frame of reference for the particular type of *lysu* in question. A genitive construction with *hwæt* occurs in the Kentish laws only in Æthelberht 3

[63] Fell, 'A *friwif locbore*', 164.
[64] *Ibid.* 163.

and 73, but is paralleled in three clauses within Alfred's *domboc*. In Alfred 37,2, the phrase *hwæt yfla* 'any wrong' functions as a blanket term to cover any kind of criminal conduct,[65] while in Alfred 40,1, the phrase *ðisses hwæt* 'any of this' refers back to a list of offences detailed in the earlier part of the clause.[66] Alfred 38 is of particular interest in this connection:

Gif mon beforan cyninges ealdormen on gemote gefeohte, bete wer 7 wite, swa hit ryht sie, 7 beforan þam CXX scill. ðam ealdormen to wite.	If anyone fights in a meeting in the presence of the king's ealdorman, he is to pay wergild and fine, as it is the law, and before that, 120 shillings to the ealdorman as a fine.
38,1. Gif he folcgemot mid wæpnes bryde árære, ðam ealdormen hundtwelftig scill. to wite.	38,1. If he disturbs a public meeting by drawing a weapon, [he is to pay] 120 shillings to the ealdorman as a fine.
38,2. Gif ðises hwæt beforan cyninges ealdormonnes gingran gelimpe oððe cyninges preoste, XXX scill. to wite.[67]	38,2. If any of this takes place in the presence of the deputy of the king's ealdorman, or of the king's priest, 30 shillings [is to be paid] as a fine.[68]

Again, it may be noted that the presence of a high-ranking official leads to increased penalties not for sexual or financial irregularity, but for violence. The phrase *ðises hwæt* in 38,2 relates to the offences described in 38 and 38,1, and I suggest that *lyswæs hwæt* in Æthelberht 3 refers back in a similar way to the type of offence discussed in ch. 2, and *leswæs hwæt* in Æthelberht 73 to the types of assault outlined in chs. 33–72, indicating in the first instance that two-fold compensation is payable for violence perpetrated in the king's presence, and in the second that a fine of thirty shillings is payable for violence committed by a woman in a position of responsibility. Ch. 73 would thus provide the same kind of transition between the personal injury tariff and the sequence on women as does ch. 85 between the latter and the final section on servants and slaves.

It is curious that while Æthelberht 73 has generally been treated in isolation from the surrounding laws, the following clause 74 has

[65] *Gesetze,* ed. Liebermann I, 70.
[66] *Ibid.* 72 and 74.
[67] *Ibid.* 70 and 72.
[68] *English Historical Documents*, ed. Whitelock, p. 414.

consistently been associated with the personal injury tariff from which it is separated by ch. 73. Ch. 74 is one of the shortest and most laconic of Æthelberht's laws, presumably because its meaning was self-evident to a contemporary audience:

> Mægþbot sy swa friges mannes.

The key term *mægþbot* 'maiden compensation' is unique, but editors are united in assuming that it refers to compensation payable *to* the maiden, and in taking the clause as a whole to mean that injuries to a young woman or virgin are to be compensated at the same rate as injuries to a free man. This was the reading offered by Hickes in 1703–05 ('Virginis aut virginitatis compensatio sit ut liberi hominis'[69]) and followed by Wilkins in 1721 ('Virginis compensatio sit ut liberi hominis'[70]), and interpretation has altered little in the last three hundred years. Nineteenth-century editors translated as 'Let "maiden-bōt" be as that of a free-man' (Thorpe[71]) and 'Die Buße einer Jungfrau sei wie die eines freien Mannes' (Schmid[72]), while in the twentieth century there is general agreement between Liebermann ('[Die für Verletzung einer] Jungfrau [zu entrichtende] Busse sei so [hoch] wie [für die Verletzung] eines freien Mannes'[73]), Attenborough ('Compensation [for injury] to be paid to an unmarried woman, shall be on the same scale as that paid to a freeman'[74]) and Whitelock ('The compensation for [injury to] a maiden is to be as for a freeman'[75]). Lendinara does not translate the clause in its entirety, but defines *mægþ bōt* along similar lines as 'fine for assault on an unmarried woman,'[76] and the same definition is given – though with a question mark indicating uncertainty – by Clark Hall.[77] The accepted interpretation is summed up by Doris Stenton when she writes:

> The second law simply states that injury, of whatever kind, to a free

[69] G. Hickes, *Linguarum Vett. Septentrionalium Thesaurus Grammatico-Criticus et Archaeologicus*, 2 vols. (Oxford, 1703–05) II, 91.
[70] *Leges Anglo-Saxonicae Ecclesiasticae & Civiles*, ed. D. Wilkins (London, 1721), p. 6.
[71] *Ancient Laws*, ed. Thorpe, p. 8.
[72] *Die Gesetze der Angelsachsen*, ed. R. Schmid, 2nd ed. (Leipzig, 1858), p. 8.
[73] *Gesetze,* ed. Liebermann I, 7.
[74] *The Laws,* ed. Attenborough, p. 15.
[75] *English Historical Documents*, ed. Whitelock, p. 393.
[76] Lendinara, 'The Kentish Laws', p. 223.
[77] J. R. Clark Hall, *A Concise Anglo-Saxon Dictionary*, 4th ed. (Cambridge, 1960), p. 225, s.v. *mægðbōt*.

> maiden must be paid for at the same rate as injury to a free man. The king at this point is looking back to a long and detailed list of injuries for which compensation has already been provided in the laws, and is making this tariff generally applicable to women as well as men.[78]

Despite the unanimity of opinion, however, there are problems with this reading. Firstly, ch. 74 does not make the personal injury tariff 'generally applicable to women'. It singles out one particular type of woman, the unmarried girl, giving no indication of the scale of compensation appropriate to a married woman or widow. Secondly, if the aim of this clause were indeed to establish the same rates of compensation for women as for men, Æthelberht's laws would be unique among the barbarian codes in so doing. Personal injury tariffs are a common feature of early Germanic legislation, and it is usual for injuries to women to attract a higher penalty than injuries to men. In the Alamannic laws of *c.* 717–19, for instance, a lengthy catalogue of compensation for injuries of various kinds in chs. 57–59 is followed by the direction that women are to receive twice the amount:

59,2. Haec omnia conpositio, quod ad viris indicavimus, ad feminis eorum omnia dupliciter conponatur.[79]	59,2. Let all this compensation that we have determined for men be rendered twofold to their women.[80]

The following ch. 60 is concerned with manslaughter, and reiterates the principle of double compensation for women:

60,1. Si quis autem liber liberum occiderit, conponat eum bis octuaginta solidis ad filios suos. Si autem filios non reliquid nec heredes habuit, solvat eum 200 solidis.	60,1. If, however, any freeman kills another freeman, let him compensate for him with twice eighty solidi to his children. If, however, he leaves no children and has no relatives, let him [the killer] pay 200 solidi for him.
60,2. Feminas autem eorum semper in duplum.[81]	60,2. Women, however, [are] always [to be compensated] twofold.[82]

[78] Stenton, *The English Woman*, p. 7.
[79] *Leges Alamannorum*, ed. by K. A. Eckhardt, Monumenta Germaniae Historica, Legum Sectio I: Leges nationum Germanicarum 5.1 (Hanover, 1966), 129.
[80] Rivers, *Laws of the Alamans*, p. 90.
[81] *Leges Alamannorum*, ed. Eckhardt, 129–30.

The first series of Lombard laws contains a list of compensations for injuries to freemen in chs. 45–74, followed in chs. 76–102 by a corresponding tariff for injuries to the half-free or to household slaves, and in chs. 103–27 by another list relating to field slaves, but free women are mentioned only in ch. 75, which stipulates that a pregnant woman and her unborn child are to be compensated for separately in the event of manslaughter.[83] The Bavarian laws of *c.* 744–48 also include three tariffs (sections IV, V and VI) relating to freemen, freedmen and slaves, and as noted above, IV,30 stipulates that a free woman is to be compensated double for injuries unless she has chosen to fight. Discussing this and other clauses, Rivers argues persuasively that the double compensation allocated to women under both Bavarian and Alamannic law is a direct corollary of their legal inability to defend themselves with weapons.[84] It seems unlikely that the Anglo-Saxon laws would stand alone in assigning equal compensation to both sexes, and indeed the personal injury tariff in Alfred 44–77, which is generally agreed to have been modelled on that of Æthelberht,[85] contains no hint of such a thing.

I wish to suggest that Æthelberht 74 refers to the penalty payable not *to* but *by* the *mægþ*. This is how *mægþbot* was understood by Toller, who defines it as 'the fine to be paid by an unmarried woman' and translates the whole clause as 'let the fine to be paid by an unmarried woman be the same as that by a free man (for the same offence)'.[86] Toller's interpretation is acknowledged as an alternative possibility by Attenborough[87] and presumably underlies Wormald's summary analysis of the opening of the women's sequence as 'offences by senior *and junior* women' (my italics),[88]

[82] Rivers, *Laws of the Alamans*, p. 90.
[83] *Leges Langobardorum*, ed. Bluhme, 20–30.
[84] T. J. Rivers, 'The Legal Status of Freewomen in the Lex Alamannorum, *Zeitschrift der Savigny-Stiftung für Rechtsgeschichte, Germanistische Abteilung* 91 (1974), 175–79. Rivers points out that women receive double compensation only for those crimes which also apply to men, and not for those appertaining exclusively to women such as abduction and sexual molestation.
[85] See for instance *Councils and Synods with Other Documents Relating to the English Church. I: A.D. 871–1204*, Part I: 871–1066 ed. D. Whitelock, M. Brett and C. N. L. Brooke (Oxford, 1981), p. 18, and S. Keynes and M. Lapidge, *Alfred the Great: Asser's "Life of King Alfred" and Other Contemporary Sources* (London, 1983), pp. 310–11 n. 33.
[86] *An Anglo-Saxon Dictionary*, ed. Toller, p. 658, s.v. *mægþ-bót*. Toller draws attention to the fact that 'This regulation follows one that settles the fine to be paid by "fri wif locbore"'.
[87] *The Laws*, ed. Attenborough, p. 178.
[88] Wormald, '"Inter cetera bona…', 972.

but it was rejected by Liebermann on the grounds that this type of construction is not paralleled in other compounds in *-bot*:

> In den 23 Wörtern, deren zweites Glied *-bot* ... bildet, drückt das erste entweder Quantität oder Qualität der Busse aus oder aber das, was (wofür) gebüsst wird ... aber niemals das büssende Subjekt.[89]

This may bear further examination. In the first place, compounds in *-bot* do not conform to a standard pattern. Those cited by the editors of the Toronto *Dictionary of Old English* are *brycgbot*, *burhbot*, *cynebot*, *cyricbot*, *dædbot*, *dægbot*, *dolgbot*, *eftbot*, *fæhþbot*, *feohbot*, *gearbot*, *godbot*, *hadbot*, *hloþbot*, *mannbot*, *mægbot*, *mægþbot*, *monaþbot*, *sarbot*, *synnbot*, *weofodbot*, *woruldbot* and *wucubot*.[90] Of these, *brycgbot* and *burhbot* refer to the obligatory maintenance of a bridge or fortification respectively, *cyricbot* to church repairs, and *eftbot* to restoration or renewal, while *dædbot* and *synnbot* refer to ecclesiastical penance and *dægbot*, *gearbot*, *monaþbot* and *wucubot* to penance for a period of a day, year, month or week.[91] None is relevant to the interpretation of *mægþbot*. The sense 'compensation for injury' occurs in *dolgbot* 'fine or compensation for a wound', *fæhþbot* 'compensation incurred as the result of a feud, compensation for manslaughter (committed against one's kin)', *feohbot* 'compensation in money', *godbot* 'reparation made to the church', *hadbot* 'a recompense, compensation, or atonement for injury done to persons in holy orders', *sarbot* 'compensation paid for inflicting a wound', *weofodbot* 'a fine to be paid to the bishop for the injury done to the church by doing wrong to one in holy orders', and *woruldbot* '*bot* prescribed by the secular power'. In none of these does the first element denote either the victim or the perpetrator of the offence. This leaves just four compounds – too few to be statistically significant – referring to a person or group of people by whom, for whom, or to whom compensation is to be paid. Both *cynebot* 'king's compensation, payment made to the people for the slaying of the king' and *mannbot* 'a fine to be paid to the lord of a man slain' refer to the person to be compensated *for* rather than to the payer or the recipient. By analogy, *mægþbot* might be taken to represent the compensation payable to the family of the *mægþ* in the event of her manslaughter, but in the absence of any supportive evidence for such an interpretation, the possibility seems a remote one. Finally, *hloþbot* 'compensation or fine

---

[89] *Gesetze,* ed. Liebermann III, 13–14.

[90] DOE, s.v. *bōt*.

[91] Definitions here and throughout this paragraph are taken from DOE (A–G), and otherwise from Toller, with *Supplement* and *Addenda* (1972).

to be paid by a member of a *hloþ* for the wrong committed by any one of them' designates the persons responsible for paying compensation, while *mægbot* 'the *bot* paid to the kinsmen of a slain man for the slaying of the latter' designates those entitled to receive it.[92] The odds would therefore appear to be evenly balanced with regard to the interpretation of *mægþbot* as compensation payable either *to* or *by* the girl herself.

It should also be noted that it is uncertain whether the nonce occurrence *mægþbot* represents a compound or two separate words. Word division counts for little in the manuscript, but for what it is worth, the two elements of *mægþ/bot* are divided at a line-ending while *botsy* is written together.[93] Comparison with the position of *locbore* at the end of the previous line shows that there was sufficient space for *bot* to have been written on the same line as *mægþ*, so the fact that the scribe chooses to begin a new line may just possibly indicate that word division is intended. If this is the case, it might be acceptable to punctuate the clause as follows: *Mægþ: bot sy swa friges mannes* 'A maiden: compensation is to be ...' The syntax would, however, be unlike that of other Kentish laws, and since the compounds discussed above provide abundant evidence of parallel formations from a noun followed by *bot*, the traditional punctuation seems preferable.

There is thus a reasonable case for taking Æthelberht 73 and 74 as a sequence dealing in turn with the compensation payable by a *fri wif* and a *mægþ*. Toller's reading, however, provides no clue as to the nature of the offence or offences in question, and it remains unclear why the *mægþ* rather than the married woman or widow should be singled out for parity of treatment with a free man. To the best of my knowledge there are no other instances of such a pairing in either continental Germanic or later Anglo-Saxon legislation, and in fact the closest parallel I have been able to trace for a woman of any kind explicitly being required to pay the same compensation as a free man is from seventh-century Visigothic law, and concerns not an unmarried girl but a free adult. The Visigothic Code VI.iii.2–3 reads as follows:

---

[92] Formally, *mægþbot* could be a doublet of *mægbot*, from OE *mægþ* in the sense 'kindred' rather than 'maiden'. The two terms are bracketed together in the (unpaginated) Index to Thorpe, and could be taken to be alternative spellings of the same compound. I explored this possibility in a paper given some years ago to the Research Group on Manuscript Evidence at the Parker Library, Corpus Christi College, Cambridge, but I no longer believe it to be tenable.

[93] *Textus Roffensis*, 3r15–16. Letter *y* is written over an erasure.

2. Si quis mulierem gravidam percusserit quocumque hictu aut per aliquam occasionem mulierem ingenuam abortare fecerit, et exinde mortua fuerit, pro homicidio puniatur. Si autem tantumodo partus excutiatur, et mulier in nullo debilitata fuerit, et ingenuus ingenue hoc intulisse cognoscitur, si formatum infantem extincxit, CL solidos reddat; si vero informem, C solidos pro facto restituat.	2. If anyone should cause a freeborn woman to abort by a blow, or by any other means, and she should die from the injury, he shall be punished for homicide. But if only an abortion should be produced in consequence, and the woman should be in no wise injured; where a freeman is known to have committed this act upon a freewoman, and the child should be fully formed, he shall pay two hundred *solidi*; otherwise, he shall pay a hundred *solidi*, by way of satisfaction.
3. Si mulier ingenua per aliquam violentiam aut occasionem ingenue partum excusserit aut eam ex hoc debilitasse cognoscitur, sicut et ingenui superioris damni pena multetur.[94]	3. Where a freeborn woman, either by violence or by any other means, causes another freeborn woman to abort, whether, or not, she should be seriously injured as a result of said act, she shall undergo the same penalty provided in the cases of freeborn men.[95]

Again, the law-givers acknowledge the possibility of female violence, and attempt to contain it within the framework of statute law. Other laws assign the same penalty to both men and women of equal rank: for instance, in the Visigothic Code VI.iv.3, a detailed tariff of compensations for injuries inflicted by slaves, freedmen or persons of free birth is followed by the direction that *Omnes autem sententie legis huius tam in viris quam in feminis observande sunt*[96] 'All the provisions of this law shall apply to the cases of men as well as to those of women'.[97] Nowhere, however, is an equation made between free men and unmarried girls as either criminals or victims, and indeed it is difficult to see why it should be.

---

[94] *Leges Visigothorum*, ed. K. Zeumer, Monumenta Germaniae Historica, Legum Sectio I: Legum nationum Germanicarum 1 (Hanover, 1902), 261.

[95] S. P. Scott, *The Visigothic Code* (Boston, MA, 1910), pp. 206–7.

[96] *Leges Visigothorum*, ed. Zeumer, 266.

[97] Scott, *The Visigothic Code*, p. 214.

It seems to me that the crucial flaw both in Toller's translation and in the traditional reading of Æthelberht 74 lies in the unproven assumption that the final word of the clause means 'man' in the modern sense 'adult of the male sex'. It is too well known to require demonstration here that OE *man(n)* had a much wider semantic range than its Present Day English reflex, referring to human beings of both sexes and sometimes even specifically to women.[98] Unequivocal examples of the term used both in a general and in a female sense are to be found in the law-codes. VI Æthelstan 2, for instance, makes provision for a subscription to be paid by *ælc man*. That this applies to both sexes is shown by the fact that the law goes on to exempt impecunious widows:

... 7 scute ælc man his scll', þe hæfde *þæt* yrfe *þæt* wǣre XXX pænig̃ wurð, buton earmre wúdewan, þe nænne forwyrhtan næfde ne nán lánd.[99]	...And each man was to pay his shilling who had property that was worth 30 pence, except for a poor widow, who had no one working for her and no land.[100]

Alfred 18 sets the penalty for sexual assault on nuns at twice the amount payable for a lay *man*:

Gif hwa nunnan mid hæmeðþinge oððe on hire hrægl oððe on hire breost butan hire leafe gefó, sie hit twybete swa we ær be læwdum men fundon.[101]	If anyone in lewd fashion seizes a nun either by her clothes or her breast without her leave, the compensation is to be double that we have established for a lay person.[102]

---

[98] See for instance the discussion in C. Fell, C. Clark and E. Williams, *Women in Anglo-Saxon England and the Impact of 1066* (London, 1984), pp. 17–18. J. P. Stanley and C. McGowan, 'Woman and Wife: Social and Semantic Shifts in English', *Papers in Linguistics* 12 (1979), 491–502, observe that the semantic range of *man* narrowed during the Old English period, so that the once generic term came to designate a male human being towards the end of the ninth century, at about the same time as the word *wif* began to mean a married woman. Both shifts would thus significantly post-date the laws of Æthelberht.

[99] *Gesetze,* ed. Liebermann I, 174–5.

[100] *English Historical Documents*, ed. Whitelock, p. 425.

[101] *Gesetze,* ed. Liebermann I, 58.

[102] *English Historical Documents*, ed. Whitelock, p. 411. The cross-reference is to Alfred 11, which deals with various forms of sexual attack from rape downwards, and which I have discussed in detail in 'Alfred's *Domboc* and the Language of Rape: a Reconsideration of Alfred, ch. 11', *Medium Ævum* 66 (1997), 1–27, reprinted in this volume.

Alfred 26 deals with the rape of underage girls, and again uses the word *mann* in an unambiguously female sense:

Gif mon ungewintrædne wifmon to niedhæmde geðreatige, sie ðæt swa ðæs gewintredan monnes bot.[103]	If anyone rapes a girl not of age, that is to be the same compensation as for a woman past child-bearing age.[104]

Once the possibility is allowed that *mann* in Æthelberht 74 may similarly mean 'person' or even 'woman' rather than 'man', it becomes evident that the purpose of the clause may be to equate the *mægþ* not with a free man, but with a free woman. Depending on the alternative interpretations of *mægþbot* discussed above, the meaning could be either that an unmarried girl was entitled to the same level of compensation as an adult woman, or that she was liable to pay the same fine. Juxtaposition with ch. 73 strongly suggests the latter, especially as it would be highly unusual under Germanic law for a girl to receive the same compensation for injury as a woman of child-bearing age. This is a topic that I have discussed elsewhere,[105] so it may here suffice to cite a single example from the early-eighth-century Alamannic laws, where ch. 56 sets out a scale of compensation for different forms of sexual attack against virgins, and goes on to state that adult women are to receive twice the amount:

56,2. Si autem muliere haec contingerit, omnia dupliciter componat, sicut antea diximus de virgine.[106]	56,2. If, however, this happens to an adult woman, let him compensate all things twice what we said above concerning the virgin.[107]

Standard practice under Salic and Ripuarian law was for the homicide of adult women to be compensated at three times the rate of unmarried

---

[103] *Gesetze,* ed. Liebermann I, 64 and 66.

[104] This interpretation is proposed in my article, 'A New Reading of Alfred, ch. 26', *Nottingham Medieval Studies* 41 (1997), 1–12, reprinted in this volume. Previous interpretations take *gewintredan* to mean 'adult'.

[105] See Hough 'A New Reading'. When I wrote that article, I accepted the traditional interpretation of Æthelberht 74, and assumed that the personal injury tariff in Alfred's code also applied equally to both sexes. These are views that I no longer hold.

[106] *Leges Alamannorum*, ed. Eckhardt, 115–16.

[107] Rivers, *Laws of the Alamans*, 85.

girls,[108] so it would again be surprising to find equal compensation for all age groups in seventh-century England. I therefore suggest that Æthelberht 74 concerns the compensation payable neither *to* nor *for* but *by* an unmarried woman, and that the clause relates not to the personal injury tariff in chs. 32–72 but to the immediately preceding law concerning the *fri wif* in ch. 73.

It remains to be pointed out that the case for taking the *wif* of Æthelberht 73 and the *mann* of Æthelberht 74 to be one and the same is strengthened by the use of the same descriptor (*fri(g)*) in both instances. Also relevant is the fact that OE *wif* is the generic term for a woman who is not a *mægþ*. As discussed above, the two words are in complementary distribution; and this provides a fairly clear indication that chs. 73 and 74 are to be read in conjunction with each other.[109] Far from allocating unmarried girls the same rate of compensation for injury as free men, the purpose of ch. 74 may rather be to penalize them equally with married women and widows for acts of unwomanly violence.

In conclusion, I suggest that Æthelberht 73 and 74 define the penalty for physical assault by females of free birth, dealing first with adult women and then with unmarried girls. This offers several advantages over previous readings of the two laws. Firstly, it restores the coherence of this section of Æthelberht's code, allowing chs. 73 and 74 to be read as a self-contained pair of clauses covering women of all age groups, with links both to the preceding personal injury tariff and to the following women's sequence. Secondly, it establishes a plausible semantic range for OE *lysu* in chs. 3 and 73, identifying the offence as one that features prominently elsewhere in the early law-codes and could reasonably be expected to attract the penalties stated. Thirdly, it removes the anomalies inherent in the supposed equation between unmarried women and free men in ch. 74, and is more consistent with evidence from continental Germanic legislation

[108] *Pactus Legis Salicae*, ch. 41,15 and 41,16; *Lex Ribuaria*, chs. 12 and 13.

[109] The significance of the contrast between *wif* and *mægþ* has been obscured by the consistent misinterpretation of *wif* either as 'virgin' – by those who take *locbore* to mean 'long hair' and long hair to be a symbol of virginity – or as 'married woman'. The latter is, of course, the meaning of the Present Day English reflex *wife*, and although the Old English word is well known to have had a wider semantic range, it is all too easy to assume a connection with its modern counterpart. Even Fell falls into the trap, commenting of Æthelberht 73: 'This is the only place in the laws of Æðelbert where a woman is required to pay a fine, and it makes obvious sense to see this as the other side of the picture in which she is freed from responsibility for her husband's theft' (*Women in Anglo-Saxon England,* p. 61). The law concerning theft by the husband does not in any case occur in Æthelberht's code, but is Ine 57.

and later Anglo-Saxon law. I therefore propose the following interpretation of the two clauses:

73. Gif fri wif locbore leswæs hwæt gedeþ, XXX scll' gebete.	73. If a free woman in a position of responsibility commits any violence, she is to pay 30 shillings compensation.
74. Mægþbot sy swa friges mannes.	74. The compensation payable by an unmarried girl is to be the same as that payable by a free woman.

6.

THE WIDOW'S *MUND* IN ÆTHELBERHT 75 AND 76*

First published 1999: *Journal of English and Germanic Philology* 98, 1–16.

Chs. 75 and 76 of the law-code issued by King Æthelberht of Kent during the early seventh century contain important evidence relating to the legal status of widows in early Anglo-Saxon society. The consensus of scholarly opinion is that both clauses deal with the abduction of widows, who apparently occupied a subordinate position under the protection or guardianship of members of their kin. This interpretation does not seem to me to accord with the text, and I wish to propose an alternative reading indicating that it was the widows themselves who were able to extend protection to their household and dependants, and who were entitled to compensation for any violation of their rights.

The two clauses in question read as follows, with Dorothy Whitelock's translation:

75 Mund þare betstan widuwan eorlcundre L scillinga gebete.	75 [Breach of] guardianship over a noble-born widow of the highest class is to be compensated for with 50 shillings;
75.1 Đare oþre XX scll', ðare þriddan XII scll', þare feorðan VI scll'.	75.1 that over one of the second class, with 20 shillings; over one of the third class, with 12 shillings; over one of the fourth, with six shillings.

*This article is dedicated to the memory of Christine E. Fell, who died 2 July 1998.

76 Gif man widuwan unagne genimeþ, II gelde seo mund sy.[1]	76 If a man takes a widow who does not belong to him, the [penalty for breach of the] guardianship is to be doubled.[2]

Interpretation of the word *mund* is clearly crucial. It normally refers to the concept of protection, and editors of the laws have assumed that in the case of Æthelberht 75, this means protection of the widow, or guardianship over her. Thorpe suggested, by analogy with Longobardic law, that the *mund* may have been the amount payable by the widow's family to regain the tutelage over her that was transferred to her husband's family on her marriage.[3] This is not generally accepted, however, and seems particularly unlikely since the verb *gebetan* usually refers to compensation for a crime. As Attenborough points out, the possibility that *mund* may correspond to ON *mundr*, referring to the marriage price of the widow, is also incompatible with the use of *gebetan*.[4] Liebermann, like Whitelock, interprets *mund* as the fine for breach of guardianship, and he introduces a new character, the *Vormund* or guardian, as the recipient of the fine: 'Das Schutzrecht über die vornehmste Wittwe vom Adelstande büsse [wer es verletzt] mit 50 Schillingen; [75,1] [das] über die [an Range] zweite mit 20 Schll., [das] über die dritte mit 12 Schll., [das] über die vierte mit 6 Schll. [an ihren Vormund]'[5] Attenborough is more cautious, leaving *mund* untranslated,[6] but he suggests in a note that 'from cap. 76 below it would seem that the *mund* belongs, not to the widow herself, but

[1] *Die Gesetze der Angelsachsen*, ed. F. Liebermann, 3 vols. (Halle, 1903–16) I, 7. All quotations from legal texts are taken from this edition unless otherwise stated (henceforth cited as *Gesetze*). I also use Liebermann's numbering system for the laws of Æthelberht, since individual clauses are not numbered in the only extant manuscript, the twelfth-century *Textus Roffensis* (Maidstone, Kent Archives Office, DRc/R1, fols. 1r-3v).

[2] *English Historical Documents c.500-1042*, ed. D. Whitelock, 2nd ed. (London, 1979), p. 393.

[3] *Ancient Laws and Institutes of England*, ed. B. Thorpe, folio edition (London, 1840), p. 8.

[4] *The Laws of the Earliest English Kings*, ed. F. L. Attenborough (Cambridge, 1922), p. 178. Interestingly, the possibility that some Kentish place-names may derive from OE *mund* used in a similar sense to that of OE *morgengifu* 'morning-gift to a bride' is raised in R. Coates, 'Towards an Explanation of the Kentish *-mondens*', *Journal of the English Place-Name Society* 18 (1985–86), 40–7, at 42.

[5] *Gesetze*, ed. Liebermann I, 7.

[6] *The Laws*, ed. Attenborough, p. 15.

to a person responsible for her (*mundbora*), *i.e.*, that it is a value of guardianship'.[7]

This reading would appear to indicate that the widow was subject in some way to a member or members of her kin, a view that has been accepted by many scholars. Lancaster, for instance, writes: 'We may assume also that she [the widow] was the direct responsibility of some members of the *mægð*. This is the significance of the early laws of Æthelbert (Kent, ?602–3) penalizing breaches of the guardianship of widows'.[8] Fell stresses the concept of protection rather than of guardianship, but the principle is similar: 'Law 75 specifies the compensation to be made for abducting widows of various classes of society. . . I take it to mean that a man who removes a widow from the protection of her kin (whether kin by blood or law) without an appropriate contract is required to pay an appropriate compensation'.[9] So too Rivers comments that 'all women in medieval society were under the protection (*mundium*) of men, either fathers, husbands, brothers, or other male guardians'.[10]

There is, however, an alternative view. Without entering into any discussion of Æthelberht 75, Doris Stenton states that it 'attempts a classification of widows, and sets out the sums due for violating the right of protecting her dependants enjoyed by a widow of noble birth, and by widows said to be of the second, the third, and the fourth class'.[11] This would suggest that widows enjoyed a much higher status in early Kentish society than is indicated by the traditional reading of the clause, and it seems to me to accord better with the use of *mund* in other texts. As I aim to show, the word *mund* in Old English normally refers to protection *by* rather than protection *of*, so this is the most logical inference in Æthelberht 75. If, as most scholars assume, *mund* here refers to a breach of guardianship over a widow, or to her unlawful removal from the protection of her kin, it would represent a unique usage of a by no means uncommon word. Other occurrences of *mund* in the laws refer to a very specific legal concept, and firm evidence would be needed to justify a substantially different reading in this single instance.

---

[7] *Ibid.* p. 178.

[8] L. Lancaster, 'Kinship in Anglo-Saxon Society: I', *British Journal of Sociology* 9 (1958), 230–50, at 241.

[9] C. Fell, C. Clark and E. Williams, *Women in Anglo-Saxon England and the Impact of 1066* (London, 1984), p. 61.

[10] T. J. Rivers, 'Widows' Rights in Anglo-Saxon Law', *American Journal of Legal History* 19 (1975), 208–15, at 208.

[11] D. M. Stenton, *The English Woman in History* (London, 1957), p. 9.

The meaning of *mund* in a legal context can only be demonstrated from its usages in other Anglo-Saxon laws. Because of the irregular practice of word-division in the manuscripts and the significance of individual elements of compound nouns, it is useful also to consider other relevant words that begin with this syllable. These are *mundbora* 'protector', *mundbyrd* 'protection', and *mundbrice* 'breach of protection'. The most frequent is *mundbora*, with a total of sixty-nine occurrences listed in *A Microfiche Concordance to Old English*.[12] Only three are from legal texts, and all occur in versions of the same law, Edward and Guthrum 12, VIII Æthelred 33, and II Cnut 40:

40 Gyf man gehadodne oððe ælþeodigne þurh ænig þingc forræde æt feo oððe æt feore, þonne sceal him cingc beon for mæg 7 for mundboran, butan he elles oðerne (hlaford) hæbbe.	40 If a man in holy orders or a foreigner is for any reason defrauded of property or of life, the king shall then be for him in the place of a kinsman and protector, unless he has another.
40.1 7 bete man þam cingce, swa hit gebyrige, oððe he ða dæde wrece swiþe deope.	40.1 And compensation is to be paid to the king, as is fitting, or he is to avenge the deed very severely.
40.2 Cristenan kyningce gebyrað swyðe rihte, þæt he Godes æbylgðe wrece swyðe deope, be ðam þe seo dæd si.[13]	40.2 It belongs very rightly to a Christian king to avenge very severely offences against God, in proportion to the deed.[14]

As honorary kinsman and protector to clerics and foreigners, the king is responsible for exacting compensation for offenses which are in effect violations of his *mund* in the sense discussed below. All other occurrences of *mundbora* in Old English can similarly be translated 'protector'.

Mundbyrd is also a common compound, occurring fifty-one times in the Old English corpus.[15] Its primary meaning is 'protection', and it is often found in religious contexts. In legal texts it has a specialized meaning based on the Anglo-Saxon concept of *mund*. The word occurs in the following laws: Æthelberht 8 and 15, Hlothhere and Eadric 14,

[12] A. DiPaolo Healey and R. L. Venezky, *A Microfiche Concordance to Old English* (Toronto, 1980), s.v. *mundbora, mundboran, mundborum, mundburan.*

[13] *Gesetze*, ed. Liebermann I, 340.

[14] *English Historical Documents*, ed. Whitelock, p. 461.

[15] Healey and Venezky, *A Microfiche Concordance to Old English*, s.v. *mundbyrd, mundbyrda, mundbyrde*.

Wihtred 2, Alfred 3 and 5, and IV Æthelstan 6,2. In addition, there are two occurrences in the text known as *Grið* (8 and 14), which also deals with legal matters. In every instance, the legislation either specifies the financial value of the *mundbyrd* of a particular class (Æthelberht 8 and 15, Alfred 3) or of the church (Wihtred 2, *Grið* 8), or describes circumstances under which this sum became payable (Hlothhere and Eadric 14, Alfred 5, IV Æthelstan 6,2, *Grið* 14).

It is evident from these laws that *mundbyrd* in a legal context refers to the value of a person's *mund*, a word difficult to translate since it represents a concept which has not survived into modern society. The nearest equivalent is 'breach of the peace', but this is inadequate both because it is only expressed in negative terms, and because it is a public concept, whereas in Anglo-Saxon England all classes of society were entitled to a personal *mundbyrd*. As Finberg comments in his discussion of the Kentish *ceorl*, 'The clearest indication of his social status is his *mundbyrd*, the fine payable for an offense against one of his dependants'.[16] That of a *ceorl* was worth six shillings according to Æthelberht 15:

15 Ceorles mundbyrd: VI scillingas.[17]	15 The [breach of a] *ceorl*'s protection: six shillings.[18]

This is of course the same amount as the *mund* of a widow of the lowest class mentioned in Æthelberht 75,1. The sum was payable for violation of personal security, or in the case of the church, for breach of sanctuary. For instance, Hlothhere and Eadric 14 stipulates that a householder is entitled to receive payment of his *mundbyrd* if brawling takes place within his house and stains it with blood:

14 Gif þ*æt* flet geblodgad wyrþe, forgylde þem mæn his mundbyrd 7 cyninge L scill'.[19]	14 If the house is stained by bloodshed, he is to pay to the man [the price for breach of] his protection, and 50 shillings to the king.[20]

The first occurrence of the term *mundbyrd* is in Æthelberht 8:

---

[16] H. P. R. Finberg, 'English Society in the Seventh Century', *The Agrarian History of England and Wales* I, 2: *A.D. 43–1042*, ed. H. P. R. Finberg (Cambridge, 1972), p. 430–48, at p. 432.
[17] *Gesetze*, ed. Liebermann I, 4.
[18] *English Historical Documents*, ed. Whitelock, p. 392.
[19] *Gesetze*, ed. Liebermann I, 11.
[20] *English Historical Documents*, ed. Whitelock, p. 395.

8 Cyninges mundbyrd: L scillinga.[21]	8 The [breach of the] king's protection, 50 shillings.[22]

Whitelock glosses the term here as 'Offences against anyone or any place under the king's protection, but also including various acts showing lack of respect', and goes on to point out that 'Other persons than the king had their *mund(byrd)* "(right of giving) protection"'.[23] I suggest that one such person was the widow, and that unless the word *mund* can be shown to have had another meaning in Old English legal texts, this is the interpretation that should be adopted for Æthelberht 75.

The financial value of *mundbyrd* was also the fine payable for its violation. This concept begins to be expressed as *mundbrice* in extant texts from the mid-tenth century onwards. The latter term may have evolved to replace the specialized usage of *mundbyrd*, which occurs mainly in earlier law-codes. There are fifteen surviving instances of *mundbrice*, all from legal documents.[24] Apart from a few occurrences in charters, none earlier than the eleventh century, the term appears only in II Edmund 6, VI Æthelred 34, VIII Æthelred 3, I Cnut 2,5 and 3,2, II Cnut 12 and 42, and *Grið* 6 and 11. In all cases it refers to a breach of *mund* in the sense discussed above, or to the fine payable for that offense. In II Edmund 6, II Cnut 12, and all the charter references, *mundbrice* is linked with *hamsocn*, a term which also refers to a serious violation of personal security.[25] As Whitelock notes,[26] the earliest occurrence of *mundbrice* in the laws is in II Edmund 6:

6 Eac we cwædon be mundbrice 7 be hamsocnu*m*: se ðe hit ofer ðis dó, ðæt he þolige ealles ðæs he age, 7 si on cyninges dome, hwæðer he lif age.[27]	6 Further, we have declared concerning *mundbryce* and *hamsocn*, that anyone who commits it after this is to forfeit all that he owns, and it is to be for the king to decide whether he may preserve his life.[28]

[21] *Gesetze*, ed. Liebermann I, 3.
[22] *English Historical Documents*, ed. Whitelock, p. 391.
[23] *Ibid.* n.6.
[24] Healey and Venezky, *A Microfiche Concordance to Old English*, s.v. *mundbrice, mundbrices, mundbryce, mundbryces*.
[25] R. V. Colman, '*Hamsocn*: its Meaning and Significance in Early English Law', *American Journal of Legal History* 25 (1981), 95–110.
[26] *English Historical Documents*, ed. Whitelock, p. 428, n.2.
[27] *Gesetze*, ed. Liebermann I, 188.
[28] *English Historical Documents*, ed. Whitelock, p. 428.

In a note to this law, Whitelock writes, 'This term [*mundbryce*] means the violation of anyone's right of protection over others, but here it is clearly the king's right which is meant'.[29] The other laws mentioned above also refer to the king's *mundbrice*; but *Grið* includes other ranks, with ch. 6 equating an archbishop with the king, and ch. 11 specifying the amounts due in compensation to both laymen and ecclesiastics:

6 7 on Cantwara lage cyning 7 arceb*iscop* agan gelicne and efen dyrne mundbryce.	6 And under the law of the Kentish people, king and archbishop have an equal [fine for] breach of protection.
11 7 gif hwa cynges mundbrice elles gewyrce, gebete þ*æt* mid V pundum on Engla lage, arceb*iscopes* 7 æþelinges mundbrice mid þri*m* pundum, oðres biscpæs 7 ealdormannes mid II pundum.[30]	11 And if anyone otherwise commits a breach of the king's protection, he is to compensate with five pounds under the law of the English people; [if he commits a breach] of an archbishop's or *æþeling*'s [protection, he is to compensate] with three pounds; [if he commits a breach] of a bishop's or *ealdormann*'s [protection, he is to compensate] with two pounds.[31]

By the time this treatise was drawn up in the eleventh century, crimes of *mundbrice* were rated according to their seriousness, a point which I shall suggest may also be relevant to the interpretation of Æthelberht 75 and 76. The worst offense involved fighting in church or in the king's house, and was penalized by forfeiture of all possessions and possible loss of life according to *Grið* 9.[32] This was the standard penalty for *mundbrice* or *hamsocn* according to II Edmund 6, quoted above.

The uncompounded term *mund* does not occur elsewhere in Æthelberht's laws, but instances of the word in later codes will repay close examination. In addition to Æthelberht 75 and 76, OE *mund* occurs eleven times in legal texts, including ecclesiastical laws and the treatises known

[29] *Ibid.* n.2.
[30] *Gesetze*, ed. Liebermann I, 470.
[31] Author's translation.
[32] *Gesetze*, ed. Liebermann I, 470.

as *Wergeld*, *Geþyncþo*, and *Grið*.[33] The closest both geographically and chronologically to Æthelberht is ch. 8 of the late-seventh-century laws of Wihtred, setting out the rights and obligations of the manumittor of a slave:

> 8 Gif man his mæn an wiofode freols gefe, se sie folcfry; freolsgefa age his erfe ænde wergeld 7 munde þare hina, sie ofer mearce ðær he wille.[34]

> 8 If anyone gives his man freedom at the altar, he is to have the rights of a freeman of that people; his manumittor is to have his inheritance and his wergild and protection over his household, even if he live beyond the boundary, wherever he wishes.[35]

This was a necessary safeguard for the former slave, who could have been attacked or killed with impunity if he had had no one to avenge crimes against him or to collect his *wergild*. The principle is similar to that of Edward and Guthrum 12, VIII Æthelred 33, and II Cnut 40, quoted above, where the king is appointed *for mæg 7 for mundboran* 'as kinsman and as protector' to foreigners and members of the clergy.

The most common usage of *mund* in Anglo-Saxon law is in relation to the king's peace. II Edmund 7,3 and *Wergeld* 4 refer to this in identical terms: *ðonne rære man cyninges munde* 'then the king's peace is to be established'.[36] As Whitelock comments, 'This clause means that any act of violence after that will be regarded as a breach of the king's special protection'.[37] VI Æthelred 34 specifies the king's *mund* as a fine for damaging or destroying a warship, using the term interchangeably with *mundbrice*. The penalty is in addition to the payment of full compensation:

> 34 7 gyf hwa folces fyrdscip awyrde, gebete *þæt* georne, 7 cyninge þa munde; 7 gif hit man amyrre, *þæt* hit ænote weorðe, forgylde hit fullice, 7 cyninge þone mundbrice.[38]

> 34 And if anyone damages a national warship, he shall with all diligence make compensation for it, and shall pay to the king the fine due for breach of his 'mund'; and if it be destroyed so

[33] Healey and Venezky, *A Microfiche Concordance to Old English*, s.v. *mund, munde*.
[34] *Gesetze*, ed. Liebermann I, 13.
[35] *English Historical Documents*, ed. Whitelock, p. 397.
[36] *Gesetze*, ed. Liebermann I, 190 and 392.
[37] *English Historical Documents*, ed. Whitelock, p. 429, n.1.
[38] *Gesetze*, ed. Liebermann I, 254.

as to be useless, he shall pay for it in full, and shall give the king the fine due for breach of his 'mund'.[39]

Again, the value of *mund* depends on the rank of the person entitled to receive compensation, not on the value of property or rank of dependants under that person's protection.

Two occurrences of *mund* occur in versions of the same law, VIII Æthelred 5,1 and I Cnut 3,2, giving a scale of fines for violating the sanctuary of churches of varying status:

3.2 Heafodmynstres griðbryce is æt botwyrþum þingu*m* be cingces munde, þ*æt* is mid V pundum on Engla lage (7 on Centlande æt þa*m* mundbryce V pund þa*m* cingce 7 þreo þa*m* arcebi*scope*), 7 medemran mynstres mid CXX scill', þæt is be cingces wite, 7 þonne gyt læssan, þær lytel þeowdom sig, 7 legerstow þeah sig, mid XL scill', and feldcyricean, þær legerstow ne sig, mid XXX scyll'.[40]

3.2 Amends for violation of the protection of a principal church, in cases in which compensation can be paid, shall be made by payment of the fine for breach of the king's *mund*, *i.e.* £5 in districts under English law, (and in Kent for breach of the *mund*, £5 to the king and £3 to the Archbishop), and in the case of a church of medium rank, by the payment of 120 shillings, *i.e.* by the fine due to the king (for insubordination), and in the case of one still smaller where there is little divine service but where, however, there is a graveyard, by the payment of 60 shillings, and in the case of a country chapel where there is no graveyard, by the payment of 30 shillings.[41]

The fact that a principal church is to be compensated by payment of the king's *mund* is not intended to indicate that the offense is against the king, but to show that the church is entitled to equal rights of giving

[39] *The Laws of the Kings of England from Edmund to Henry I*, ed. A. J. Robertson (Cambridge, 1925), p. 101.

[40] *Gesetze*, ed. Liebermann I, 282.

[41] *The Laws*, ed. Robertson, pp. 157–9.

protection. Throughout the Anglo-Saxon period, the church's *mundbyrd* tended to be equated with that of the king, as in Wihtred 2:

2 Ciricean mundbyrd sie L scll' swa cinges.[42]

2 The [breach of] the Church's protection is to be 50 shillings like the king's.[43]

and *Grið* 8:

8 7 Chr*ist*es cyrican mundbyrd is efne swa cynges.[44]

8 And the [breach of] the protection of Christ's church is the same as the king's.[45]

A problematic but significant phrase is *mæðe 7 munde*, recorded in *Geþyncðo* 7, in a context which clearly refers to the attainment of high status:

7 And gif leornere wære, þe þurh lare geþuge, þ*æt* he had hæfde 7 þenode Criste, wǽre se siððan mæðe 7 munde swa micelre wyrðe, swa ðonne þa*m* hade gebirede mid rihte, gif he hine heolde, swa swa he scolde.[46]

7 And if there were a scholar who prospered with his learning so that he took orders and served Christ, he should afterwards be entitled to so much more honour and protection as belonged by rights to that order, if he kept himself [chaste] as he should.[47]

The preceding clauses describe the procedures whereby people of various ranks could rise in the social scale, and the achievement of *mæðe 7 munde* is reserved for the high-ranking clergy. Whitelock's translation 'honour and protection' does not explain what type of protection was involved, and at first sight, Thorpe's translation 'rank and power'[48] might be preferred. However, the same phrase occurs in a similar context in ch. 3 of *Grið*, a compilation dealing largely with the rights of king, church, and ecclesiastical dignitaries to *mund* in the technical, legal sense. *Grið* contains two references to *mundbyrd* (8 and 14), as well as three of

---

[42] *Gesetze*, ed. Liebermann I, 12.

[43] *English Historical Documents*, ed. Whitelock, p. 396.

[44] *Gesetze*, ed. Liebermann I, 470.

[45] Author's translation.

[46] *Gesetze*, ed. Liebermann I, 458.

[47] *English Historical Documents*, ed. Whitelock, p. 469.

[48] *Ancient Laws*, ed. Thorpe, p. 82.

the fifteen extant occurrences of *mundbrice* (6 and 11). It seems reasonable to suggest that *mund* in *Grið* 3 has a similar semantic range, so that both here and in *Geþyncðo* 7 the reading would be, 'honor and [a high value placed on the right to give] protection'. This interpretation is strengthened by the heading, *Be griðe 7 be munde*, for the word *grið* also refers to sanctuary or personal security, and is used in this sense throughout the text. Liebermann translates the heading, 'Von Sonderfrieden und von Schutzgewalt' ('Of Special Peace and of Power of Protection').[49] Both here and in other legal contexts, 'power of protection' or 'right of protection' is probably the most accurate translation of *mund*.

Two further instances of *mund* in Anglo-Saxon law remain to be considered. The first occurs in Edmund's code concerning the blood-feud. II Edmund 1,1 states that the kindred of a man who has killed another may be absolved from the obligation to pay compensation on his behalf or to take part in the feud provided that they disown him and never afterwards give him *mete ne munde*.[50] This clearly means 'food nor protection', for the following clause stipulates a severe penalty for any of the kindred who subsequently harbor the slayer. Here again, the word *mund* refers to protection *by* rather than to protection *of*. The kindred can no longer include the slayer within their *mund*, their right of giving protection, and they are therefore no longer entitled to claim the *mundbrice* fine if he is attacked. It is evident from the whole tenor of the code that this aspect of *mund* is uppermost in the legislator's mind. Ch. 2 is concerned with the violation of sanctuary given by the church or the king, a clear case of *mundbrice* even though the term is not introduced until ch. 6 (*be mundbrice 7 be hamsocnum*), which states that the perpetrator is to forfeit all possessions and to be at the king's mercy.[51] The final clause, II Edmund 7,3, deals with the king's peace, as discussed above. It would therefore be surprising if the use of *mund* in II Edmund 1,1 did not lie within this semantic range.

Finally, *mund* also occurs in the eleventh-century ecclesiastical code known as the *Law of the Northumbrian Priests*. Ch. 19 deals with the violation of church sanctuary:

19 Gif man ciricgrið abrece, bete be circan mæðe 7 be þa*m* þe hire mund sy.[52]	19 If anyone violates sanctuary, he is to pay compensation in proportion to the status of

[49] *Gesetze*, ed. Liebermann I, 470.
[50] *Ibid.* I, 186.
[51] *Ibid.* I, 188.
[52] *Ibid.* I, 381.

the church and according to
what its right of protection is.[53]

This is perfectly straightforward, and there can be no doubt that compensation is payable to the church according to the value of its *mund*, its right of giving protection. As I have attempted to demonstrate, this is the sense in which *mund* is consistently used throughout the surviving corpus of Anglo-Saxon legal texts.

With regard to the interpretation of Æthelberht 75 and 76, it seems to me that the burden of proof lies with those who support a reading of *mund* which is considerably at odds with its usual meaning in legal contexts. There is no evidence that the word could refer to guardianship, nor to the protection of the widow by unspecified kinfolk.[54] There is, on the other hand, a good deal of evidence that it referred to the power of giving protection. It may be significant that the sums involved occur elsewhere in the same code as compensation for the violation of *mundbyrd*. As already noted, Æthelberht 8 assesses the king's *mundbyrd* at fifty shillings,

---

[53] *English Historical Documents*, ed. Whitelock, p. 473.

[54] The semantic range of OE *mund* is further discussed by D. Day in 'Hands across the Hall: The Legalities of Beowulf's Fight with Grendel' *Journal of English and Germanic Philology* 98 (1999), 313–24, who cites a tenth-century charter (S 1447) where the grantor Ecgferth conveys his property to Archbishop Dunstan *to mundgenne his lafe 7 his bearne* 'in order that he might act as guardian to his widow and child' (*Anglo-Saxon Charters*, ed. A. J. Robertson, 2nd ed. (Cambridge, 1956), no. 44, pp. 90–2) as evidence that 'widows and minor children were at times at least technically under the *mund* of male religious figures or of religious institutions'. It does not seem to me that the charter supports this interpretation. The circumstances surrounding Ecgferth's death by drowning are obscure, and it is uncertain whether he committed suicide, as some scholars believe, or was executed, as I personally consider more probable. However, it is at any rate clear that, as Robertson notes, 'Ecgferth had been guilty of some serious crime', as a result of which his property was subject to forfeiture (p. 338). In transferring his estate to Dunstan, he was attempting to secure some form of support for his widow and child, who would have otherwise been left in desperate straits and might even have been considered to be implicated in his guilt. The situation is not comparable with that pertaining to the majority of widows in Anglo-Saxon England, and indeed appears to be more closely analogous to that outlined in S 1445, where the criminal Helmstan transfers ownership of his estate at Fonthill to Ealdorman Ordlaf in return for the latter's support and protection during the course of a tricky lawsuit (S. Keynes, 'The Fonthill Letter', *Words, Texts and Manuscripts: Studies in Anglo-Saxon Culture Presented to Helmut Gneuss on the Occasion of his Sixty-Fifth Birthday*, ed. M. Korhammer (Cambridge, 1992), pp. 53–97).

the same amount as the *mund* of a widow of the highest class, while Æthelberht 15 assesses a *ceorl*'s *mundbyrd* at six shillings, the same amount as the *mund* of a widow of the lowest class.[55] One way in which *mundbrice* could be perpetrated was through fighting or bloodshed within the area under protection, and this is the subject of Æthelberht 13, which assesses the compensation for manslaughter on the premises of an *eorl* at twelve shillings,[56] the same as the *mund* of a widow of the third class.

Interpretation of Æthelberht 75 has been heavily influenced by the traditional reading of the following clause, which all editors take to refer to the abduction of a widow characterized as *unagne*. The penalty is twice the *mund*, and from this it is assumed that the values of *mund* given in Æthelberht 75 represent the standard penalties for abducting a widow. This is not a valid inference, for two reasons. Firstly, the idea of abduction is not introduced until ch. 76. The preceding clause defines the value of a widow's *mund*, which is a legal concept in its own right. Secondly, if the aim of Æthelberht 76 were to increase the compensation due for widows characterized as *unagne*, their *mund* would presumably be assessed at a higher rate. This is not the case. The *mund* remains the same, but the crime itself attracts a heavier penalty. The crime, therefore, must be different.

Other texts make it clear that violations of *mund* could vary in gravity and in the compensation required. *Grið* 9, for instance, specifies forfeiture of all possessions and possible loss of life for fighting in the king's house or in church,[57] while *Grið* 11 gives a fixed financial penalty for other forms of *mundbrice*.[58] Alfred 5 stipulates payment of the king's *mundbyrd* and that of the church for forcibly removing a fugitive from a church consecrated by a bishop, but if more than one person is seized, the fine is increased accordingly: *mare, gif he ðær mare ófgefo* 'more, if he seizes more from there'.[59] I wish to suggest that Æthelberht 76 refers to

---

[55] The connection is also made by Finberg, 'English Society in the Seventh Century', p. 433, who equates the term *mund* in Æthelberht 75 with *mundbyrd*, commenting: 'Four classes of widow are distinguished by the gradations of their *mundbyrd* (75). These gradations are presumably determined by the standing of their late husbands. The lowest, 6 shillings, is identical with the *mundbyrd* of the *ceorl*; the highest, 50 shillings, with that of the king. The first-class widow is said to be nobly born, perhaps a lady of the royal house. If so, the 20-shilling widow may be a non-royal noble-woman and the 12-shilling one the widow either of a lesser gentleman or of a freeman'.

[56] *Gesetze*, ed. Liebermann I, 4.

[57] *Ibid.* I, 470.

[58] *Ibid.* I, 471.

[59] *Ibid.* I, 50.

a particularly serious violation of the widow's *mund*, a situation where an offense is committed not against one of her dependants but against herself.

The issue is obscured by the fact that the form *unagne* does not occur elsewhere in the surviving corpus of Old English[60] and is of uncertain meaning. It appears to be a syncopated accusative singular form of the adjective *unagen*, defined as 'not one's own, not in a person's possession or under his control' by Toller,[61] who cites the occurrence in this law as 'a widow of whom he is not the guardian'. Liebermann, Attenborough, and Whitelock all adopt this reading.[62] However, this is to presuppose that Æthelberht 75 refers to a breach of trust by the supposed guardian himself, a theory which is unsupported by the text and which would negate the argument that the guardian is the recipient of the fine. Doris Stenton interprets Æthelberht 76 along traditional lines despite her reading of the preceding clause: 'Yet another law regulates the compensation due from a man who 'takes a widow who does not belong to him' to the man who is her lawful guardian'.[63] Fell provides an alternative reading of *unagen*, but one which assumes that the theme of abduction is common to both clauses: '*Unagen* can only mean if she is without protecting kin. Thus, as her vulnerability increases, so also does the amount of fine to be paid'.[64] Rivers claims that Æthelberht 75 deals with assault, Æthelberht 76 with the same offense aggravated by abduction: 'If a widow was not only assaulted but also abducted, double the *mundium* was required. This two-fold payment was probably required in order to compensate the widow's guardian, especially if the abductor wished to keep the woman as a wife'.[65] If, as I suggest, Æthelberht 75 is in fact concerned with the widow's right of protection over her dependants, an alternative interpretation must also be offered for Æthelberht 76.[66]

---

[60] Healey and Venezky, *A Microfiche Concordance to Old English.*

[61] *An Anglo-Saxon Dictionary Based on the Manuscript Collections of the Late Joseph Bosworth*, ed T. N. Toller (Oxford, 1898), p. 1089.

[62] *Gesetze*, ed. Liebermann I, 7; *The Laws*, ed. Attenborough, p. 15; *English Historical Documents*, ed. Whitelock, p. 393.

[63] Stenton, *The English Woman in History*, p. 9.

[64] Fell et al., *Women in Anglo-Saxon England*, p. 61.

[65] Rivers, 'Widows' Rights in Anglo-Saxon Law', p. 210.

[66] One possibility which has been suggested to me is that the adjective *unagen* may be used here to mean 'dependent, not in control of one's affairs', as reflected in definition I.c of the entry for the positive semantic counterpart *own* in the *Oxford English Dictionary*, 2nd ed. (Oxford, 1989): 'to be one's own man (or woman): to be master of oneself; to be independent; to have the full control or use of one's faculties'. This would make good sense, allowing the two clauses to be read as a consecutive sequence with Æthelberht 75 dealing in descending social order with

Comparison with the positive form of the adjective *agen* in Old English may be useful here. The primary meaning is 'own', as indeed is reflected in Toller's definition of *unagen* as 'not one's own'. In a legal context, however, and in relation to women, the frame of reference is not guardianship but lawful marriage. This is definition A.12.a.i. of the headword *āgen* in the Toronto *Dictionary of Old English*: 'in a legal context, perhaps with the sense 'lawful': *(his) agen wif* '(his) lawful wife'.[67] By analogy, *unagen* in Æthelberht 76 may be taken to have the sense 'unlawful', referring to a widow who has not consented to marriage with the man who carries her off. It is clear from other sections of Æthelberht's code that marriage in early Kentish society represented a legal contract between consenting parties, and indeed the theme is continued in the following clause, Æthelberht 77, which is directly concerned with the marriage contract:

77 Gif mon mægþ gebigeð, ceapi geceapod sy, gif hit unfacne is.	77 If anyone buys a maiden, she is to be bought with a [bride] payment, if there is no fraud.
77,1 Gif hit þonne facne is, ef þær æt ham gebrenge, 7 him man his scæt agefe.[68]	77,1 If, however, there is any fraud, she is to be taken back home, and he is to be given back his money.[69]

I give Whitelock's translation for convenience, although the associations of the Modern English verb 'buy' give the impression that the girl was

widows who enjoy the right of protection over their dependants and Æthelberht 76 describing the fifth and lowest category: the widow who has lost her own independence and is in need of protection herself. The suggestion also derives some support from comparison with continental legislation, since *Lex Baiwariorum* VIII,7 imposes heavy financial penalties on the abductor of a widow who has been reduced to poverty (*Lex Baiwariorum*, ed. E. von Schwind, Monumenta Germaniae Historica, Legum Sectio I: Leges nationum Germanicarum 5.2 (Hanover, 1926), 356–57). There is, however, a problem in applying this interpretation to Æthelberht 76. The reference to *seo mund* clearly refers back to the various amounts enumerated in the preceding clause, and this in turn suggests that the ruling applies equally to the four classes of widow listed there rather than to a fifth and lowest class.

[67] Dictionary of Old English Project, *Dictionary of Old English A–G.* Version 2.0. CD-ROM, 2008, s.v. *āgen.*

[68] *Gesetze*, ed. Liebermann I, 7–8.

[69] *English Historical Documents*, ed. Whitelock, p. 393.

treated as a chattel, which is almost certainly incorrect.[70] Æthelberht 77 begins a short sequence of laws concerning lawful marriage (77–81), which is followed by two clauses (82–83) concerning the illegal seizure of a maiden, described in Æthelberht 82 in wording closely similar to that of Æthelberht 76:[71]

82 Gif man mægþmon nede genimeþ: ðam agende L scillinga 7 eft æt þam agende sinne willan ætgebicge.[72]	82 If anyone carries off a maiden by force, [he is to pay] to the owner 50 shillings, and afterwards buy from the owner his consent [to the marriage].[73]

The legislator's concern here is evidently to ensure that the offender is not able to avoid the usual financial costs by using force to secure a wife

[70] The Anglo-Saxon marriage contract has been the subject of considerable discussion. Some scholars take it to show that the girl was sold to her future husband, a view expressed by R. Hill, 'Marriage in Seventh Century England', *Saints, Scholars and Heroes: Studies in Medieval Culture in Honour of Charles W. Jones*, ed. M. H. King and W. M. Stevens (Collegeville, MN, 1979), pp. 67–75, at p. 69; A. L. Klinck, 'Anglo-Saxon Women and the Law', *Journal of Medieval History* 8 (1982), 107–21, at 109; and (more cautiously) Stenton, *The English Woman in History*, p. 8. Other scholars, however, have pointed out that the semantic range of OE *gebigan* is not identical to that of its modern descendant, the verb 'to buy', so that this interpretation may be inappropriate: see especially Lancaster, 'Kinship in Anglo-Saxon Society', p. 243; E. Young, 'The Anglo-Saxon Family Law', *Essays in Anglo-Saxon Law*, ed. H. Adams (Boston, MA, 1876), pp. 121–82, at p. 164; F. Mezger, 'Did the Institution of Marriage by Purchase Exist in Old Germanic Law?', *Speculum* 18 (1943), 369–71, at 369–70; and Fell et al., *Women in Anglo-Saxon England*, p. 16.

[71] It should be noted that in neither clause is it certain whether the verb *geniman* refers to abduction or to rape. As Fell comments in connection with a discussion of Æthelberht 82 and 83: 'it is not clear that Old English *geniman* necessarily and always has a significance different from that of *niman*. If is perfectly possible that these two laws refer not to abduction or, as it has romantically been termed, "marriage by capture", but more simply to sexual intercourse, perhaps rape . . . The abduction theme has been based on an assumption that the *ge* prefix adds the "away" sense to "take", an assumption that is certainly open to challenge. . . . *Genimeð* is the verb used in Æthelberht 76 where equally it could mean "abducts" or "sleeps with" and is normally translated "takes"'. ('An Appendix to Carole Hough's Article "A Re-appraisal of Æthelberht 84"', *Nottingham Medieval Studies* 37 (1993), 7–8, at 7.)

[72] *Gesetze*, ed. Liebermann I, 8.

[73] *English Historical Documents*, ed. Whitelock, p. 393.

instead of going through the proper legal channels. A similar concern may very possibly underlie Æthelberht 76.

Legality is also a theme in continental Germanic law concerning the remarriage of widows. It has long been recognized that the code issued by the Frankish king Clovis during the early sixth century has particularly close affinities with Æthelberht's laws,[74] and it is thus relevant to point out that *Pactus Legis Salicae* 44 specifies in some detail the legal formalities to be observed before a widow may remarry:

44,1 Sicut adsolet homo moriens et uiduam dimiserit, qui eam uoluerit accipere, antequam eam accipiat ante thunginum aut centenarium, hoc est ut thunginus aut centenarius mallum indicant, et in ipso mallo scutum habere debet, et tres homines tres causas demandare debent.	44,1 If it happens that a man dies, leaving a widow, and [a prospective bridegroom] wishes to take her [in matrimony], let him take her in the presence of the *thunginus* or the *centenarius*, that is, let the *thunginus* or the *centenarius* announce [this fact] in court. And he must have a shield in the same court, and three men [as witnesses] must be asked three questions [by the *thunginus* or the *centenarius*].
44,2 Et tunc ipse, qui uiduam accipere debet, tres solidos aeque pensantes et denarium habere debet. Et tres erunt, qui solidos <illius> pensare <*uel habere*> uel probare debent, et hoc factum, si eis conuenit, <sic eam> accipiat *cui debentur*.	44,2 And then, he who wants to take the widow should have three solidi of equal weight and a denarius. And these three [men] must have weighed the solidi or must prove that the solidi have been weighed, and [when] this deed occurs, if it is agreeable to them, let him to whom she belongs take her.
44,3 Si uero istud non fecerit et sic eam acciperit, mallobergo reipus nichalesinus hoc est, MMD denarios qui faciunt solidos LXII semis, cui reipi debentur, exsoluere debet.[75]	44,3 But if he does not do this and he [still] takes her (known in the malberg as *reipus nichalesinus*) he must pay 2500 denarii, which make sixty-two and one-half solidi, to

[74] See, for instance, J. M. Wallace-Hadrill, *Early Germanic Kingship in England and on the Continent* (Oxford, 1971), p. 38.

[75] *Pactus Legis Salicae*, ed. K. A. Eckhardt, Monumenta Germaniae Historica,

	whomever the ring-money belongs.[76]

As Rivers comments, 'That the procedure for remarriage of a widow took place in court indicates the desirability of a woman who had acquired an inheritance from her late husband. The presence of the court was to oversee that the widow was not exploited'.[77]

Anglo-Saxon law too was concerned to protect widows from exploitation and from being illegally forced into remarriage, a situation still envisaged as late as the early eleventh century. This is evident from II Cnut 73, which emphasizes that a widow is to choose for herself, and goes on to state that if she remarries within a year she is to forfeit her late husband's possessions *even if she has been married by force*:

73 7 sitte ælc wuduwe werleas XII monað, ceose syððan *þæt* heo sylf wylle. . . .	73 And each widow is to remain unmarried for 12 months; she is afterwards to choose what she herself will. . . .
73,2 7 þeah heo nydnumen weorðe, þolige þæra æhta, butan heo fram þam ceorle sylle eft ham ongean 7 næfre heo eft his ne weorðe.[78]	73,2 And even if she was married by force, she is to forfeit those possessions, unless she wishes to leave the husband and return home and never afterwards become his.[79]

I suggest that a similar commitment to safeguard the widow's freedom of choice is reflected in Æthelberht 76, imposing a heavy financial penalty on any man who attempts to force her into marriage without a proper contract.

In sum, I would suggest that the traditional readings of both Æthelberht 75 and Æthelberht 76 require substantial revision. OE *mund* is well documented as a legal term referring to the right to give protection, and this is the interpretation which should be placed on its usage in Æthelberht 75. Æthelberht 76 refers to a situation where the widow herself is unlawfully seized, a flagrant violation of her rights for which twice the usual compensation is due. I propose the following translation:

Legum Sectio I: Leges nationum Germanicarum 4.1 (Hanover, 1962), 168–9.

[76] T. J. Rivers, *Laws of the Salian and Ripuarian Franks* (New York, 1986), p. 90.

[77] *Ibid.* p. 21.

[78] *Gesetze*, ed. Liebermann I, 360.

[79] *English Historical Documents*, ed. Whitelock, pp. 465–6.

75 Mund þare betstan widuwan eorlcundre L scillinga gebete.	75 The right of protection of a widow of the highest class of nobility is to be compensated for at 50 shillings;
75.1 Ðare oþre XX scll', ðare þriddan XII scll', þare feorðan VI scll'.	75.1 that of one of the second class, at 20 shillings; of one of the third class, at 12 shillings; of one of the fourth class, at 6 shillings.
76 Gif man widuwan unagne genimeþ, II gelde seo mund sy.	76 If anyone takes a widow who is not his own [legal wife], [the penalty] is twice the value of the right of protection.

7.

THE EARLY KENTISH "DIVORCE LAWS": A RECONSIDERATION OF ÆTHELBERHT, CHS 79 AND 80

First published 1994: *Anglo-Saxon England* 23, 19–34.

Evidence concerning the position of women in Anglo-Saxon England, particularly during the early period, is sparse and often difficult to assess. Surviving law-codes constitute an important source of information, but due to their cryptic phraseology and sometimes archaic vocabulary they are notoriously open to misinterpretation. Two clauses from the earliest extant code, issued by King Æthelberht of Kent towards the beginning of the seventh century, are commonly treated as evidence of the independent status of divorced women in early Kentish society.[1] So far as I am aware this view has never been challenged, although it remains uncorroborated by other sources and is by no means the only possible interpretation of the text. In this paper I wish to put forward an alternative reading.

The laws in question are chs. 79 and 80 of Æthelberht's code.[2] These occur within a small group of clauses dealing with marriage, and in particular with the financial position of a woman whose marriage

---

[1] C. Fell, *Women in Anglo-Saxon England and the Impact of 1066* (London, 1984), p. 57, writes: 'According to the laws of Æðelbert a woman had the right to walk out of a marriage that did not please her, though I do not find this particular freedom reiterated in the later laws. Since, if she took the children with her, she was also entitled to take half the property, she seems to have had reasonable independence and security'.

[2] The numbering of clauses has no manuscript authority and therefore no significance. The only copy of Æthelberht's law-code is contained in the twelfth-century manuscript *Textus Roffensis* (Maidstone, Kent Archives Office, DRc/R1), where the whole code is written consecutively. However, it is convenient to refer to clauses by number, and I shall use the system found in the standard edition of the Anglo-Saxon laws, *Die Gesetze der Angelsachsen*, ed. F. Liebermann, 3 vols. (Halle, 1903–16).

is brought to an end either through the death of her husband or by some other means. The sequence reads as follows (the parallel translation is Whitelock's):

77 Gif man mægð gebigeð, ceapi geceapod sy, gif hit unfacne is.

77 If anyone buys a maiden, she is to be bought with a [bride] payment, if there is no fraud.

77.1 Gif hit þonne facne is, ef þær æt ham gebrenge, 7 him man his scæt agefe.

77.1 If, however, there is any fraud, she is to be taken back home, and he is to be given back his money.

78 Gif hio cwic beam gebyreþ, healfne scæt age, gif ceorl ær swylteþ.

78 If she bears a living child, she is to have half the goods, if the husband dies first.

79 Gif mid bearnum bugan wille, healfne scæt age.

79 If she wishes to go away with the children, she is to have half the goods.

80 Gif ceorl agan wile: swa an bearn.

80 If the husband wishes to keep [the children], [she is to have the same share] as a child.

81 Gif heo beam ne gebyreð, fæderingmagas fioh agan 7 morgengyfe.[3]

81 If she does not bear a child, [her]paternal kinsmen are to have [her] goods and the 'morning-gift'.[4]

To begin with, this appears straightforward enough. The first clause in the sequence, ch. 77, states that a marriage agreement is to stand unless there is evidence of fraud. If there is fraud, the woman is to be returned home and the bridegroom's money refunded. Ch. 78 deals with the position of a widow, stating that a woman who has borne a child is entitled to half the property on the demise of her husband. The next two clauses, chs. 79 and 80, are very cryptically expressed. These are interpreted by all editors of the laws in terms of divorce or legal separation, with the woman retaining her right to half the property if she leaves with the children, but receiving only the same amount as a child if they remain in the custody of

[3] *Gesetze*, ed. Liebermann I, 7–8.

[4] *English Historical Documents c. 500–1042*, ed. D. Whitelock, 2nd ed. (London, 1979), p. 393.

her ex-husband. Finally, ch. 81 discusses the position of a woman who has not borne a child. Scholars are divided as to whether this follows in sequence from chs. 79 and 80, referring to a woman who is separated from her husband, or whether it should be read in connection with ch. 78, referring to a widow[5].

It seems to me that there is inadequate linguistic evidence to associate Æthelberht, chs. 79 and 80, with the subject of divorce. Interpretation of the verb *bugan* in ch. 79 is crucial. All editors take this to refer to departure. Hickes and Wilkins translate it as 'recedere'; Schmid and Liebermann agree on 'ausscheiden'; Attenborough gives 'to depart', and Thorpe, like Whitelock, has 'to go away'.[6] However, this is not the usual meaning of the verb in Old English. The position is complicated by the fact that the verbs *bu(g)an* and *bugan* are etymologically distinct[7] but cannot always be differentiated in written texts. Both must therefore be taken into consideration here. Bosworth-Toller's *Dictionary* defines the first as 'to dwell, live' or 'to inhabit, occupy', and the second as 'to inhabit' or 'to bow or bow down oneself, bend, swerve, give way, submit, yield, turn, turn away, flee'. Toller's *Supplement* adds a number of

---

[5] Liebermann (*Gesetze* I, 8) takes ch. 81 to continue the theme of divorce, so that on dissolution of the marriage a childless woman's property passes back into the possession of her relatives. L. Lancaster, 'Kinship in Anglo-Saxon Society: II', *British Journal of Sociology* 9 (1958), 359–77, at 368, agrees that 'a childless woman (who had left her husband?) had to hand over her possessions and her "morning gift"... to her paternal kin'. G. MacCormack, 'Inheritance and Wergild in Early Germanic Law–I', *Irish Jurist* ns 8 (1973), 143–63, at 153, argues that ch. 81 contrasts with 78 rather than with 79–80, and 'should be taken as dealing with the situation in which the marriage ends through the death of the husband not through the departure of the wife'. T. J. Rivers, 'Widows' Rights in Anglo-Saxon Law', *American Journal of Legal History* 19 (1975), 208–15, at 212, appears to endorse this view, claiming that 'the paternal inheritance destined for widows was more a provision for the children than for the widows, since widows were not entitled to inherit from their late husbands if they had no children'. Fell (*Women in Anglo-Saxon England*, p. 75) suggests that ch. 81 may concern a woman who dies childless rather than one whose marriage has ended for whatever reason.

[6] G. Hickes, *Linguarum Vett. Septentrionalium Thesaurus Grammatico-Criticus et Archæologicus* (Oxford, 1703–5) IV (*Dissertatio Epistolaris*), p. 92; *Leges Anglo-Saxonica Ecclesiasticae & Civiles*, ed. D. Wilkins (London, 1721), p. 7; *Die Gesetze der Angelsachsen*, ed. R. Schmid, 2nd ed. (Leipzig, 1858), p. 9; *Gesetze*, ed. Liebermann I, 8; *The Laws of the Earliest English Kings*, ed. F. L. Attenborough (Cambridge, 1922), p. 15; *Ancient Laws and Institutes of England*, ed. B. Thorpe, folio edition (London, 1840), p. 9.

[7] J. Pokorny, *Indogermanisches Etymologisches Wörterbuch*, 2 vols. (Bern, 1959–69) I, 149 and 153.

sub-sections to the latter, of which IIIa is 'of retirement, withdrawal'.[8] Only three examples are cited: two are concerned with entering a monastery or convent, and the third is Æthelberht, ch. 79.

The Toronto *Dictionary of Old English*[9] has an extensive entry for *būan, būgan, būgian*. This comprises four main sections:

1 to inhabit, dwell in (something/a place *acc.*)
2 to possess, inherit (something *acc.*)
3 to live, dwell
4 of land, to lie

Again there is a separate entry under *bugan*. This presents a wider range of alternatives, including 'to bow or bend', and 'to turn, change direction (without expressed object)'. A sub-section 3a 'to go away (without expressed object)' is created specially to accommodate Æthelberht, ch. 79. There are no other recorded instances of this meaning, and thus there is no external support for the reading.

Like many of the early laws, this group of clauses leaves much unsaid. The subject is omitted from ch. 79, but is understood to be the woman referred to as *mægþ* in ch. 77 and as *hio* in ch. 78. If *bugan* has its usual meaning of 'to live or inhabit', ch. 79 could well mean that if the widow wishes to live with her children, and presumably to provide for them as they grow up, she is entitled to half the property left by her husband, her full allowance under the terms of ch. 78. It is unnecessary to postulate an unattested meaning for the verb in this context.

This reading is supported by similar provisions in law-codes from the later seventh century. Æthelberht's code is followed in the only extant manuscript by a further series of Kentish laws in the joint names of Kings Hlothhere and Eadric (673–86), and these also deal with a widow's right both to financial provision and to custody of her children. Hlothhere and Eadric, ch. 6, reads as follows:

Gif ceorl acwyle be libbendum wife 7 bearne, riht is þæt hit, þæt bearn, medder folgige, 7 him mon an his fæderingmagum	If a husband dies leaving wife and child, it is right that the child should accompany the mother, and he is to be given

[8] *An Anglo-Saxon Dictionary Based on the Manuscript Collections of the Late Joseph Bosworth*, ed. T. N. Toller (Oxford, 1898), pp. 132–3; *Supplement* (Oxford, 1921), p. 110

[9] Dictionary of Old English Project, *Dictionary of Old English A–G*. Version 2.0. CD-ROM, 2008.

wilsumne berigean gefelle, his feoh to healdenne, oþ þæt he X wintra sie.[10]	one of his paternal kinsmen as a willing protector, to look after his property until he is ten years old.[11]

The same theme occurs in the West Saxon laws of Ine, originally issued towards the end of the seventh century although now preserved only as an appendix to the great *domboc* compiled by King Alfred about 200 years later. Ine, ch. 38, emphasizes that a widow is entitled to custody of her children as well as to adequate provision for their maintenance:

Gif ceorl 7 his wif bearn hæbben gemæne, 7 fere se ceorl forð, hæbbe sio modor hire bearn 7 fede: agife hire mon VI scill. to fostre, cu on sumera, oxan on wintra; healden þa mægas þone frumstol, oð ðæt hit gewintred sie.[12]	If a husband and wife have a child together, and the husband dies, the mother is to have her child and rear it; she is to be given six shillings for its maintenance, a cow in summer, an ox in winter; the kinsmen are to take charge of the paternal home, until the child is grown up.[13]

There are no such parallels to the traditional reading of Æthelberht, ch. 79, and some evidence against it. A penitential handbook based on the judgements of Archbishop Theodore (669–90) and apparently compiled in Northumbria during the early eighth century[14] stipulates clearly that a marriage could only be dissolved by mutual consent. The *Theodore Penitential* (II.xii.7) states:

7 Legitimum conjugium non licet frangi sine consensu amborum.[15]	7 A legal marriage may not be broken without the consent of both parties.[16]

[10] *Gesetze*, ed. Liebermann I, 10.
[11] *English Historical Documents*, ed. Whitelock, p. 394.
[12] *Gesetze*, ed. Liebermann 1, 104–6.
[13] *English Historical Documents*, ed. Whitelock, p. 403.
[14] *Councils and Ecclesiastical Documents Relating to Great Britain and Ireland*, ed. A. W. Haddan and W. Stubbs, 3 vols. (Oxford, 1869–73) III, 173.
[15] *Ibid.* III, 199.
[16] J. T. McNeill and H. M. Gamer, *Medieval Handbooks of Penance* (New York, 1938), p. 209.

This militates against the view that a woman could legally leave her husband. Indeed, the same source (xii.10) goes on to say that an adulteress who had been repudiated by her husband was allowed to retain only a fourth of her property, and even this only on condition that she entered a nunnery:

10 Mulier si adultera est et vir ejus non vult habitare cum ea, si vult ilia monasterium intrare, quartam partem sux hereditatis optineat; si non vult, nihil habeat.[17]	11 If a woman is an adulteress and her husband does not wish to live with her, if she decides to enter a monastery she shall retain the fourth part of her inheritance. If she decides otherwise, she shall have nothing.[18]

There is no suggestion that the woman could initiate the divorce, nor that she was entitled to any financial entitlement, except as a special concession if she retired from secular life. Conditions in eighth-century Northumbria cannot of course be taken to mirror those in seventh-century Kent; but a drastic change must have occurred if Whitelock's translation of Æthelberht, ch. 79, is correct.

Continental evidence is also important here. As Wallace-Hadrill has shown, Anglo-Saxon law is closely related to other Germanic legislation, so that comparison with continental codes can often throw light on interpretation.[19] Again, the traditional reading of Æthelberht, ch. 79, in terms of divorce is unparalleled in Germanic law, whilst a widow's right to custody of her children is a recurrent theme. To take a single example, ch. 85.1 of the Burgundian code issued by King Gundobad during the late fifth century reads as follows:

Si mater tutelam suscipere voluerit, nulla ei parentela praeponatur.[20]	If a mother wishes to assume guardianship, no other relationship shall be placed before her.[21]

---

[17] *Councils and Ecclesiastical Documents*, ed. Haddan and Stubbs III, 199.

[18] McNeill and Gamer, *Medieval Handbooks of Penance*, p. 209.

[19] J. M. Wallace-Hadrill, *Early Germanic Kingship in England and on the Continent* (Oxford, 1971), pp. 33–7, discusses the interdependence of the barbarian codes: 'We need to place Æthelberht's laws where they belong, within the body of a legal tradition that goes back to the codex of the Visigoth king Euric, composed in southern Gaul between 466 and 484' (p. 33); 'Æthelberht's legislation must be seen in its place among other Germanic laws, and we must suppose that its inspiration was not unlike theirs' (p. 36).

[20] *Leges Burgundionum*, ed. L. R. de Salis, Monumenta Germaniae Historica, Legum Sectio I: Leges nationum Germanicarum 2.1 (Hanover, 1892), p. 107.

[21] K. F. Drew, *The Burgundian Code* (Philadelphia, PA, 1949), p. 78.

The verb *voluerit* may be compared with *wille* in Æthelberht, ch. 79, emphasizing that the mother has freedom of choice in this matter. Similar provisions occur in Visigothic law, to which I shall return shortly.

The problem with this reading of Æthelberht, ch. 79, is that it clashes with the accepted interpretation of the following clause. Æthelberht, ch. 80, is also very cryptically expressed, yet there is general agreement as to its purport. All editors take *ceorl* to be the subject of *agan wile*, with the object understood to be the children mentioned in ch. 79. Thus it seems that ch. 80 must refer to an alternative scenario where the husband, clearly very much alive, takes custody of the children and in so doing reduces the divorce settlement due to his ex-wife.

However, the wording of this clause would support an alternative interpretation. Grammatically, *ceorl* may be nominative or accusative. There is nothing in the construction of ch. 80 to indicate that this is the subject rather than the object of the verb. Indeed, comparison with chs. 79 and 81 may suggest that *hio* is to be understood as the subject in all three instances. In this case, the *ceorl* of ch. 80 must be a new character, not the widow's first husband, I would read the clause along the lines, 'If [she] wishes to take [another] husband...'

This too ties in with information from other sources. Continental legislation confirms that it was customary under early Germanic law for a widow to lose some of her inheritance rights from a first marriage on entering a second. Again the late-fifth-century Burgundian code may be particularly relevant. Ch. 42 allocates a third of the husband's property to a childless widow, to be forfeited if she remarries within a year:

[1] ... Idcirco praesenti constitutione decernimus: ut, si mulier, defunct sine filiis coniuge suo, ad secunda vota non ierit, tertiam totius substantiae mariti usque ad diem mortis suae secura possideat; sic tamen, ut post transitum eius ad legitimos mariti heredes omnia revertantur.

1 ... Therefore we decree in the present constitution that if a woman whose husband has died without children has not taken her vows a second time, let her possess securely a third of all the property of her husband to the day of her death; with the further provision that after her death, all will revert to the legitimate heirs of her husband.

[2] De morginegiva vero, quod priori a tempore obitus prioris mariti intra annum nubere voluerit, habeat liberam potestatem et tertiam

2 Let that remain in effect which has been stated previously concerning the morning gift. For if she wishes to marry within a year from the

substantiae partem, quam permissa fuerat possidere, dimittat. Ceterum si emenso anno vel biennio maritum accipere voluerit, omnia sicut dictum est, quae de priore marito habuit, derelinquat et pretium, quod de nuptiis eius inferendum est, accipiat cuius partibus defuncti parentis debetur hereditas.[22]

time of the death of her first husband, let her have full right to do so, but let her give up that third part of the property possess. However, if she wishes to take a husband after a year or two have passed, let her give up all as has been stated above which she received from her first husband, and let the heirs in whose portion the inheritance of her former husband belongs receive the price which must be paid for her (second) marriage.[23]

Ch. 59 allocates guardianship of the children with all their possessions to the grandfather if a widow remarries, but emphasizes that both children and property are to remain in their mother's custody whilst she continues as a widow:

Nepos amisso patre cum rebus omnibus ad avi ordinationem vel crediderit eligendas. Ceterum si nubere electa castitate distulerit, filii cum omni facultate in eius solatio et potestate consistant. sollicitudinem conferatur: ea tamen ratione, si mater eius secundas nuptias[24]

If the father is dead, let a grandchild with all his possessions be given over to the supervision and care of the grandfather if his mother has decided upon a second marriage. Moreover, if she fails to remarry because she has chosen chastity, let her children with all their property remain in her care (custody) and power.[25]

This juxtaposition of the themes of guardianship and second marriage may have implications for the interpretation of Æthelberht, chs. 79–80. Ch. 62 of the Burgundian code confirms that a widow forfeited the majority of her financial rights on remarriage:

---

[22] *Leges Burgundionum*, ed. de Salis, p. 73.
[23] Drew, *The Burgundian Code*, pp. 50–1.
[24] *Leges Burgundionum*, ed. de Salis, p. 92.
[25] Drew, *The Burgundian Code*, pp. 65.

[1] Filius unicus, defuncto patre, tertiam partem facultatis matri utendam relinquat; si tamen maritum alterum non acceperit. Nam si ad alias nuptias transierit, omnia perdat.

1 Let an only son, if his father is dead, leave a third part of his property for the use of his mother, provided nevertheless she does not take another husband; for if she enters another marriage, let her lose all.

[2] Dotem sane suam, quam a marito suo acceperat, quamdiu vixerit utatur, filio proprietate servata.[26]

2 Nevertheless, let her use her wedding gift which she received from her husband, as long as she lives, and let the ownership be reserved for the son.[27]

Ch. 74 revises earlier legislation concerning widows and their offspring. Under the new arrangement, a widow could divide the property with her sons; but this again depended on her not remarrying, and was also affected by whether or not she wished her adult sons to live with her. The second clause reads as follows:

[2] Quaecumque sane mulier, coniuge suo in fato conlapso, ad secundi mariti vota non ierit, ac si earn adulti iam filii secum esse noluerint, hac ratione cum eis defuncti mariti dividat facultatem, ut, si unum filium habuerit, praedictae substantiae tertiam consequatur; si duos aut très vel quatuor aut plures erunt filii, quartam accipiat portionem, quam tamen post obitum eius ad filios ipsius piacuit remeare.[28]

2 If any woman whose husband has died does not take vows to a second husband, or does not wish her sons, now grown, to live with her, she may accordingly divide the property of the dead husband with them. If she has one son only, let her obtain the above-mentioned third; if there are two or three or four or more sons, let her receive a fourth part; nevertheless after her death, let the property return to the sons.[29]

This may present a parallel with the scenario described so elliptically in Æthelberht's code.

---

[26] *Leges Burgundionum*, ed. de Salis, p. 93.
[27] Drew, *The Burgundian Code*, pp. 66.
[28] *Leges Burgundionum*, ed. de Salis, p. 98.
[29] Drew, *The Burgundian Code*, pp. 71.

Visigothic law also emphasizes both the widow's right to custody and the reduction of her entitlements on remarriage. The Visigothic Code (III.i.7) gives a mother the authority to choose spouses for her children only whilst she remains a widow:

Patre mortuo utriusque sexus filiorum coniunctio in matris potestate consistât; matre vero mortua, aut si ad alias nuptias forte transierit, fraters eligant, cui dignius puer vel puella iungatur.[30]	If the father should be dead, the right to dispose of the children of both sexes in marriage shall belong to the mother. If the mother also should be dead, or if she should have married a second time, the brothers shall have the right to select the husband or wives for the other children.[31]

The Code goes on to affirm that the mother is to have custody of her children unless she remarries (IV.iii.3):

Si patre mortuo in minori etate filii relinquantur, mater eorum tutela, si voluerit, suscipiat, si tamen in viduitate permanserit; ... Quod si mater alium maritum acceperit, …[32]	After the death of the father, the mother shall have the guardianship of the minor children, if she should wish it, provided she remains a widow; ...But if the mother should marry again, …[33]

Interestingly, this corresponds to a similar provision concerning the rights of a widowed father (IV.ii.13):

Matre mortua filii in patris potestate consistant.[34]	If the mother should die, the children shall remain under the control of the father.[35]

The father's position was also affected by remarriage. Although still entitled to custody of his children, he was obliged to draw up an inventory

---

[30] *Leges Visigothorum*, ed. K. Zeumer, Monumenta Germaniae Historica, Legum sectio I: Leges nationum Germanicarum 1 (Hanover, 1902), p. 130.
[31] S.P. Scott, *The Visigothic Code* (Boston, MA, 1910), p. 81.
[32] *Leges Visigothorum*, ed. Zeumer, pp. 190–1.
[33] Scott, *The Visigothic Code*, p. 132.
[34] *Leges Visigothorum*, ed. Zeumer, p. 178.
[35] Scott, *The Visigothic Code*, p. 123.

of their property and to carry out other legal procedures to safeguard their inheritance. This clause continues:

> Quod si marito suppreste uxor forsitan moriatur, filii, qui sunt ex eodem coniugio procreati, in patris potestate consistant, et res eorum, si novercam non superduxerit, ... Quod si pater novercam superduxerit, quia valde indignum est, ut filii eius, patris potestate vel gubernatione relicta, in alterius tuitione deveniant, filios suos pater ille, qui novercam duxerit, non relinquat; sed filios et res eorum iuxta superiore modum tuitionis ordine regat; ita tamen, ut inventarium de rebus filiorum suorum manu sua conscriptum coram iudice vel heredibus defuncte mulieris strenue faciat, et tali se placiti cautione in heredum illorum nomine constringat, quibus tutela ipsa pertinere, si pater defuisset, legitime poterat, ut nihil de rebus filiorum suorum evertat, sed filiorum suorum vitam sollicito voto vel actu salvare intendat, et res eorum absque aliqua perditionis diminution tuendas accipiat; si tamen voluerit.[36]

> And, if she should die while her husband is still living and he should not marry again, he shall have charge of the children born of the marriage, and may retain possession of their property, ... If, however, the father should marry again, he shall not relinquish the care of the children, because it is not just that his authority over them having been abandoned, they should be placed under the guardianship of another; but he shall still retain control over them and their property, as hereinbefore mentioned. But he must at once draw up an inventory of their property in his own hand, in the presence of a judge, or of the heirs of his deceased wife; and he must also bind himself by a written obligation, that those relatives who are legally entitled to it shall have the guardianship of the children in the case of his death; in order that none of the property of the latter may be lost, but may be protected by him, in every way, from injury or diminution in value.[37]

The following clause continues the theme of inheritance, stating that a widow was to share equally in the income from her late husband's estate with her children, who were to receive her share on her death or remarriage (IV.ii.14):

[36] *Leges Visigothorum*, ed. Zeumer, pp. 178–9.
[37] Scott, *The Visigothic Code*, pp. 123–4.

Mater, si in viduitate permanserit, equalem inter filios suos, id est qualem unusquisque ex filiis, usufructuariam de facultate mariti habeat portionem; quam usque ad tempus vite sue usufructuario iure possideat. Ceterum nec donare nec vindere nec uni ex filiis conferre présumât... Post obitum vero matris portio, quam mater acceperat, ad filios equaliter revertatur, quia non possunt de paternam hereditatem fraudari. Quod si mater ad alias nuptias forte transierit, ex ea die usufructuariam portionem, quam de bonis mariti fuerat consecuta, filii inter reliquas res paternas, qui ex eo nati sunt coniugio, vindicabunt.[38]	A mother, during her lifetime, or so long as she remains a widow, shall share equally with her children in the income derived from the estate of her deceased husband. But she cannot give away, or sell, or bestow upon any of her children her share of the aforesaid property... After the death of the mother, whatever she received from her husband shall be equally distributed among the children, because they must not be defrauded of their paternal inheritance. If the mother should marry again, from that very day the children can claim as their own that portion of their father's property which their mother received at his death.[39]

A widow who remarries within a year is to forfeit half her property, in case a woman pregnant by her first husband might destroy her offspring (III.ii.1):

Si qua mulier post mortem mariti sui se alio infra annum coniunxerit vel adulterium fecerit, medietatem rerum suarum filii sui ex priori coniugio procreati aut, si filii desunt, alii propinquiores defuncti viri heredes per iudicis instantiam ipsarum rerum consequantur medietatem. Quam idcirco mulierem precipue huic volumus subiacere dispendio, ne hec, que a marito gravida relinquitur, dum immoderato desiderio ad	If any woman, within a year after the death of her husband, should marry another, or commit adultery, the children by her first marriage shall receive half of her property; or, if there are no children, the nearest heirs of the deceased husband shall receive half of her property, by order of the court. We have especially prescribed this penalty lest the woman, having been left pregnant by her husband, and desiring to enter into a second

[38] *Leges Visigothorum*, ed. Zeumer, p. 182.
[39] Scott, *The Visigothic Code*, p. 125.

secundi coniugii vota festinat vel adulterium perpetrat, spem partus, priusquam nascatur, extinguat.[40]	marriage, should destroy her unborn offspring.[41]

The same reasoning may underlie certain rulings in the eleventh-century Anglo-Saxon laws of Æthelred and Cnut, which will be discussed shortly.

Similar provisions concerning remarriage occur in other Germanic codes. According to the mid-eighth-century Bavarian laws, a widow with children inherited a share of the property equal to each of her sons, but forfeited it to them if she took another husband (XIV.7–8):

VII [De viduis.] De viduis quae post mortem mariti sui in viduitate permaneant, aequalem inter filios suos, id est qualem unus ex filiis usufructuariam habeat portionem, quem usque ad tempus vitae suae usufructuario iure possedeat.	7 Concerning widows. Let her who remains in widowhood after the death of her husband have a portion in usufruct equal to her sons', that is, as if she were one of the sons. For as long as she lives, let her legally possess it by right of usufruct.
VIII [De secundis nuptiis.] Quodsi mater ad alias nuptias forte transient, ea die usufructuariam portionem, quam de bonis mariti fuerat consecuta, filii inter reliquas res paternas qui ex eo nati sunt coniugio, vindicabunt. Mater vero si habet proprias res et cum dote sua quam per legem habet, egrediat. Et si ibi nec filios nec filias generavit, post mortem eius omnia quae de filiis suis detulit, ad illos revertatur.[42]	8 But if a mother contracts another marriage, on that day let the sons who are born of the earlier marriage take over her portion of the usufruct from her husband's property, whatever remains of the paternal inheritance. However, let a mother depart if she has her own property, [with] her morning gift, which she possesses legally. And if she has borne neither sons nor daughters [from her former marriage], let everything she took away from [the late husband's] children [that is, those of a former marriage] be returned to them after his death.[43]

---

[40] *Leges Visigothorum*, ed. Zeumer, p. 133.
[41] Scott, *The Visigothic Code*, p. 83.
[42] *Lex Baiwariorum*, ed. E. von Schwind, Monumenta Germaniae Historica, Legum Sectio I: Leges nationum Germanicarum 5.2 (Hanover, 1926), pp. 426–7.
[43] T. J. Rivers, *Laws of the Alamans and Bavarians* (Philadelphia, PA, 1977), p. 159.

Ch. 10 states that a childless widow was entitled to half the property until her death or remarriage:

> De eo qui sine filiis et filiabus mortuus est, mulier accipiat portionem suam, dum viduitatem custodierit, id est medietatem pecuniae. Medietas autem ad propinquos mariti pertineat. Si autem mulier mortua fuerit aut alium maritum tulit, tunc quod proprium habet et de mariti rebus quae per legem ei debentur, accipiat; ceteras res propinqui prions mariti accipiant.[44]

> Concerning him who dies without sons and daughters. Let a wife keep her portion as long as she is provided by her widowhood, that is, half the property; however, let half belong to the relatives of the husband. If, however, the wife dies or takes another husband, then let him keep what is his own and what was to be given to her from the property of the husband according to the law. Let the relatives of the former husband keep the remaining property.[45]

It seems most likely that Æthelberht, ch. 81, refers similarly to the position of a childless widow, following directly on from the discussion of a widow with children in the preceding clauses of the sequence.

Alamannic law also refers to the possibility of a widow giving up the property from her first marriage in order to contract a second. The *Leges Alamannorum*, ch. 54, begin as follows:

> 1 Si quis liber mortuus fuerit, reliquit uxorem sine filios aut filias, et de ilia hereditate exire voluerit, nubere sibi alium coaequalem sibi, sequatur earn dotis legitima …[46]

> 1 If any freeman dies leaving a wife without sons or daughters and she wishes to give up the inheritance to marry another of equal status to her own, let a lawful dowry accompany her …[47]

Here it is clearly regarded as axiomatic that the widow would forfeit her inheritance on remarriage.

---

[44] *Lex Baiwariorum*, ed. von Schwind, p. 429.

[45] Rivers, *Laws of the Alamans and Bavarians*, p. 160.

[46] *Leges Alamannorum*, ed. K. A. Eckhardt, Monumenta Germaniae Historica, Legum Sectio I: Leges nationum Germanicarum 5.1 (Hanover, 1966), 112.

[47] Rivers, *Laws of the Alamans and Bavarians,* p. 84.

The laws issued by the Lombard King Aistulf in 755 limit strictly the amount of property that a man was allowed to bequeath to his wife, stipulating in ch. 14.5 that it was to revert to the children if she died or remarried:

> 14.5 Si quis Langobardus decidens uxori suae usumfructum de rebus suis iudicare voluerit, et filius vel filias ex ea reliquerit, non amplius ei pro usumfructum iudicare possit, quam medietatem ex sua substantia super illut, quod ei in morgincap et metam secundum legem datum fuerit. Et si filius aut filias ex alia uxore reliquerit unum aut duos, possit uxori suae tertiam portionem ad usumfructum relinquere; si fuerint tres, quartam partem; si amplius, per eo numero conputetur; morgincap et meta, quod ei legibus data est, habeat inantea. Si quidem nupserit postea, aut mortua fuerit, usumfructum in integrum ad heredes revertatur, de meta vero et morgincap fiat secundum anterior edictum.[48]

> 14.5 That Lombard who on dying wishes to grant to his wife a usufruct from his property, if he leaves sons or daughters by her, cannot grant more to her for her usufruct than a half of his property since he has already given her a morning gift and a marriage portion according to law. And if he leaves one or two sons or daughters from a previous wife, he can leave only a third portion of his property for the usufruct of his surviving wife; if there are three [children from the previous marriage, he can leave her] a fourth part; if there are more children, her share shall be determined according to this progression. But she shall have the complete morning gift and marriage portion which her husband gave her according to law. If she marries again or if she dies, the usufruct [of her portion] shall revert in entirety to the heirs and, concerning the marriage portion and the morning gift, let it be observed as provided in the earlier law.[49]

Again the position is perfectly clear, with a second marriage leading to the forfeiture of property from the first.

I have quoted at length from continental legislation in order to demonstrate the strength of support for my suggested interpretation of

---

[48] *Leges Langobardorum,* ed. F. Bluhme, Monumenta Germaniae Historica, Leges 4 (Hanover, 1869), pp. 200–1.

[49] K. F. Drew, *The Lombard Laws* (Philadelphia, PA, 1973), p. 234.

Æthelberht, chs. 79–80. Most English sources concern the later Anglo-Saxon period; but these too indicate that a widow's inheritance was reduced if she remarried. V Æthelred, ch. 21, dating from the early eleventh century, simply forbids remarriage within a year:

21 7 sy ælc wydewe, þe hy sylfe mid rihte gehealde, on Godes griðe 7 on þæs cynges.	21 And every widow who conducts herself rightly is to be under the protection of God and the king.
22.1 7 sitte ælc XII monað werleas; ceose syððan þæt heo sylf wille.[50]	21.1 And each [widow] is to remain unmarried for twelve months; she is afterwards to choose what she herself will.[51]

This is repeated in VI Æthelred, ch. 26,[52] but II Cnut, ch. 73, adds a further proviso, setting out the financial implications:

73 7 sitte ælc wuduwe werleas XII monað, ceose syððan þæt heo sylf wylle.	73 And each widow is to remain unmarried for 12 months; she is afterwards to choose what she herself will.
73a 7 gif heo binnan geares fæce wer geceose, þonne þolige heo þære morgengyfe 7 ealra þæra. æhta, þe heo þurh ærran wer hæfde; 7 fon þa. nehstan frynd to ðam landan 7 to þan æhtan, þe heo ær hæfde.[53]	73a And if she chooses a husband within the year's space, she is then to forfeit the morning-gift and all the possessions which she had through her former husband; and the nearest kinsmen are to succeed to the lands and to the possessions which she had before.[54]

As in several of the continental laws mentioned above, the crucial period here is the first year of widowhood. However, other evidence suggests that remarriage at a later date, though not illegal, could still result in financial loss. The late Old English text known as *Be Wifmannes Beweddunge*

[50] *Gesetze*, ed. Liebermann I, 242.
[51] *English Historical Documents*, ed. Whitelock, p. 445.
[52] *Gesetze*, ed. Liebermann I, 254.
[53] *Ibid.* I, 360.
[54] *English Historical Documents*, ed. Whitelock, p. 465.

('Concerning the Betrothal of a Woman') makes it clear that a widow would lose her inheritance on remarriage. Chs. 3 and 4 read as follows:

3 Đonne syððan cyþe se brydguma, hwæs he hire geunge, wið þam ðet heo his willan geceose, 7 hwæs he hire geunge, gif heo læng sy ðonne he.	3 Then afterwards the bridegroom is to announce what he grants her in return for her acceptance of his suit, and what he grants her if she should live longer than he.
4 Gif hit swa geforword bið, þonne is riht, ðæt heo sy healfes yrfes wyrðe – 7 ealles, gif hy cild gemæne habban – bute heo eft wær ceose.[55]	4 If it is thus contracted, then it is right that she should be entitled to half the goods–and to all, if they have a child together–unless she marries again.[56]

Surviving wills tell the same story. In the mid-ninth century, the reeve Abba left property to his wife on condition that she did not take a second husband (S 1482):

is min willa gif me God bearnes unnan wille, ðæt hit foe to londe æfter me 7 his bruce mid minum gemeccan; ... Gif me ðonne gifeðe sie, ðæt ic bearn begeotan ne mege, þonne is min willa þæt hit hæbbe min wiif ða hwile ðe hia hit mid clennisse gehaldan wile... Gif min wiif ðonne hia nylle mid clennisse swæ gehaldan, 7 hire liofre sie oðer hemed to niomanne, ðonne foen mine megas to ðem londe 7 hire agefen hire agen.[57]	it is my desire that if God will give me a child, he shall have the land after me, and enjoy it with my wife; ... If, however, it is my lot not to have a child, then I desire that my wife shall have it as long as she is willing to keep it without marrying again... If, however, my wife is not willing to remain unwedded, and prefers to contract another marriage, then my kinsmen are to take the land and to give her own property to her.[58]

---

[55] *Gesetze*, ed. Liebermann I, 442.

[56] *English Historical Documents*, ed. Whitelock, p. 465.

[57] In references to Anglo-Saxon charters, S = *Anglo-Saxon Charters: an Annotated List and Bibliography*, ed. P. H. Sawyer, Royal Historical Society Guides and Handbooks 8 (London, 1968). A revised version is now available at http://www.esawyer.org.uk.

[58] *Select English Historical Documents of the Ninth and Tenth Centuries*, ed. F.E. Harmer (Cambridge, 1914), pp. 3 and 40–1 (no. 2).

This is perfectly logical, since a second marriage contract would itself provide for the widow's financial security.

Earl Ælfred's will (S 1508), dating from the late ninth century, refers to a verbal agreement that his wife will not remarry. To be on the safe side, he stipulates that two thousand pigs are to be hers only on condition that she keeps this promise:

> Ic Ęlfred dux sello Werburge 7 Alhdryðe uncum gemenum bearne, æfter minum dege, þas lond mid cwice ęrfe 7 mid earðe 7 mid allum ðingum ðe to londum belimpað; 7 twa þusendu swina ic heom sello mid þem londum, gif hio hio gehaldeð mid þare clęnnisse þe uncer wordgecweodu seondan.

> I, Earl Ælfred, give these estates, after my time, to Werburg and to Alhthryth, the child of us both, with livestock and with produce and with everything pertaining thereto; and I give them two thousand swine with the estates, if she remains unmarried in accordance with our verbal agreements.[59]

Evidently there was no legal obligation on Werburg to remain unmarried. Two thousand pigs would no doubt represent a powerful inducement.

Finally, the mid-eleventh-century will of Eadwine of Caddington (S1517) deals with the issues of both guardianship and inheritance. Eadwine leaves property to his widow until she remarries, at which time she is also to lose custody of their child:

> 7 minan wife ꝥ land æt Westtune, 7 æt Cnybbanwyrðe, 7 þæne bryce ealra þæra landa him bam gemæne þa hwile ðe heo on wudewanhade riste, 7 seððan hio wer nime, fo Æþelwine to þam cilde, 7 to ealre þære are þe ic him becweden hæbbe, oð ðæt hit sylf gemagod sy.

> And to my wife the land at Weston and Knebworth, and the use of all the lands common to them both, for as long as she remains a widow; and when she takes a husband, Æthelwine is to take care of the child, and of all the property which I have bequeathed to him, until the child is himself capable.[60]

Keynes comments that Ethelwine 'seems from what follows to have been the testator's brother';[61] and again the transference of custody to

59 *Select English Historical Documents*, ed. Harmer, pp. 13 and 47 (no. 10).

60 S. Keynes, 'A Lost Cartulary of St Albans Abbey', *Anglo-Saxon England* 22 (1993), 253–79, at 275–6.

61 *Ibid*. p. 277.

the paternal relatives at this point accords with the continental evidence discussed above. I would suggest that the phrase *seððan hio wer nime* corresponds to the more cryptically expressed *Gif ceorl agan wile* in Æthelberht, ch. 80.

In short, it is clear that in Anglo-Saxon England as in continental Germanic society, the inheritance and custody rights of a widow were substantially reduced on her remarriage. There is, on the other hand, no evidence at all that a married woman who left her husband was entitled either to custody of her children or to a financial settlement. I suggest therefore that the pair of clauses known as Ethelberht, chs. 79 and 80, do not deal with the position of a divorcee, but with that of a widow. Two courses of action are open to her. Either she remains celibate, retaining her legal inheritance and custody of her children, or she may remarry, forfeiting the former and possibly the latter. The first alternative is outlined in ch. 79, the second in ch. 80. I propose the following translation:

77 Gif man mægð gebigeð, ceapi geceapod sy, gif hit unfacne is.	77 If anyone pays for a maiden, the bargain is to stand, if there is no fraud.[62]
77.1 Gif hit þonne facne is, ef þær æt ham gebrenge, 7 him man his scæt agefe.	77.1 If, however, there is any fraud, she is to be taken back home, and he is to be given back his money.
78 Gif hio cwic beam gebyreþ, healfne scæt age, gif ceorl ær swylteþ.	78 If she bears a living child, she is to have half the goods, if the husband dies first.
79 Gif mid bearnum bugan wille, healfne scæt age.	79 If she wishes to live with the children, she is to have half the goods.
80 Gif ceorl agan wile: swa an bearn.	80 If she wishes to take [another] husband, [she is to have the same share] as a child.

[62] I also revise Whitelock's translation of Æthelberht, ch. 77, since I accept Fell's arguments concerning the use of the verb *bicgan* in marriage contexts: 'there is a vast range of evidence... for the fact that the money the bridegroom had to pay (the *morgengifu*) was payment to the woman herself, intended to guarantee her financial security and independence within marriage. *Bicgan* has the meaning "to pay for" and there is evidence that it could be used in the sense of paying money within a contractual framework' (*Women in Anglo-Saxon England*, p. 16).

81 Gif heo bearn ne gebyreð, faederingmagas fioh agan 7 morgengyfe.	81 If she does not bear a child, [her] paternal kinsmen are to have [her] goods and the 'morning-gift'.

There are three advantages in adopting this interpretation in preference to the traditional reading given at the beginning of this paper. In the first place, it disposes of the need to assume that the verb *bugan* in Æthelberht, ch. 79, is being used in a way unparalleled in the extant corpus of Old English. Secondly, it allows the group of clauses comprising Æthelberht, chs. 77–81, to be read as a consecutive sequence rather than as a sequence which is interrupted and then resumed. Thirdly, it is supported by evidence from other sources, both English and continental.[63]

[63] I am very grateful to Christine Fell, Simon Keynes and Patrick Wormald for their advice whilst this paper was in preparation.

8.

A REAPPRAISAL OF ÆTHELBERHT 84

First published 1993: *Nottingham Medieval Studies* 37, 1–6.

The cryptic style and often archaic vocabulary of the law-code attributed to King Æthelberht of Kent can lead to difficulties in interpretation, and these are compounded by the fact that the *domas* are written continuously, without chapter headings or numbering. Whether or not this was originally the case is uncertain. Whereas the laws themselves appear to have been issued towards the end of the sixth or the beginning of the seventh century, the only surviving copy is found in the twelfth-century manuscript *Textus Roffensis*.[1] This contains a collection of legal material from the Anglo-Saxon period, including later codes also extant in other manuscripts. Where comparison is possible, the *Textus Roffensis* copy can often be seen to be defective; and so the unique text of the early Kentish laws is unlikely to be free from corruption.

Æthelberht's code was first printed by Hickes at the beginning of the eighteenth century.[2] Hickes numbered the clauses from 1 to 89, and provided a Latin translation. Hickes' numbering has been followed with certain modifications by later editors; and I shall use the system found in Liebermann's standard edition of the Anglo-Saxon laws.[3] This provides a convenient way of referring to individual sections of the code, but has no manuscript authority or structural significance.

I emphasize this point since I shall be concerned in this paper with a clause which has traditionally been regarded as part of a related group of laws within Æthelberht's code. From the eighteenth century onwards, Æthelberht, ch. 84, has been treated as a continuation of chs. 82–83, although neither the wording nor the manuscript layout suggests that these

---

[1] N. R. Ker, *Catalogue of Manuscripts Containing Anglo-Saxon* (Oxford, 1957), no. 373. Facsimile edited by P. Sawyer, Early English Manuscripts in Facsimile 7 (Copenhagen, 1957).

[2] G. Hickes, *Linguarum Vett. Septentrionalium Thesaurus Grammatico-Criticus et Archæologicus* (Oxford, 1703-5) IV (Dissertatio Epistolaris), 89–92.

[3] *Die Gesetze der Angelsächsen*, ed. F. Liebermann, 3 vols. (Halle, 1903–16).

three clauses form a related sequence. I wish to re-examine this grouping, and to suggest an alternative approach to ch. 84.

Æthelberht, ch. 84, appears on lines 7 and 8 of folio 3v of *Textus Roffensis,* and reads as follows:

Gif gængang geweorðeþ xxxv scill' 7 cyninge xv scillingas.	If *gængang* occurs, 35 shillings and 15 shillings to the king.

Like other clauses in this code, it begins with a capital letter and concludes with a raised point; and raised points are also used to surround the numerals. The two elements of *gængang* are separated by a small space, a division which has little significance in view of the late date of the manuscript and the fact that Anglo-Saxon copyists frequently split up compounds in this way. The last two letters are written over an erasure, the final *g* being much taller than this scribe's norm. Hickes omitted this letter, whilst Wilkins, whose edition of the Anglo Saxon laws was the first to contain the early Kentish codes, transcribed it as *s*.[4] However, the flat top and curving tail identify Minuscule *g;* and in fact it is not uncommon for the *Textus Roffensis* scribe to use elongated letters when making alterations. On folio 15r line 11, for instance, *ðysum* is changed to *ðyssum* by the addition of a second *s* which is almost twice the height of the original letter. Two lines further down, *ge* is inserted before *deme,* and as on folio 3v the *g* has a very tall ascender.

The compound *gængang* is unrecorded in this form elsewhere in Old English, and its meaning is wholly uncertain. However, it has been widely assumed that the two preceding clauses provide a framework for interpretation. Æthelberht, chs. 82-83, deal with abduction, and read:

82. Gif man mægþmon nede genimeþ ðam agende L scillinga 7 eft æt þam agende sinne willan ætgebicge.
83. Gif hio oþrum mæn in sceat bewyddod sy xx scillinga gebete.

Some of the vocabulary here is debatable, but for the purposes of this article I give Whitelock's translation:

82. If anyone carries off a maiden by force, [he is to pay] to the owner 50 shillings, and afterwards buy from the owner his consent [to the marriage].

[4] *Leges Anglo-Saxonicæ Ecclesiasticæ & Civiles*, ed. D. Wilkins (London, 1721), p. 7.

> 83 If she is betrothed to another man at a [bride] price, he is to pay 20 shillings compensation.[5]

Following on from this, successive editors of the code have taken ch. 84 to specify an additional or alternative fine in the event that the girl becomes *gængang*. Wilkins suggested that the word refers to pregnancy, deriving from a colloquial usage of *gange*.[6] Although there is no evidence of this semantic range in Old English, Thorpe agrees in a footnote that, 'Its signification, though quite uncertain, yet, judging from the context, seems to be "pregnant"'.[7]

The same translation is offered by Bosworth-Toller,[8] but Grimm[9] found it unacceptable on linguistic as well as contextual grounds. His alternative suggestion that the reference is to the return of the girl by her abductor is discussed in a footnote by Schmid,[10] and is followed by Liebermann, Attenborough and Whitelock.[11] This is much more convincing etymologically. Although *gængang* itself is unique, both elements are well documented and occur frequently in compounds. *Gang* usually refers in some sense to a journey or a road; whilst the early use of *gain* as a prefix is described as follows by the *Oxford English Dictionary*:

> Its senses are chiefly those of opposition, return, or reversal, answering to Lat. *re-*.[12]

Old English variants are listed here as *gegn* and *géan*; but the spelling *gæn* is fully in keeping with the Kentish dialect of Æthelberht's laws. As Campbell explains, the disappearance of *æ, oe* and *y* from the Kentish

---

[5] *English Historical Documents c. 500-1042*, ed. D. Whitelock, 2nd ed. (London, 1979), p. 393.

[6] 'Gængans derivatur a gange *ambulare*, & Germanis usitatam loquendi formulam signat, qua mulier gravida *ambulans* dicitur: Sie hat noch so viel Wochen zu Gehen'. (*Leges*, ed. Wilkins, p. 404).

[7] *Ancient Laws and Institutes of England*, ed. B. Thorpe, folio edition (London, 1840), p. 10.

[8] *An Anglo-Saxon Dictionary Based on the Manuscript Collections of the Late Joseph Bosworth*, ed. T. N. Toller (Oxford, 1898) p. 356. The entry is not updated in Toller's *Supplement* (1921), nor in the subsequent *Addenda* by A. Campbell (1972).

[9] J. Grimm, *Göttingische Gelehrte Anzeigen* (1841), 357–8.

[10] *Die Gesetze der Angelsachsen*, ed. R. Schmid, 2nd ed. (Leipzig, 1858), p. 8.

[11] *Gesetze*, ed. Liebermann I, 8; *The Laws of the Earliest English Kings*, ed. F. L. Attenborough (Cambridge, 1922), p. 15; *English Historical Documents*, ed. Whitelock, p. 393.

[12] *Oxford English Dictionary*, 2nd ed. (Oxford, 1989), 's.v. *gain-*, *prefix*.'

sound-system meant that these symbols came to be used interchangeably with *e*:

> The spellings of *KG* [Kentish Glosses to Proverbs] make it clear that by the tenth century *ǣ* of whatever origin had been raised to *ē* in Kt. [Kentish], while *ōē* had been unrounded to *ē*, and *ȳ* unrounded and lowered to *ē*. These changes are proved by the glosses both by direct orthographical evidence (the symbol *e* appearing for *æ, œ, y)* and by inverted spellings, in which *ce, y* appear for *e* (e.g. *wær, byrene* for *wer* man, *berene* g.s. she-bear).[13]

Bearing in mind that *Textus Roffensis* is a twelfth-century copy of the early laws, *gæn* could therefore represent either an original form preserved through a good manuscript tradition, or a late inverted spelling. The latter is more probable. Other examples of *æ* for *e* on the same page include ch. 83 *mæn* and ch. 89 *Ðeowæs,* whilst *y* for *e* appears in ch. 83 *bewyddod* and ch. 85 *cwynan.* Not all forms are Kentish, however, suggesting that the *Textus Roffensis* scribe may not have consistently reproduced the orthography of his exemplar. West Saxon *sceat* also occurs in ch. 83, for instance, although the Kentish spelling *scæt* is more common in this code.

Grimm's translation of *gængang* is thus perfectly plausible, and can be supported by comparison with other compounds listed in *A Microfiche Concordance to Old English*[14] such as *geanfar, geancyr, ongengang, ongeancyme, ongeanfær, ongeanryne* and *ongængan.* All of these have a sense of 'return'. However, such a reading does not account for the fact that a fine is payable to the king if, and only if, *gængang* occurs. This seems completely inappropriate in the context of either of the suggested interpretations of this word. Other possibilities should be explored.

It seems to me that the most striking parallels are provided by the nonce occurrences *gegnpaþe* and *gaegngeong,* both of which have connotations of violence or opposition. *Gegnpaþe* occurs in one of the *Exeter Book* Riddles and appears to mean the track along which dog and badger travel before meeting to fight.[15] *Gaegngeong* glosses the word *obbiatio,* 'hostile encounter', in the *Durham Ritual* (Durham, Cathedral

[13] A. Campbell, *Old English Grammar* (Oxford, 1959), p. 122.

[14] A. di Paolo Healey and R. L. Venezky, *A Microfiche Concordance to Old English* (Toronto, 1980).

[15] G. P. Krapp and E. van K. Dobbie, *The Exeter Book,* The Anglo-Saxon Poetic Records III (London, 1936), p. 188, Riddle 15 line 26. Dictionary of Old English Project, *Dictionary of Old English A–G.* Version 2.0. CD-ROM, 2008 (hereafter DOE), s.v. *gēan-pæþ*, *gegn-pæþ*, defines as 'hostile path, opposing road'.

MS A.IV.19).[16] Whitelock refers to the gloss in a footnote as though *gaegngeong* were identical with *gængang*;[17] and although this is not actually the case, it is reasonable to assume that the semantic range of the two compounds will be closely similar.

Comparison with *gencyme* may also be useful. In several texts this refers to the coming of Christ; but elsewhere it denotes some form of danger or attack. Thus the Leechbooks offer protection *Wið ealle yfele gencymas* and *Wiþ þ(æt) þu nane yfele gencymas þe ne ondræde,* which Cockayne translates as 'Against all evil gaincomers' and 'That thou may dread no evil gaincomers'.[18] The first of these chapter-headings refers to a charm involving *felt wyrt:*

> Gyf hwa mid hym þysse wyrte ane tealgre byrð ne bið he bregeð mid ænigum ogan ne him wildeor ne dereþ ne ænig yfel geancyme.[19]

I give Cockayne's idiosyncratic translation:

> If one beareth with him one twig of this wort, he will not be terrified with any awe, nor will a wild beast hurt him, or any evil coming near.[20]

The second ascribes similar properties to *wudu þistel*:

Wiþ þ(æt) ðu nane yfele	In order that thou may dread no
geancymas ðe ne ondræde genim	ill gaincomers, take this same
þas ylcan wyrte carduum	wort carduus silvaticus, in early
silfaticum on ærne mergen þonne	morning, when first the sun
seo sunne ærest upgange 7 þ(æt)	upgoeth; and let that be when
sy þonne se mona sy in	the moon is in Capricorn, and

---

[16] Ker, *Catalogue,* no. 106. Facsimile edited by R. J. Brown, Early English Manuscripts in Facsimile 16 (Copenhagen, 1969). The gloss appears on folio 87v line bl4:
latine obbiatio id est antiqui plebis
on læd gaegngeong þæt is ða aldo folcum
I am greatly indebted to Professor Simon Keynes for drawing this to my attention. The last two letters of *gaegngeong* are not visible in the facsimile, nor, due to the tightness of the binding, in the manuscript itself. I therefore rely on the reading presented in the Glossary to the facsimile edition (p.68).

[17] *English Historical Documents*, ed. Whitelock, p. 393, n. 7

[18] T. O. Cockayne, *Leechdoms, Wortcunning, and Starcraft of Early England* (London, 1864) I, 30–31, 44–45. Other manuscripts contain the alternative spelling *gean.*

[19] *Ibid.* 176.

[20] *Ibid.* 177.

capricornu 7heald hy mid þe swa lange swa ðu hy mid þe byrst nan with yfeles þe ongean cymeð.	retain it. As long as thou bearest it with thee, naught of evil cometh against thee.[21]

The latter is of particular interest, demonstrating the relationship between the noun *geancyme* and verb *ongean cyman.* Unfortunately it is not clear from the Leechbooks what these *yfele geancymas* are, or even whether they are corporeal or supernatural; but they appear to represent a source of danger to travellers comparable with the risk of encountering a wild animal.[22] Footpads, perhaps? It may be only a short step from this to a law against *gængang.*

Parallels between Anglo-Saxon and other Germanic law-codes are often illuminating, and may be particularly so in this instance. Early continental codes include references to an act of aggression not apparently represented in the extant Old English laws. This involved blocking the road to someone else, a form of assault to which travellers were vulnerable and which could conceivably underlie the references to *yfele geancymas* in the Leechbooks. Under Lombard law this offence was known as *wegworin* and attracted a heavy penalty. *Rothair's Edict* 27 stipulates twenty *solidi* compensation to a freeman whose road is blocked by another, in addition to payment for any injuries caused. This is the same amount as for a chest wound, and compares with twelve *solidi* for a broken bone, and sixteen for the loss of a front tooth or an index finger. Interestingly, if the offence is committed against a woman, the penalty rockets to 900 *solidi,* half of which is payable to the king (*Rothair's Edict* 26).[23] We may remember that in Æthelberht, ch. 84, the fine is also split between the king and the offended party.

Alamannic law too compensates women at a higher rate than men for *wegalaugen. Pactus Legis Alamannorum* 18 establishes six *solidi* as the penalty for waylaying a free man, twelve *solidi* for a free woman.[24] These again are substantial sums: twelve *solidi* was the price of a thumb or a chest injury, whilst a broken limb might only cost three. Even if committed against a slave, compensation for this crime is set at twenty

---

[21] *Ibid.* 224–225.

[22] DOE, s.v. *gēan-cyme*, published after this essay first appeared, defines the occurrences in the Leechbooks as 'meeting, encounter'.

[23] *Leges Langobardorum*, ed. F. Bluhme, Monumenta Germaniae Historica, Leges 4 (Hanover, 1869).

[24] *Leges Alamannorum*, ed. K. A. Eckhardt, Monumenta Germaniae Historica, Legum Sectio I: Leges nationum Germanicarum 5.1 (Hanover, 1966), p. 26.

solidi (*Rothair's Edict* 28), or three *solidi* (*Pactus Legis Alamannorum* 18,3).

Possibly the closest affinities with Æthelberht's laws are to be found in the code issued by the Frankish king Clovis during the early sixth century.[25] It may therefore be particularly significant that this includes road-blocking in the tariff for personal injuries and insults. *Pactus Legis Salicae* 31 gives the penalty for obstructing a free man as fifteen *solidi,* which is trebled to forty-five *solidi* for a free woman or girl.[26] By comparison, fifteen *solidi* is payable for cutting off an ear (29,14), forty-five *solidi* for libelling a free woman as a prostitute (30,3). Similarly, the laws of the Ripuarian Franks specify a fine of fifteen *solidi* for blocking the road to a free man (*Lex Ribuaria* 83).[27]

I think that we have here a possible parallel with the early Kentish offence of *gængang.* If so, there are two possibilities. One is that Æthelberht, ch. 84 has no connection with the theme of abduction in chs. 82 and 83. There is no manuscript evidence to associate it with the preceding clauses, and its construction may in fact suggest a change of topic. Most of Æthelberht's laws express the passive tense through the impersonal pronoun *man,* a typical opening being *Gif man* ... . The phrasing of ch. 84, *Gif gængang geweorðeþ,* is unlike any other in the code with the notable exception of the personal injury sequence in chs. 33–72. This begins, *Gif feaxfang geweorð,* and continues in similar fashion for the next thirty-nine clauses. The use of an almost identical construction in ch. 84 may indicate that this is another law of the same type rather than a continuation of chs.82 and 83. It is at least a remarkable coincidence that references to *wegworin* and *wegalaugen* in continental codes occur in connection with personal injury tariffs.

The alternative possibility is that Æthelberht, ch. 84 does indeed form a related group with chs. 82 and 83, referring to an abduction aggravated by violence or involving an attack on the open road. Hayashi argues that in

---

25 J. M. Wallace-Hadrill, *Early Germanic Kingship in England and on the Continent* (Oxford, 1971), p. 38, points out that at least nineteen of Æthelberht's laws have parallels in *Lex Salica.*

26 *Pactus Legis Salicae*, ed. K. A. Eckhardt, Monumenta Germaniae Historica, Legum Sectio I: Leges nationum Germanicarum 4.1 (Hanover, 1962), pp. 120–1.

27 F. Beyerle and R. Buchner, *Lex Ribuaria* (Monumenta Germaniae Historica, Legum Sectio I: Leges nationum Germanicarum 3.2 (Hanover, 1954), p. 130. Useful translations of the codes mentioned above may be found in K. F. Drew, *The Lombard Laws* (Philadelphia, PA, 1973); T. J. Rivers, *Laws of the Alamans and Bavarians* (Philadelphia, PA, 1977); and T. J. Rivers, *Laws of the Salian and Ripuarian Franks* (New York, NY, 1986).

continental law, waylaying was regarded as the prelude to rape or assault. Discussing *Lex Salica,* he comments:

> Again, 'interruption of way' (of somebody), of Title 31, deals really with how such rule as social politeness demands, but consists of stipulations punishing acts of this sort as preparatory stages either for robbery ('waylaying') in cases of interrupting the way of a freeman, or for rape in cases of interrupting the way of a woman.[28]

This would certainly explain why the penalty was so much higher in continental codes if the victim was a woman, and it ties in well with the apparent context of Æthelberht, ch. 84.

In conclusion, it is worth noting an entry in the *Middle English Dictionary.* One of the meanings of the verb *ayen-stonden* is given as 'To be firmly lodged; block (someone's) way, obstruct'.[29] I suggest that the early usage of *gængang* in Æthelberht, ch. 84, should be construed along similar lines.[30]

---

[28] H. Hayashi, 'The Lost Laws of Anglo-Saxon Kings. Part 2: Some Observations on the Nature of Anglo-Saxon Laws (1)', *Gakushuin Review of Law and Politics* 25 (1990), 147–215, at 206.

[29] H. Kurath and S. M. Kuhn, *Middle English Dictionary* (Ann Arbor, 1956), I, 593.

[30] I presented an earlier version of this paper at a workshop organised by the Research Group on Manuscript Evidence at the Parker Library, Corpus Christi College, Cambridge, and have profited from the comments and advice of those present, including Christine Fell, Ray Page and Patrick Wormald. I am also grateful to Simon Keynes for reading this through and making helpful suggestions. DOE, s.v. *gēan-gang*, published after this essay first appeared, explains the occurrence in the Durham Ritual gloss as 'meeting, encounter', and offers the following summary of possible interpretations for the occurrence in Æthelberht 84: 'legal term of uncertain meaning, with interpretations based on whether or not the sentence is interpreted as independent of, or a continuation of, the preceding two sentences; if the sentence is independent, suggestions include '(the offence of) waylaying (on the open road)'; if the sentence is a continuation, 'attack, fight (on the open road)' related to an abduction mentioned earlier; or 'return (of an abducted woman to her guardian or fiancé)'; or 'meeting (between an abductor and a woman who came willingly to meet him)'.

9.

A RECONSIDERATION OF INE, CH. 23: WITH A NOTE ON *JULIANA*, LINE 242A

First published 1997: *Neuphilologische Mitteilungen* 98, 43–51.

The law-code issued by King Ine of Wessex towards the end of the seventh century survives only as an appendix to the great *domboc* compiled by Alfred the Great some two centuries later.[1] It is therefore uncertain whether the extant text of Ine's laws represents the original code in its entirety or is a selection edited by Alfred. Current scholarly opinion tends towards the former view. Drawing attention to various discrepancies between Ine's code and that of Alfred himself, for instance, Keynes and Lapidge comment: 'The fact that such discrepancies were allowed to stand suggests that the received text of Ine's code was respected, and was not edited by Alfred to suit his own purposes'.[2] This does not of course mean that Ine's code has survived in its original form. Many changes might already have taken place in the two centuries preceding Alfred's reign, and indeed there are a number of indications that this was so. Attenborough notes that 'the language of the laws of Ine has been brought into conformity with that of Alfred's time in regard to the form of words, though not to the same extent in syntax and vocabulary',[3] while Richardson and Sayles identify a block of clauses from Ine, chs. 55–69 which are in a laconic style out of keeping with the rest of the code, commenting: 'The contrast in styles is so marked that the inference seems justified that there has been an amalgamation of two or more texts

[1] M. P. Richards, 'The Manuscript Contexts of the Old English Laws: Tradition and Innovation', *Studies in Earlier Old English Prose*, ed. P. E. Szarmach (Albany, NY, 1986), pp. 171–92.
[2] S. Keynes and M. Lapidge, *Alfred the Great: Asser's 'Life of King Alfred' and Other Contemporary Sources* (Harmondsworth, 1983), p. 311.
[3] *The Laws of the Earliest English Kings*, ed. F. L. Attenborough (Cambridge, 1922), p. 35.

of different dates and perhaps of different origin'.[4] Less attention has as yet been paid to the integrity of individual clauses within the extant code. The purpose of this article is to examine a single clause, Ine, ch. 23,[5] and to discuss problems relating both to interpretation and to textual transmission.

The full text of Ine, ch. 23 survives in three manuscripts. Cambridge, Corpus Christi College MS 173, dates from the mid-tenth century, while the *Textus Roffensis* (Maidstone, Kent Archives Office, DRc/R1) and Cambridge, Corpus Christi College MS 383, both date from the early twelfth. The opening section of the clause is also preserved in British Library, Burney MS 277, dating from the early eleventh century, and there is a Latin version in the *Quadripartitus*, a legal compilation dating from the twelfth. The following text is from Cambridge, Corpus Christi College MS 173, generally considered the most reliable of the extant witnesses:

> Be elðeodies monnes slege.
>
> 23. Gif mon elðeodigne ófslea, se cyning ah twædne dǽl weres, þriddan dæl sunu oððe mægas.
> 23,1. Gif he ðonne mægleas sie, healf kyninge, healf se gesið.
> 23,2. Gif hit ðonne abbod sie oððe abbodesse, dælen on þa ilcan wisan wið þone kyning.
> 23,3. Wealh gafolgelda CXX scill., his sunu C, ðeowne LX, somhwelcne fiftegum; Weales hyd twelfum.[6]

The standard translation is provided by Whitelock:

> 23. If a foreigner is slain, the king has two-thirds of the wergild, his son or kinsmen the third part.
> 23.1. If, however, he is without kinsmen, half [goes to] the king, half to the *gesith*.
> 23.2. If, however, it is an abbot or an abbess, they are to share in the same way with the king.
> 23.3. A Welsh rent-payer [has a wergild of] 120 shillings, his son, 100; a slave [is to be paid for with] 60, some with 50; a Welshman's hide with 12 [shillings].[7]

---

[4] H. G. Richardson and G. O. Sayles, *Law and Legislation from Æthelberht to Magna Carta* (Edinburgh, 1966), p. 15.
[5] I follow the numbering system printed in square brackets in the standard edition of the Anglo-Saxon laws, *Die Gesetze der Angelsachsen*, ed. F. Liebermann, 3 vols. (Halle, 1903–16). This is not the same as the manuscript numbering.
[6] *Gesetze*, ed. Liebermann I, 22, 98, 100.
[7] *English Historical Documents c. 500–1042*, ed. D. Whitelock, 2nd ed. (London, 1979), p. 401.

It has often been pointed out that the final provision is not wholly consistent with the terms of Ine, ch. 32, where a slightly different scale of valuation is presented:

32. Gif Wilisc mon hæbbe hide londes, his wer bið CXX scill.; gif he þonne healfes hæbbe, LXXX scill.; gif he nænig hæbbe, LX scillinga.[8]	32. If a Welshman has a hide of land, his wergild is 120 shillings; if, however, he has a half hide, 80 shillings; if he has none, 60 shillings.[9]

The implications of this are difficult to assess, although it is possible as Attenborough suggests that the discrepancy 'may point to a composite origin... or to additions having been made after the time of Ine'.[10] More surprising are internal inconsistencies within the text of Ine, ch. 23 itself, which have hitherto attracted little discussion. This article will attempt to define these inconsistencies, and to explore their implications.

It is necessary to begin by outlining the interpretive difficulties surrounding this clause. Ine, ch. 23 is of immediate interest to students of women's history, since the linking of *abbod* and *abbodesse* in ch. 23,2 suggests that the abbess ranked equally with her male counterpart. Indeed, it is often taken to indicate that an abbess was entitled to claim part of the *wergild* for a foreigner towards whom she had acted as protector. Fell notes that 'This law belongs to the end of the seventh century, the period in which the great double foundations in charge of abbesses were being constructed', and adds: 'It is the first clear statement in the laws of a woman's right to receive *wergild* for those under her protection'.[11] Unfortunately the issues are less clear-cut than this statement implies. Firstly, the antecedent of *hit* in ch. 23,2 is ambiguous. It may indeed be the word *gesið*, as most editors assume: alternatively, however, the pronoun could refer to the victim of the crime. Liebermann discusses the latter possibility, pointing out that the abbot or abbess could be regarded as having become *mægleas* through leaving their kin-group to enter religious orders.[12] The interpretation is supported by later Anglo-Saxon laws linking together foreigners and members of the clergy. VIII Æthelred, chs. 33 and 34, for instance, state that compensation is

[8] *Gesetze*, ed. Liebermann I, 102.
[9] *English Historical Documents*, ed. Whitelock, p. 402.
[10] *The Laws*, ed. Attenborough, p. 185.
[11] C. E. Fell et al., *Women in Anglo-Saxon England and the Impact of 1066* (London, 1984), p. 123.
[12] *Gesetze*, ed. Liebermann III, 72.

payable to the king for injuries either to foreigners or to those in religious orders:

33. And gif man gehadodne oððe ælþeodigne man þurh ænig þinc forræde æt feo oððe æt feore, oððe hine bænde oððe hine beate oððe gebismrige on ǽnige wisan, þonne sceal him cyngc beon for mæg 7 for mundboran, buton he elles oðerne hæbbe.	33. And if a man in holy orders or a foreigner is for any reason defrauded of property or of life, or is bound or beaten or insulted in any way, the king shall then be for him in the place of a kinsman and protector, unless otherwise he has another.
34. And bete man ægðer ge him ge þam cynge, swa swa hit gebirige, be þam þe séo dæd sy, oððe he ða dæde wrece swiðe deope.[13]	34. And compensation is to be paid both to him and to the king, as is fitting, in proportion to the deed, or he is to avenge the deed very severely.[14]

The ruling is repeated in II Cnut, ch. 40, and may well have implications for the interpretation of Ine, ch. 23,2. But there is a more serious difficulty with this sub-clause. However it is to be understood, the plural verb *dælen* is out of place. Whitelock's translation 'they are to share' glosses over the fact that only one person – whether the *gesið*, the abbot, or the abbess – is actually to share the *wergild* with the king. The verb should therefore be singular. It is also puzzling that whereas the abbot and abbess are ostensibly singled out for special treatment, the terms stated in ch. 23,2 are no different from those generally applicable under ch. 23,1: an equal division of *wergild* applies in each case. This element of superfluity is totally out of keeping with the usually concise expression of the Old English law-codes. Despite the unanimity of the extant manuscripts, the reading can scarcely be original.

A further problem with the traditional interpretation of Ine, ch. 23 is that the basis on which the abbot or abbess may be able to claim a share in the deceased's *wergild* is not entirely clear. It depends on the meaning of *gesið*, a word whose semantic range in this context is far from certain. Attenborough translates as 'magnate', explaining in a note that it refers to 'the man under whose protection he has been',[15] and this interpretation is

[13] *Ibid.* I, 267.
[14] *English Historical Documents*, ed. Whitelock, p. 451.
[15] *The Laws*, ed. Attenborough, pp. 43, 185.

followed by Whitelock[16] and Fell.[17] If correct, this would indeed indicate that an abbess no less than an abbot was able to act as protector towards visiting foreigners, with important implications for the legal standing of women at this period. However, there are few if any precedents for such a reading. The simplex term *gesið* is recorded elsewhere in Ine's laws only in ch. 50, where it refers to social class:

50. Gif gesiðcund mon þingað wið cyning oððe wið kyninges ealdormonnan for his inhiwan oððe wið his hlaford for ðeowe oððe for frige, nah he þær nane witerædenne, se gesið, forðon he him nolde ær yflcs gestieran æt ham.[18]	50. If a *gesith-born* man intercedes with the king or the king's ealdorman or with his lord for members of his household, slaves or freemen, he, the *gesith*, has no right to any fines, because he would not previously at home restrain them from wrongdoing.[19]

The compounds *gesiðcund* and *gesiðmon* also occur in Ine, chs. 30, 45, 51, 54, 63 and 68, and again are used consistently to designate a particular rank in society. Ine, chs. 30, 51 and 54 contrast the ranks of *gesið* and *ceorl*:

30. Gif mon cierliscne monnan fliemanfeorme teo, be his agnum were geladige he hine; gif he ne mæge, gielde hine his agne were; 7 se gesiðmon swa be his were.[20]	30. If a *ceorl* is accused of harbouring fugitives, he is to exculpate himself by [an oath of the amount of] his own wergild; if he cannot, he is to pay for [harbouring] him his own wergild; and the man of *gesith* rank similarly by his wergild.[21]
51. Gif gesiðcund mon landagende forsitte fierd, geselle CXX scill. 7 ðolie his landes; unlandagende LX scill.; cierlisc XXX scill. to fierdwite.[22]	51. If a *gesith-born* man, who owns land, neglects military service, he is to give 120 shillings and to forfeit his land; one who owns no land, 60 shillings, a *ceorl* 30 shillings, as

[16] *English Historical Documents*, ed. Whitelock, p. 401 n.4.
[17] Fell et al., *Women in Anglo-Saxon England and the Impact of 1066*, p. 123.
[18] *Gesetze*, ed. Liebermann I, 110, 112.
[19] *English Historical Documents*, ed. Whitelock, p. 404.
[20] *Gesetze*, ed. Liebermann I, 102.
[21] *English Historical Documents*, ed. Whitelock, p. 402.
[22] *Gesetze*, ed. Liebermann I, 112.

fine for [neglect of] military service.[23]

54. Se þe bið werfæhðe betogen 7 he onsacan wille þæs sleges mid aðe, þonne sceal bion on þære hyndenne an kyningæde be XXX hida, swa be gesiðcundum men swa be cierliscum, swa hwæþer swa hit sie.[24]

54. He who is accused of homicide, and wishes to deny the slaying with an oath – then there shall be in the hundred [hides] a man entitled to swear a king's oath at 30 hides, both in the case of a *gesith-born* man or a *ceorl*, whichever it be.[25]

Ine, ch. 45 gives a scale of compensation for house-breaking according to the rank of the victim:

45. Burgbryce mon sceal betan CXX scill. kyninges 7 biscepes, þær his rice bið; ealdormonnes LXXX scill.; cyninges ðegnes LX scill.; gesiðcundes monnes landhæbbendes XXXV; 7 bi ðon ansacan.[26]

45. Forcible entry into the residence of the king or the bishop, within his own diocese, one shall compensate with 120 shillings; [into that] of an ealdorman, with 80 shillings; [into that] of a king's thegn, with 60 shillings; [into that] of a *gesith-born* man who owns land, with 35 shillings; and deny it correspondingly.[27]

So too Ine, chs. 63 and 68 use the term *gesiðcund* with reference to social class:

63. Gif gesiðcund mon fare, þonne mot he habban his gerefan mid him 7 his smið 7 his cildfestran.[28]

63. If a *gesith-born* man moves elsewhere, he may then have with him his reeve and his smith and his children's nurse.[29]

[23] *English Historical Documents*, ed. Whitelock, p. 404.
[24] *Gesetze*, ed. Liebermann I, 112, 114.
[25] *English Historical Documents*, ed. Whitelock, p. 405.
[26] *Gesetze*, ed. Liebermann I, 108.
[27] *English Historical Documents*, ed. Whitelock, p. 404.
[28] *Gesetze*, ed. Liebermann I, 118.
[29] *English Historical Documents*, ed. Whitelock, p. 406.

68. Gif mon gesiðcundne monnan adrife, fordrife þy botle, næs þære setene.[30]	68. If a *gesith-born* man is evicted, he is to be evicted from the dwelling, but certainly not from the cultivated land.[31]

Elsewhere in legal texts, *gesið* and its compounds occur only in ch. 11 of *Norðleoda Laga*, a tenth-century compilation primarily concerned with status, and in ch. 5 of the late-seventh-century laws of King Wihtred of Kent, whose code is roughly contemporary with that of Ine himself.[32] The relevant sections read as follows:

11. And gif his sunu 7 his sunu sunu þæt geþeoð, þæt hi swa micel landes habban, siððan bið se ofsprinc gesiðcundes cynnes be twam þusendum.[33]	11. And if his son and his son's son prosper, so that they have so much land, then the offspring is of *gesith-born* class, at 2,000 [*thrymsas*].[34]
5. Gif ðæs geweorþe gesiþcundne mannan ofer þis gemot, þæt he unriht hæmed genime ofer cyngæs bebod 7 biscopes 7 boca dom, se þæt gebete his dryhtne C scll' an ald reht.	5. If after this meeting, any *gesith-born* man chooses to enter into an illicit union in spite of the command of the king and the bishop and the decree of the books, he is to pay to his lord 100 shillings according to ancient law.
5,1. Gif his ceorlisc man sie, gebete L scll'; 7 gehwæder þæt hæmed mid hreowe forlæte.[35]	5,1. If it is a *ceorl*, he is to pay 50 shillings; and both of them are to abandon the union, with repentance.[36]

Again, the frame of reference is social class, and there are no documented occurrences of *gesið* in relation to protection.

In non-legal contexts, the most usual meaning of *gesið* is 'companion, comrade', as in *Beowulf*, line 29:

---

[30] *Gesetze*, ed. Liebermann I, 118.

[31] *English Historical Documents*, ed. Whitelock, p. 406.

[32] A. diP. Healey and R. L. Venezky, *A Microfiche Concordance to Old English* (Toronto, 1980), was invaluable as a tool for tracing occurrences of *gesið* and its compounds.

[33] *Gesetze*, ed. Liebermann I, 460.

[34] *English Historical Documents*, ed. Whitelock, p. 470.

[35] *Gesetze*, ed. Liebermann I, 12.

[36] *English Historical Documents*, ed. Whitelock, p. 397.

> Hī hyne þā ætbǣron tō brimes faroðe,
> swǣse gesīþas, swæ hē selfa bæd,...[37]

> They who were his dear comrades then carried him to the seashore as he had himself commanded...[38]

Toller gives an extensive list of examples, including the occurrence in Ine, ch. 23, which he translates as 'if one slay a foreigner, if he be kinless, half the king [has], half the companion'.[39] His reading is followed by Liebermann, who draws attention to a parallel with the phrase *þam gegildan* in Alfred, ch. 28.[40] The latter clause directs that if a man without relatives is killed, the *wergild* is to be divided between the king and the deceased's companions:

28. Gif mon swa geradne mon ofslea, gif he mægas nage, gielde mon healfne cyninge, healfne þam gegildan.[41]	28. If anyone kills a man so placed, if he has no kinsmen, he is to pay half to the king, half to the associates.[42]

The situation here is very similar to that described in Ine, ch. 23. As in Ine, ch. 23,1, inheritance is in default of kin, and in both instances there is a two-way split with the king. There must therefore be a strong possibility that *gesið* in Ine, ch. 23 functions in a similar way to *gegilda* in Alfred, ch. 28.

Liebermann's suggestion has received little scholarly support. Fell ignores it altogether,[43] while Whitelock comments that Attenborough's interpretation 'makes better sense of the next clause'.[44] There is, however, a logistic difficulty with their reading. If the term *gesið* refers to a protector, it is illogical for him or her to receive a share of the *wergild* only if there are no surviving relatives. Compensation for a man under one's protection should on the contrary be payable irrespective of the inheritance rights of the kin-group. It makes much better sense for the

---

[37] Fr. Klaeber, *Beowulf and The Fight at Finnsburg*, 3rd ed. (Lexington, MA, 1950), p. 2.
[38] S. A. J. Bradley, *Anglo-Saxon Poetry* (London, 1982), p. 412.
[39] *An Anglo-Saxon Dictionary Based on the Manuscript Collections of the Late Joseph Bosworth*, ed. T. N. Toller (Oxford, 1898), p. 442, s.v. *ge-síþ*.
[40] *Gesetze*, ed. Liebermann III, 72.
[41] *Ibid.* I, 66.
[42] *English Historical Documents*, ed. Whitelock, p. 413.
[43] Fell et al., *Women in Anglo-Saxon England and the Impact of 1066*, p. 123.
[44] *English Historical Documents*, ed. Whitelock, p. 401 n.4.

relatives' share to devolve to a close associate of the dead man. Bearing in mind therefore that the meaning 'protector' is unattested elsewhere in the extant corpus of Old English whereas the meaning 'companion' is securely established, it seems to me that the balance of probability is very much in favour of Liebermann's interpretation.

Finally, I wish to draw attention to certain anomalies in the text of Ine, ch. 23 which lead me to suspect that the received version may be corrupt. Two points already mentioned are the plural form of the verb *dælen* in ch. 23,2 and the fact that the allocation of *wergild* in this sub-clause is the same as in ch. 23,1. Another suspicious feature is the lack of grammatical concord between the two phrases placed in apposition in ch. 23,1. Whereas the word *kyninge* has a dative singular inflection, *se gesið* is clearly nominative. This is difficult to account for. Thorpe emends to *kyningc*, commenting that this is 'undoubtedly the true reading',[45] but since the form does not occur in any of the extant manuscripts, his confidence may be misplaced. The *Textus Roffensis* has *cyninge*, again with a dative inflection, while Cambridge, Corpus Christi College 383, where the text is often inferior, has the uninflected form *cyning*. The reading *se gesið* is common to all three extant manuscripts.

The most peculiar aspect of Ine, ch. 23, however, lies in the fact that according to ch. 23,1, the proportion of *wergild* due to the king is reduced from two-thirds to a half if the deceased had no relatives. Logically, the reverse should be the case, for since the *gesið* inherits only in default of kin, it is wholly inappropriate for him or her to receive more than would have fallen to the *mægas*. Something must be wrong.

It is noticeable that three of the four anomalies identified above focus on Ine, ch. 23,1. This is where the grammar goes awry, where information given in ch. 23,2 is pre-empted, and where the illogical division of *wergild* occurs. I suggest therefore that Ine, ch. 23,1 has been miscopied at an early stage of textual transmission, and that the original reading may have allocated a majority share of the *wergild* to the king. Since the extant manuscripts are substantially in agreement, it would appear that the text available to Alfred towards the end of the ninth century was already defective, and this may have serious implications also for the integrity of other clauses within Ine's code.

---

45 *Ancient Laws and Institutes of England*, ed. B. Thorpe, folio edition (London, 1840), p. 51.

Appendix: A Note on *Juliana*, Line 242a

The above discussion of Ine, ch. 23 notes that OE *gesið*, a term crucial to the interpretation of this clause, is otherwise unrecorded with the meaning 'protector'. There is, however, one occurrence where such an interpretation, though not previously suggested, would make very good sense. Lines 238b–242a of the poem *Juliana* in the Exeter Book read as follows:

Symle heo wuldorcyning
herede æt heortan, heofonrices god,
in þam nydclafan, nergend fira,
heolstre bihelmad. Hyre wæs halig gæst
singal gesið.[1]

The word *gesið* in line 242a is usually taken to mean 'companion', as in Bradley's translation:

> Constantly she praised the King of glory in her heart, the God of the heaven-kingdom within that place of confinement and the Saviour of men, enveloped in darkness. To her the Holy Ghost was a constant companion.[2]

So too Woolf's standard edition of the poem gives 'companion' as the glossary definition for *gesīð*.[3] However, the context would support an alternative interpretation. At this point in the poem, Juliana is in prison, undergoing a selection of the usual torments inflicted on female saints in hagiographical literature. In two previous speeches, she has declared her trust in God as her *mundbora* 'protector':

'Næfre þu gelærest þæt ic leasingum,
dumbum ond deafum deofolgieldum,
gæste geniðlum gaful onhate,
þam wyrrestum wites þegnum,
ac ic weorðige wuldres ealdor
middangeardes ond mægenþrymmes,
ond him anum to eal biþence,
þæt he mundbora min geweorþe,
helpend ond hælend wið hellsceaþum.'[4] (lines 149–57)

---

[1] B. J. Muir, *The Exeter Anthology of Old English Poetry: An Edition of Exeter Dean and Chapter MS 3501*, 2 vols. (Exeter, 1994) I, 199.
[2] S. A. J. Bradley, *Anglo-Saxon Poetry* (London, 1982), p. 308.
[3] R. Woolf, *Juliana* (New York, 1966), p. 78.
[4] Muir, *The Exeter Anthology of Old English Poetry* I, 196.

'Never shall you teach me to offer oblations to spurious things, to dumb and deaf devil-images, to the soul's enemies, to the worst ministrants of torment, but I honour the glorious Lord of earth and of the heavenly host and in him alone I put my whole trust that he shall be my protector, my helper and my saviour against hell-fiends.'[5]

'Ne ondræde ic me domas þine,
awyrged womsceaða, ne þinra wita bealo.
Hæbbe ic me to hyhte heofonrices weard,
mildne mundboran, mægna waldend,
se mec gescyldeð wið þinum scinlace
of gromra gripe, þe þu to godum tiohhast...'[6] (lines 210–5)

'I do not fear your judgments, you condemned sinner, nor the hurt of your tortures: I have as my hope the Guardian of heaven, the merciful Protector, the Lord of hosts, who will shield me against your delusion and from the clutches of the demons whom you regard as gods...'[7]

It would therefore be dramatically appropriate for the Holy Spirit to be described as Juliana's 'protector' in prison. The traditional rendering 'companion' is perfectly acceptable, and may well be correct. But an alternative translation 'protector' would give a stronger sense in the context.

[5] Bradley, *Anglo-Saxon Poetry*, p. 306.
[6] Muir, *The Exeter Anthology of Old English Poetry* I, 198.
[7] Bradley, *Anglo-Saxon Poetry*, p. 307.

10.

ALFRED'S *DOMBOC* AND THE LANGUAGE OF RAPE: A RECONSIDERATION OF ALFRED, CH. 11

First published 1997: *Medium Ævum* 66, 1–27.

The great *domboc* issued by Alfred the Great towards the end of the ninth century represents an important source of information on both social and legal traditions in early Anglo-Saxon England. It comprises a collection of his own laws to which are appended the late-seventh-century laws of King Ine of Wessex, and is generally attributed to the latter part of Alfred's reign (871–99).[1] A more precise dating is difficult to establish: Liebermann suggested 892–3,[2] while, more recently, Simon Keynes and Michael Lapidge comment that the code 'was probably drawn up in the late 880s or early 890s'.[3] No previous legislation survives from any of the early Anglo-Saxon kingdoms except Kent, where the seventh-century codes of Kings Æthelberht, Hlothhere and Eadric, and Wihtred, offer some fascinating but fragmentary insights into local practice.[4] Alfred, whose

---

[1] *English Historical Documents c. 500–1042*, ed. D. Whitelock, 2nd ed. (London, 1979), p. 407, comments: 'The code was probably issued late in his [Alfred's] reign'.

[2] *Die Gesetze der Angelsachsen*, ed. F. Liebermann, 3 vols. (Halle, 1903–16) III, 34.

[3] S. Keynes and M. Lapidge, *Alfred the Great: Asser's 'Life of King Alfred' and Other Contemporary Sources* (Harmondsworth, 1983), p. 163.

[4] All three are preserved only in the early-twelfth-century *Textus Roffensis* manuscript (Maidstone, Kent Archives Office, DRc/R1). It is unknown how much legislation has been lost from the early Anglo-Saxon kingdoms, but at least two codes are no longer extant. In *Historia ecclesiastica gentis Anglorum*, III, viii, Bede describes laws issued to enforce the Christian religion by Æthelberht's grandson Eorcenberht, who ruled from 640 to 664 (*Bede's Ecclesiastical History of the English People*, ed. B. Colgrave and R. A. B. Mynors (Oxford, 1969), pp. 236–7), while the Preface to Alfred's *domboc*, ch. 49,9, names Offa of Mercia

laws are described by Stenton as 'the great code with which the continuity of English legislation begins',[5] was the first English ruler to legislate for the country as a whole,[6] and in ch. 49,9 of the Preface to his *domboc*, he claims to bring together the legal systems of Kent and Mercia as well as of Wessex:

Ic ða Ælfred cyning þás togædere gegaderode 7 awritan het, monege þara þe ure foregengan heoldon, ða ðe me licodon; 7 manege þara þe me ne licodon ic áwearp mid minra witena geðeahte, 7 on oðre wisan bebead to healdanne. Forðam ic ne dorste geðristlæcan þara minra awuht fela on gewrit settan, forðam me wæs uncuð, hwæt þæs ðam lician wolde ðe æfter ús wæren. Ac ða ðe ic gemette awðer oððe on Ines dæge, mines mæges, oððe on Offan Mercna cyninges oððe on Æþelbryhtes, þe ærest fulluhte onfeng on Angelcynne, þa ðe me ryhtoste ðuhton, ic þa heron gegaderode, 7 þa oðre forlét.[7]	Then I, King Alfred, collected these together and ordered to be written many of them which our forefathers observed, those which I liked; and many of those which I did not like I rejected with the advice of my councillors, and ordered them to be differently observed. For I dared not presume to set in writing at all many of my own, because it was unknown to me what would please those who should come after us. But those which I found, which seemed to me most just, either in the time of my kinsman, King Ine, or of Offa, king of the Mercians, or of Ethelbert, who first among the English received baptism, I collected herein, and omitted the others.[8]

---

alongside Æthelberht of Kent and Ine of Wessex as one of Alfred's legislative models. However, a Latin capitulary of 786 provides an important source of evidence on Mercian legislation; and, indeed, it has recently been suggested that the text of Offa's laws to which Alfred refers may have been not a vernacular code but the capitulary itself (P. Wormald, 'In Search of King Offa's "Law-code"', *People and Places in Northern Europe 500–1600: Essays in Honour of Peter Hayes Sawyer*, ed. I. Wood and N. Lund, (Woodbridge, 1991), pp. 25–45).

[5] F. M. Stenton, *Anglo-Saxon England*, 3rd ed. (Oxford, 1971), p. 72.

[6] An alternative view is expressed by D. A. E. Pelteret, who believes that the description of Alfred as *Westseaxna cyning* in the Preface, ch. 49,10 'is important because it implies that his was not a national code but one that had application only to West-Saxon territory' (*Slavery in Early Mediaeval England: From the Reign of Alfred Until the Twelfth Century* (Woodbridge, 1995), p. 81). As Keynes and Lapidge point out, however, Alfred himself 'seems to be conscious of a wider conception of his position', and 'thought of himself as successor to all three traditions of royal legislation' (*Alfred the Great*, p. 39).

[7] *Gesetze*, ed. Liebermann I, 46. All quotations from Anglo-Saxon law are taken

Not all pronouncements by Anglo-Saxon kings can be taken at face value, however, and it is doubtful to what extent Alfred actually did incorporate other laws into the West Saxon *domboc*. There are no documented instances of direct borrowing between Alfred and earlier legislators, as there are, for instance, between Cnut and Æthelred during the later Anglo-Saxon period.[9] Although the personal injury tariff in Alfred, chs. 44–77 may have been inspired by the corresponding section of Æthelberht's code (chs. 33–72),[10] the differences between the two sequences are too substantial for a close link to be envisaged;[11] while scholarly attempts to identify Mercian features in Alfred's laws have not met with success.[12] Alfred's claim is more plausibly to be interpreted as a powerful statement of political unity than as a factual account of legislative methodology.

The importance of the *domboc* is attested by the number of extant manuscripts. The earliest is Cambridge, Corpus Christi College, MS 173, dating from the mid-tenth century, but complete copies also survive in two twelfth-century legal collections, the *Textus Roffensis* (Maidstone, Kent Archives Office, DRc/R1), and the Latin *Quadripartitus*. Incomplete versions appear in London, British Library, MS Cotton Otho B.xi, dating from the early eleventh century, and in Cambridge, Corpus Christi College, MS 383, dating from the early twelfth. The mid-eleventh-century London, British Library, MS Cotton Nero A.i, contains the *capitula* and

---

from this edition unless otherwise stated.

[8] *English Historical Documents*, ed. Whitelock, pp. 408–9.

[9] It has long been recognised that the laws of both Æthelred and Cnut were drafted by Archbishop Wulfstan. See esp. D. Whitelock, 'Wulfstan and the Laws of Cnut', *English Historical Review* 63 (1948), 433–52.

[10] *Councils and Synods With Other Documents Relating to the English Church: I A.D. 871–1204*, ed. D. Whitelock, M. Brett and C. N. L. Brooke, Part I: *871–1066* (Oxford, 1981), p. 18, comment 'From the laws of Æthelberht he [Alfred] got the idea of including a detailed list of compensations for injuries'; while Keynes and Lapidge agree that Æthelberht's schedule 'clearly served as the model for the tariff in Alfred's code' (*Alfred the Great*, p. 310).

[11] Alfred's tariff is much more comprehensive than that attributed to Æthelberht. It is also differently ordered, is based on the West Saxon monetary system, and betrays no obvious verbal dependence on the Kentish model. Since personal injury tariffs are a feature common to many early Germanic law-codes, it is fully possible that Alfred's could derive from another source. A detailed comparative analysis of the personal injury tariffs in Germanic law, which appeared since this essay was first published, is L. Oliver, *The Body Legal in Barbarian Law* (Toronto, 2011).

[12] Arguments for a Mercian element in Alfred's code are summarized and refuted by Wormald, 'In Search of…', pp. 27–8.

the beginning of the introduction only; and the first part of Ine's laws is also preserved in London, British Library, MS Burney 277, dating from *c.* 1030.[13] In all manuscripts, chapter headings for both codes appear together at the beginning, and the numbering for Ine's laws follows on consecutively from those of Alfred, the complete collection being divided into 120 chapters.[14]

The relationship of any of the early law-codes to actual practice in Anglo-Saxon England is highly uncertain. Modern historians have established that the purpose of much early medieval legislation was not for practical use in a court of law, but to enhance the public image of the king.[15] In particular, there are a number of discrepancies between Alfred's own laws and those of Ine that suggest that the composite *domboc* was not designed to be applied in a court of law. For instance, the fine for *burhbryce* 'forced entry' is assessed differently in Alfred, ch. 40[16] and Ine, ch. 45.[17] Under Ine, a bishop was entitled to compensation of 120 shillings, the same as a king, while an ealdorman was entitled to 80 shillings. Under Alfred, both bishop and ealdorman received 60 shillings, only half as much as the king. Similarly, the felling of trees calls forth different penalties in Alfred, ch. 12[18] and Ine, ch. 43,[19] and there

---

[13] Parallel texts from all extant manuscripts of the *domboc* are printed in *Gesetze*, ed. Liebermann I, 16–123, with notes on the manuscripts themselves at I, xviii-xlii, and a diagrammatical stemma at III, 32. A cogent discussion of manuscript history is provided in M. P. Richards, 'The manuscript contexts of the Old English laws: tradition and innovation', *Studies in Earlier Old English Prose*, ed. P. E. Szarmach (Albany, NY, 1986), pp. 171–92.

[14] The number 120 symbolises canon law, being the age at which Moses died and the number of members of the early Church. Its significance in the context of the *domboc* is discussed in P. Wormald, '*Lex Scripta* and *Verbum Regis*: Legislation and Germanic Kingship, from Euric to Cnut', *Early Medieval Kingship*, ed. P. H. Sawyer and I. N. Wood, (Leeds, 1977), pp. 105–38 (p. 132).

[15] See esp. Wormald, '*Lex Scripta* and *Verbum Regis*'. With specific reference to Alfred's *domboc*, Keynes and Lapidge, *Alfred the Great*, p. 39, comment: 'the law-code was evidently intended to be more than a collection of pronouncements on matters of current concern to the king. The act of law-making was a public display of a king's royal power, and provided an opportunity for him to express his political and ideological aspirations in legal form'.

[16] Cyninges burgbryce bið CXX scill., ærcebiscepes hundnigontig scill., oðres biscepes 7 ealdormonnes LX scill., twelfhyndes monnes XXX scill., syxhyndes monnes XV scill.; ceorles edorbryce V scill.

[17] Burgbryce mon sceal betan CXX scill. kyninges 7 biscepes, þær his rice bið; ealdormonnes LXXX scill.; cyninges ðegnes LX scill.; gesiðcundes monnes landhæbbendes XXXV; 7 bi ðon ansacan.

[18] For Alfred, ch. 12, see p. 188 below.

are different rules relating to sanctuary in Alfred, ch. 2[20] and Ine, ch. 5.[21] These anomalies indicate that the *domboc* may not represent a reliable guide to contemporary legal practice but they detract little from its essential value to the historian. Although Alfred's purpose appears to have been political rather than primarily legislative, the compilation is none the less a crucial source-document for the study of ninth-century England. As Keynes and Lapidge point out, it not only presents 'a dramatic assertion of his [Alfred's] role as the shepherd and guardian of an amalgamated English people', but 'affords valuable evidence of those matters which the king considered to be of particular importance for ensuring social and political order'.[22]

Several clauses within the *domboc* relate directly to women, and these are of special significance in reflecting the role and status of women in early English society. Ine, chs. 7 and 57 define the limits of a married woman's responsibility for a theft committed by her husband;[23] Ine, ch. 23 treats an abbess on the same terms as an abbot;[24] Ine, ch. 31 deals with

---

[19] 43. Đonne mon beam on wuda forbærne, 7 weorðe yppe on þone ðe hit dyde, gielde he fulwite: geselle LX scill.; forþamþe fýr bið þeof.
43,1. Gif mon afelle on wuda wel monega treowa, 7 wyrð eft undierne, forgielde III treowu ælc mid XXX scill.; ne ðearf he hiora má geldan, wære hiora swa fela swa hiora wære: forþon sio ǽsc bið melda, nalles ðeof.

[20] 2. Gif hwa þara mynsterhama hwelcne for hwelcere scylde gesece, þe cyninges feorm to belimpe, oððe oðerne frione hiered þe árwyrðe sie, age he þreora nihta fierst him to gebeorganne, buton he ðingian wille.
2,1. Gif hine mon on ðam fierste geyflige mid slege oððe mid bende oððe þurh wunde, bete þara æghwelc mid ryhte ðeodscipe, ge mid were ge mid wite, 7 þam hiwum hundtwelftig scill. ciricfriðes to bote 7 næbbe his agne forfongen.

[21] 5. Gif hwa sie deaðes scyldig 7 he cirican geierne, hæbbe his feorh 7 bete, swa him ryht wisige.
5,1. Gif hwa his hyde forwyrce 7 cirican geierne, sie him sio swingelle forgifen.

[22] Keynes and Lapidge, *Alfred the Great*, p. 39.

[23] Be stale.
7. Gif hwa stalie, swa his wif nyte 7 his bearn, geselle LX scill. to wite.
7,1. Gif he ðonne stalie on gewitnesse ealles his hiredes, gongen hie ealle on ðeowot.
7,2. X wintre cniht mæg bion ðiefðe gewita.
For Ine, ch. 57, see p. 179–80 below.

[24] Be elðeodies monnes slege.
23. Gif mon elðeodigne ófslea, se cyning ah twædne dǽl weres, þriddan dæl sunu oððe mægas.
23,1. Gif he ðonne mægleas sie, healf kyninge, healf se gesið.
23,2. Gif hit ðonne abbod sie oððe abbodesse, dælen on þa ilcan wisan wið þone kyning.

a breach of the marriage contract;[25] Ine, ch. 38 establishes a widow's right to guardianship of her children together with an allowance for their upkeep;[26] Alfred, ch. 8 condemns intercourse with a nun and nullifies the inheritance rights of any child born from such a union;[27] Alfred, ch. 9 defines the penalty for the manslaughter of a pregnant woman;[28] Alfred, ch. 10 deals with compensation for adultery;[29] Alfred, ch. 11 is concerned with assaults on women;[30] Alfred, ch. 18 covers assaults on nuns as well as sexual misconduct by engaged women;[31] Alfred, chs. 25 and 26 deal respectively with the rape of slave-women and of underage girls;[32] and Alfred, ch. 42,7 allows vengeance to be taken against

---

23,3. Wealh gafolgelda CXX scill., his sunu C, ðeowne LX, somhwelcne fiftegum; Weales hyd twelfum.

[25] Be þon þe mon wif byccge, 7 þonne sio gift tostande.

31. Gif mon wíf gebyccge, 7 sio gyft forð ne cume, agife þæt feoh 7 forgielde 7 gebete þam byrgean, swa his borgbryce sie.

[26] Be þon ðe ryhtgesamhiwan bearn hæbben, 7 þonne se were gewite.

38. Gif ceorl 7 his wif bearn hæbben gemæne, 7 fere se ceorl forð, hæbbe sio modor hire bearn 7 fede: agife hire mon VI scill. to fostre, cu on sumera, oxan on wintra; healden þa mægas þone frumstol, oð ðæt hit gewintred sie.

[27] Be nunnan hæmede.

8. Gif hwa nunnan of mynstere ut álæde butan kyninges lefnesse oððe biscepes, geselle hundtwelftig scill', healf cyninge, healf biscepe 7 þære cirican hlaforde, ðe ðone munuc age.

8,1. Gif hio leng libbe ðonne se ðe hie utlædde, nage hio his ierfes owiht.

8,2. Gif hio bearn gestriene, næbbe ðæt ðæs ierfes ðon mare ðe seo modor.

8,3. Gif hire bearn mon ofslea, gielde cyninge þara medrenmæga dǽl; fædrenmægum hiora dǽl mon agife.

[28] Be bearneacnum wífe ofslægenum.

9. Gif mon wíf mid bearne ófslea, þonne þæt bearn in hire sie, forgielde ðone wifman fullan gielde, 7 þæt bearn be ðæs fædrencnosles were healfan gelde.

[29] Be twelfhyndes monnes wife forlegenum.

10. Gif mon hæme mid twelfhyndes monnes wife, hundtwelftig scill. gebete ðam were; syxhyndum men hundteontig scill. gebete; cierliscum men feowertig scill. gebete.

[30] For Alfred, ch. 11, see p. 177 below.

[31] Be nunnena onfenge.

18. Gif hwa nunnan mid hæmeðþinge oððe on hire hrægl oððe on hire breost butan hire leafe gefó, sie hit twybete swa we ær be læwdum men fundon.

18,1. Gif beweddodu fæmne hie forlicgge, gif hio sie cirlisc, mid LX scill. gebete þam byrgean, 7 þæt sie on cwicæhtum feogodum, 7 mon nænigne mon on ðæt ne selle.

18,2. Gif hio sie syxhyndu, hundteontig scill. geselle þam byrgean.

18,3. Gif hio sie twelfhyndu, CXX scill. gebete þam byrgean.

[32] Be ungewintredes wifmonnes nedhæmde.

the perpetrator of adultery with a close female relative.[33] Unfortunately the interpretation of these clauses is not always straightforward. In Ine, ch. 31, for instance, dealing with a breach of the marriage contract, it is not wholly clear whether the defaulting party is the bride or the groom, and hence whether the clause is designed to protect the interests of the man or of the woman.[34] Alfred, ch. 8, dealing with the case of a nun who is removed from her minster, is taken to refer to abduction by a majority of scholars, including Chaney,[35] Colman,[36] Duckett,[37] Judd,[38] and Richards and Stanfield;[39] but Fell takes an opposing view, arguing cogently that the clause 'obviously relates to nuns who willingly stayed away from their nunneries'.[40] Most recently, Yorke comments that the abducted nun 'was presumed to have acquiesced in the act', citing this clause as evidence of a double standard whereby 'women were judged differently from men in West Saxon lawcodes and generally not to their advantage'.[41] In other laws relating to sexual misconduct, it may similarly be unclear whether or not the woman was a willing party, and this has major implications for the cultural attitudes involved. On the one hand, the imposition of

---

26. Gif mon ungewintrædne wifmon to niedhæmde geðreatige, sie ðæt swa ðæs gewintredan monnes bot.
For a discussion of this clause, see C. Hough, 'A New Reading of Alfred, ch. 26', *Nottingham Medieval Studies* 41 (1997), 1–12, reprinted in this volume. For Alfred, ch. 25, see p. 182 below.

[33] 42,7. 7 mon mot feohtan órwige, gif he gemeteð oþerne æt his æwum wife, betynedum durum oððe under anre réon, oððe æt his dehter æwumborenre (oððe æt his swistær borenre) oððe æt his medder ðe wære to æwum wife forgifen his fæder.

[34] For a discussion of this clause, see C. Hough, 'Place-name Evidence Relating to the Interpretation of Old English Legal Terminology', *Leeds Studies in English* 27 (1996), 19–48.

[35] W. A. Chaney, *The Cult of Kingship in Anglo-Saxon England* (Manchester, 1970), p. 232.

[36] R. V. Colman, 'The Abduction of Women in Barbaric Law', *Florilegium* 5 (1983), 62–75.

[37] E. Duckett, *Alfred the Great and His England* (London, 1957), p. 89.

[38] E. Judd, 'Women Before the Conquest: A Study of Women in Anglo-Saxon England', *Papers in Women's Studies (University of Michigan)* 1 (1974), 127–49 (p. 144).

[39] M. P. Richards and B. J. Stanfield, 'Concepts of Anglo-Saxon Women in the Laws', *New Readings on Women in Old English Literature*, ed. H. Damico and A. H. Olsen, (Bloomington and Indianapolis, IN, 1990), pp. 89–99 (p. 96).

[40] C. E. Fell et al., *Women in Anglo-Saxon England and the Impact of 1066* (London, 1984), p. 124.

[41] B. Yorke, *Wessex in the Early Middle Ages* (London, 1995), p. 280.

penalties for intercourse with a consenting female partner would seem to indicate that the offence was perceived as a violation of male rights, the woman herself being regarded as a chattel. This is the case in the early Kentish laws relating to intercourse with slaves, as for instance Æthelberht, chs. 10, 11, 14 and 16:

10. Gif man wið cyninges mægdenman geligeþ, L scillinga gebete.	10. If anyone lies with a maiden belonging to the king, he is to pay 50 shillings compensation.
11. Gif hio grindende þeowa sio, XXV scillinga gebete. Sio þridde: XII scillingas.	11. If it is a grinding slave, he is to pay 25 shillings compensation; [if a slave of] the third [class], 12 shillings.
14. Gif wið eorles birele man geligeþ, XII scill' gebete.	14. If anyone lies with a nobleman's serving-woman, he is to pay 20 shillings compensation.
16. Gif wið ceorles birelan man geligeþ, VI scillingum gebete; aet þære oþere ðeowan L scætta; aet þare þriddan XXX scætta.	16. If anyone lie with a *ceorl*'s serving-woman, he is to pay six shillings compensation; [if] with a slave-woman of the second [class], 50 *sceattas*; [if with one of] the third [class], 30 *sceattas*.)[42]

As Fell comments, 'the compensation doubtless went to the owner, as it did if a male slave was injured',[43] and it has been suggested that this reflects 'a significant honor or prestige component in the master's maintenance of control over the sexual activity of his slave'.[44] Penalties for forced intercourse and other forms of sexual attack, on the other hand, would appear to be aimed at the protection of the woman herself, thus testifying to some measure of personal independence. The main purpose of

---

[42] *English Historical Documents*, ed. Whitelock, pp. 391–2. For a discussion of Æthelberht, ch. 10, see Hough, 'Place-name Evidence'.

[43] Fell et al., *Women in Anglo-Saxon England*, p. 62.

[44] R. M. Karras, 'Desire, Descendants, and Dominance: Slavery, the Exchange of Women, and Masculine Power', *The Work of Work: Servitude, Slavery, and Labor in Medieval England*, ed. A. J. Frantzen and D. Moffat (Glasgow, 1994), pp. 16–29 (p. 21).

this article is to examine a ruling generally taken to fall within the former category of intercourse with a consenting female partner, and to suggest that the situation described is actually one of rape.

The clause in question is Alfred, ch. 11, an important but highly problematic law. It reads as follows:

Be cirliscre fæmnan onfenge.	On seizing a maiden of the ceorl class.
11. Gif mon on cirliscre fæmnan breost gefó, mid V scill. hire gebete.	11. If anyone seizes a maiden of the ceorl class by the breast, he is to pay her 5 shillings' compensation.
11,1 Gif he hie oferweorpe 7 mid ne gehæme, mid X scill. gebete.	11,1 If he throws her down and does not lie with her, he is to pay 10 shillings' compensation.
11,2 Gif he mid gehæme, mid LX scill. gebete.	11,2 If he lies with her, he is to pay 60 shillings' compensation.
11,3 Gif oðer mon mid hire læge ǽr, sie be healfum ðæm þonne sio bot.	11,3 If another man has lain with her before, the compensation is then to be half that.
11,4 Gif hie mon teo, geladiege hie be sixtegum hida, oððe ðolige be healfre þære bote.	11,4 If she is accused, she is to clear herself with an oath of 60 hides, or forfeit half the compensation.
11,5 Gif borenran wifmen ðis gelimpe, weaxe sio bót be ðam were.[45]	11,5 If this happens to a better-born woman, the compensation is to increase according to the wergild.)[46]

The opening and closing sections are reasonably straightforward. Chs. 11 and 11,1 define the compensation payable for various kinds of assaults on women; this is based on the *ceorl* class but allows in 11,5 for increased

[45] *Gesetze*, ed. Liebermann I, 16, 56.

[46] *Councils and Synods*, ed. Whitelock, Brett and Brooke, pp. 27–8. Whitelock's translation does not include the rubric. The clause is omitted from her translation of Alfred's laws in *English Historical Documents*, pp. 407–16.

amounts to be paid to victims of higher social rank.[47] By comparing these sums with the penalties for other forms of personal injury listed in the same law-code, it is possible to assess the gravity with which such assaults were regarded.[48] The personal injury tariff is also based on the *ceorl* class, as can be seen from the fact that some of the sums correspond to a *wergild* of 200 shillings,[49] and so the two scales are directly comparable. Five shillings is the value of a little toe or of a thumbnail according to Alfred, chs. 64,4[50] and 56,1:[51] not a great sum, but more than the worth of a back tooth or a finger-nail as defined in chs. 49,1[52] and 57–60.[53] To seize a woman by the breast was therefore roughly equivalent to the infliction of a small but permanent injury on a man – or rather, since most provisions within the personal injury tariff appear to be equally applicable to both men and women, on an adult of either sex. To throw her to the ground was twice as serious. Ten shillings is the compensation stipulated in Alfred, ch. 35, for either binding, or cutting the hair of,

---

47 The form *borenran* is a nonce occurrence, but its meaning is transparent. The term has no entry in Dictionary of Old English Project, *Dictionary of Old English A–G*. Version 2.0. CD-ROM, 2008, although one occurrence is noted of *geboren* 'with reference to status or rank at birth' (*ibid*., s.v. *(ge)boren* B.1.f). W. Lambarde, *Archaeionomia: sive De Priscis Anglorum Legibus*, 2nd ed., ed. A. Wheloc (Cambridge, 1644) p. 26, reads *æþelborenran*; and Liebermann (*Gesetze* I, 57) notes that *æþel* is a sixteenth-century addition to the text in Cambridge, Corpus Christi College, MS 383. Indeed, since the term *æþelboren* is recorded mostly in late texts, particularly in the writings of Ælfric (DOE, s.v. *æþel-boren*), it might be postulated that it replaced an earlier usage of *(ge)boren*. The word *bett* is added above the line in the *Textus Roffensis* manuscript (fol. 18r, line 16), probably by the main scribe.

48 Brief comparisons along these lines are also made in Fell et al., *Women in Anglo-Saxon England*, p. 64.

49 With regard to Alfred, ch. 47, for instance, stipulating a penalty of 66 shillings, 6⅓ pennies for knocking out an eye, Attenborough comments: 'Obviously a third of the wergeld (200 shillings) is the amount intended' (*The Laws of the Earliest English Kings*, ed. F. L. Attenborough (Cambridge, 1922), p. 199).

50 Gif sio lytle ta sie ófaslegen, geselle him V scill.

51 Gif se nægl bið ófaslegen, ðam sculon V scill. to bote.

52 Gif hit sie se wongtoð, geselle IIII scill. to bote.

53 57. Gif se scytefinger bið ófaslegen, sio bót bið XV scill.; his nægles bið III scill.
58. Gif se midlesta finger sie ófaslegen, sio bot bið XII scill.; 7 his nægles bot bið II scill.
59. Gif se goldfinger sie ófaslegen, to þam sculon XVII scill. to bote; 7 his nægles IIII scill. to bote.
60. Gif se lytla finger bið ófaslegen, ðam sceal to bote VIIII scill., 7 an scill. his nægles, gif se sie ófaslegen.

an unoffending *ceorl*.[54] It is in excess of the value of a little finger as defined in ch. 60.[55] The implication is that sexual offences were treated with some severity under the law.

Equally important is the fact that compensation was payable to the woman herself. The phrase *hire gebete* 'pay her compensation' in the opening clause of Alfred, ch. 11 constitutes the earliest explicit reference in the extant Anglo-Saxon laws to a woman's right to receive compensation for offences against herself. The word *hire* is recorded both in Cambridge, Corpus Christi College, MS 173, and in the *Textus Roffensis* manuscript. It is omitted from the inferior text preserved in Cambridge, Corpus Christi College, MS 383, but has been added there by a sixteenth-century hand.[56] The reading is highly significant; indeed, Fell comments that 'the most notable point in this law is the unambiguous use of the pronoun *hire* "her", in the phrase *hire gebete*, "compensate her", i.e. it is the woman herself who is specified as the recipient of the compensation'.[57] As a dative singular pronoun, *hire* could formally be taken to mean 'for her' rather than 'to her', but a translation 'compensate for her' is untenable here for two reasons. Firstly, other laws within the *domboc* identify the recipient of compensation in similar terms. Examples include Alfred, ch. 10 (*gebete ðam were* 'compensate the husband'), Alfred, ch. 18,1 and Ine, ch. 31 (*gebete þam byrgean* 'compensate the surety'), Alfred, chs. 25 and 39 (*gebete þam ceorle* 'compensate the *ceorl*'), and Alfred, chs. 48 and 65 (*gebete him* 'compensate him'). There is no reason to believe that *hire gebete* is being used in a different sense in Alfred, ch. 11. Secondly, ch. 11,4 allows the plaintiff to bring oath-helpers to defend her right to maximum compensation. This is one of two references within the *domboc* to a woman's right to clear herself on oath from a false accusation. The other occurs in Ine, ch. 57:

Gif ceorl ceap forstilð 7 bireð into his ærne, 7 befehð þærinne mon, þonne bið se his dǽl synnig butan þam wife anum,	If a husband steals any cattle and brings it into his house, and it is seized therein, he is guilty for his part, but without his

[54] 35. Gif mon cierliscne mon gebinde unsynnigne, gebete mid X scill. 35,3. Gif he hine on bismor to homolan bescire, mid X scill. gebete.

[55] See n. 53 above.

[56] *Gesetze*, ed. Liebermann I, 56–57.

[57] Fell et al., *Women in Anglo-Saxon England*, p. 63.

forðon hio sceal hire ealdore hieran: gif hio dear mid aðe gecyðan, þæt hio þæs forstolenan ne onbite, nime hire ðriddan sceat.	wife, for she must obey her lord; if she dare declare with an oath that she did not taste of the stolen meat, she is to receive her third portion.[58]

Charter evidence too indicates that women were considered oath-worthy in Anglo-Saxon times. A charter dating from 804[59] records a will made by Æthelric, son of Æthelmund, in which he bequeaths estates at Westbury and Stoke to his mother, Ceolburh, and authorizes her to defend her right to the property on oath:

Et si aliquis homo in aliqua contentione juramentum ei decreverit contra Berclingas . liberrima erit ad reddendum cum recto consilio propinquorum meorum . qui mihi donabant hereditatem et meo quo ei dabo.[60]	And if any man in any dispute decrees from her an oath against the Berkeley people, she will be most free to give it with the true counsel of my kinsfolk, who granted me the inheritance, and with mine, with which I will give it to her.[61]

Æthelric's reasons for anticipating opposition from Berkeley are obscure,[62] as are many other circumstances surrounding his dispositions;[63] but it is at any rate clear that his mother was entitled to swear an oath in support of her own claims. Another charter, concerning a late tenth-century dispute over land at Hagbourne and Bradfield in Berkshire between Wynflæd and

---

[58] *English Historical Documents*, ed. Whitelock, p. 405.

[59] *Anglo-Saxon Charters: An Annotated List and Bibliography*, ed. P. H. Sawyer, Royal Historical Society Guides and Handbooks 8 (London, 1968), no. 1187. A revised version is now available at http://www.esawyer.org.uk.

[60] W. de G. Birch, *Cartularium Saxonicum*, 3 vols. and index (London, 1885–99) I, 439.

[61] *English Historical Documents*, ed. Whitelock, p. 513.

[62] It is evident from later developments that he was right to do so. F. M. Stenton, *The Latin Charters of the Anglo-Saxon Period* (Oxford, 1955), p. 43, comments: 'The arrangements which the great Mercian noble Æthelric son of Æthelmund made for the disposition of his inheritance gave rise to pleas which began in 804 and were not settled for the next twenty years'.

[63] A detailed discussion is presented in P. Wormald, 'Charters, Law and the Settlement of Disputes in Anglo-Saxon England', *The Settlement of Disputes in Early Medieval Europe*, ed. W. Davies and P. Fouracre (Cambridge, 1986), pp. 149–68 (pp. 152–7).

Leofwine,[64] records that the case was resolved on production of an oath by Wynflæd and her supporters of both sexes:

> þa getæhte man Wynflæde þæt hio moste hit hyre geahnian . þa gelædde hio þa ahnunga mid Ælfþryþe fultume þæs cyninges modor . þæt is þonne ærest Wulfgar abbud . 7 Wulfstan priost . 7 Æfic þara æþelinga discsten . 7 Eadwine . 7 Eadelm . 7 Ælfelm . 7 Ælfwine . 7 Ælfweard . 7 Eadwold . 7 Eadric . 7 Ælfgar . 7 Eadgyfu abbudisse . 7 Liofrun abbudisse . 7 Æþelhild . 7 Eadgyfu æt Leofecanoran . 7 hyre swustor . 7 hyre dohtor . 7 Ælfgy[fu 7 hyr]e dohtor . 7 Wulfwyn . 7 Æþelgyfu . 7 Ælfwaru . 7 Ælfgyfu . 7 Æþelflæd . 7 menig god þegen . 7 god wif þe we ealle atellan ne magon þæt [þær] forþcom eal se fulla ge on werum ge on wifum.[65]

> Then Wynflæd was informed that she might prove her ownership of the estate, and she adduced proof of her ownership with the help of Ælfthryth, the king's mother, her supporters being first Abbot Wulfgar and Wulfstan the priest and Æfic, the Æthelings' seneschal, and Edwin and Eadhelm and Ælfhelm and Ælfwine and Ælfweard and Eadwold and Eadric and Ælfgar and the Abbess Eadgifu and the Abbess Leofrun and Æthelhild and Eadgifu of Lewknor and her sister and her daughter and Ælfgi[fu and her] daughter and Wulfwyn and Æthelgifu and Ælfwaru and Ælfgifu and Æthelflæd and many a good thegn and good woman, all of whom we cannot enumerate, so that the full number was produced, including both men and women.[66]

This is an important point since it militates strongly against the notion of women as property which has been advanced by a number of Anglo-Saxon scholars. Klinck, for instance, argues that 'Ine and Alfred, like Ethelbert, indicate that women are subject to male guardianship', and goes on to claim: 'Like Ethelbert, Alfred tabulates penalties for sexual offences against women according to the rank of the woman's guardian

[64] *Anglo-Saxon Charters: An Annotated List and Bibliography*, ed. Sawyer, no. 1454. The case is no. 49 in P. Wormald, 'A Handlist of Anglo-Saxon Lawsuits', *Anglo-Saxon England* 17 (1988), 247–81, where it is dated to 990.
[65] *Anglo-Saxon Charters*, ed. A. J. Robertson (Cambridge, 1939), p. 136. Abbreviations have silently been expanded.
[66] *Ibid*. p. 137.

(Alfred 10-18)'.[67] So too, in a recent discussion of Old English terminology relating to slavery, Girsch comments:

> For a woman, the set of conditions defining servitude would have been not altogether removed from the existence she might expect as a free woman – the property of her father until he gave her to a husband, largely without autonomy except in trivial affairs, without legal standing in many or even most situations, and almost certainly required to display, and probably impelled to feel, humility. . . . In the secular world, a free woman might expect to be in the power of a man for most or all of her life.[68]

The legal evidence, as represented in the extant charters and in laws such as Ine, ch. 57 and Alfred, ch. 11, presents a powerful argument against this view.

It is in the middle section of Alfred, ch. 11 where difficulties of interpretation arise. Ch. 11,2 deals with the penalty for sexual intercourse, but there is no consensus of opinion as to whether it refers to seduction or to rape. Whitelock's translation 'lies with' is non-committal, while the woman is seen as a willing party by Fell,[69] but as a rape victim by Richards and Stanfield.[70] The latter reading seems to follow from the situation outlined in 11,1, where the woman has been thrown to the ground by her assailant. On the other hand, the verb recorded in all three manuscripts is *gehæman* 'to have sexual intercourse' rather than *niedhæman*, the specific term for rape which appears in Alfred, chs. 25 and 26. The Latin version of ch. 11,2 preserved in the unreliable *Quadripartitus* manuscript reads *Si concubuerit*,[71] again with no suggestion of constraint. The fact that compensation is payable to the woman herself implies that intercourse must have taken place without her consent; yet the sum mentioned – 60 shillings – is actually less than the total penalty for raping a *ceorl*'s slave-woman according to Alfred, ch. 25. The latter is the first of two consecutive laws concerning rape in the *domboc*, preceding a ruling on the rape of underage girls in ch. 26. It reads as follows:

---

[67] A. L. Klinck, 'Anglo-Saxon Women and the Law', *Journal of Medieval History* 8 (1982), 107–21 (p. 110).

[68] D. S. Girsch, 'Metaphorical Usage, Sexual Exploitation, and Divergence in the Old English Terminology for Male and Female Slaves', *The Work of Work*, ed. A. J. Frantzen and D. Moffat, pp. 30–54 (pp. 46, 50).

[69] Fell et al., *Women in Anglo-Saxon England and the Impact of 1066*, pp. 63–64.

[70] Richards and Stanfield, 'Concepts of Anglo-Saxon Women', p. 96.

[71] *Gesetze*, ed. Liebermann I, 57.

25. Gif mon ceorles mennen to nedhæmde geðreatað, mid V scill. gebete þam ceorle; 7 LX scill. to wite.	25. If anyone rapes a *ceorl*'s slave-woman, he is to pay five shillings compensation to the *ceorl*, and 60 shillings fine.
25,1. Gif ðeowmon þeowne to nedhæmde genede, bete mid his eowende.	25,1. If a slave rape a slave-woman, he is to pay by suffering castration.[72]

This amounts to a hefty total of 65 shillings, whereas a woman of *ceorl* class who was unable to muster the necessary oath-helpers to testify to her virginity would receive only 30. Fell comments that the discrepancy between the two penalties 'shows the severity with which rape was regarded where rape of a slave comes more expensive than seduction of a free-woman'.[73] The contrast would indeed be a striking one, but should not be accepted without closer investigation. A more detailed analysis of the clause will suggest that Alfred, ch. 11,2 is concerned with rape rather than with seduction, and that the total penalty would in fact be in excess of the 65 shillings payable for raping a slave under the terms of Alfred, ch. 25.

It is difficult to believe either that compensation would be paid to a woman who had willingly allowed herself to be seduced, or that mutual consent is compatible with the form of assault described in Alfred, ch. 11,1. There are instances elsewhere within the *domboc* where the topic changes in the middle of a clause.[74] For instance, Alfred, ch. 9, *Be bearneacnum wife ofslægenum* 'On the manslaughter of a pregnant woman', also covers theft and kidnapping; while the manuscript grouping for Alfred, ch. 26, *Be ungewintredes wifmonnes nedhæmde* 'On the rape of an underage girl', includes offences committed by kinless men. However, no such discontinuity is evidenced in ch. 11, which is concerned throughout with penalties for sexual offences. Here the phrasing provides evidence of continuity, with a direct parallel between chs. 11,1 *Gif he hie . . . mid ne gehæme*, and 11,2 *Gif he mid gehæme*. Indeed, the omission of the accusative pronoun *hie* from ch. 11,2 means that it cannot be read other than in conjunction with the preceding sub-clause. These are quite clearly alternative courses of action in the same situation.

---

72 *English Historical Documents*, ed. Whitelock, p. 413.

73 Fell et al., *Women in Anglo-Saxon England*, p. 64.

74 The division of the composite *domboc* into 120 chapters is, as Keynes and Lapidge comment, 'often effected with apparent disregard for content' (*Alfred the Great*, p. 304).

It is essential to recognize the importance of context in the interpretation of Old English sexual vocabulary. Where the context leaves no doubt that the situation is one of constraint, the general term *gehæman* 'to have sexual intercourse' may be used rather than the more explicit *niedhæman* 'to rape'. This is certainly the case with other literary occurrences, both in texts associated with Alfred and elsewhere. Describing the rape of Dinah by the Hebrew prince Shechem, for instance, the Alfredian translation of Pope Gregory's *Pastoral Care* states:

> & ða gelicode hio him, & he hi genam niedenga, & hire mid gehæmde.
>
> and she pleased him, and he took her by force, and lay with her.[75]

Here the verb *niedhæman* 'to rape' would be superfluous in conjunction with the adverb *niedenga* 'by force'. Similarly, the penitential work most recently edited under the title *A Late Old English Handbook for the Use of a Confessor* includes the following provision in Section 4:

> Gyf hwa mid his lotwræncum oðres mannes folgere fram him apæce for hæmedþinge, and hire unwilles wið hi hæme, gif he bið gehadod man, ðolige his hades; gif he beo læwede, beo he amansumad fram eallum Cristenum þingum.[76]
>
> If anyone by deceit seduces another man's follower away from him for intercourse, and has intercourse with her against her will, if he is a man in holy orders, he is to forfeit his orders; if he is lay, he is to be excommunicated from all Christian practices.

In this instance, the phrase *hire unwilles* 'against her will' expresses the idea of constraint, so that again a general term for sexual intercourse suffices. So too, the verb *hæman* 'to have sexual intercourse' is used in connection with the phrase *hire unðances* 'against her will' to refer to rape in the 1086 entry from the Peterborough MS of the *Anglo-Saxon Chronicle*: 'Gif hwilc carl man hæmde wið wimman hire unðances, sona he forleas þa limu þe he mid pleagode'[77] ('And if any man had intercourse

[75] *King Alfred's West-Saxon Version of Gregory's 'Pastoral Care'*, ed. H. Sweet, 2 vols., Early English Text Society 45, 50 (London, 1871; reprtd 1958), pp. 414, 415.

[76] R. Fowler, 'A late Old English handbook for the use of a confessor', *Anglia* 83 (1965), 1–34 (p. 23).

[77] *Two of the Saxon Chronicles Parallel*, ed. J. Earle and C. Plummer, 2 vols. (Oxford, 1892–9) I, 220.

with a woman against her will, he was forthwith castrated').[78] In all three cases, the verb *(ge)hæman* occurs in the same sentence as an expression of constraint, and its meaning is therefore beyond dispute. In the case of Alfred, ch. 11,2, the idea of constraint is expressed in the previous sub-clause, but the implications are equally clear. There can be few less ambiguous scenarios than one where a woman has already been thrown violently to the ground, and this almost certainly accounts for the non-occurrence of the verb *niedhæman* 'to rape' in this law.

Linguistically, then, there is no real difficulty in interpreting the verb *gehæman* in Alfred, ch. 11,2 in terms of rape. What is inconceivable is that the penalty for raping a free woman in Alfred, ch. 11 could be less than the penalty for raping a slave in Alfred, ch. 25. A closer comparison of the two clauses may dispel this impression. The offender in Alfred, ch. 25 forfeits a total of 65 shillings, but this is made up of 5 shillings' compensation (payable to the slave's owner) plus a fine of 60 shillings. Alfred, ch. 11,2 mentions only the amount of compensation required. Does this mean that there was no fine, or that the fine is left unstated? Liebermann indicates the latter,[79] with good reason. Compensation (*bot*) is normally accompanied by a fine (*wite*) in the early laws, the appropriate scale being set out in Alfred, ch. 9,1:

A sie þæt wite LX scill', oð ðæt angylde árise to XXX scill'; siððan hit to ðam árise þæt angylde, siððan sie þæt wite CXX scill'.	The fine is always to be 60 shillings until the simple compensation rises to 30 shillings; when the simple compensation has risen to that, the fine is afterwards to be 120 shillings.[80]

This makes it possible to work out the *wite* corresponding to the various *bot*s defined in Alfred, ch. 11. For a minor assault as described in Alfred, chs. 11 or 11,1, the *wite* is 60 shillings, whereas for rape (chs. 11,2 and 11,3), it rises to 120 shillings, bringing the total penalty to 180 shillings, or 150 shillings if the woman was not a virgin. This is much more plausible in comparison with the total penalty for raping a slave in Alfred, ch. 25.

---

[78] D. Douglas and G. W. Greenaway, *English Historical Documents II*: *1042–1189* (London, 1953), p. 164.

[79] Liebermann, *Gesetze* III, 54, comments: 'Nebenher geht Strafgeld für den Richter'.

[80] *English Historical Documents*, ed. Whitelock, p. 411.

It should be noted, however, that the range of application of Alfred, ch. 9,1 is less than clear, and it is not wholly certain whether or not the sums listed as compensation for personal injuries in Alfred, chs. 44–77 were to be accompanied by a fine. Such an interpretation certainly seems to be implied by a passage in ch. 42,4, which refers to *wite* in addition to compensation for wounds:

> Gif he wille on hond gan 7 his wæpenu sellan, 7 hwa ofer ðæt on him feohte, gielde swa wer swa wunde swa he gewyrce, 7 wite 7 hæbbe his mæg forworht.

> If he is willing to surrender, and to give up his weapons, and after that anyone fights against him, he [who does] is to pay wergild or compensation for wounds according to what he has done, and a fine, and is to have forfeited [the right to avenge] his kinsman.[81]

Furthermore, there are references throughout the *domboc* to an interrelationship between fine and compensation. Alfred, chs. 29, 31, and 38 refer to *wer 7 wite* '*wergild* and fine', while Alfred, ch. 30 refers to *wer 7 fulwite* '*wergild* and full fine' – all implying that the respective amounts could easily be determined. Alfred, ch. 7,1 defines payment as *swa wer swa wite* 'both *wergild* and fine', and Alfred, ch. 37,2 stipulates that anyone who employs an absconding workman is to pay a fine of 120 shillings in addition to compensation for any of his past offences:

> Gif he hwæt yfla gedon hæbbe ðær he ær wæs, bete ðæt se ðe hine ðonne to men onfo, 7 cyninge CXX scill. to wite.

> If he has committed any wrong where he was before, he who now receives him as his man is to pay compensation for it, and 120 shillings to the king as fine.[82]

Two clauses in particular show that the *wite* was directly related to the amount of compensation. Alfred, ch. 6 deals with the theft of church property:

> Gif hwa on cirican hwæt geðeofige, forgylde þæt angylde, 7 ðæt wite swa to ðam angylde belimpan wille, 7 slea

> If anyone steals anything in church, he is to pay the simple compensation and the fine normally belonging to that

[81] *Ibid*. p. 415.
[82] *Ibid*. p. 414.

mon þa hond óf ðe he hit mid gedyde.	simple compensation, and the hand with which he did it is to be struck off.[83]

Here the words 'ðæt wite swa to ðam angylde belimpan wille' indicate that the fine as well as the compensation depended on the value of the item stolen. So too, Alfred, ch. 31,1 gives the collective penalty for a group of marauders accused of murder:

Gif hloð ðis gedó 7 eft oðswerian wille, tio hie ealle; 7 þonne ealle forgielden þone wer gemænum hondum 7 ealle án wite, swa to ðam were belimpe.	If a band of men does this and afterwards wishes to deny it on oath, they are all to be accused; and then they are all collectively to pay the wergild, and all one fine, as is accordant to the wergild.[84]

Again the *wite* is based directly on the level of compensation, in this instance comprising the *wergild* of the slain man.

On the other hand, it would appear that the payment of compensation was not always accompanied by a fine. Alfred, ch. 36 defines a situation where no fine would be incurred. In the event of accidental death from a spear carried over the shoulder, the *wergild* alone is payable:

Eac is funden: gif mon hafað spere ofer eaxle, 7 hine mon on asnaseð, gielde þone wer butan wite.	Moreover, it is established: if anyone has a spear over his shoulder, and a man is transfixed on it, the wergild is to be paid without the fine.[85]

The issue here is that the crime is one of accident as opposed to intention. Only if the offender is unable to refute an accusation of deliberate intent does the fine come into effect:

36,1. Gif beforan eagum asnase, gielde þone wer; gif hine mon tio gewealdes on ðære dæde, getriowe hine be þam wite 7	36,1. If he is transfixed before his eyes, he is to pay the wergild; if anyone accuses him of intention in this act, he is to

[83] *Ibid.* p. 410.
[84] *Ibid.* p. 413.
[85] *Ibid.* p. 414.

mid ðy þæt wite afelle.

clear himself in proportion to the fine, and by that [oath] do away with the fine.[86]

This is particularly interesting in relation to Alfred, ch. 11,4, as in both cases the oath required is equal in value to the amount of money at issue. There is also a close similarity of terminology and of word-order between ch. 11,4, 'Gif hie mon teo' and ch. 36,1 'gif hine mon tio'. Even though the offender in Alfred, ch. 36 may escape payment of the *wite*, this in itself shows that there was a recognised *wite* to be enforced.

The only clause besides Alfred, ch. 25 to define both compensation and fine is ch. 12, concerning tree-felling:

Gif mon oðres wudu bærneð oððe heaweð unaliefedne, forgielde ælc great treow mid V scill., 7 siððan æghwylc, sie swa fela swa hiora sie, mid V pæningum; 7 XXX scill. to wite.

If a man burns or fells the wood of another, without permission, he is to pay for each large tree with five shillings, and afterwards for each, no matter how many there are, with fivepence; and 30 shillings as a fine.[87]

Here the equation is not in accordance with the scale given in ch. 9,1, as the *wite* is 30 shillings rather than 60 for a *bot* of 5 shillings or less. It is difficult to know what to make of this discrepancy. One possibility is that the fines mentioned in ch. 9,1 were not generally applicable, perhaps referring only to penalties for theft. In this case it could be misleading to extrapolate from the treatment of theft to the treatment of other crimes such as rape, despite the striking correspondence with the terms of Alfred, ch. 25. Alternatively, however, it may be that the sum of 30 shillings mentioned in Alfred, ch. 12 is an error, or indeed that the fine is included simply because it constituted an exception to the usual rule. A further possibility is that Alfred, ch. 12 may relate to an older scale of assessment. It is clear from ch. 9,2 that the new method has been introduced to rationalize an existing system:

Geo wæs goldðeofe 7 stodðeofe 7 beoðeofe, 7 manig witu maran ðonne oþru; nu sint eal gelic buton manðeofe: CXX scill'.

Formerly, [the fine] for the stealer of gold, the stealer of stud-horses, the stealer of bees, and many fines, were greater

[86] *Ibid.*

[87] *Ibid.* p. 411.

than others; now all are alike, except for the stealer of a man: 120 shillings.[88]

Although this refers directly only to theft, it suggests that a less structured relationship between *wite* and *bot* was already in existence, a supposition that can be supported from earlier laws such as ch. 9 of the code issued by King Æthelberht of Kent towards the beginning of the seventh century:

Gif frigman freum stelþ, III gebete, 7 cyning age þæt wite 7 ealle þa æhtan.

If a freeman steals from a freeman, he is to pay three-fold, and the king is to have the fine or all the goods.[89]

Chs. 11–13 of the later seventh-century Kentish laws of Kings Hlothhere and Eadric are concerned with offences committed in someone else's house, each stipulating a fine of 12 shillings to the king in addition to varying amounts of compensation to the householder:

11. Gif man mannan an oþres flette manswara hateþ oððe hine mid bismærwordum scandlice grete, scilling agelde þam þe þæt flet age, 7 VI scill' þam þe he þæt word togecwæde, 7 cyninge XII scll' forgelde.

11. If anyone in another's house calls a man a perjurer, or shamefully accosts him with insulting words, he is to pay a shilling to him who owns the house, and 6 shillings to him to whom he spoke that word, and to pay 12 shillings to the king.

12. Gif man oþrum steop asette ðær mæn drincen, buton scylde, an eald riht scll' agelde þam þe þæt flet age, 7 VI scll' þam þe man þone steap aset, 7 cynge XII scll'.

12. If anyone removes a cup from another where men are drinking, without provocation, he shall according to ancient law pay a shilling to him who owns the house, and 6 shillings to him whose cup was removed, and 12 shillings to the king.

13. Gif man wæpn abregde þær mæn drincen 7 ðær man yfel ne deþ, scilling þan þe þæt flet age, 7 cyninge XII scll'.

13. If anyone draws a weapon where men are drinking, and yet no injury is done there, [he is to pay] a shilling to him who owns

[88] *Ibid.* p. 411.
[89] *Ibid.* p. 391.

the house and 12 shillings to the king.[90]

Hlothhere and Eadric, ch. 14 deals with bloodshed in similar circumstances, stipulating a fine of 50 shillings to the king in addition to payment of the householder's *mundbyrd* 'fine for breach of protection':

14. Gif þæt flet geblodgad wyrþe, forgylde þem mæn his mundbyrd 7 cyninge L scill'.	14. If the house is stained by bloodshed, he is to pay to the man [the price for breach of] his protection, and 50 shillings to the king.[91]

Once it is realized that the sums mentioned as compensation in the early Old English laws did not represent the entire monetary penalty, and that the damages outlined in Alfred, ch. 11 would have been supplemented by a substantial fine, the apparent discrepancy between the penalties stipulated in Alfred, chs. 11 and 25 disappears. Taking into account the traditional fine of 60 shillings, the total penalty for the offence of *breost gefon* 'seizing by the breast' would come to a minimum of 65 shillings for the lowest class of freewoman, the equivalent of the penalty for rape of a slave. For raping a woman of *ceorl* rank, the total penalty would amount to 180 shillings, with correspondingly greater sums for assaults against women of higher social class. Although a woman who was sexually experienced was entitled to less compensation than a virgin, the fine or *wite* for such an offence would still be very substantial, thus acting as a powerful deterrent.

It remains to be considered whether or not the treatment of sexual assault in Alfred, ch. 11 was based on an established legislative tradition. Discussing the impact of the Germanic invasions on Western society, Brundage refers to 'the introduction of primitive Germanic legal systems, which did not much concern themselves with the protection of women from violent assault', and goes on to comment: 'it was the law of the western Church that strove to penalize such assaults during the early middle ages'.[92] It might therefore appear that Alfred's *domboc* was innovative in this respect. The question will, however, repay further examination. Although the early Kentish laws are largely silent on

[90] *Ibid.* p. 395.

[91] *Ibid.* p. 395.

[92] J. A. Brundage, 'Rape and Marriage in the Medieval Canon Law', *Revue de droit canonique* 28 (1978), 62–75, (p. 64).

the topic of sexual assault, it has recently been suggested that two clauses generally taken to refer to abduction may in fact be concerned with rape. The standard reading of Æthelberht, chs. 82 and 83, is as follows:

82. Gif man mægþmon nede genimeþ: ðam agende L scillinga 7 eft æt þam agende sinne willan ætgebicge.	82. If anyone carries off a maiden by force, [he is to pay] to the owner 50 shillings, and afterwards buy from the owner his consent [to the marriage].
83. Gif hio oþrum mæn in sceat bewyddod sy, XX scillinga gebete.	83. If she is betrothed to another man at a [bride] price, he is to pay 20 shillings compensation.[93]

Fell offers an alternative interpretation, commenting:

> it is not clear that Old English *geniman* necessarily and always has a significance different from that of *niman*. It is perfectly possible that these two laws refer not to abduction or, as it has romantically been termed, 'marriage by capture', but more simply to sexual intercourse, perhaps rape, not otherwise mentioned in this law-code but suggested by the word *nede*.[94]

If this proposal is correct, the ruling on rape in Alfred, ch. 11,2 may be exceptional only inasmuch as compensation is paid directly to the woman.

Similar difficulties of interpretation occur in continental Germanic legislation, and may usefully be discussed here before returning to a more detailed consideration of Æthelberht, chs. 82 and 83. The Latin term *raptus* in the continental codes is often taken to refer to rape, but its primary meaning more probably relates to the abduction of a woman, possibly against her will, but more crucially in defiance of the proper legal formalities for marriage.[95] According to Rivers's translation, for instance, a decree issued by the Frankish King Childebert II in 595 is concerned with rape, a crime for which the perpetrator could forfeit his life (*Decretio Childberti* ch. 2,2):

---

[93] *English Historical Documents*, ed. Whitelock, p. 393.

[94] C. Fell, 'An Appendix to Carole Hough's Article "A Re-appraisal of Æthelberht 84"', *Nottingham Medieval Studies* 37 (1993), 7–8.

[95] P. J. Payer, *Sex and the Penitentials: the Development of a Sexual Code 550–1150* (Toronto, 1984), argues strongly that *raptus* does not connote sexual rape. See especially pp. 38, 60–61, 117.

Pari conditione conuenit Kalendas Martias omnibus adunatis, ut ad(m)o(d)um quicumque praesumpserit facere raptum, unde impiissimus uitius adcreuerat, uitae periculum feriatur, et nullus de obtimatibus nostris praesumat pro ipso praecari, sed unusquisque ad(m)o(d)um inimicum Dei persequatur. Qui uero <uel> edictum nostrum transcendere praesumpserit, in cuiuslibet iudicis pago primitus admissum fuerit, ille iudex collectum solacium ipsum raptorem occidat et iaceat <eum> forbatuos. Et si ad ecclesiam confugium fecerit, reddendos ad episcopo absque ullam praecationem separentur <et> in exilio deputentur. Certe si ipsa mulier raptum consenserit, ambo pariter <in> exilio transmittantur <et>, si foris ecclesia capti fuerint, ambo pariter occidantur, et facultatem eorum parentibus <eorum> legitimis, et quod fisco nostro debetur adquiratur.[96]

By similar judgment it was agreed on the calends of March [595] when everyone was assembled that whoever attempts to rape [a woman], whereby a dishonorable crime is perpetrated, let him realize that his life is in peril, and let none of our magnates attempt to ask for him, but let each one of them be pursued in such a manner as an enemy of God. But whoever attempts to transgress our edict, in whichever county he is surrendered, that judge by public proclamation may kill the rapist, and no wergild is required for him. And if he flees to a church, let him be apprehended without any pleading after being surrendered to the bishop, and let him be sent into exile. If perhaps the woman agreed to be seduced, let them both be sent into exile together, and if they flee to a church, let them both be killed together. And let their property be acquired by their lawful relatives and let our public treasury acquire what is owed it.[97]

The translation 'rape' is, however, scarcely compatible with the possibility that the woman may have consented to the crime ('si ipsa mulier raptum consenserit'), or with the threat that she too may face the death penalty. As with the abducted nun in Alfred, ch. 8, the woman's consent comprises an aggravating rather than an extenuating circumstance. It therefore appears that Childebert's ruling is essentially concerned with the unlawful

---

[96] *Pactus Legis Salicae*, ed. K. A. Eckhardt, Monumenta Germaniae Historica, Legum Sectio 1: Leges nationum Germanicarum 4.1 (Hanover, 1962), 268.

[97] T. J. Rivers, *Laws of the Salian and Ripuarian Franks* (New York, 1986), pp. 145–6.

removal of the woman, the offence being committed against her kin rather than against herself.

It is clear too from the Burgundian laws compiled by King Gundobad towards the end of the fifth century that *raptus* did not necessarily involve sexual rape, since ch. 12 of the *Lex Gundobada* both allows for the possibility that the victim may be returned unviolated and makes provision for a situation where the girl herself is a willing party:

XII. De raptibus puellarum.	XII. On the stealing of girls.
[1.] Si quis puellam rapuerit, pretium, quod pro puella daturus erat, in novigildo cogatur exsolvere, et multae nomine solidos XII.	1. If anyone shall steal a girl, let him be compelled to pay the price set for such a girl ninefold, and let him pay a fine to the amount of twelve solidi.
[2.] Si vero puella, quae rapta est, incorrupta redierit ad parentes, sexies puellae pretium raptor exsolvat, multae autem nomine solidos XII.	2. If a girl who has been seized returns uncorrupted to her parents, let the abductor compound six times the wergeld of the girl; moreover, let the fine be set at twelve solidi.
[3.] Quod si raptor solutionem suprascriptam unde solvere non habuerit, puellae parentibus adsignetur, ut faciendi de eo quod ipsi maluerint habeant potestatem.	3. But if the abductor does not have the means to make the above-mentioned payment, let him be given over to the parents of the girl that they may have the power of doing to him whatever they choose.
[4.] Si vero puella sua sponte expetierit virum et ad domum illius venerit, et ille se cum illa miscuerit, nuptiale pretium in triplum solvat; si autem incorrupta redierit ad domum suam, remota omni calumnia revertatur.	4. If indeed, the girl seeks the man of her own will and comes to his house, and he has intercourse with her, let him pay her marriage price threefold; if moreover, she returns uncorrupted to her home, let her return with all blame removed from him.

[5.] Romana vero puella, si sine parentum suorum voluntate aut conscientia se Burgundionis coniugio sociaverit, nihil se de parentum facultate noverit habituram.[98]	5. If indeed, a Roman girl, without the consent or knowledge of her parents, unites in marriage with a Burgundian, let her know she will have none of the property of her parents.[99]

A similar situation applied under Visigothic law, where as Scott comments:

> The crime of rape was considered by the Visigothic legislator in the original and broader acceptation of the term, and not according to the more limited significance attaching to it at the present day. It included, therefore, the offences of abduction and kidnapping.[100]

The association between abduction and rape evidenced in the continental Germanic law-codes may also be reflected in Æthelberht, chs. 82 and 83, and would help to explain the subsequent clause in the vernacular sequence. Æthelberht, ch. 84 reads as follows:

Gif gængang geweorðeþ, XXXV scill' 7 cyninge XV scillingas.	If *gængang* occurs, [he is to pay] 35 shillings and 15 shillings to the king.

I have argued elsewhere that the nonce-occurrence *gængang* refers to road-blocking or way-laying, a recurrent theme in continental Germanic codes, so that ch. 84 either represents a change of topic from the preceding clauses on abduction, or refers to an abduction involving an attack on the open road.[101] Comparison with continental law will support the latter alternative. Particularly close links have been identified between Anglo-Saxon and Frankish legislation, and are worth exploring further.[102]

---

98 *Leges Burgundionum*, ed. L. R. de Salis, Monumenta Germaniae Historica, Legum Sectio 1: Leges nationum Germanicarum 2.1 (Hanover, 1892), pp. 51–2.

99 K. F. Drew, *The Burgundian Code, Book of Constitutions or Law of Gundobad, Additional Enactments* (Philadelphia, PA, 1949), p. 31.

100 S. P. Scott, *The Visigothic Code* (Boston, MA., 1910), p. 89 n. I.

101 C. Hough, 'A Reappraisal of Æthelberht 84', *Nottingham Medieval Studies* 37 (1993), 1–6, reprinted in this volume. Previous scholars take *gængang* to refer to the pregnancy or return of the girl.

102 J. M. Wallace-Hadrill, *Early Germanic Kingship in England and on the Continent* (Oxford, 1971), pp. 37–8, discusses parallels between Æthelberht's laws and *Lex Salica*.

Pactus Legis Salicae, ch. 13,4 stipulates a heavy financial penalty for a *raptor*, translated by Rivers as 'rapist':

Raptor uero ILMD den. qui fac. sol. LXIII culp. iud.[103]	For a rapist, let him be held liable for 2500 denarii, which make sixty-two and one-half solidi.[104]

Again, there are difficulties with this translation, since both the preceding and following clauses are concerned with abduction rather than with sexual assault, giving a scale of penalties depending on the place from which the girl is taken, the number of men involved, and the use or non-use of weapons. Drew's translation is more circumspect: 'The abductor shall be liable to pay twenty-five hundred denarii (i.e., sixty-two and one-half solidi)'.[105] A much higher penalty is demanded in the final clause of the sequence, ch. 13,14, where the situation is unambiguously one of sexual rape:

Si quis puella sponsata dructe ducente [ad maritum et eam] in uia [aliquis] adsallierit et cum ipsa uiolenter moechatus fuerit, mallobergo gangichaldo, sunt denarii VIIIM qui faciunt solidos CC culpabilis iudicetur.[106]	If anyone follows a betrothed girl in a wedding procession who is on her way to be married and assaults her on the road and forces her to engage in sex (known in the malberg as *gangichaldo*), let him be held liable for 8000 denarii, which make 200 solidi.[107]

This may represent a direct parallel to Æthelberht, ch. 84, referring to an abduction involving an attack on the open road.[108] The possibility is strengthened by the fact that in both codes, the preceding clause is concerned with compensation to the girl's original fiancé. *Pactus Legis Salicae*, ch. 13,13 reads as follows:

---

[103] *Pactus Legis Salicae*, ed. Eckhardt, 61.
[104] Rivers, *Laws of the Franks*, p. 56.
[105] K. F. Drew, *The Laws of the Salian Franks* (Philadelphia, PA, 1991), p. 78.
[106] *Pactus Legis Salicae*, ed. Eckhardt, 63.
[107] Rivers, *Laws of the Franks*, p. 57.
[108] I am very grateful to Mr Stanley Rubin for drawing my attention to the parallel between Æthelberht, ch. 84 and *Pactus Legis Salicae*, ch. 13,14, and for raising the possibility of a connection between OE *gængang* and the Frankish term *gangichaldo* preserved in the continental law.

Incontra sponsum uero, cuius sponsa est, solidos XV culpabilis iudicetur.[109]

For the benefit of the bridegroom, whose fiancée she is, let [the abductor] be liable for fifteen solidi.[110]

Although more cryptically worded, Æthelberht, ch. 83 is also generally taken to refer to compensation payable to the former fiancé,[111] and the sum of 20 shillings would thus correspond to the 15 solidi stipulated under the continental law. I therefore propose the following interpretation of the sequence from Æthelberht, chs. 82–84:

82. Gif man mægþmon nede genimeþ: ðam agende L scillinga 7 eft æt þam agende sinne willan ætgebicge.

82. If anyone carries off a maiden by force, [he is to pay] to the guardian[112] 50 shillings, and afterwards buy from the guardian his consent [to the marriage].

83. Gif hio oþrum mæn in sceat bewyddod sy, XX scillinga gebete.

83. If she is betrothed to another man at a [bride] price, he is to pay 20 shillings compensation.

84. Gif gængang geweorðeþ, XXXV scill' 7 cyninge XV scillingas.

84. If she is assaulted on the road, [he is to pay] 35 shillings and 15 shillings to the king.

Æthelberht's code may thus indeed contain an allusion to sexual assault, although in a context quite different from that of Alfred, ch. 11.

There are indications elsewhere that continental legislators were concerned to protect women against sexual molestation. *Pactus Legis Salicae*, ch. 20 contains a range of provisions relating to this topic:

20. De eo qui ingenua mulieri manum uel brachium <aut digitum> extrinxerit.

20. Concerning him who touches a freewoman's hand, arm or finger.

---

[109] *Pactus Legis Salicae*, ed. Eckhardt, 63.

[110] Rivers, *Laws of the Franks*, p. 57.

[111] *The Laws*, ed. Attenborough, p.178; Colman, 'The Abduction of Women in Barbaric Law', p. 69.

[112] Fell, 'An Appendix to Carole Hough's Article', 7, points out that the word *agend* is 'better translated "guardian" than by the Whitelockian "owner" though "guardian" has some awkward overtones too'.

1. Si quis ingenuus homo ingenuae mulieri uel qualibet <feminae> <manum uel brachium aut> digitum extrinxerit, cui fuerit adprobatum, mallobergo chamin hoc est, DC denarios qui faciunt solidos XV culpabilis iudicetur.

1. If a freeman touches a freewoman's or any woman's hand, arm or finger (known in the malberg as *chamin*), and it can be proven that he did this, let him be held liable for 600 denarii, which make fifteen solidi.

2. Si brachium presserit, mallobergo chamin sunt, denarios MCC qui faciunt solidos XXX culpabilis iudicetur.

2. If he presses her arm (known in the malberg as *chamin*), let him be held liable for 1200 denarii, which make thirty solidi.

3. Certe si super cubitum manum miserit <cui fuerit adprobatum>, mallobergo chamin malicharde hoc est, MCCCC denarios qui faciunt solidos XXXV culpabilis iudicetur.

3. If he definitely places his hand above her elbow (known in the malberg as *chamin malicharde*), and it can be proven that he did this, let him be held liable for 1400 denarii, which make thirty-five solidi.

4. Si quis mamillam mulierem strinxerit <aut sciderit, quod sanguis egressus fuerit>, mallobergo de bructe, <M(D)CCC denarios qui faciunt> solidos XLV culpabilis iudicetur.[113]

4. If anyone touches a woman's breast or cuts it so that blood comes forth (known in the malberg as *de bructe*), let him be held liable for 1800 denarii, which make forty-five solidi.[114]

Possibly the closest parallel to Alfred, ch. 11 occurs in the Alamannic laws dating from the early eighth century. *Lex Alamannorum*, ch. 56 defines the compensation due for sexual assault as follows:

56,1. Si quis libera femina virgo vadit itinere suo inter duas villas, et obviavit eam aliquis, per raptum denudat caput eius, cum sex solidis conponat. Et si eius vestimenta levaverit, usque

56,1. If any free virgin woman [maiden] goes on a journey between two estates, and anyone meets her [and] uncovers her head, let him compensate with six solidi. And

[113] *Pactus Legis Salicae*, ed. Eckhardt, pp. 83–4.

[114] Rivers, *Laws of the Franks*, p. 63.

ad genucula denudet, cum sex solidis conponat. Et si cam denudaverit, usque genetalia eius appareant vel posteriora, cum 12 solidis conponat. Si autem ab ea fornicaverit contra voluntate eius, 40 solidos conponat.

if he raises her clothing to the knee, let him compensate with six solidi. And if he exposes her so that her genitalia or posterior appears, let him compensate with twelve solidi. If, however, he fornicates with her against her will, let him compensate with forty solidi.

56,2. Si autem muliere haec contingerit, omnia dupliciter componat, sicut antea diximus de virgine.[115]

56,2. If, however, this happens to an adult woman, let him compensate all things twice what we said above concerning the virgin.[116]

As in Alfred, ch. 11, there is a scale of penalties graded according to the severity of the assault and the status of the victim, and it is clear that the rape is carried out against her will: 'Si autem ab ea fornicaverit contra voluntate eius'. Again, comparison with the corresponding personal injury tariff is illuminating. Six *solidi* is the compensation payable for cutting off half an ear or the top of a thumb according to *Lex Alamannorum*, chs. 57,10 and 57,41, while 12 *solidi* corresponds to a whole ear (ch. 57,8) or a whole thumb (ch. 57,42).[117] Forty *solidi* are payable for the loss of a major faculty such as hearing (ch. 57,9) or speech (ch. 57,26), or for cutting off the lower part of an arm (ch. 57,39) or an entire foot (ch. 57,66).[118] The same injuries inflicted on women attract a double compensation according to ch. 59,2:

Haec omnia conpositio, quod ad viris indicavimus, ad feminis eorum omnia dupliciter conponatur.[119]

Let all this compensation that we have determined for men be rendered twofold to their women.[120]

[115] *Leges Alamannorum*, ed. K. A. Eckhardt, Monumenta Germaniae Historica, Legum Sectio 1: Leges nationum Germanicarum 5.1, rev. ed. (Hanover, 1966), pp. 115–6.

[116] T. J. Rivers, *Laws of the Alamans and Bavarians* (Philadelphia, PA, 1977), p. 85.

[117] *Leges Alamannorum*, ed. Eckhardt, pp. 118, 124.

[118] *Ibid.* 118, 121, 124, 128.

[119] *Ibid.* 129.

[120] Rivers, *Laws of the Alamans and Bavarians*, p. 90.

So too in the event of homicide, double compensation is to be paid for women. Ch. 60 begins as follows:

1. Si quis autem liber liberum occiderit, conponat eum bis octuaginta solidis ad filios suos. Si autem filios non reliquid nec heredes habuit, solvat eum 200 solidis.	1. If, however, any freeman kills another freeman, let him compensate for him with twice eighty solidi to his children. If, however, he leaves no children and has no relatives, let him [the killer] pay 200 solidi for him.
2. Feminas autem eorum semper in duplum.[121]	2. Women, however, [are] always [to be compensated] twofold.)[122]

Rivers accounts for this two-fold compensation in terms of women's inability to defend themselves with weapons, necessitating a higher level of protection for them as the weaker members of society: 'Ordinarily, since women cannot defend themselves, they have to be protected with higher (double) compensation'.[123] The provision is not paralleled in Anglo-Saxon law, where as noted above, the personal injury tariff in Alfred's code appears to apply equally to both sexes.

Whether single compensation was required, as in the Anglo-Saxon codes, or double compensation, as under Alamannic legislation, a constant feature is the commitment to ensure the safety of women against attack.

The theme of sexual assault is continued in later Anglo-Saxon law. Only two post-Alfredian codes specify penalties for rape,[124] but both indicate that the crime was regarded as a serious one. VI Æthelred, ch. 39 is concerned with assaults on nuns and widows:

7 gif hwa nunnan gewemme oþþe wydewan nydnæme, gebete þæt deope for Gode 7 for	And if anyone injures a nun or does violence to a widow, he shall make amends to the

[121] *Leges Alamannorum*, ed. Eckhardt, pp. 129–30.

[122] Rivers, *Laws of the Alamans and Bavarians*, p. 90.

[123] T. J. Rivers, 'The Legal Status of Freewomen in the Lex Alamannorum', *Zeitschrift der Savigny-Stiftung für Rechtsgeschichte, Germanistische Abteilung* 91 (1974), 175–9 (p. 176).

[124] Discussing the late Old English period, Girsch comments that 'rape of free women was much more costly than rape of slaves' ('Metaphorical Usage', p. 49). This appears to imply recourse to a wider range of legislation than I have been able to trace from late Anglo-Saxon England, but Girsch unfortunately cites no evidence in support of her statement.

worolde.	utmost of his ability both towards church and state.[125]

This is partly repeated in the law-code issued by the Danish king Cnut during the early eleventh century. II Cnut, ch. 52 stipulates that a rapist was to pay his own *wergild* as compensation:

52. Gif hwa wudewan nydnæme, gebete þæt be were.	52. If anyone takes by force a widow, he is to compensate for it with the wergild.
52,1. Gif hwa mæden nydnæme, gebete þæt be were.	52,1. If anyone takes by force a maiden, he is to compensate for it with the wergild.[126]

Here the recipient of the compensation is unstated, so although it may most logically be taken to be the woman, there can be no certainty on this point. Karras, indeed, claims a similar ambiguity for Alfred, ch. 11,2, commenting: 'even if the 60 shilling compensation here is in addition to a fine to the king, there is nothing to indicate that it went to the woman rather than her kin'.[127] Her reading, however, overlooks the crucial phrase *hire gebete* 'compensate her' in the opening section of Alfred, ch. 11, which – in the laconic style characteristic of the Old English law-codes – clearly applies equally to each of the following sub-clauses.

The severity with which rape was regarded during the later Anglo-Saxon period is also illustrated by penitential literature. Despite Payer's statement that rape 'in the predominant sense of sexual relations forced on a woman, with some degree of violence against her person, is certainly not present as a subject in the penitential and non-penitential literature before Gratian',[128] the offence occurs in the *Pseudo-Egbert Penitential*[129] where book 2, ch. 13 specifies excommunication as the standard penalty:

---

[125] *The Laws of the Kings of England from Edmund to Henry I*, ed. A. J. Robertson (Cambridge, 1925), p. 103.

[126] *English Historical Documents*, ed. Whitelock, p. 463.

[127] Karras, 'Desire, Descendants, and Dominance', p. 28 n. 43.

[128] Payer, *Sex and the Penitentials*, p. 117.

[129] The manuscript traditions of the vernacular penitentials known as the *Pseudo-Egbert Penitential* and the *Pseudo-Egbert Confessional* are discussed by A. J. Frantzen, *The Literature of Penance in Anglo-Saxon England* (New Brunswick, NJ, 1983), pp. 133–9.

Gif hwá mid his ofercræfte wíf oððe mæden nydinga nimð to unrihthǽmede, hire únwilles, beo he amánsumod.[130]	If anyone by fraud takes a woman or a girl in unlawful intercourse, forcibly against her will, he is to be excommunicated.

The same provision is repeated in section 4 of *A Late Old English Handbook for the Use of a Confessor*, immediately before the passage cited above (p. 187).[131] In both instances, the phrase *hire unwilles* reflects the fact that the woman's independent right of volition was recognised by the Church no less than by the State.

Finally, rape also features in the post-Conquest laws attributed to William I. The manuscripts and authenticity of the *Leis Willelme* are discussed by Liebermann, who attributes the compilation to a date prior to 1135, and identifies as primary sources the laws of Cnut and of Alfred.[132] It is therefore interesting to note that ch. 18 offers a direct parallel to Alfred, ch. 11, describing a situation where a woman is assaulted and thrown to the ground for purposes of rape. There is a significant difference, however. It is clear from the *Leis* that the victim is no longer legally independent, for, as in the early Kentish laws concerning intercourse with slaves, compensation is paid to the woman's lord rather than to herself:

18. Cil ki purgist femme a force forfeit ad les menbres.	18. If anyone assaults a woman he shall suffer castration as a penalty.
18,1. Ki abat femme a terre pur fere lui force, la munte al seinur X sol.	18,1. If anyone throws a woman to the ground in order to offer violence to her, the compensation to her lord for breach of his *mund* shall be 10 shillings.
18,2. S'il la purgist, forfait est de membres.	18,2. If he assaults her, he shall suffer castration.[133]

130 *Ancient Laws and Institutes of England*, ed. B. Thorpe, folio edition (London, 1840), p. 369.
131 Fowler, 'A Late Old English Handbook', p. 23.
132 *Gesetze*, ed. Liebermann III, 283–6.
133 *The Laws*, ed. Robertson, pp. 262–3.

By this time, rape was evidently regarded as a crime not against the woman but against her lord. The contrast between the victim's role here and in Alfred, ch. 11 illustrates a drastic fall in the legal status of women between the late ninth and early twelfth centuries.[134]

In conclusion, Alfred, ch. 11 provides vital evidence of the seriousness with which crimes against women were regarded in early Anglo-Saxon England, and of cultural attitudes towards women in ninth-century society. Both in its immediate application within the *domboc*, and in the wider context of English and continental legislation, it testifies to a firm commitment to the protection of women against sexual attack, with important implications for the legal status of women at this period. A woman who was entitled to receive compensation on her own behalf for crimes committed against her person cannot have been regarded as a mere chattel. On the contrary, she would appear to have enjoyed a degree of legal autonomy which was broadly comparable with that of her male contemporaries, and a personal independence which would have been the envy of her post-Conquest successors. As Doris Stenton commented some forty years ago: 'The evidence which has survived from Anglo-Saxon England indicates that women were then more nearly the equal companions of their husbands and brothers than at any other period before the modern age'.[135] The reading of Alfred, ch. 11 presented in this paper offers strong support for this position.[136]

[134] The impact of the Norman Conquest on the legal status of women has been much discussed in recent years: see esp. P. Stafford, 'Women in Domesday', *Reading Medieval Studies* 15 (1989), 75–94; and 'Women and the Norman Conquest', *Transactions of the Royal Historical Society*, 6th ser., 4 (1994), 221–49.

[135] D. M. Stenton, *The English Woman in History* (London, 1957), p. 348.

[136] I am grateful to the anonymous referee of *Medium Ævum* for some very helpful comments on an earlier version of this article.

11.

A NEW READING OF ALFRED, CH. 26

First published 1997: *Nottingham Medieval Studies* 41, 1–12.

Chapter 26 of the law-code issued by King Alfred the Great towards the end of the ninth century is concerned with compensation for the rape of underage girls.[1] The clause is usually taken to set the level of compensation at the same rate as for adult women. The purpose of this article is to put forward an alternative interpretation, based on linguistic criteria and on comparative evidence from continental Germanic legislation.

The Old English text of Alfred, ch. 26, survives in three manuscripts. The earliest and most reliable is Cambridge, Corpus Christi College MS 173, dating from the mid-tenth century. Here the clause reads as follows:

> Gif mon ungewintrædne wifmon to niedhæmde geðreatige, sie ðæt swa ðæs gewintredan monnes bot.[2]

The standard translation is provided by Whitelock:

> If anyone rapes a girl not of age, that is to be the same compensation as for an adult.[3]

The other manuscripts are Maidstone, Kent Archives Office, DRc/R1 (*Textus Roffensis*) and Cambridge, Corpus Christi College MS 383, both dating from the early twelfth century, and there is also a Latin version in the twelfth-century legal collection known as *Quadripartitus*. Substantial

[1] The sequence of clauses from Alfred, ch. 25, to Alfred, ch. 31, differs between manuscripts, and this makes it difficult to refer to numbered clauses without ambiguity. I follow the numbering system printed in square brackets in the standard edition of the Anglo-Saxon laws *Die Gesetze der Angelsachsen*, ed. F. Liebermann, 3 vols. (Halle, 1903–16).

[2] *Gesetze*, ed. Liebermann I, 64, 66.

[3] *English Historical Documents c. 500-1042*, ed. D. Whitelock, 2nd ed. (London, 1979), p. 413.

textual variants affect the rubric rather than the clause itself. Whereas Cambridge, Corpus Christi College MS 173, has *Be ungewintredes wifmonnes nedhæmde* 'Concerning the rape of an underage girl',[4] the chapter-heading in the *Textus Roffensis* copy is *Be tyngewintredes monnes nydhæmede* 'Concerning the rape of a ten year old person'.[5] This was not the original reading, for as Liebermann notes, the letters *tyn* have been written over an erasure.[6] The scribe was perhaps influenced by the fact that ten is given as the age of majority in ch. 7,2 of the seventh-century West Saxon laws of Ine,[7] a compilation which survives only as an appendix to Alfred's own code. Like the other two manuscripts, the *Textus Roffensis* has *ungewintredne* in the main clause. The rubric to Cambridge, Corpus Christi College MS 383, is yet more idiosyncratic, reading *slæge* 'manslaughter' rather than *nedhæmde* 'rape';[8] but this conflicts with the clause itself and is probably to be regarded as a straightforward error in a notoriously unreliable manuscript. The rubric alone also survives in two further manuscripts, British Library, Cotton Otho MS B.xi (*Be ungewintr:des monnes wif nedhæmd*), and British Library, Cotton Nero MS A.i (*Be ungewintredes wifmannes niedhæmde*), both dating from the eleventh century.[9]

The terminology of Alfred, ch. 26, may repay closer investigation than it has hitherto received. The term *ungewintred* occurs only in this law,[10] but its meaning is transparent, referring to a girl who has not reached the age of majority. The term *gewintred* is more ambiguous. Like Whitelock, all previous editors of the Anglo-Saxon laws take it to mean 'adult'. Lambarde has 'qui adultam',[11] Wilkins 'qui adultæ servæ',[12] Thorpe 'a full-aged person',[13] Schmid 'ut adultae mulieris',[14] Liebermann

[4] *Gesetze*, ed. Liebermann I, 18.
[5] *Ibid.* I, 19.
[6] *Ibid.* I, 19.
[7] *Ibid.* I, 92.
[8] *Ibid.* I, 64.
[9] *Ibid.* I, 18.
[10] A. DiP. Healey and R. L. Venezky, *A Microfiche Concordance to Old English* (Toronto, 1980).
[11] W. Lambarde, *Archaeionomia: sive De Priscis Anglorum Legibus*, 2nd ed. by Abraham Wheloc (Cambridge, 1644), p. 28.
[12] *Leges Anglo-Saxonicae Ecclesiasticae & Civiles*, ed. D. Wilkins (London, 1721), p. 40.
[13] *Ancient Laws and Institutes of England*, ed. B. Thorpe, folio edition (London, 1840), p. 35.
[14] *Die Gesetze der Angelsachsen*, ed. R. Schmid, 2nd ed. (Leipzig, 1858), p. 87.

'für die erwachsene Person',[15] and Attenborough 'an adult'.[16] However, this is not the only meaning of *gewintred* in Old English. Toller's definition is 'grown to full age, full-aged, aged',[17] and the majority of extant occurrences in fact refer not to adulthood but to old age. The term is elsewhere recorded seven times in the literary corpus,[18] and in six instances out of the seven, the meaning is 'of advanced age'. A brief examination of all seven will be appropriate here.

Two occurrences are within a homily for the Monday in Rogationtide, where the frame of reference is the attainment of spiritual maturity:

> Þonne is seo æftre accennednyss gastlicu . Syððan se mann gewintrod bið . . . Þonne is seo þridde accennednyss æft*er* þam soðan andetnyssa syððan se mann gewintrad bið . *and* he hine sylfne gemedmað þurh þa soðan anddetnysse . *and* þurh his scriftes fultu*m* . þæt he bið andfenge drihtenes sylfes lichaman . *and* his blode .[19]

> Then is the second spiritual birth, after the man has grown older. . . . Then is the third birth according to the true confession after the man has grown older and he shows himself worthy through true confession and through the aid of his confessor that he should receive God's own body and his blood.

In both instances, the term clearly refers to advancing age rather than to the transition from childhood to adulthood. The glossary to Tristram's

[15] *Gesetze*, ed. Liebermann I, 67.

[16] *The Laws of the Earliest English Kings*, ed. F. L. Attenborough (Cambridge, 1922), p. 77.

[17] *An Anglo-Saxon Dictionary Based on the Manuscript Collections of the Late Joseph Bosworth*, ed. T. N. Toller (Oxford, 1898); *Supplement* by T. N. Toller (1921); s.v. *ge-wintred*. Toller's entry for this word may not be wholly reliable, translating as he does the phrase *Ðæs gewintredan monnes* in Alfred, ch. 26, as 'a full-aged *man*' (my italics).

[18] Healey and Venezky, *A Microfiche Concordance to Old English*, s.vv. *gewintrad*, *gewintred*, *gewintredan*, *gewintrede*, *gewintrod*. Two separate entries are listed for *gewintrede*, but these are in effect the same, representing almost identical versions of one chapter-heading from the Alfredian translation of the *Pastoral Care*.

[19] H. L. C. Tristram, *Vier altenglische Predigten aus her heterodoxen Tradition, mit Kommentar, Übersetzung und Glossar sowie drei weiteren Texten im Anhang* Freiburg i. Br. dissertation, 1970, p. 179. I am very grateful to Professor Tristram for kindly sending me a copy of her doctoral dissertation, and for advising me on the interpretation of *gewintrod* in the Rogation Day homily.

edition, noting that *ge-wintrian* is not evidenced in dictionaries, defines it as *älter werden, altern* 'to grow old, to age'.[20]

A third occurrence is within a homily on the Nativity of Mary the Virgin:

Ða wæs þonon geworden, *þæt* Ioseph wæs gehaten sum gewintrod man, eode þyder mid iungum mannum and his gyrde bær.[21]	Then it came about, that a certain aged man called Joseph went there with the young men and carried his staff.

Here the contrast with the phrase *mid iungum mannum* 'with the young men' suggests that *gewintrod* is used with the sense 'aged', and this is confirmed a few sentences later when the homilist states that Joseph was overlooked *forðan þe he wæs eald* 'because he was old'.[22] The glossary to Assmann's edition defines *gewintrod* as *alt* 'old'.[23]

A fourth occurrence is as a gloss to Latin *annosam* 'full of years, long-lived' in a manuscript of Sedulius; *Carmen Paschale*.[24]

The only unambiguous use of *gewintred* to mean 'adult, having reached the age of legal majority' occurs in ch. 38 of the late-seventh-century laws of Ine:

Gif ceorl 7 his wif bearn hæbben gemæne, 7 fere se ceorl forð, hæbbe sio modor hire bearn 7 fede: agife hire mon VI scill. to fostre, cu on sumera, oxan on wintra; healden þa mægas þone fru*m*stol, oð ðæt hit gewintred sie.[25]	If a husband and wife have a child together, and the husband dies, the mother is to have her child and rear it; she is to be given six shillings for its maintenance, a cow in summer, an ox in winter; the kinsmen are to take charge of the paternal home, until the child is grown up.[26]

---

[20] *Ibid.* p. 423.

[21] B. Assmann, *Angelsächsiche Homilien und Heiligenleben*, Bibliothek der Angelsächsischen Prosa 3 (Kassel, 1889), p. 130.

[22] *Ibid.* p. 131.

[23] *Ibid.* p. 281.

[24] H. D. Meritt, *Old English Glosses: A Collection* (New York and London, 1945, reprtd 1971), p. 29. The manuscript in which the gloss is recorded (as *ḡwintrā*) is Cambridge, Corpus Christi College 173, but did not originally form part of the same compilation as the manuscript of Alfred's law-code with which it is now bound (N. R. Ker, *Catalogue of Manuscripts Containing Anglo-Saxon* (Oxford, 1957), p. 59).

[25] *Gesetze*, ed. Liebermann I, 104–6.

This may carry particular weight, since the laws of Ine are appended to Alfred's own code in all extant manuscripts, forming part of the composite *domboc*. On the other hand, the two remaining occurrences of *gewintred* are also in texts associated with Alfred, and in both instances the term is used with a sense of old age. The first is a chapter heading in Alfred's translation of Gregory's *Cura Pastoralis*:

Ðætte on oðre wisa sint to maniannne ða ðe medo*m*lice cunnon læran, & ðeah for mi(c)lu*m* ege & for micelre eaðmodnesse forwandiað; & on oðre wisan ða ðe ðon*ne* giet to ðæm gewintrede ne beoð ne geðiegene, & ðeah for hrædhydignesse bioð to gegripene.	That those who are capable of teaching properly, and yet from great fear and humility refuse, are to be admonished in one way; and in another those who are not yet old or experienced enough for it, and yet from hasty zeal undertake it.[27]

Here again the context suggests a sense of maturity – later adulthood – rather than the attainment of legal majority at the age of ten. The final occurrence is even less ambiguous. It appears in the West Saxon translation of *Orosius*' *Histories Against the Pagans*, a work commissioned by Alfred although no longer considered to be his work:[28]

On þæm dagum Ilirice gesetton Ueteromonem þone mon to hiora anwealde, to þon þæt hie siþþan mehten winnan wið Magnentiuse, 7 hi hiene nieddon to leornunga, þeh he gewintred wære.[29]	In those days, the Illyrians appointed the man Vetranio to their government, so that they could then wage war against Magnentius, and they forced him to learning, although he was advanced in years.

[26] *English Historical Documents*, ed. Whitelock, p. 403.

[27] *King Alfred's West-Saxon Version of Gregory's Pastoral Care*, ed. H. Sweet, 2 vols., Early English Text Society 45, 50 (London, 1871, reprinted 1958) II, 375. The reading here is from the Hatton MS; the Cotton MS reading, cited separately by Healey and Venezky (see n.18), is identical as regards the use of the term *gewintrede*.

[28] *The Old English Orosius*, ed. J. Bately, Early English Text Society supplemental series 6 (London, 1980), p. lxxv, comments: 'the overwhelming weight of evidence is that if Alfred was the author of Bo[ethius] and So[liloquies], he could not also have been responsible for Or[osius]'.

[29] *Ibid*. pp. 149–50.

The glossary to Bately's edition defines *gewintred* as 'old in years, aged'.[30]

Comparison with the use of the term elsewhere, then, suggests that *gewintred* in Alfred, ch. 26, may refer to advanced age rather than to adulthood. The distinction is an important one. According to the established reading, the burden of this clause is to equate compensation for all women irrespective of age. If on the other hand *gewintred* were to be taken to denote advanced age, the result would be to equate compensation for the young and the elderly – presumably those before and after the age of child-bearing – in contradistinction to women in the prime of life. Either interpretation is linguistically possible, and either would make sense on contextual grounds. The traditional reading is supported by the Latin rendering *adulte mulieris* in the *Quadripartitus* text,[31] but this must be discounted as evidence in view of the well-known deficiencies of this version. As Whitelock comments, 'The author was probably not an Englishman, and did not always understand his originals'.[32] One reason why an interpretation of *gewintred* as 'past child-bearing age' has not previously been considered may be the fact that compensation for women of advanced age is not defined separately within Alfred's *domboc*, so that there would be no means of establishing the corresponding *gewintredan monnes bot*. The same difficulty may apply, however, to the traditional reading 'adult'. The only clause that might be taken to define the penalty for adult rape is Alfred, ch. 11,2:

Gif he mid gehæme, mid LX scill. gebete.[33]	If he lies with her, he shall pay [her] 60 shillings compensation.[34]

Unfortunately the interpretation of this clause is itself problematic. Although it occurs within a sequence concerning sexual assault, and

[30] *Ibid.* p. 404.

[31] *Gesetze*, ed. Liebermann I, 67.

[32] *English Historical Documents*, ed. Whitelock, p. 360. An authoritative discussion is P. Wormald, '*Quadripartitus*', *Law and Government in Medieval England and Normandy: Essays in Honour of Sir James Holt*, ed. G. Garnett and J. Hudson (Cambridge, 1994), pp. 111–47. A summary account appears in his *The Making of English Law: King Alfred to the Twelfth Century. volume I: Legislation and its Limits* (Oxford, 1999), pp. 236–44.

[33] *Gesetze*, ed. Liebermann I, 56.

[34] *The Laws*, ed. Attenborough, p. 71.

I personally take it to refer to rape,[35] it is usually interpreted in terms of non-violent intercourse.[36]

Lambarde[37] and Wilkins[38] attempt to resolve the difficulty by taking the corresponding *bot* to be that established for the rape of slaves in the preceding clause, Alfred, ch. 25:

25. Gif mon ceorles mennen to nedhæmde geðreatað, mid V scill. gebete þam ceorle; 7 LX scill. to wite.	25.If anyone rapes a *ceorl's* slave-woman, he is to pay five shillings compensation to the *ceorl*, and 60 shillings fine.
25,1. Gif ðeowmon þeowne to nedhæmde genede, bete mid his eowende.[39]	25,1. If a slave rape a slave-woman, he is to pay by suffering castration.[40]

They treat Alfred, ch. 26, as a continuation of ch. 25, under an inclusive chapter-heading *Be nydhæmed*, reading *gewintredes mennes bot* rather than *gewintredan monnes bot* in the main text of the clause. The reading is without manuscript authority, and is not accepted by modern scholars.

The solution may simply be that the phrase *gewintredan monnes bot* in Alfred, ch. 26, refers to a well-known but unwritten scale of damages. It has long been recognised that extant Anglo-Saxon legislation does not represent a complete codification of contemporary law. As Whitelock comments, 'A great amount of customary law . . . was probably never put into writing at all, being too well known and too fixed to require written statement'.[41] It is perhaps significant that whereas Alfred, ch. 18, concerning assaults on nuns, refers directly to a corresponding penalty given elsewhere in the *domboc* (*sie hit twybete swa we ær be læwdum men fundon*[42] 'the compensation is to be double that we have established for a lay person'[43]), no such claim is made in ch. 26. There is therefore no

[35] C. Hough, 'Alfred's *Domboc* and the Language of Rape: A Reconsideration of Alfred, ch. 11', *Medium Ævum* 66 (1997), 1–27, reprinted in this volume.

[36] For instance, C. E. Fell et al., *Women in Anglo-Saxon England and the Impact of 1066* (London, 1984), pp. 63-4, take Alfred, ch. 11,2, to refer to the 'seduction of a free-woman'.

[37] Lambarde, *Archaeionomia: sive De Priscis Anglorum Legibus*, p. 28.

[38] *Leges*, ed. Wilkins, p. 40. The interpretation is reflected in Wilkins' translation 'qui adultæ servæ' quoted above.

[39] *Gesetze*, ed. Liebermann I, 62, 64.

[40] *English Historical Documents*, ed. Whitelock, p. 413.

[41] *English Historical Documents*, ed. Whitelock, p. 362.

[42] *Gesetze*, ed. Liebermann I, 58.

[43] *English Historical Documents*, ed. Whitelock, p. 411.

overwhelming necessity to assume that a corresponding *gewintredan monnes bot* must appear within the *domboc*.

Two points have emerged from the above discussion. Firstly, the term *gewintred* in Old English may mean either 'adult' or 'of advanced age', the latter meaning being predominant in the extant corpus. Secondly, contextual evidence offers no conclusive support in favour of either reading in Alfred, ch. 26. But there is another range of evidence to be explored. Comparison with continental Germanic legislation often throws light on problematic areas of Anglo-Saxon law, and may usefully be applied here. It is in fact highly unusual in Germanic law for this type of compensation to be equal for all age-groups. Under Alamannic law, for instance, an adult woman received twice as much compensation as a girl for sexual attack. *Leges Alamannorum*, ch. 56, defines the various amounts due to an unmarried girl for a wide range of sexual offences including rape, and goes on to state that double the compensation is payable to an adult woman:

56,1. Si quis libera femina virgo vadit itinere suo inter duas villas, et obviavit eam aliquis, per raptum denudat caput eius, cum sex solidis conponat. Et si eius vestimenta levaverit, usque ad genucula denudet, cum sex solidis conponat. Et si cam denudaverit, usque genetalia eius appareant vel posteriora, cum 12 solidis conponat. Si autem ab ea fornicaverit contra voluntate eius, 40 solidos conponat.	56,1. If any free virgin woman [maiden] goes on a journey between two estates, and anyone meets her [and] uncovers her head, let him compensate with six solidi. And if he raises her clothing to the knee, let him compensate with six solidi. And if he exposes her so that her genitalia or posterior appears, let him compensate with twelve solidi. If, however, he fornicates with her against her will, let him compensate with forty solidi.
56,2. Si autem muliere haec contingerit, omnia dupliciter componat, sicut antea diximus de virgine.[44]	56,2. If, however, this happens to an adult woman, let him compensate all things twice what we said above concerning the virgin.[45]

[44] *Leges Alamannorum*, ed. K. A. Eckhardt, Monumenta Germaniae Historica, Legum Sectio I: Leges nationum Germanicarum 5.1, rev. ed. (Hanover, 1966), pp. 115–6.
[45] T. J. Rivers, *Laws of the Alamans and Bavarians* (Pennsylvania, PA, 1977), p. 85.

With regard to other serious offences such as homicide, it is most common for young and old women to be ranked together at a lower rate, with higher compensation for those of child-bearing age. This was the case under Salic law, where *Pactus Legis Salicae*, ch. 41,15, defines two hundred *solidi* as the penalty for killing a free girl before she is able to have children:

Si quis puellam ingenuam, *antequam infantes habere possit*, occiderit, mallobergo hismala sunt, denarios VIIIM qui faciunt solidos CC culpabilis iudicetur.[46]	If anyone kills a girl who is free-born before she can have children (known in the malberg as *hismala*), let him be held liable for 8000 denarii, which make 200 solidi.[47]

Ch. 41,17 gives the same penalty for killing a woman past middle age who is no longer capable of child-bearing:

Post media uero etate et postquam infantes non potest habere, qui eam occiderit VIIIM denarios qui faciunt solidos CC culpabilis iudicetur.[48]	But after middle age and after she can have no more children, let him who kills her be held liable for 8000 denarii, which make 200 solidi.[49]

At the same time, ch. 41,16 values a woman who has begun to bear children at six hundred *solidi*:

Si quis mulierem ingenuam, postquam ceperit nutrire, occiderit, XXIVM denarios qui faciunt solidos DC culpabilis iudicetur.[50]	If anyone kills a freewoman after she has begun to nurse, let him be held liable for 24,000 denarii, which make 600 solidi.[51]

These provisions are repeated in ch. 65e,2–4, with the additional information that a *puella* is defined as a girl up to twelve years of age, while a mature woman is entitled to maximum compensation up to sixty,

[46] *Pactus Legis Salicae*, ed. K. A. Eckhardt, Monumenta Germaniae Historica, Legum Sectio I: Leges nationum Germanicarum 4.1 (Hanover, 1962), p. 160.
[47] T. J. Rivers, *Laws of the Salian and Rapuarian Franks* (New York, NY, 1986), p. 88.
[48] *Pactus Legis Salicae*, ed. Eckhardt, p. 161.
[49] Rivers, *Laws of the Salian and Ripuarian Franks*, p. 88.
[50] *Pactus Legis Salicae*, ed. Eckhardt, p. 161.
[51] Rivers, *Laws of the Salian and Ripuarian Franks*, p. 88.

the official age-limit for child-bearing.[52] Pointing out that the *wergild* of a freeman was 200 *solidi*, Rivers comments: 'it is evident that a woman's principal contribution to Frankish society was bearing and rearing children. This fact is made manifest by the extremely high wergeld assigned to women of childbearing years'.[53]

Similar clauses are found in Ripuarian law, except that here the upper age-limit for child-bearing is set at a more realistic forty years. *Lex Ribuaria*, chs. 12 and 13, define a penalty of two hundred *solidi* for killing either a girl or a woman over forty years, while a woman of child-bearing age up to forty years is rated at six hundred *solidi*:

12,1. Si quis feminam Ribvariam interfecerit, postquam parere coeperit usque ad quadragesimum annum, sexcentos sold. culpabilis iudicetur. Aut si negaverit, cum 70 duobus iuret.	12,1. If anyone kills a Ripuarian woman, from the time that she begins to have children until age forty, let him be held liable for 600 solidi. Or if he denies it, let him swear with seventy-two [oathtakers].
13. Si quis puellam Ribvariam interfecerit, 200 solid. culpabilis iudicetur. Aud si negaverit, cum 12 iuret.	13. If anyone kills a Ripuarian girl, let him be held liable for 200 solidi. Or if he denies it, let him swear with twelve oathtakers.
13a. Si quis f[eminam Ribva]ria[m p]os[t qu]adrag[esimum annum .... inter]fecerit .... CC sol. culpabilis iudicetur aut cu[m 12 (?) iu]ret.[54]	13a. If anyone kills a Ripuarian woman who is older than forty, let him be held liable for 200 solidi, or let him swear with twelve [oathtakers].[55]

Again, there is no question of equal compensation for all age groups.

[52] *Pactus Legis Salicae*, ed. Eckhardt, p. 235; Rivers, *Laws of the Salian and Ripuarian Franks*, p. 111.
[53] Rivers, *Laws of the Salian and Ripuarian Franks*, p. 22.
[54] F. Beyerle and R. Buchner, *Lex Ribvaria*, Monumenta Germaniae Historica, Legum Sectio I: Leges nationum Germanicarum 3.2 (Hanover, 1954), pp. 78–9.
[55] Rivers, *Laws of the Salian and Ripuarian Franks*, p. 175.

Although the continental evidence is mostly concerned with homicide rather than with rape,[56] a clear principle emerges whereby underage girls are equated with women past child-bearing age for purposes of compensation, receiving only half or a third of the amount due to women in the prime of life. The theme is less prominent in Anglo-Saxon legislation, but it is notable that the early-eleventh-century laws of Cnut deal in a single clause with the rape of maidens and of widows, specifying the same penalty in either case. II Cnut, ch. 52, reads as follows:

52. Gif hwa wudewan nydnæme, gebete þ*æt* be were.	52. If anyone takes by force a widow, he is to compensate for it with the wergild.
52,1. Gif hwa mæden nydnæme, gebete þ*æt* be were.[57]	52,1. If anyone takes by force a maiden, he is to compensate for it with the wergild.[58]

The corresponding penalty for the rape of a married woman is not stated: what is significant, however, is that as in the continental laws, both groups of women outside the child-bearing class are grouped together for purposes of compensation. By analogy, the penalty for underage rape in Alfred, ch. 26, may most logically be associated with the penalty for raping a woman past child-bearing age.[59]

To sum up, recorded meanings of *gewintred* in Old English are compatible with an interpretation of the term in Alfred, ch. 26, as either 'adult' or 'of advanced age', with the balance of evidence in favour of the latter. Comparison with continental evidence strongly supports the

---

[56] It is interesting in this connection that, as noted above, the scribe of Cambridge, Corpus Christi College 383 gives the rubric to Alfred, ch. 26, as *Be . . . slæge* 'Concerning manslaughter'.

[57] *Gesetze*, ed. Liebermann I, 346.

[58] *English Historical Documents*, ed. Whitelock, p. 463.

[59] It is interesting to note that the three-fold distinction between women before, during and after the age of child-bearing, while strongly represented in the laws, is barely visible in the place-name corpus that comprises another major source of evidence for women in Anglo-Saxon society. This and other issues are discussed in my 'Women in Place-Names', *Perceptions of Place: Twenty-First-Century Interpretations of English Place-Name Studies*, ed. J. Carroll and D. N. Parsons (Nottingham, 2013), pp. 251–81, which appeared since this essay was first published. A corpus of Old English and Old Norse feminine personal names in English place-names was compiled for my 'Women in English place-names', *'Lastworda Betst': Essays in Memory of Christine E. Fell with her Unpublished Writings*, ed. C. Hough and K. A. Lowe (Donington, 2002), pp. 41–106.

meaning ‘past child-bearing age’. I therefore suggest the following translation of the clause:

> If anyone rapes a girl not of age, that is to be the same compensation as for a woman past child-bearing age.

PART III:

LAW AND MANUSCRIPTS

12.

PALAEOGRAPHICAL EVIDENCE FOR THE COMPILATION OF *TEXTUS ROFFENSIS*[1]

First published 2001: *Scriptorium* 55, 57–79.

The *Textus Roffensis* (Medway Archive and Local Studies Centre, MS DRc/R1) is widely recognized as one of the most important post-Conquest manuscripts of Anglo-Saxon legal material. Written throughout by a single scribe and datable on internal evidence to 1122–1123, it appears to have been designed as a two-part volume, comprising a collection of legislative texts in Old English and Latin (fols. 1–118) followed by a cartulary of Rochester Cathedral Priory (fols. 119–235). The two parts are reproduced as separate volumes in the Early English Manuscripts in Facsimile series, and are discussed in some detail in the introductions to those volumes by Peter Sawyer and in subsequent studies by Mary P. Richards and Patrick Wormald.[2]

---

[1] This paper was written while I was in receipt of a Leverhulme Research Fellowship from October 1999–March 2000. I am very grateful to the directors of the Leverhulme Trust for their support and to Professor Simon Keynes for his constructive comments on an earlier version of this paper. I am also grateful to the staff of Medway Archives and Local Studies Centre for their helpfulness and efficiency during my visits to Strood to work on the manuscript, and in particular to Mr Stephen Dixon, Borough Archivist.

[2] *Textus Roffensis: Rochester Cathedral Library Manuscript A.3.5. Part I*, ed. P. H. Sawyer, Early English Manuscripts in Facsimile 7 (Copenhagen, 1957); *Textus Roffensis: Rochester Cathedral Library Manuscript A.3.5. Part II*, ed. P. H. Sawyer, Early English Manuscripts in Facsimile 11 (Copenhagen, 1962); M. P. Richards, 'Texts and Their Traditions in the Medieval Library of Rochester Cathedral Priory', *Transactions of the American Philosophical Society* 78.3 (1988), esp. 43–60, '*The Textus Roffensis*'; P. Wormald, '*Laga Eadwardi*: the *Textus Roffensis* and its Context', *Anglo-Norman Studies* 17 (1995), 243–66, reprinted in his *Legal Culture in the Early Medieval West: Law as Text, Image and Experience* (London, 1999), pp. 115–38 (all page references are to the reprint); P. Wormald, *The Making of English Law: King Alfred to the Twelfth Century* I:

The purpose of this paper is to examine the palaeographical evidence for the compilation of the manuscript, focusing on the Old English sections of Part I. The vernacular texts are differentiated from the Latin not only by the use of the Anglo-Saxon letters *þ*, *ð* and *wynn* and of different letter-forms for *d*, *f*, *g*, *h* and *r*, but by the use of an insular form of *s* in addition to the caroline and round forms also used for Latin, and of curving and *f*-shaped forms of *y* in addition to the straight-limbed form also used for Latin. An uncial form of *r* also appears occasionally in Old English. This uncial *r* had gone out of fashion by the twelfth century, as had the curving and *f*-shaped forms of *y*; and Sawyer noticed that all three are used in *Textus Roffensis* only up to fol. 37. At the same point, linguistic corrections, common at the beginning of the manuscript, almost disappear. Sawyer therefore concluded that the scribe had begun by reproducing fairly accurately both the language and the script of his exemplar, but had decided from fol. 38 to update both as he went along:

> Before, but not after fo. 38 the scribe made many linguistic alterations. It is likely that before he altered them the texts were a fairly close copy of his immediate source and it is also probable that the unusual letter forms show the influence of that source. The changes at fo. 38 may mean that when the scribe reached that point he decided to modernise both the script and the language of his source.[3]

Believing, as Sawyer did, that the legal material in Part I had been copied largely from a single source, there was no reason to explore the matter further.[4] More recently, however, Wormald has demonstrated that the collection was in fact assembled from a range of different sources by the scribe himself, and re-ordered so that as far as possible each quire was self-contained and began with a new text.[5] In the light of this, the deployment of letter-forms takes on a new significance. While Sawyer simply noted that the use of an archaic form of *y* at the beginning of the manuscript 'probably means that the source used by the scribe ... also had this letter form', the realisation that more than one source was actually used raises the possibility that the distribution of this and of other variant letter-forms may repay closer examination. Archaic graphs are not uniformly distributed throughout fols. 1–37, nor indeed within individual

---

Legislation and its Limits (Oxford, 1999), 244–53.

[3] *Textus Roffensis Part I*, ed. Sawyer, p. 14.

[4] Sawyer, following Liebermann, thought that *Textus Roffensis*, Cambridge, Corpus Christi College 383, and *Quadripartitus* derived from a common source, a lost Canterbury manuscript designated 'hbq' in Liebermann's stemma.

[5] '*Laga Eadwardi*'.

quires. They are found in certain texts but not in others, while the incidence of *þ* / *ð* and of alternative forms of *s* also varies across different texts, not only within folios 1–37 but throughout the manuscript. It therefore seems possible that the choice of letter-forms may be related to the use of different exemplars, so that the distribution of alternative graphs may help to differentiate between these exemplars and to provide additional information on the composition and structure of the manuscript.

1. The Cartulary

The hypothesis that the use of variant letter-forms in the Old English sections of *Textus Roffensis* Part I may derive from the manuscript's exemplars can be tested with reference to the cartulary texts in Part II. These are mainly written in Latin but include boundary clauses and other passages in Old English. Single-sheet originals are extant for five of the charters containing Old English, so that the scribe's choice of graphs may in these instances be compared directly with his sources.[6] Since archaic forms of *r* and *y* are almost entirely absent from Part II, the following analysis is based on the distribution of *þ* and *ð* and of the variant forms of *s*.

The first vernacular passage which can be compared with a single-sheet original is the boundary clause to S 35 on 130r2–12.[7] Here the *Textus Roffensis* copy uses insular *s* exclusively (nineteen occurrences), with eight occurrences of *ð* but none of *þ*. In the eighth-century original, London, British Library, Cotton Charter viii. 34, insular *s* and *ð* are also exclusively used.[8] The bounds of S 266 on 131r1–6 similarly use only insular *s* (ten occurrences), with seven occurrences of *ð* and a single *þ* in 131r3 *þæt*. In the single-sheet original, London, British Library, Cotton Charter vi. 4, insular *s* and *ð* are exclusively used.[9] The boundary clause

[6] *Charters of Rochester*, ed. A. Campbell, AS Charters 1 (London, 1973), pp. xiii–xiv, finds it 'highly likely that the *Textus Roffensis* texts of the charters found also on single sheets were derived from the single sheets which are still extant', and comments that 'The texts of the ... charters in the *Textus Roffensis*, when compared with the single sheets, inspire considerable confidence in the care, honesty, and accuracy of the scribe of the *Textus Roffensis*'.

[7]. In references to Anglo-Saxon charters, S = *Anglo-Saxon Charters: an Annotated List and Bibliography*, ed. P. H. Sawyer, Royal Historical Society Guides and Handbooks 8 (London, 1968), followed by the number of the document. A revised version is now available at http://www.esawyer.org.uk.

[8]. E. A. Bond, *Facsimiles of Ancient Charters in the British Museum*, 4 vols. (London, 1873–8) II, 4.

[9] Bond, *Facsimiles of Ancient Charters* IV, 5.

to S 327 on 135r22–135v7 again prefers insular *s* and *ð*, with a single occurrence of *þ* in 135v6 *þare*. Unfortunately the single-sheet version, London, British Library, Cotton Charter viii. 29, is generally considered to be a late copy,[10] and is therefore of limited value for purposes of comparison. It may nonetheless be relevant to note that here too *ð* is exclusively used, although there are four occurrences of Anglo-Saxon long *s* alongside the insular form.[11]

The short boundary clause to S 165 on 136v21–3 is written in caroline script, with caroline forms of *f*, *g* and *r* as well as *s*, so it is unsurprising that it bears little resemblance to the ninth-century original, London, British Library, Cotton Charter viii. 31.[12] S 1458, an account of the history of several estates in Kent on 147r12–148r19, has seven occurrences of caroline *s*, with fifty-eight occurrences of *ð* (thirty-seven in word-initial position, seventeen medial, four final) and twenty-three of *þ* (twenty initial, one medial, two final).[13] Comparison with the tenth-century single-sheet original, London, British Library, Cotton Charter viii. 20, shows that in seventy-nine out of eighty-one instances, the choice of *þ* or *ð* coincides with that of the exemplar.[14] The two exceptions are 148r11 *suð* and 148r14 *ðam*, where the original has *suþ* and *þā* respectively: the final letter of *suþ*, however, is barely visible at a line-ending, so it is possible that the *Textus Roffensis* scribe may have been uncertain which graph was intended. Of the seven occurrences of caroline *s* in the cartulary text, three correspond to Anglo-Saxon long *s* in the single-sheet original: 148r10 *east*, 148r10 *west* and 148r13 *east*. In the other four instances (147r15–16 *bi/scope*, 147r19 *æfstan*, 147v21 *cristes*, 148r12 *west*), Cotton Charter viii. 20 has insular *s*; while it also has a further occurrence of long *s* represented by the insular variety in *Textus Roffensis* 147v19 *dunstane*. In short, both sets of graphs reflect the influence of the exemplar, with *þ* and *ð* corresponding very closely to the original. On the other hand, no attempt is made to reproduce archaic letter-forms such as tall *e* or curving *y*. The latter appears twice in the single-sheet charter, but is represented by straight-sided *y* in *Textus Roffensis* 147r15 *yrfe* and 147r24 *yrfe*. This lends credence to Sawyer's view that the disappearance of old-fashioned

---

[10] *Anglo-Saxon Charters*, ed. Sawyer, p. 152. Campbell considers that 'the copy may be before 900' (*Charters of Rochester*, p. xiv) or alternatively 'about 975' (*ibid.* p. xxiv).

[11] Bond, *Facsimiles of Ancient Charters* II, 35.

[12] *Ibid.* II, 10.

[13] Caroline *s* is also used for an addition above 148r13, corresponding to insular *s* in the charter original.

[14] Bond, *Facsimiles of Ancient Charters* III, 34.

graphs from about fol. 37 represents a change in scribal policy rather than a change of exemplar.

The use of *þ* and *ð* is regularized in the bounds to S 671 on 151r20–3 and 151r24–151v9, with *þ* used initially, *ð* medially and finally, and there are four instances of caroline *s*, all before *t*. Here the distribution of *þ* and *ð* corresponds precisely to that of the tenth-century original, London, British Library, Cotton Charter viii. 33, but the use of *s* is substantially different, with only one of the four instances of caroline *s* in the *Textus Roffensis* copy coinciding with long *s* in the original (151v9 *east*).[15] In the other three instances, the single-sheet version has insular *s*, while it also has no less than nine occurrences of long *s* represented in *Textus Roffensis* by the insular variety.[16]

Although the remaining cartulary texts of Part II cannot be compared with single-sheet originals, the occurrence of identifiable patterns within but not between texts again suggests a close adherence to exemplars. The will of Dunn on 140r20–140v8 (S 1514) uses insular *s* exclusively, with eleven occurrences of *ð* (in all positions) and three of *þ* (two initial, one medial). The Old English bound to S 339 on 141r1–14 has several instances of *þ* in initial position but continues to prefer *ð* and to use only the insular form of *s*, as is also the case in the bounds to S 321 142r7–12 and to S 514 on 143v4–14. The will of Brihtric and Ælfswith on 144r5–145r (S 1511), however, is quite different, using caroline *s* six times before *t* and twice in word-final position.[17] The distribution of letter-forms

[15] *Ibid.* III, 26.

[16] All are within the second part of the bounds (151v1 *sulunga*, 151v2 *Ærest*, 151v2 *eastan*, 151v4 *beorges*, 151v5 *stanes* [first letter], 151v6 *bewestan*, 151v6 *wichammes*, 151v6–7 *ham/mes*, 151v7 *hāmes*). There seems at first sight to be a change in practice within the single-sheet charter itself, since the first part of the bounds (*billanoran ... trind hyrst*) is written in a fairly compressed script using insular *s*, the second (*Þis synt þara tyn sulunga land gemæro ...*) in a more spacious script with much taller ascenders, wider spacing, and predominantly caroline *s*. On closer examination, however, it appears that the first section of the bounds may not be original. The second section starts at the beginning of a line, and the spacing between it and the Latin text two lines above corresponds to the usual line-spacing within the charter. The Latin text of that line concludes after three words, and a short description of land boundaries in Latin and Old English has subsequently been inserted, using a smaller script in order to compress two lines of text into the space available. Curiously, the letter-forms of the *Textus Roffensis* copy correspond more closely to the first, non-original part of the bounds than to the second.

[17] This folio is also notable for an isolated example of curving *y* in 144r13 *kyne*, though not written by the main scribe.

changes again in the boundary clause to S 885 on 153v19–154v3), where caroline *s* occurs five times before *t*, once each before *c* and *u*, and once in word-final position. *Þ* is now more common than *ð*, occurring mainly in initial position whereas *ð* is mainly used medially and finally. In the account of a lawsuit between Bishop Godwine and Leofwine on 155r20–156v1 (S 1456), *þ* substantially outnumbers *ð*, although the latter occurs in all positions, the former mainly at the beginnings of words. The incidence of caroline *s* has increased, with four occurrences before *c*, three before *d*, one before *i* and twelve before *t*. The use of *þ* and *ð* is regularised in the boundary clause to S 893 on 158v5–18), with *þ* consistently being used in initial position, *ð* medially and finally. Insular *s* predominates, but caroline *s* occurs three times before *t*, and once before *y*. In the boundary clause to S 926 on 161v16–162r17, on the other hand, *ð* has taken over from *þ* as the preferred graph, occurring in all positions while *þ* occurs only initially, and caroline *s* occurs six times before *t*, once before *c* and three times in final position. *Þ* and *ð* are fairly evenly distributed in the list of serfs on 162r19–162v11, and caroline *s* occurs twice before *t*; whereas the seven-line list of manumissions on 162v13–19 bristles with no less than five occurrences of caroline *s* (preceding *c*, *e*, *i*, *s* and *wynn* respectively) alongside ten of insular *s*, and has seven occurrences of *þ* (in all positions) with only two of *ð* (both final). In contrast, the lengthy account of disputes concerning land at Snodland and elsewhere, which follows on 162v20–163v16 (S 1457) has only three occurrences of caroline *s*, all before *t*, while *ð* outnumbers *þ* by more than four to one. The first page of the list of estates liable for work on Rochester Bridge on 166v is a replacement leaf in another hand, but the final section of text on 167r uses *þ* exclusively rather than *ð* (there are, however, no instances of the graph in word-final position), and uses mainly insular *s*, with five occurrences of caroline *s*, three before *t* and one each before *c* and *y*. Finally, the vernacular translation of a Charter of William I on 171r4–14 has a single occurrence of caroline *s* before *t* and regularises the use of *þ* and *ð* to position the former consistently at the beginnings of word, the latter in the middle and at the end.

From this evidence, it is reasonable to conclude that the choice of letter-forms by the *Textus Roffensis* scribe was strongly influenced by his sources, particularly as regards the use of *þ* and *ð*. Having established this, we may proceed to an examination of the legal texts in Part I.

2. The Legal Collection

Table 12.1 analyses the use of variant letter-forms within the Old English sections of *Textus Roffensis* Part I, the contents of which are outlined in the Appendix.[18] It shows the incidence of curving, *f*-shaped and straight-sided forms of letter *y* within each text, given both as actual numbers and as percentages rounded to one decimal place, together with the number of occurrences of uncial *r*. Also included is the distribution of *þ* and *ð*, and of the three types of letter *s* – insular, rounded and caroline – together with a breakdown of occurrences in word-initial, word-medial, and word-final position.[19] Whereas Sawyer is correct in stating that all three forms of *s* are 'used in all positions' in the Old English sections of Part I as a whole,[20] patterns of use are clearly differentiated across the various texts, being regularized in some but not in all. The crucial factor with regard to caroline *s* appears to be the letter following, for in some but not all texts caroline *s* occurs mainly or exclusively before letter *t*, traditionally preceded in Anglo-Saxon Minuscule script by the native 'long' *s*, to which the *Textus Roffensis* form occasionally bears a close resemblance.[21] Letters preceded by caroline *s* in individual texts are analyzed in **Table 12.2**. The tables exclude occurrences of capital *S*, which are invariably based on the uncial form, and also exclude emended letter-forms since the choice of graph may in such instances have been influenced by the space available.[22] Interlinear and marginal additions

---

[18] Quire 10 has been misplaced, and belongs between the present quires 4 and 5.

[19] The identification of initial, medial or final position relates to spacing in the manuscript rather than to modern word division, but ignores tironian signs attached to a following word. There are many instances where it is uncertain whether a space is intended, and so the figures should be regarded only as a rough guide in this respect. The word 'various' indicates that a letter-form is used indiscriminately, not that every possible combination in which it might appear is represented on the page.

[20] *Textus Roffensis Part I*, ed. Sawyer, p. 13.

[21] *Ibid.* pp. 13–14, notes that 'The descender of caroline *s* generally ends on the line but it sometimes continues below the line and curves to the left', as in 6r22 *standen* and 37v24 *stande*. This extended, curving *s* is very similar to Anglo-Saxon long *s*, and where it consistently appears in the same position, most commonly before letter *t*, the implication would appear to be that it was copied directly from an early exemplar.

[22] For instance, on most occasions where *i* or *ie* is converted to *y*, the minim stroke of the original letter *i* is used as the basis for the straight-limbed version of *y*, as in 4r11 *acwyle*. In 4v7 *nylle*, however, a curving *y* is produced to fit into the narrow space between the original *n* and *l*.

in – so far as one can tell – the main hand are counted separately, with the figures italicized and underlined respectively. They are not included in the percentages, since again other factors may be involved.[23]

This range of evidence throws light on a number of different aspects of the manuscript including the range of sources used in compiling the collection, the number of exemplars available for individual items, the authorship of the rubrics, and the codicology of individual quires. Each of these areas will be discussed separately below.

2.1 Sources

It is immediately evident from **Tables 12.1** and **12.2** that different texts display different patterns in the deployment of letter-forms. For instance, archaic letter-forms – curving and f-shaped *y* and uncial *r* – occur in both the Kentish laws (fols. 1–6) and the Alfred/Ine *domboc* (fols. 9–31v20),[24] but not – with the sole exception of a curving *y* in 7r2 *syndan* – in *Hadbot* (7r–7v10) or the West Saxon Regnal Table (7v12–8v) positioned between them at the end of quire 1. The two groups of texts are also differentiated by the use of other graphs. Whereas the Kentish laws and Alfred/Ine are united in a preference for round *s* (54.7% and 52.7% respectively), closely followed by insular *s* (38.2% and 42.2%), both *Hadbot* and the Regnal Table use caroline *s* for more than 70% of all occurrences. Over 50% of occurrences of caroline *s* in both the Kentish laws and Alfred/Ine precede letter *t*, a pattern not reflected in *Hadbot* or the Regnal Table, and while the Kentish laws and Alfred/Ine use round *s* in all positions, but with a majority of occurrences at the beginnings of words, round *s* occurs in the Regnal Table only in word-final position, and in *Hadbot* mainly in word-final position. Quite clearly, these texts were not copied as a group from a single exemplar. The palaeographical evidence offers strong support for Wormald's assertion that the scribe himself was responsible for re-ordering the material, inserting *Hadbot* and the Regnal Table after the Kentish laws in order to fill up the quire.[25] Moreover, the fact that linguistic corrections occur in the former texts as well as in those with archaic letter-forms confirms that the sparsity of such corrections from

[23] With interlinear additions, *þ* may be preferred to *ð* because its descender can be elongated to double as an omission marker, as in 14r16 '*þu*'; while the use of caroline *s* for additions on pages where this form is otherwise unrepresented may testify to the use of a second exemplar, as discussed below.

[24] Figures for fols. 11, 12, 13 and 16 are omitted from the totals for Alfred/Ine for reasons discussed below.

[25] '*Laga Eadwardi*', p. 120.

fol. 38 reflects a change in scribal practice rather than the use of a more up-to-date exemplar.[26]

Whether or not any of the texts in quires 1–3 may derive from a common source is more difficult to establish. No source is known for the Kentish laws, and Wormald tentatively suggests a 'home grown' Rochester manuscript as a possible exemplar for these as well as for the first version of Alfred/Ine.[27] Despite the similarities noted above, however, the two sets of laws are differentiated by the use of *þ* and *ð*, with the Kentish codes strongly favouring *þ* (69.2%) while Alfred/Ine shows a slightly less marked preference for *ð* (63.2%). The same graphs serve to differentiate *Hadbot* from the Regnal Table, since the former uses *þ* for 72.7% of all occurrences, the latter for only 23.8%. *Hadbot* is one of a group of anonymous texts attributed to Archbishop Wulfstan, also including *Að* (39v5–13), *Mircna Laga* (39v14–22), *Geþyncðo* (93r16–93v23) and *Norðleoda Laga* (93v23–94r).[28] Wormald suggests that these may have belonged together in the scribe's exemplar, being split up in *Textus Roffensis* in order to fill available spaces within quires.[29] All show a comparable preference for *þ* over *ð*, but again the palaeographical evidence is inconclusive as the heavy use of caroline *s* in *Hadbot* is not paralleled by any others in the group.

In marked contrast with all the preceding texts, *Be Blaserum* and *Forfang* in quire 4 (31v21–32r8) use insular *s* almost exclusively, with only two occurrences each of round and caroline *s*, while *þ* outnumbers *ð* by six to one. Evidently this reflects a change of exemplar. This is particularly significant since Liebermann's case for a common source for *Textus Roffensis*, Cambridge, Corpus Christi College 383, and *Quadripartitus* depended crucially on the fact that in all three manuscripts, Alfred/Ine is followed by *Be Blaserum* and *Forfang*. Wormald argues that the *Textus Roffensis* scribe was responsible for spontaneously adding *Be Blaserum* to Ine's code, as evidenced by the use of darker ink and larger lettering from 31v21–32v24, and by the fact that on 11r, the rubric to *Be Blaserum* is written over the opening initial of Alfred's preface and must therefore be a later addition.[30] The case is already a strong one, and is placed beyond reasonable doubt by the palaeographical evidence. *Ordal*

[26] Examples include *Hadbot* 7r6 *hi* → *hy*, Regnal Table 8v4 *Hi* → *Hy* and 8v24 *ofspring* → *ofspryng*.

[27] '*Laga Eadwardi*', p. 132.

[28] D. Bethurum, 'Six Anonymous Old English Codes', *Journal of English and Germanic Philology* 49 (1950), 449–63.

[29] '*Laga Eadwardi*', p. 120.

[30] *Ibid.* p. 122.

(32r10–32v21) is different again, with the first appearance of caroline *r* in 32r12 *arceb[iscopes]*,[31] and a higher incidence of caroline *s* than in any other text except the three-line *Walreaf* on 32v22–4. The two texts are also linked by the use of letter *w* in the rubric to *Ordal* (32r10) and the first word of *Walreaf* (32v22), and by the regularization of *þ* and *ð*, with *þ* occurring exclusively in word-initial position, *ð* medially and finally. The only occurrence of *þ* in non-initial position on 32v is in the rubric to II Æthelstan in the last line, which also signals the re-introduction of round *s*. Following on from this, II Æthelstan (32v24–37r6) uses *þ* and *ð* indiscriminately, and round *s* extensively, as do V Æthelstan (37r7–38r5) and the IV Æthelstan fragment (38r5–18).

It is also clear from **Table 12.1** that the disappearance of old-fashioned letter-forms after fol. 37 does not result from the scribe consistently substituting his own preferred graphs for those of his exemplar. If this were the case, the script would be all of a piece from fol. 38. Instead, different texts continue to reflect different patterns of use for *þ* / *ð* and for the variant types of *s*. Whereas the three sets of Æthelstan's laws on 32v24–38r18 are united in a preference for round s in all positions, with insular s a close second and caroline s hardly featuring at all, the beginning of *Pax* at 38r20 marks a change to the use of caroline *s* for a majority of instances in both this and the following text *Swerian*. The two also concur in a preference for *ð* as opposed to *þ*, the latter occurring only initially but the former in all positions, whereas both graphs are used indiscriminately in the Æthelstan texts. It is particularly interesting to see what happens on 39v, where the last four lines of *Swerian* in 1–4 are followed by *Að* (5–13) and *Mircna Laga* (14–22). Insular *s* is hardly represented at all in either *Pax* (38r20–4) or *Swerian* (38v–39v4), but makes a dramatic comeback in *Að* – not, however, at the beginning of the text in line 5, but in line 10, where a new section begins with an enlarged initial *T*. The first section of *Að* on 39v5–9 uses caroline *s* almost exclusively, but this disappears in favour of the insular form in 39v10–13, where *ð* also replaces *þ* as the preferred graph. It is difficult to know what to make of this, but it may suggest that the scribe took the two parts of *Að*, which appear in reverse order in other manuscripts, from different sources.

Insular *s* continues to predominate in *Mircna Laga* (39v14–22) and in most texts in quires 5, 6 and 10, but is outnumbered by caroline *s* in II Edward (43r22–44r22), *Geþyncðo* (93r16–93v23), *Be Wifmannes Beweddunge* (94v–95r9) and *Hit Becwæð* (95r23–95v18). In none of these is caroline *s* followed by letter *t* as systematically as in the Kentish laws

[31] Except in the Latin words *Veritatem and mentior* on 6r19 and 6r20, and *ælfred* in the rubric to Alfred/Ine on 9r1.

and Alfred/Ine, although such a tendency does appear at the beginning of Edward and Guthrum, where seven out of ten occurrences of caroline *s* on 40r precede *t*. William I's writ On Exculpation (47r23–47v) stands out as the only item (apart from the very short *Walreaf*) to make no use of round *s*. It also contains two occurrences of *w*, not seen since *Ordal* and *Walreaf* on fol. 32: all three texts are uniquely preserved in this manuscript. Round *s* otherwise represents between 6% and 20% of occurrences of *s* in each text within quires 5, 6 and 10 – substantially less than in the Kentish codes, Alfred/Ine, or II, V and IV Æthelstan. As in *Hadbot* and the Regnal Table in quire 1, it now occurs mainly or exclusively in word-final position. The use of *þ* and *ð* is also regularized in some but not all texts in these quires. *Wergeld* (41v19–42r21), I and II Edward (42r22–44r22), and I and II Edmund (44r22–46r11) all show a strong preference for *ð* in all positions, with *þ* being restricted largely or entirely to initial use. In Edward and Guthrum (40r–41v19), I Æthelred (46r11–47r23), William I (47r23–47v), III Æthelred (48r–49v18), VI Æthelstan (88r–93r16), *Geþyncðo* (93r16–93v23) and *Norðleoda Laga* (93v23–94r), the use of both graphs is regularized, with *þ* occurring mainly in initial position, *ð* medially and finally.[32] In the three sets of Æthelstan's laws in quire 4, on the other hand, the distribution of the two graphs is fairly even; and this suggests that the separation of VI Æthelstan from other laws by the same king may not be attributable solely to the exigencies of quire layout. Not only was this code too long to fit in the same quire, it was evidently taken from a different source. Further evidence of this is provided by the distribution of letter *s*. The three Æthelstan codes in quire 4 are united in a strong preference for round *s* (58.1% to 74.5%) followed by insular *s* (20.6% to 36.6%), with caroline *s* used for less than 8% of occurrences in any of the three. In VI Æthelstan, these preferences are reversed, with caroline *s* accounting for 42.9% of all occurrences, insular *s* for 47.5%, and round *s* making a poor showing at 9.7%. The Old English text of VI Æthelstan, like the Kentish law-codes, is extant only in the *Textus Roffensis*. It clearly did not derive from the same source as the Æthelstan laws in quire 4.[33]

---

[32] The figures would be even more overwhelming were it not that capital *Đ* is used for initials on some folios where the minuscule form occurs only medially and finally, as for instance 48r, 89r and 91r. On the other hand, the incidence of *þ* may be higher on folios with many abbreviations, as it forms the standard abbreviation for *þæt*. A comparison of initials and abbreviations across folios and texts might be enlightening, but has not been attempted at this stage.

[33] The same conclusion is reached by Wormald, *The Making of English Law*, p. 297, on the basis of textual evidence.

A striking change takes place at the beginning of *Be Wifmannes Beweddunge* on 94v, where *ð* begins to be used frequently in initial position as well as medially and finally. This practice continues through the two following texts, *Charm* (95r10–23) and *Hit Becwæð* (95r23–95v18), and results in *ð* substantially outnumbering *þ* in all three. At the same time, caroline *s* enjoys a marked increase in popularity, leaping from 13% in *Norðleoda Laga* to 53.2% in *Be Wifmannes Beweddunge*, 33.3% in the *Charm*, and 68.7% in *Hit Becwæð*. It is feasible therefore that the three final texts of quire 10 were copied as a group from a single source. Indeed, it may even be possible to identify other members of the group. Common features of these three texts are the use of *ð* in at least 75% of instances and in all positions, the restriction of *þ* to word-initial and word-medial position, the use of caroline *s* in at least 30% and of insular *s* in at least 20% of instances, and the restriction of round *s* to word-final position. **Table 12.1** shows that the only other texts which conform either exactly or very closely to the same pattern are *Swerian*, *Wergeld*, I and II Edward, and I and II Edmund. This is particularly significant since a relationship between these texts has already been adduced by Wormald on the grounds of shared idiosyncracies in the arrangement of material within *Textus Roffensis*, Cambridge, Corpus Christi College 383 and *Quadripartitus*, leading him to suggest that 'a mini-collection comprising the paired Edward and Edmund codes, Alfred–Guthrum, *Swerian*, *Be Wifmannes Beweddunge*, *Wergeld*, Charm and *Hit Becwæð* reached all three twelfth-century editors'.[34] The palaeographical evidence offers additional support for this conclusion.

It is sometimes possible to account for apparent anomalies within the extant manuscript in terms of an exemplar where the line-divisions fell in different places. As noted above, the use of *þ* and *ð* is largely regularised in certain texts, including I and III Æthelred and VI Æthelstan. Among the rare instances of *ð* in initial position within these texts are 46v18–19 *wur/ðe*, 49v14–15 *fry/ðes*, and 91v16–17 *fri/ðes*. In each case, *ð* occurs at the beginning of a line, and has therefore been classed in **Table 12.1** as the beginning of a unit as written by the scribe. However, this results from the splitting of the word at a line-ending, and clearly derives from an exemplar where it was written as a single unit with *ð* in medial position. This too suggests an element of mechanical copying, rather than the scribe substituting his own preferred graphs.

It remains a coincidence that the old-fashioned letter-forms come to an end at roughly the same point as the scribe changes his copying practice to update the language of the texts in accordance with twelfth-century

[34] *The Making of English Law*, p. 232.

phonology. The most likely explanation appears to be that he decided from fol. 38 to replace the archaic letter-forms of his exemplars, while continuing to copy other graphs as they stood. It is not my intention to suggest that the *Textus Roffensis* scribe consistently reproduced the letter-forms of his exemplars throughout the Old English sections of the manuscript. This is in my view highly unlikely. A tendency towards the clustering of individual graphs also tells against it. For example, all three instances of caroline *s* on 35r (II Æthelstan) occur within three lines of text (15–17), while all thirteen occurrences of the same letter on 45v (II Edmund) are on the bottom half of the page. The same phenomenon appears within the cartulary texts in Part II. In the will of Brihtric and Ælfswith on 144r5–145r (S 1511), for instance, six of the eight instances of caroline *s* occur towards the beginning of the will on 144r, while in the boundary clause to S 926 on 161v16–162r17, caroline *s* occurs nine times within the short section of the bounds on 161v, but only once within the much longer section on 162r. It is noticeable that the opening sections of new texts are sometimes at variance with what follows. As noted above, the opening of Edward and Guthrum on 40r shows a tendency for caroline *s* to be used mainly before *t* which is not maintained on later pages of the same text. Furthermore, twenty-three out of twenty-five instances of curving *y* in Æthelberht's code are on 1r, and almost a quarter of all occurrences of the same letter-form in Alfred/Ine are on the first two folios of quire 2. This may suggest that the scribe followed his sources closely at times of high concentration, particularly when starting on a new text, but occasionally allowed his attention to wander. My contention, then, is simply that the scribe was influenced by his sources, not that he followed them slavishly on all occasions. Where different patterns of use are discernible within different texts – and especially where new patterns coincide with the onset of new texts – it seems reasonable to conclude that they reflect to some extent the usage of different exemplars.

2.2. Interlinear and marginal corrections

The palaeographical evidence also yields information on the number of sources to which the scribe had access for individual texts. On the basis of textual amendments, Wormald suggests that more than one source was used for Alfred/Ine, with corrections taken from a second manuscript exemplar.[35] This view is corroborated by graphemic differences between the main text and the additional material. Caroline *s* accounts for only

[35] '*Laga Eadwardi*', pp. 126–30.

5.1% of occurrences in the main text of Alfred/Ine but for 77.1% of interlinear additions, and whereas the majority of occurrences in the main text precede *t*, only one of the twenty-seven interlinear additions is in this position. Curving and *f*-shaped *y* are both present in the main text but unrepresented in interlinear or marginal additions, and the predominance of *ð* (63.2%) in the main text contrasts with a strong preference for *þ* (82.5%) in the interlinear additions.

To take a specific example, three lines of text are omitted from Ine 24 on 26v and inserted in the lower margin, while the chapter number and opening word *Gif* of Ine 25 are added in the left-hand margin (**Plate 12.1**). To all appearances, the correction is contemporaneous, being written by the main scribe, in the same ink and using the same letter-forms as on the rest of the page. It could therefore be taken as an example of eye-skip, the scribe having accidentally left out three lines from his exemplar and subsequently making good the omission. That this was not the case, however, is indicated by the quite different *distribution* of letter-forms. Elsewhere on this page, the scribe uses mainly round *s*, with eleven occurrences of insular *s* and only four of caroline *s*, three of them in the traditional position before *t*. In the three lines of marginalia at the bottom of the page, round *s* is not represented at all, insular *s* twice, and caroline *s* three times, twice in word-final position and once before *d*. Evidently this was copied from a different exemplar.[36] Similarly on 22r, the words *oððe mid his swister æwumborenre* are omitted from Alfred 42,7 and added in the right-hand margin of the page (**Plate 12.2**). All three instances of letter *s* here are of the caroline variety, a letter-form otherwise represented only twice on 22r and not at all on 22v. Again, a second exemplar would appear to be indicated. By contrast, where on 6r two lines are omitted from Wihtred 20 and 21 and similarly inserted in the lower margin, the letter-forms are fully consistent with those of the main text, so that there is no reason to regard this as anything other than a simple error of omission (**Plate 12.3**).

---

[36] I am uncertain whether the whole of Ine 24 (numbered *LXVIII* in the manuscript) was missing from the first exemplar. The omission mark is at the very end of 26v15, the scribe having apparently written in as much as possible of the missing text within the space available, beginning in the space left blank after the chapter number towards the end of 26v14. It may not be a coincidence that two of the four occurrences of caroline *s* in the main text of this page (including the one not preceding *t*) are within the first part of Ine 24 in 26v15. On the other hand, this would suggest that line 15 was originally blank, which seems unlikely unless the scribe had already realised that his first exemplar was defective and planned to make good the omission without being aware of its length.

2.3 Rubrication

There is some reason to believe that the *Textus Roffensis* scribe made a practice of inserting his own titles in order to assist the reader to navigate through the manuscript. Discussing the use of headings such as *De Bromleage* and *De Hallinges* within the cartulary section, Richards comments:

> These rubrics may well be unique to the copies in the *Textus Roffensis*, for they occur neither in the originals of the charters where they still exist, nor in the fourteenth-century *Liber Temporalium*, still the property of the dean and chapter, which contains copies of most texts in the present collection.[37]

If the scribe added titles to the charter texts in Part II, he may well have done the same for the legal texts in Part I. Wormald notes that since the heading to the laws of Æthelstan on fols. 33ff. is on the last line of 32v, 'these rubrics would have been written late in the process of compilation'.[38] Drawing attention to the fact that the various rubrics to II Æthelstan 'are too inconsistent to have been provided at source', he also raises the possibility of 'scribal initiative or error'.[39] It is certainly suggestive that *Textus Roffensis* not only includes headings apparently omitted from other copies of the same texts, but also contains rubrics different from those preserved elsewhere. The laws of Ine, for instance, are rubricated in English only here and in Cambridge, Corpus Christi College 383.[40] The two rubrics are completely different – *Ines cyninges asetnysse* in *Textus Roffensis*, *Ines lage* in CCCC 383 – suggesting that at least one and probably both scribes were responsible for their own titles. The same applies to the rubric to *Swerian* on 38v1, where the scribe's responsibility for the heading *Hu se man sceal swerie* may be adduced by contrast with the corresponding rubric in CCCC 383: *Ðus man sceal swerigean hyldaðas*. Perhaps most tellingly of all, the only three occurrences of the term *asetnysse* in the extant corpus of Old English are in the rubrics to the laws of Ine, I Edmund, and William I's writ On Exculpation in the *Textus Roffensis*.[41] A single source for these three texts being out of the question on palaeographical as well as other grounds, the logical

[37] 'Texts and Their Traditions', p. 53.

[38] '*Laga Eadwardi*', p. 122 fn. 12.

[39] *The Making of English Law*, p. 300 and fn. 160.

[40] A Latin rubric also appears in *Quadripartitus*.

[41] Dictionary of Old English Project, *Dictionary of Old English A–G*. Version 2.0. CD-ROM, 2008, s.v. *ā-setnes*.

inference is that the rubrics were composed as well as penned by the scribe.

The palaeographical evidence supports this conclusion by revealing marked discrepancies between rubrication and text. On 40r (**Plate 12.4**), two of the only three occurrences of caroline *s* not preceding letter *t* are in the heading to Edward and Guthrum, which does not survive elsewhere. Of the nine instances of caroline *s* on 9r (**Plate 12.5**), no less than four occur in the one-line rubric to Alfred's laws, which is again unique to this manuscript and also contains anomalous occurrences of caroline *g* and *r*. Similarly on 24v (**Plate 12.6**), five out of seven occurrences of caroline *s* are in the rubric to Ine's laws in line 6 – again unique to this manuscript – while of the other two, one occurs before *t* (24v15 *gefæstnode*) and the other looks suspiciously like an addition (24v18 *ðas*). Between them, these two rubrics (totalling eleven words) account for a quarter of all occurrences of caroline *s* not preceding letter *t* in the combined laws of Alfred/Ine.[42] It is of course theoretically possible that the scribe may have taken them from a different source, but the most economical solution is to suppose that he added them himself.

The editorial role which the compiler of *Textus Roffensis* is now known to have adopted may necessitate the revision of many established ideas about the texts themselves.[43] Although the Kentish laws survive only in this copy, the rubric to the first code is known to be not original, since it refers in the past tense to 'the laws which King Æthelberht established in the time of Augustine', and can therefore be dated after the latter's death. Liebermann believed both this and the rubrics to the two following codes to have been drawn up by the original compiler of the series at some time between the eighth and eleventh centuries, preferring an early date before the accession of Æthelberht II in 748 on the grounds that no distinction is made between two kings of the same name, and that Augustine is not yet referred to as a saint.[44] The dating is pushed still further back, to 'no later than Wihtred's time', by Lendinara, who draws attention to the present tense formula *ðis synd wihtrædes domas* in the rubric to the third code and contrasts it with the use of the preterite in subordinate

[42] Always excepting fols. 11–13 and 16, as discussed below.

[43] On the editorial role of the *Textus Roffensis* scribe, see especially Wormald, '*Laga Eadwardi*', who demonstrates that far from being a mere copyist, he 'was not only plotting out his material with considerable care but was incorporating new stuff as he proceeded' (p. 122).

[44] *Die Gesetze der Angelsachsen*, ed. F. Liebermann, 3 vols. (Halle, 1903–16) III, 3.

clauses in the first and second.[45] These considerations may be less compelling than evidence from elsewhere in the manuscript that the scribe himself was responsible for rubricating those texts that otherwise lacked a heading. Again, it is a striking coincidence that three out of six occurrences of round *s* on 1r occur in the rubric, including the only two in non-initial position on either 1r or 1v (**Plate 12.7**). On the other hand, the rubric also includes two instances of curving *y*, an old-fashioned form unlikely to represent the scribe's personal choice unless it reflects a deliberate attempt to integrate the rubric with the rest of the page.

Liebermann's attribution of the three rubrics to a common authorship was partly based on textual similarities, as for instance the occurrence of different parts of the verb *asettan* in the first two,[46] and in this respect his conclusions may still be valid. It is therefore worth considering the possibility that the rubrics to the two later Kentish codes may also be the work not of an eighth-century compiler but of the twelfth-century scribe. The layout of quire 1 is consistent with such a theory, since no space has actually been left for headings to the laws of either Hlothhere and Eadric or Wihtred. This can be demonstrated by comparison with *Hadbot* and the West Saxon Regnal Table on fols. 7–8, neither of which is rubricated.

A blank line is left between them on 7v11, with the Regnal Table beginning on 7v12 with an enlarged initial *Đ* similar to the initials beginning the two later Kentish codes on 3v16 and 5r15 (**Plates 12.8–10**). These too would be demarcated by a blank line were it not for the rubric, which in each case begins on the line above, following directly on from the preceding text. It looks very much as though the rubrics to these laws, as to those of Æthelstan on 32v and others elsewhere in the manuscript, were added as an afterthought in the space available. Since the final line of text of Hlothhere and Eadric's code takes up more of 5r13 than that of Æthelberht's code takes up of 3v14, this would also account for the fact that the rubric to Wihtred's code is shorter than the rubrics to the two preceding series of Kentish laws. Rather than carrying the dating implications suggested by Lendinara, this may simply be because it had to be fitted into a smaller space.

---

[45] P. Lendinara, 'The Kentish Laws', *The Anglo-Saxons from the Migration Period to the Eighth Century: an Ethnographic Perspective*, ed. J. Hines (Woodbridge, 1997), pp. 211–30, at p. 213.

[46] It may not be an entire coincidence that the term *asetnysse*, which as mentioned above is uniquely recorded in the rubrics to the laws of Ine, I Edmund, and William I's writ On Exculpation in *Textus Roffensis*, is formed from this verb.

2.4 Replacement leaves

The data assembled for this study also corroborate a recent suggestion concerning the codicology of the manuscript. The orthographical corrections common throughout quires 1–4 are absent from fols. 11, 12, 13 and 16, leading Wormald to suggest that while fols. 12 and 13 are inserted leaves, 'ff. 11/16 *may be* a replacement sheet: meaning that last three lines of the rubric list, all but ff. 14r–15v of the Mosaic preface and first two pages of Alfred's laws could have been rewritten'.[47] This has obvious and important implications for the integrity of the extant text. The case is strongly supported by the palaeographical evidence. **Tables 12.3** and **12.4** present a breakdown of letter-forms on individual folios of quire 2, revealing that fols. 11–13 and 16 are sharply differentiated from the rest of the quire. These four folios stand alone in containing no occurrences of either curving or *ƒ*-shaped *y*, and in a strong tendency to restrict round *s* to word-final position. Caroline *s* appears before a wider range of letters than on other folios, while a preference for *þ* over *ð*, with a tendency for the former to be used initially, the latter medially and finally, also runs counter to the rest of the quire. Little doubt can remain that fols. 11–13 and 16 have indeed been rewritten.

3. Conclusion

The findings of the present study illustrate the value of palaeographical evidence for the composition and structure of *Textus Roffensis*, testifying to the role played by the scribe in assembling, re-organizing, and rubricating his material. It is uncertain to what extent, if any, the exemplars used may themselves have reproduced the letter-forms of earlier manuscripts. Too little is currently known about this aspect of the copying practices of Anglo-Norman scribes and their Saxon predecessors, but it is at least suggestive that differences are discernible between texts for which other evidence points towards a single source. Since the Kentish laws are otherwise unknown, it seems most likely that all three codes were derived from a single manuscript,[48] now lost, yet a number of palaeographical features appear to unite the two later series in contradistinction to those of Æthelberht. Uncial *r* occurs six times in Wihtred's laws and eight times in

---

[47] '*Laga Eadwardi*', p. 118.

[48] This is, however, not quite axiomatic. The layout of the three codes, with the pre-rubrication line-spacing and opening initials discussed above, resembles that used elsewhere in the manuscript for unrelated material rather than for sequences of texts copied *en bloc* from a single source.

those of Hlothhere and Eadric, but not at all in Æthelberht's code, while there are twenty-five occurrences of curving *y* in Æthelberht, but only one in Hlothhere and Eadric, and none in Wihtred. Caroline *s* is used before a slightly wider range of letters in Æthelberht's code than in the other two, and the preponderance of *þ* over *ð* is less pronounced. If the *Textus Roffensis* scribe was indeed responsible for the rubrication of the three sets of laws, as proposed above, it is no longer necessary to accept Liebermann's arguments that they were brought together as early as the first half of the eighth century. It would appear instead that up to a fairly advanced stage in the textual history of the Kentish laws, Æthelberht's code may have been transmitted separately from those of his successors.[49]

Even more striking is the relationship between Edward and Guthrum and *Wergeld*. The layout of 41v, where *Wergeld* follows directly on from Edward and Guthrum in the middle of line 19, indicates that the scribe failed to recognize the change of text: Wormald describes this as 'an unusual case of this manuscript reproducing its exemplar as automatically as Corpus often did'.[50] It is axiomatic therefore that the two texts derive from a single exemplar, but whereas they agree closely in the distribution of the variant forms of letter *s*, *ð* outnumbers *þ* in *Wergeld* to an extent unparalleled in Edward and Guthrum. This may suggest that the exemplar itself reflected the preferences of two different sources, raising the possibility that other copyists besides the *Textus Roffensis* scribe may regularly have reproduced variant letter-forms from one codex to another. If this does prove to be the case, palaeographical correspondences between copies of the same text may be as important as orthographical similarities in establishing transmission patterns and manuscript stemma.

---

[49] It now seems to me more likely that Æthelberht's code was transmitted alongside that of Wihtred, but separately from the laws of Hlothhere and Eadric. See my 'Numbers in Manuscripts of Anglo-Saxon Law', in *Writing and Texts in Anglo-Saxon England*, ed. A. R. Rumble (Cambridge, 2006), pp. 114–36 (p. 128), reprinted in this volume. A similar conclusion is reached on different grounds by L. Oliver, *The Beginnings of English Law* (Toronto, 2002), p. 29.

[50] *The Making of English Law*, p. 248.

TABLES

See over

Table 12.1 – Distribution of variant letter-forms in the Old English texts of *Textus Roffensis* Part I

text	insular *s*	position of insular *s*	round *s*	position of round *s*	caroline *s*	position of caroline *s*
Æth	109: 45.6%	various	115: 48.1%	106 init 6 med 13 fin	15: 6.3% *1 interlin*	11 init 3 med 1 fin *1 init*
H/E	33: 32.7%	various	61: 60.4% *1 interlin*	39 init 9 med 13 fin *1 fin*	7: 6.9%	4 init 3 med
Wih	63: 32% 4 margin	various 2 init 1 med 1 fin	118: 59.9% 2 margin	48 init 28 med 42 fin 1 init 1 fin	16: 8.1%	5 init 11 med
Kentish laws total	205: 38.2% 4 margin	various 2 init 1 med 1 fin	294: 54.7% *1 interlin* 2 margin	194 init 43 med 69 fin *1 fin* 1 init 1 fin	38: 7.1% *1 interlin*	20 init 17 med 1 fin *1 init*
Had	2: 4.1%	2 init	10: 20.4%	2 init 8 fin	37: 75.6%	26 init 5 med 6 fin
Reg Tab	2: 2%	2 init	26: 25.7%	26 fin	73: 72.3%	28 init 23 med 22 fin
Alf/Ine (**not** fols. 11-13, 16)	651: 42.2% *4 interlin* 4 margin	various *1 init* *1 med* *2 fin* 3 init 1 fin	813: 52.7% *4 interlin* 2 margin	410 init 126 med 277 fin *2 med* *2 fin* 1 init 1 fin	78: 5.1% *27 interlin* 8 margin	various *various* 2 init 2 med 2 fin
Blas/For	16: 80%	11 init 5 med	2: 10%	1 init 1 fin	2: 10%	2 init
Ord	6: 10.3%	4 init 1 med 1 fin	5: 8.6%	2 med 3 fin	47: 81%	various
Wal	0: 0%	—	0: 0%	—	3: 100%	1 init 2 fin

curving *y*	**straight *y***	**f-shaped *y***	**thorn**	**position of *þ***	**eth**	**position of *ð***	**uncial *r***
25: 38.5%	35: 53.8%	5: 7.7%	119: 58.3% *1 interlin*	49 init 17 med 53 fin *1 med*	85: 41.7%	19 init 26 med 40 fin	0
1: 2.6%	35: 89.7%	3: 7.7%	117: 81.2%	78 init 33 med 6 fin	27: 18.8%	11 init 10 med 6 fin	8
0: 0%	48: 98% 2 margin	1: 2%	85: 73.3% *1 interlin*	35 init 42 med 8 fin *1 med*	31: 26.7% 1 margin	16 init 10 med 5 fin 1 init	6
26: 17%	118: 77.1% 2 margin	9: 5.9%	321: 69.2% *2 interlin*	162 init 92 med 67 fin *2 med*	143: 30.8%	46 init 46 med 51 fin	14
1: 4.3%	22: 95.7%	0: 0%	40: 72.7%	30 init 9 med 1 fin	15: 27.3%	2 init 13 med	0
0: 0%	29: 100% 1 margin	0: 0%	25: 23.8% *1 interlin* 1 margin	23 init 1 med 1 fin *1 med* 1 med	80: 76.2% *6 interlin* 1 margin	various *5 init* *1 fin* 1 med	0
102: 17.1%	490: 82.2% *5 interlin* 9 margin	4: 0.7%	505: 36.8% *33 interlin* 7 margin	301 init 158 med 46 fin *32 init* *1 med* 5 init 1 med 1 fin	867: 63.2% *7 interlin* 5 margin	460 init 242 med 165 fin *5 init* *2 med* 2 init 2 med 1 fin	10
1: 5.6%	17: 94.4%	0: 0%	18: 85.7%	12 init 5 med 1 fin	3: 14.3%	2 init 1 fin	0
0: 0%	22: 100%	0: 0%	49: 70%	49 init	21: 30%	14 med 7 fin	0
0: 0%	0: 0%	0: 0%	2: 67%	2 init	1: 33%	1 med	0

text	insular *s*	position of insular *s*	round *s*	position of round *s*	caroline *s*	position of caroline *s*
II As	67: 20.6% *1 interlin* 1 margin	various *1 init* 1 fin	242: 74.5% *3 interlin*	98 init 50 med 94 fin *3 fin*	16: 4.9% *2 interlin* 2 margin	4 init 11 med 1 fin *2 init* 2 init
V As	34: 36.6%	various	54: 58.1% *1 interlin*	21 init 11 med 22 fin *1 fin*	5: 5.4%	2 init 2 med 1 fin
IV As	7: 25%	5 init 2 med	19: 67.9%	11 init 2 med 6 fin	2: 7.1%	2 med
Pax	1: 10%	1 init	3: 30%	3 fin	6: 60%	2 init 4 fin
Swe	3: 2.9%	2 init 1 med	25: 24.3%	1 init 24 fin	75: 72.8% *1 interlin*	various *1 init*
Að	6: 31.6%	2 init 1 med 3 fin	3: 15.8%	3 fin	10: 52.6%	2 init 6 med 2 fin
Mircna Lag	15: 78.9%	7 init 1 med 7 fin	4: 21.1%	1 init 3 fin	0: 0%	—
Ed & Guþ	98: 62%	various	23: 14.6%	23 fin	37: 23.4%	various
Wer	29: 70.7%	various	5: 12.2%	5 fin	7: 17.1%	3 init 4 fin
I Edw	32: 46.4%	various	5: 7.2%	5 fin	32: 46.4%	various
II Edw	33: 43.4% 2 margin	various 2 med	5: 6.6%	5 fin	38: 50%	various
I Edm	42: 61.8%	various	10: 14.7%	10 fin	16: 23.5%	various
II Edm	64: 61.5%	various	11: 10.6%	1 init 10 fin	29: 27.9%	various

curving *y*	**straight *y***	**f-shaped *y***	**thorn**	**position of *þ***	**eth**	**position of *ð***	**uncial *r***
17: 10.6%	142: 88.8% *3 interlin* 2 margin	1: 0.6%	174: 51.9% *9 interlin* 11 margin	133 init 37 med 4 fin *9 init* 6 init 5 med	161: 48.1% *1 interlin*	105 init 45 med 11 fin *1 fin*	1
13: 26%	37: 74%	0: 0%	53: 60.9% *1 interlin*	37 init 13 med 3 fin *1 init*	34: 39.1%	23 init 8 med 3 fin	3
0: 0%	14: 100%	0: 0%	17: 47.2%	10 init 7 med	19: 52.8%	13 init 6 med	0
0: 0%	0: 0%	0: 0%	2: 40%	2 init	3: 60%	2 init 1 fin	0
0: 0%	16: 100%	0: 0%	15: 22.4%	15 init	52: 77.6%	37 init 6 med 9 fin	0
0: 0%	8: 100%	0: 0%	10: 62.5%	7 init 2 med 1 fin	6: 37.5%	1 init 5 fin	0
0: 0%	16: 100%	0: 0%	9: 56.3%	8 init 1 med	7: 43.7%	2 init 5 fin	0
0: 0%	82: 100%	0: 0%	75: 49.3% *1 interlin* 1 margin	63 init 10 med 2 fin *1 init* 1 init	77: 50.7% 1 margin	15 init 59 med 3 fin 1 med	0
0: 0%	28: 100%	0: 0%	4: 8.3%	4 init	44: 91.7%	27 init 11 med 6 fin	0
0: 0%	37: 100%	0: 0%	24: 24.2%	20 init 3 med 1 fin	75: 75.8%	33 init 35 med 7 fin	0
0: 0%	39: 100% *1 interlin*	0: 0%	27: 30.7%	26 init 1 med	61: 69.3%	36 init 15 med 10 fin	0
0: 0%	34: 100%	0: 0%	5: 12.5%	4 init 1 fin	35: 87.5%	23 init 7 med 5 fin	0
0: 0%	52: 100%	0: 0%	17: 14.4%	17 init	101: 85.6%	55 init 30 med 16 fin	0

text	insular *s*	position of insular *s*	round *s*	position of round *s*	caroline *s*	position of caroline *s*
I Eth	68: 71.6%	various	11: 11.6%	11 fin	16: 16.8% *1 interlin*	various *1 fin*
Wil I	32: 58.2%	various	0: 0%	—	23: 41.8%	various
III Eth	63: 49.6%	various	17: 13.4%	4 init 13 fin	47: 37%	various
VI As	196: 47.5% 1 margin	various 1 fin	40: 9.7%	2 init 2 med 36 fin	177: 42.9% *1 interlin*	various *1 init*
Geþ	22: 36.1%	13 init 9 fin	12: 19.7%	1 init 11 fin	27: 44.3%	various
Nor Lag	48: 69.6%	various	12: 17.4%	12 fin	9: 13%	4 init 2 med 3 fin
Wif	23: 37.1%	11 init 6 med 6 fin	6: 9.7%	6 fin	33: 53.2%	various
Charm	10: 55.6%	7 init 2 med 1 fin	2: 11.1%	2 fin	6: 33.3%	2 init 1 med 3 fin
Bec	7: 21.9%	3 init 1 med 3 fin	3: 9.4%	3 fin	22: 68.7% *1 interlin*	various *1 init*

curving *y*	**straight *y***	**f-shaped *y***	**thorn**	**position of *þ***	**eth**	**position of *ð***	**uncial *r***
0: 0%	61: 100%	0: 0%	80: 70.8% *1 interlin*	72 init 7 med 1 fin *1 init*	33: 29.2%	8 init 16 med 9 fin	0
0: 0%	20: 100%	0: 0%	18: 40%	17 init 1 med	27: 60%	2 init 15 med 10 fin	0
0: 0%	50: 100%	0: 0%	97: 67.4% *1 interlin*	95 init 2 med *1 init*	47: 32.6%	6 init 25 med 16 fin	0
0: 0%	147: 100% 1 margin	0: 0%	327: 65.3% 3 margin	318 init 8 med 1 fin 3 init	174: 34.7% *1 interlin* 2 margin	13 init 111 med 50 fin *1 fin* 2 med	0
0: 0%	13: 100%	0: 0%	46: 62.2%	37 init 9 med	28: 37.8%	1 init 24 med 3 fin	0
0: 0%	37: 100%	0: 0%	47: 79.7%	41 init 3 med 3 fin	12: 20.3%	2 init 3 med 7 fin	0
0: 0%	28: 100%	0: 0%	13: 24.5%	12 init 1 med	40: 75.5%	29 init 7 med 4 fin	0
0: 0%	9: 100%	0: 0%	1: 8.3%	1 init	11: 91.7%	6 init 5 med	0
0: 0%	11: 100%	0: 0%	4: 12.9%	2 init 2 med	27: 87.1%	20 init 6 med 1 fin	0

Table 12.2 – Letters preceded by caroline *s* in the Old English texts of *Textus Roffensis* Part I

text	a	æ	c	d	e	f	i	l	m	n	o	p	s	t	u	wynn	y	—
Æth			4 *1*		2									8				1
H/Æ														6		1		
Wih			3											11		2		
Kent laws total			7 *1*		2									25		3		1
Had			9		4									10		1	7	6
RegTa			2		13		4	1			2	1	1	13	11	2	1	22
AE/Ine (**not** §s 11-13, 16)	1		5 1	 1	2 *5*		1 *1*		 *1*				1 *1*	42 *1* 1		6 *1* 1	5 *3*	15 *14* 4
Blas/For									1					1				
Grið			3		13						1	2	2	10		6	6	4
Wal	1																	2
II As			1		 *1*							1		13		 *1* 2		1
V As												1		3				1
IV As														2				
Pax			1				1											4
Swe		2	7		14					1	3	4	3	8		20 *1*	2	11
Að					4								2	2				2

text	a	æ	c	d	e	f	i	l	m	n	o	p	s	t	u	wynn	y	—
Mircna Lag																		
Ed & Guþ			5					10	1					8		6	1	6
Wer			1		1									1				4
I Edw			6		6							2	3	6		6		3
II Edw			8		6		1		1		1		3	5		2		11
I Edm	1		3		1					1			1	5		2		2
II Edm			4		3	1	1					2		2		3		13
I Eth			1		1			1						4		1		8 *1*
Wil I			9		3			1				1	2	4				1
III Eth	4		1		10		1	4				3	1	7		5	1	10
VI As	1		29		23			2			1	16	7	37	1	35 *1*	2	23
Geþ			2		3							2	1	5		6		8
Nor Lag			1		1			1				1	1			1		3
Wif	1		2		8					1	2	1	2	2		1		13
Charm														2		1		3
Bec	2		1		2						1			4		6 *1*		6

Table 12.3 – Distribution of variant letter-forms in *Textus Roffensis* Quire 2

fol.	insular s	position of insular s	round s	position of round s	caroline s	position of caroline s
9^{r}	19: 61.3%	various	3: 9.7%	1 init 2 med	9: 29% *1 interlin*	4 init 1 med 4 fin *1 init*
9^{v}	31: 93.9%	various	2: 6.1%	2 med	0: 0%	—
10^{r}	35: 83.3% *1 interlin*	various *1 fin*	6: 14.3%	2 init 4 med	1: 2.4% *3 interlin*	1 init *3 fin*
10^{v}	32: 78%	various	5: 12.2%	4 med 1 fin	4: 9.8%	1 init 3 med
11^{r}	22: 52.4%	various	6: 14.3%	6 fin	14: 33.3%	3 init 11 med
11^{v}	28: 60.9%	various	7: 15.2%	1 init 6 fin	11: 23.9%	6 init 1 med 4 fin
12^{r}	45: 68.2%	various	8: 12.1%	1 med 7 fin	13: 19.7%	5 init 7 med 1 fin
12^{v}	35: 71.4%	various	2: 4.1%	2 fin	12: 24.5%	8 init 3 med 1 fin
13^{r}	45: 93.7%	various	0: 0%	—	3: 6.3%	2 init 1 med
13^{v}	23: 85.2%	various	1: 3.7%	1 fin	3: 11.1%	2 init 1 med
14^{r}	28: 65.1%	various	11: 25.6%	2 init 6 med 3 fin	4: 9.3% *1 interlin*	2 init 2 fin *1 fin*

curving *y*	**straight *y***	**f-shaped *y***	**thorn**	**position of *þ***	**eth**	**position of *ð***	**uncial *r***
8: 53.3%	7: 46.7%	0: 0%	11: 52.4% *1 interlin*	9 init 2 fin *1 init*	10: 47.6%	4 init 4 med 2 fin	0
3: 60%	2: 40%	0: 0%	9: 60%	5 init 3 med 1 fin	6: 40%	3 init 2 med 1 fin	0
11: 91.7%	1: 8.3%	0: 0%	10: 33.3% *2 interlin*	9 init 1 med *2 init*	20: 66.7%	9 init 11 med	0
4: 36.4%	7: 63.6%	0: 0%	11: 47.8%	5 init 5 med 1 fin	12: 52.2% *1 interlin*	4 init 7 med 1 fin *1 init*	0
0: 0%	17: 100%	0: 0%	23: 50%	22 init 1 med	23: 50%	10 init 10 med 3 fin	0
0: 0%	28: 100%	0: 0%	35: 77.8%	29 init 6 med	10: 22.2%	3 init 6 med 1 fin	0
0: 0%	31: 100%	0: 0%	30: 60%	21 init 5 med 4 fin	20: 40%	1 init 13 med 6 fin	0
0: 0%	27: 100%	0: 0%	31: 60.8%	25 init 3 med 3 fin	20: 39.2%	2 init 17 med 1 fin	0
0: 0%	32: 100%	0: 0%	20: 51.3%	16 init 1 med 3 fin	19: 48.7%	2 init 14 med 3 fin	0
0: 0%	25: 100%	0: 0%	32: 65.3%	25 init 7 med	17: 34.7%	8 init 2 med 7 fin	0
2: 18.2%	9: 81.8%	0: 0%	24: 43.6% *1 interlin*	13 init 8 med 3 fin *1 init*	31: 56.4%	24 init 5 med 2 fin	0

fol.	insular s	position of insular s	round s	position of round s	caroline s	position of caroline s
14^{v}	22: 55%	various	13: 32.5% 1 margin	8 init 5 med 1 fin	5: 12.5% 1 margin	4 med 1 fin 1 fin
15^{r}	17: 56.7% *1 interlin*	various *1 med*	8: 26.7%	5 med 3 fin	5: 16.7%	1 init 3 med 1 fin
15^{v}	22: 71%	various	5: 16.1%	1 init 2 med 2 fin	4: 12.9% *3 interlin*	1 init 3 med *1 init* *2 med*
16^{r}	38: 82.6%	various	4: 8.7%	4 fin	4: 8.7%	3 med 1 fin
16^{v}	41: 89.1%	various	1: 2.2%	1 fin	4: 8.7%	3 med 1 fin
17^{r}	13: 34.2%	various	23: 60.5%	8 init 1 med 14 fin	2: 5.3% *1 interlin*	2 fin *1 init*
17^{v}	21: 60% 1 margin	various 1 fin	14: 40%	5 init 2 med 7 fin	0: 0% *2 interlin*	— *2 init*
18^{r}	26: 72.2%	various	10: 27.8%	6 init 1 med 3 fin	0: 0%	—
18^{v}	19: 54.3% *1 interlin*	various *1 init*	16: 45.7%	12 init 1 med 3 fin	0: 0% *1 interlin*	— *1 init*

curving *y*	**straight *y***	**f-shaped *y***	**thorn**	**position of *þ***	**eth**	**position of *ð***	**uncial *r***
2: 14.3%	12: 85.7%	0: 0%	15: 37.5% 1 margin	12 init 3 med 1 init	25: 62.5% 1 margin	16 init 6 med 3 fin 1 init	0
2: 11.8%	13: 76.5% *1 interlin*	2: 11.8%	13: 27.1%	6 init 7 med	35: 72.9%	27 init 7 med 1 fin	0
3: 37.5%	5: 62.5%	0: 0%	15: 30% *2 interlin* 1 margin	7 init 6 med 2 fin *1 init* *1 med* 1 init	35: 70%	23 init 12 med	0
0: 0%	22: 100%	0: 0%	22: 62.9%	19 init 3 med	13: 37.1%	5 init 6 med 2 fin	0
0: 0%	29: 100%	0: 0%	19: 47.5%	16 init 2 med 1 fin	21: 52.5%	3 init 18 med	0
4: 18.2%	18: 81.8%	0: 0%	15: 35.7% *1 interlin*	8 init 5 med 2 fin *1 init*	27: 64.3%	13 init 10 med 4 fin	0
0: 0%	21: 95.5%	1: 4.5%	11: 40.7% *2 interlin* 1 margin	8 init 3 med *2 init* 1 init	16: 59.3%	12 init 3 med 1 fin	0
2: 11.8%	15: 88.2% *1 interlin*	0: 0%	19: 50% *1 interlin*	7 init 11 med 1 fin *1 init*	19: 50% *1 interlin*	10 init 8 med 1 fin *1 init*	0
2: 11.1%	16: 88.9%	0: 0%	7: 21.2% *1 interlin*	3 init 4 med *1 init*	26: 78.8% *2 interlin*	10 init 15 med 1 fin *2 med*	0

Table 12.4 – Letters preceded by caroline *s* in *Textus Roffensis* Quire 2

fol.	æ	c	e	i	l	p	s	t	wynn	y	—
9^r		2						1	1 *1*	1	4
9^v											
10^r								1			*3*
10^v								4			
11^r	1		3				2	7		1	
11^v			2					1	2	2	4
12^r			1		2		1	6	2		1
12^v					2			7	2		1
13^r					2			1			
13^v								3			
14^r				1					1		2 *1*
14^v								4			1 <u>1</u>
15^r								2		2	1
15^v			*1*				*1*	3		1 *1*	
16^r								3			1
16^v		1						2			1
17^r			*1*								2
17^v								*1*		*1*	
18^r											
18^v				*1*							

Appendix:
Old English contents of *Textus Roffensis* Part I

Quire 1 (fols. 1–8)

1r–3v14	Laws of Æthelberht
3v14–5r13	Laws of Hlothhere & Eadric
5r13–6v23	Laws of Wihtred
7r–7v10	*Hadbot*
7v12–8v	West Saxon Regnal Table

Quire 2 (fols. 9–18)

9–18	Alfred/Ine

Quire 3 (fols. 19–26)

19–26	Alfred/Ine (cont.)

Quire 4 (fols. 27–39)

27r–31v20	Alfred/Ine (cont.)
31v21–32r8	*Be Blaserum* and *Forfang*
32r10–32v21	*Ordal*
32v22–4	*Walreaf*
32v24–37r6	II Æthelstan
37r7–38r5	V Æthelstan
38r5–18	IV Æthelstan (fragment)
38r20–4	*Pax*
38v–39v4	*Swerian*
39v5–13	*Að*
39v14–22	*Mircna Laga*

Quire 5 (fols. 40–7)

40r–41v19	Edward and Guthrum
41v19–42r21	*Wergeld*
42r22–43r21	I Edward
43r22–44r22	II Edward
44r22–45r4	I Edmund
45r5–46r11	II Edmund
46r11–47r23	I Æthelred
47r23–47v	William I, On Exculpation

Quire 6 (fols. 48–57)

48r–49v18	III Æthelred

Quire 10 (fols. 88–95)

88r–93r16	VI Æthelstan
93r16–93v23	*Geþyncðo*
93v23–94r	*Norðleoda Laga*
94v–95r9	*Be Wifmannes Beweddunge*
95r10–23	Charm for recovery of cattle
95r23–95v18	*Hit Becwæð*

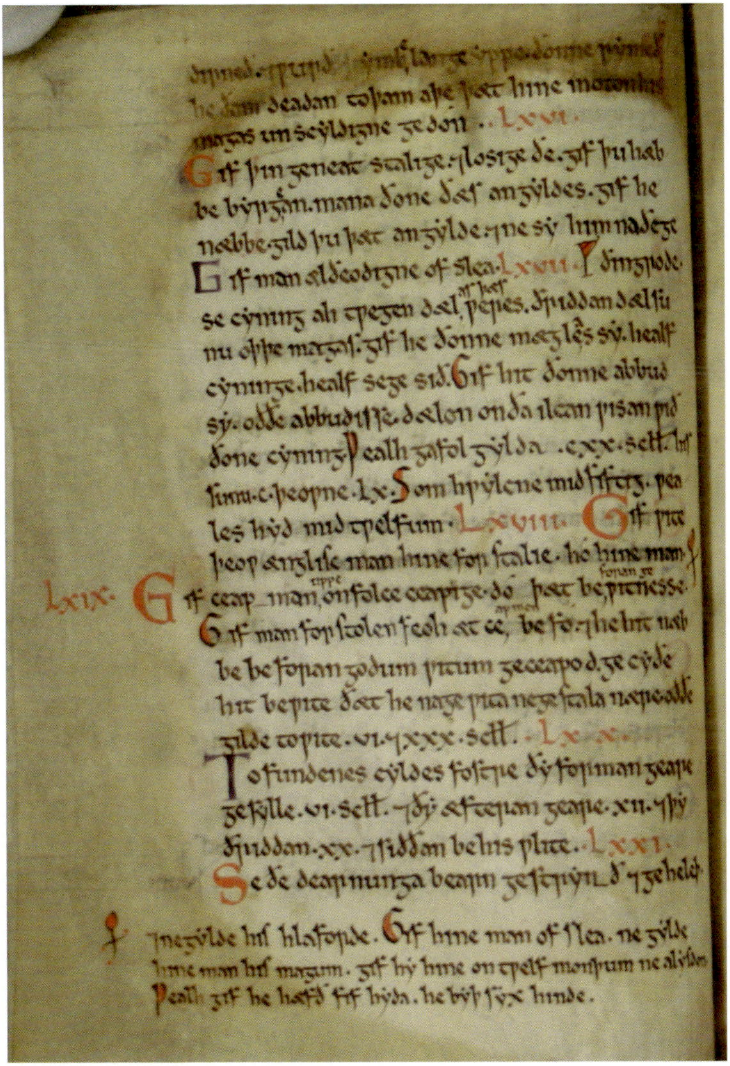

Plate 12.1 – Medway Archive and Local Studies Centre, MS DRc/R1, fol. 26v.

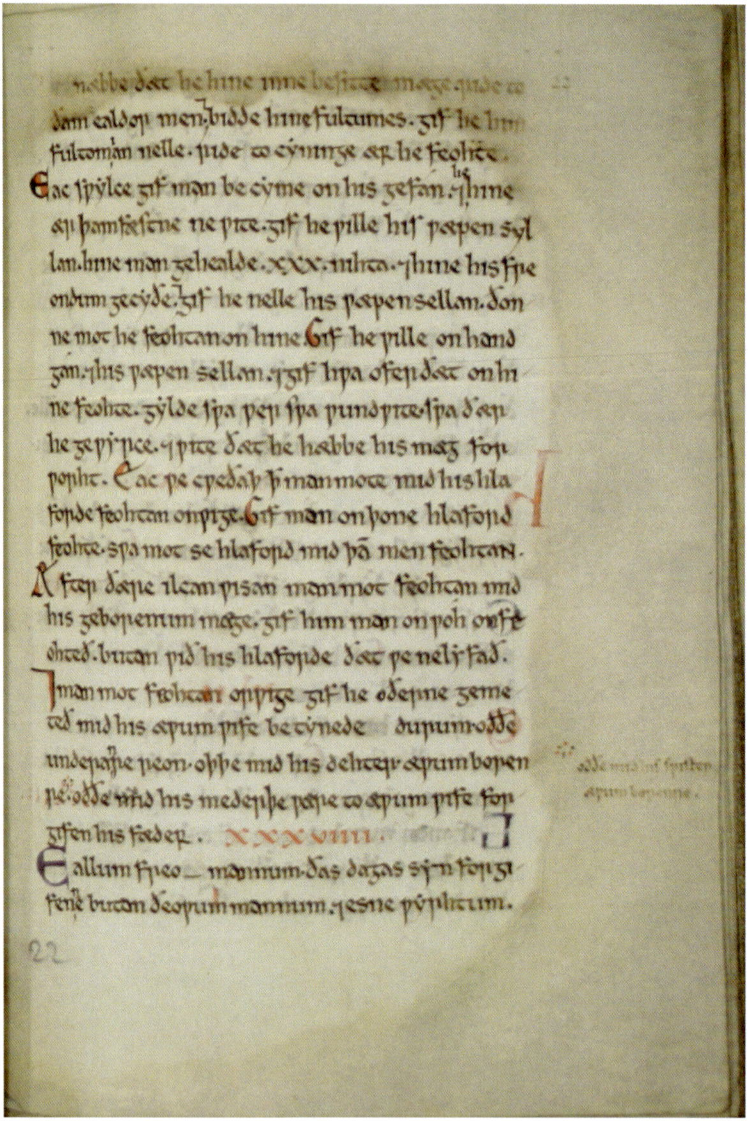

Plate 12.2 – Medway Archive and Local Studies Centre, MS DRc/R1, fol. 22r.

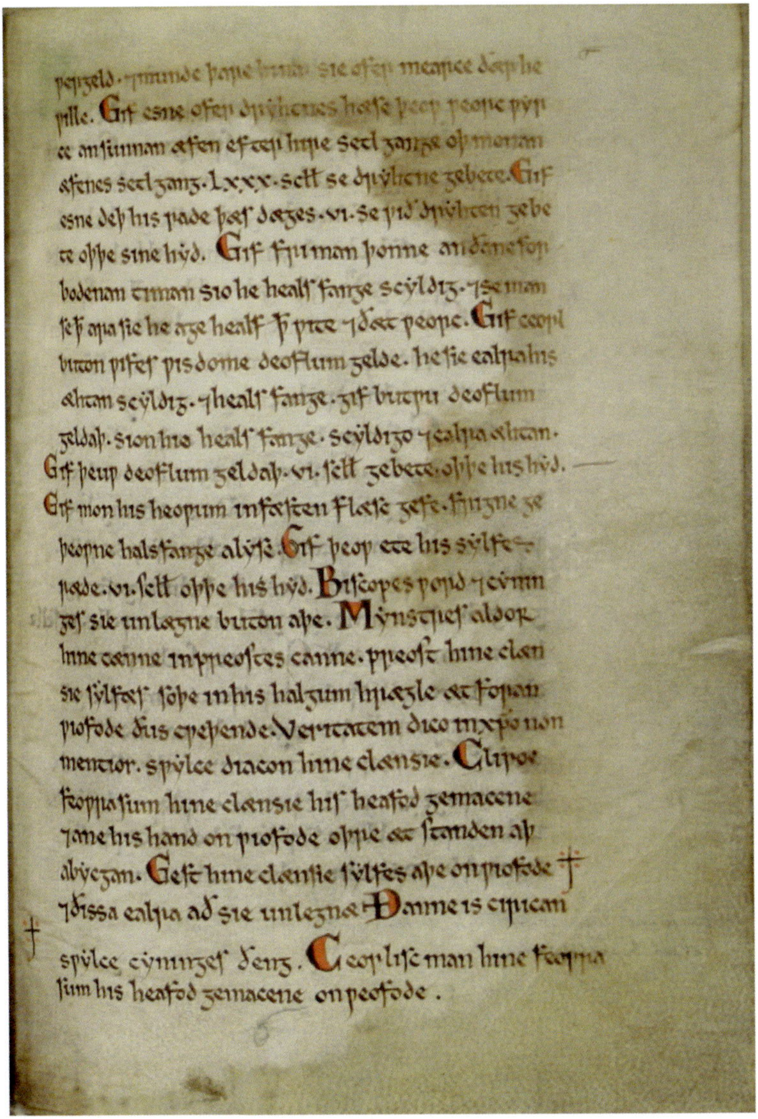

Plate 12.3 – Medway Archive and Local Studies Centre, MS DRc/R1, fol. 6r.

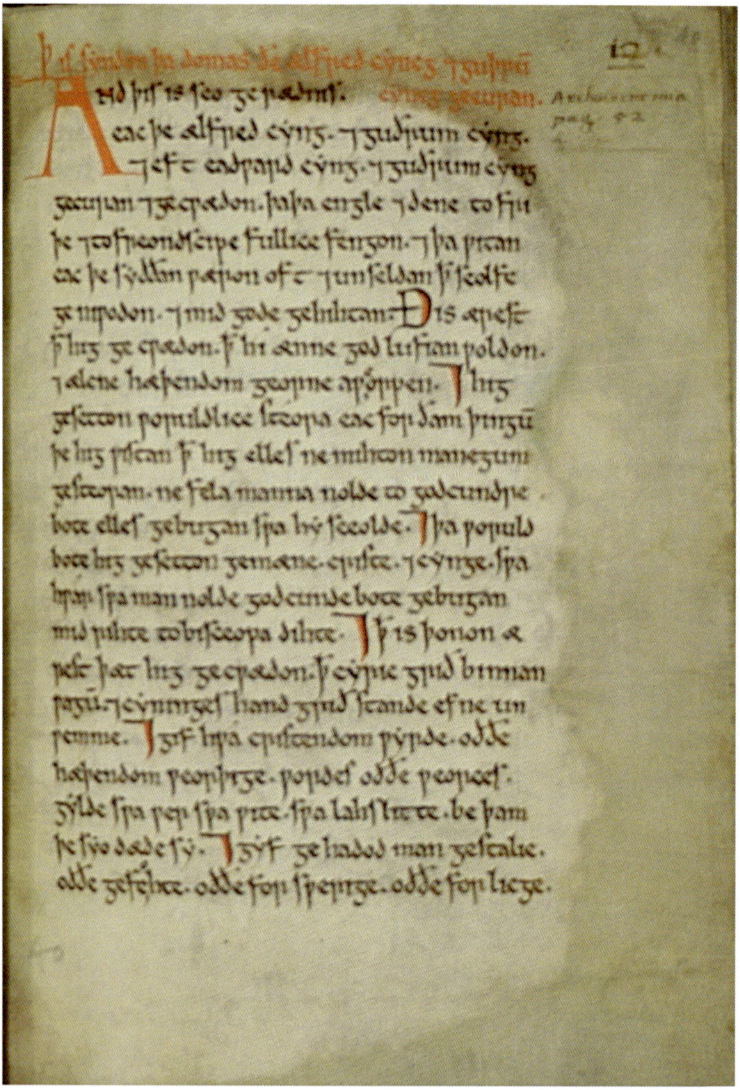

Plate 12.4 – Medway Archive and Local Studies Centre, MS DRc/R1, fol. 40r

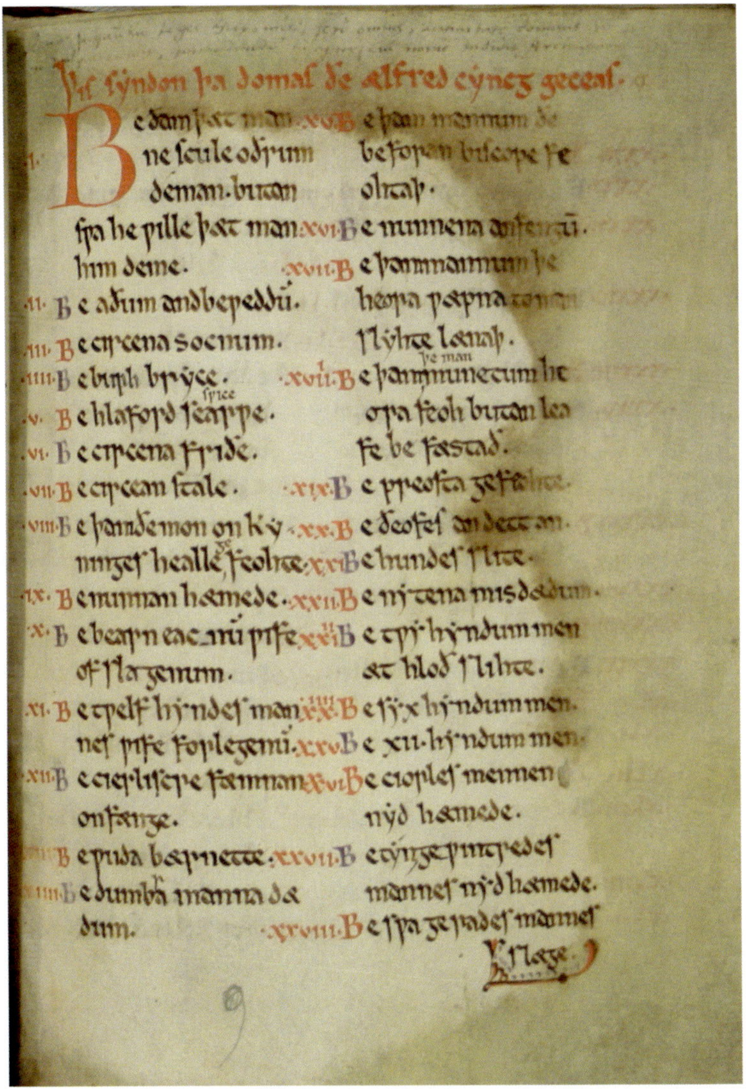

Plate 12.5 – Medway Archive and Local Studies Centre, MS DRc/R1, fol. 9r.

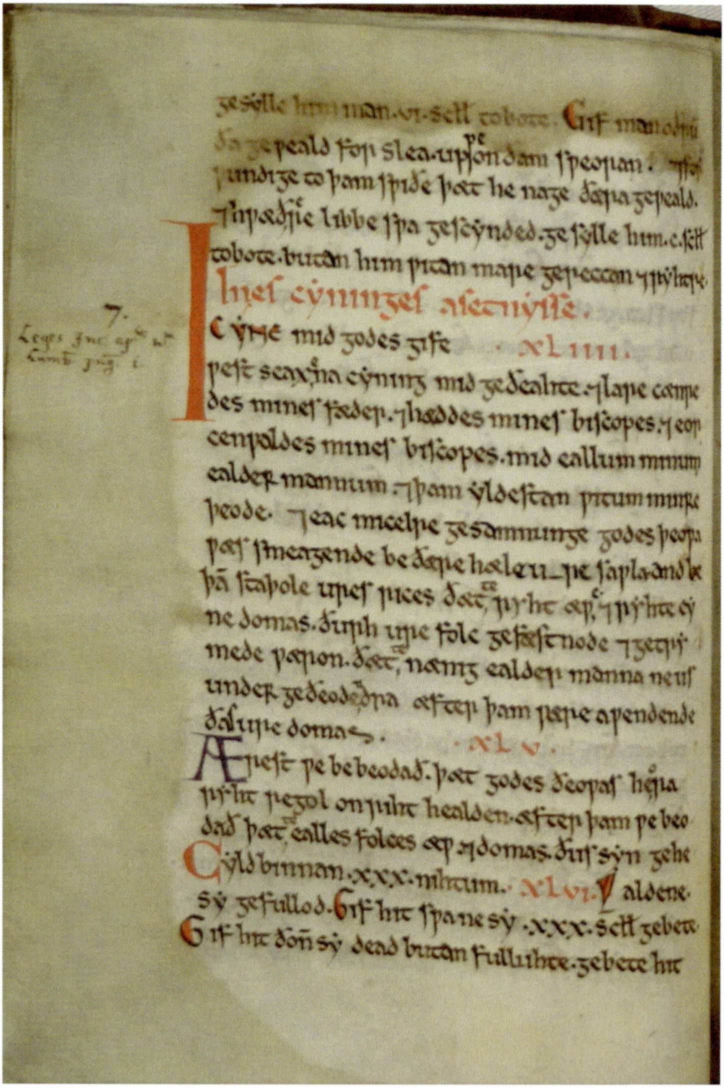

Plate 12.6 – Medway Archive and Local Studies Centre, MS DRc/R1, fol. 24v.

Plate 12.7 – Medway Archive and Local Studies Centre, MS DRc/R1, fol. 1r.

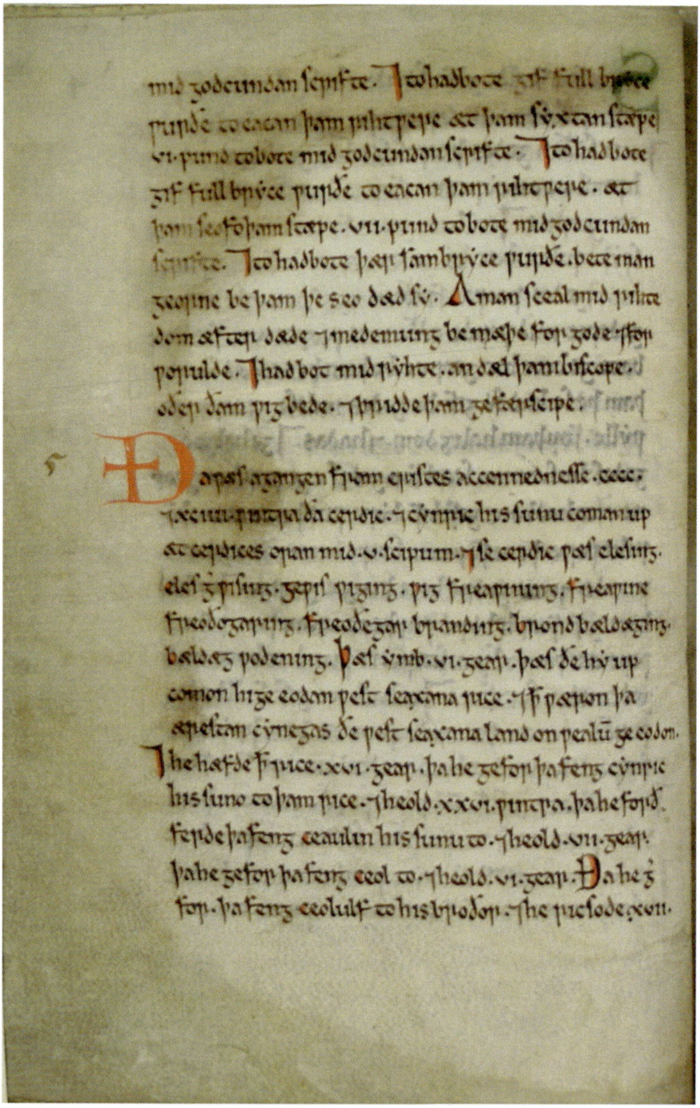

Plate 12.8 – Medway Archive and Local Studies Centre, MS DRc/R1, fol. 7v.

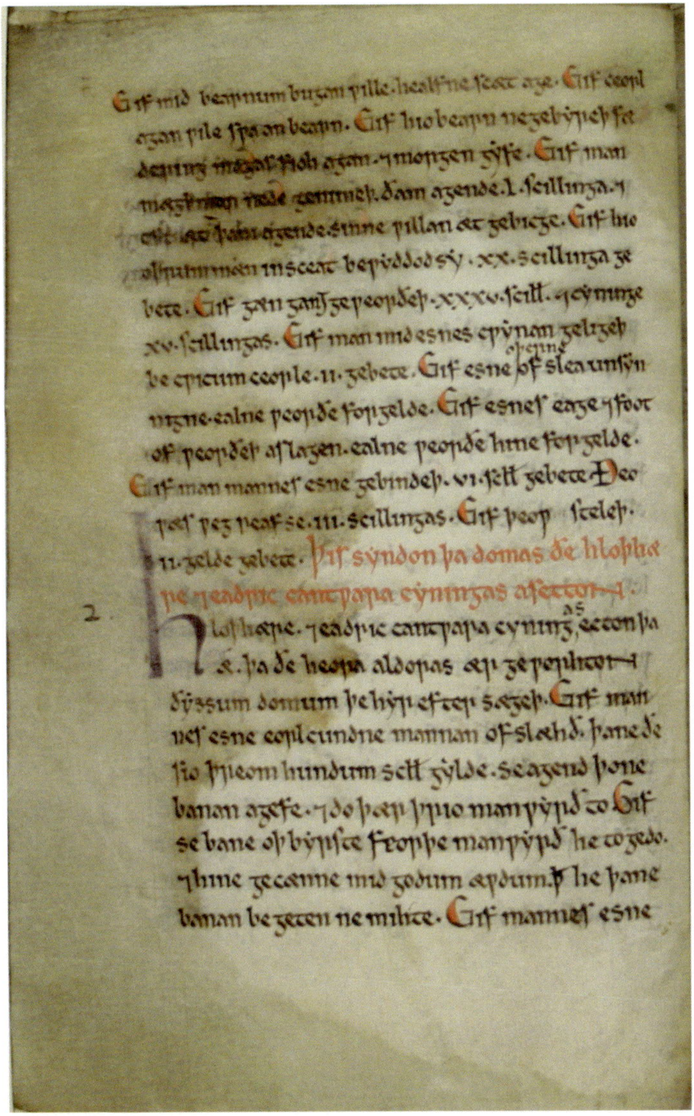

Gif mid bearnum bugan wille. healfne sceat age. Gif ceorl
agan wile swa an bearn. Gif hio bearn ne gebyreþ fæ
deringmagas fioh agan 7 morgengyfe. Gif man
mægþman nede genimeþ. ðam agende L scillinga 7
eft æt þam agende sinne willan ætgebicge. Gif hio
oþrum mæn in sceat bewyddod sy. XX scillinga ge
bete. Gif gængang geweorðeþ. XXXV scill. 7 cyninge
XV scillingas. Gif man mid esnes cwynan geligeþ
be cwicum ceorle. II gebete. Gif esne oþerne ofslea unsyn
nigne. ealne weorðe forgelde. Gif esnes eage 7 foot
of weorðeþ aslagen. ealne weorðe hine forgelde.
Gif man mannes esne gebindeþ. VI scill gebete. Ðeo
wæs weg reaf se III scillingas. Gif ðeow steleþ.
II gelde gebete. Þis syndon þa domas ðe Hloþhære
7 Eadric Cantwara cyningas asetton.
2. Hloþhære 7 Eadric Cantwara cyningas ecton þa
æ. þa ðe heora aldoras ær geworhton 7
ðyssum domum þe hyr efter sægeþ. Gif man
nes esne eorlcundne mannan ofslæhð. þane ðe
sio þreom hundum scill gylde. se agend þone
banan agefe 7 do þær þrio manwyrð to. Gif
se bane oþbyrste. feorþe manwyrð he to gedo.
7 hine gecænne mid godum æwdum þæt he þane
banan begeten ne mihte. Gif mannes esne

Plate 12.9 – Medway Archive and Local Studies Centre, MS DRc/R1, fol. 3v.

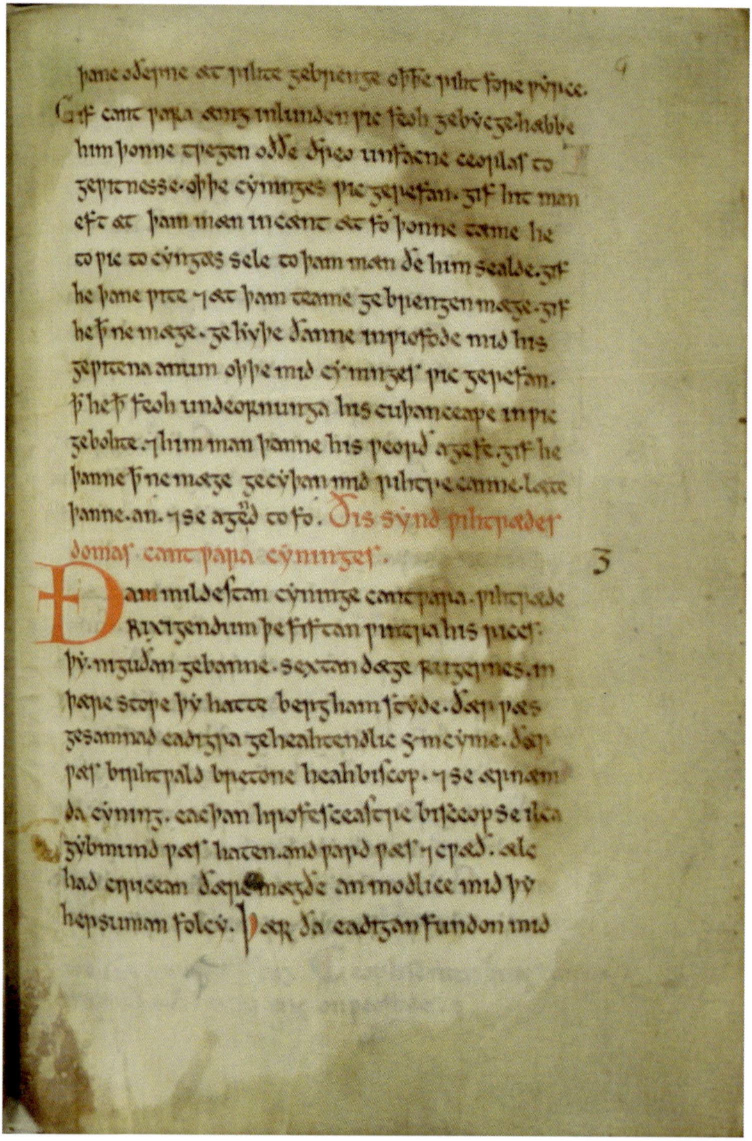

Plate 12.10 – Medway Archive and Local Studies Centre, MS DRc/R1, fol. 5r.

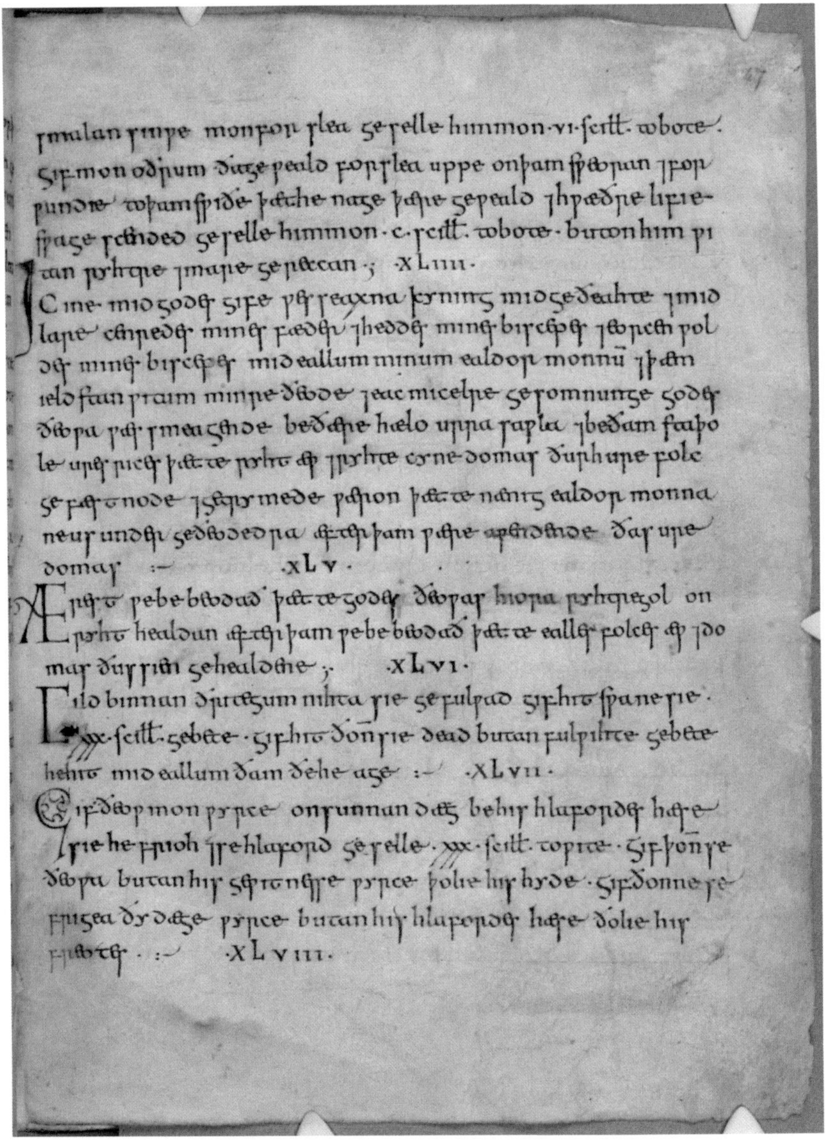

Plate 13.1 – Cambridge, Corpus Christi College 173, fol. 47r. The Alfred-Ine lawcode.

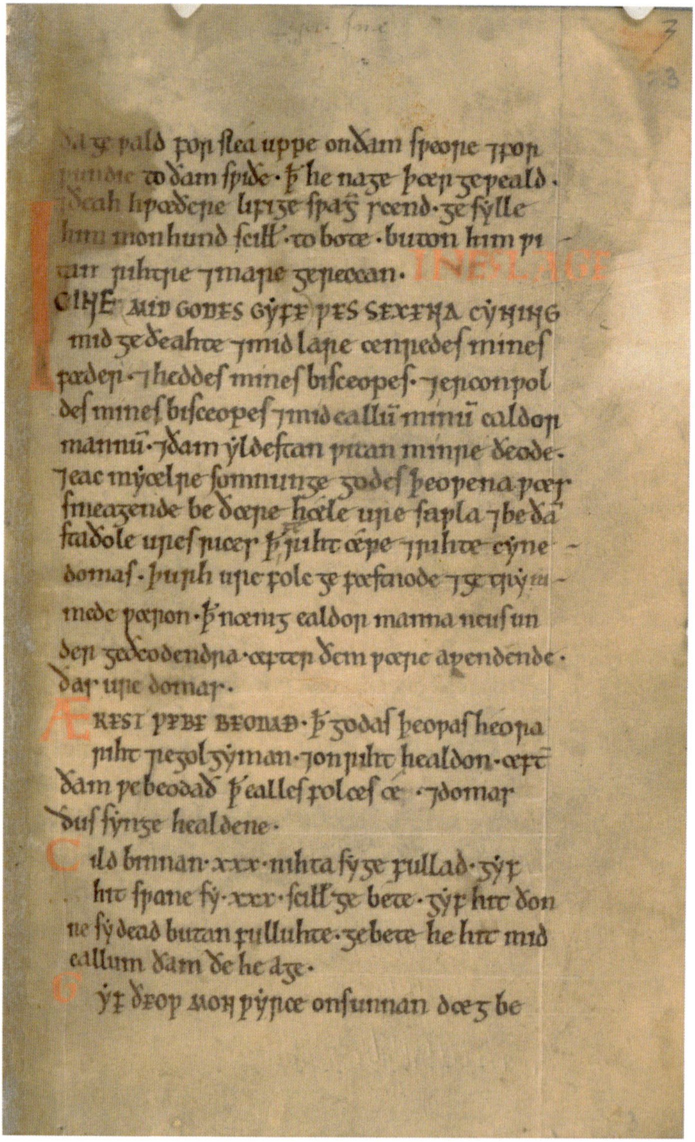

Plate 13.2 – Cambridge, Corpus Christi College 383, p. 27. The Alfred-Ine lawcode.

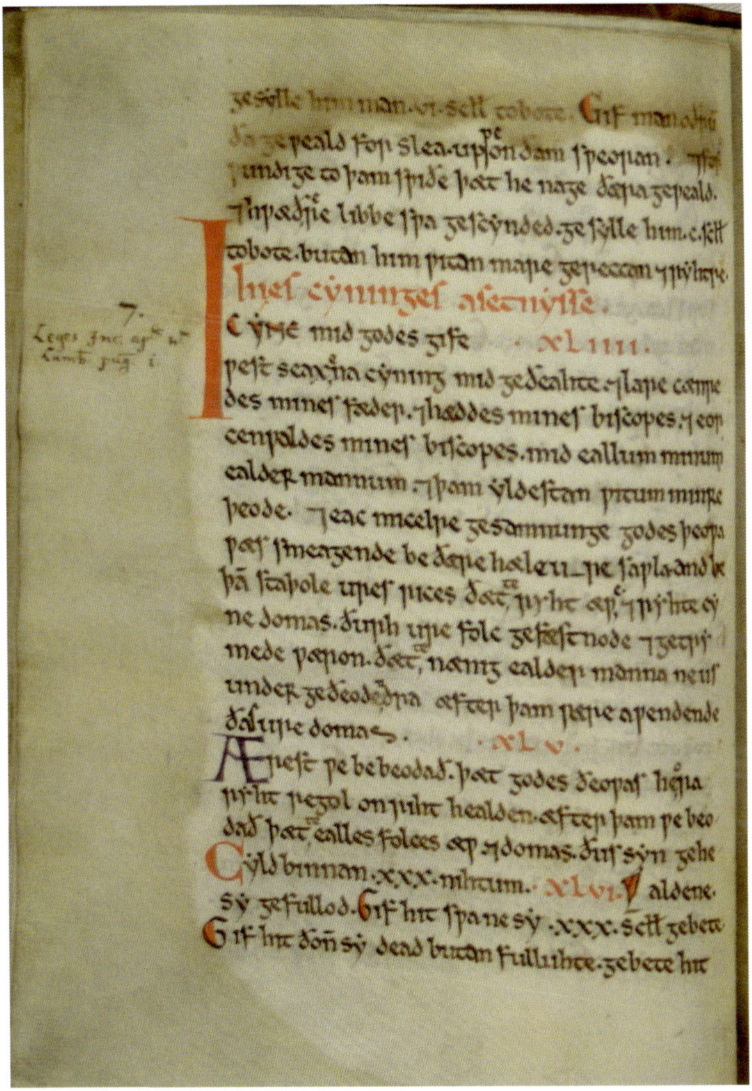

Plate 13.3 – Medway Archive and Local Studies Centre, MS DRc/R1, fol. 24v. The Alfred-Ine lawcode.

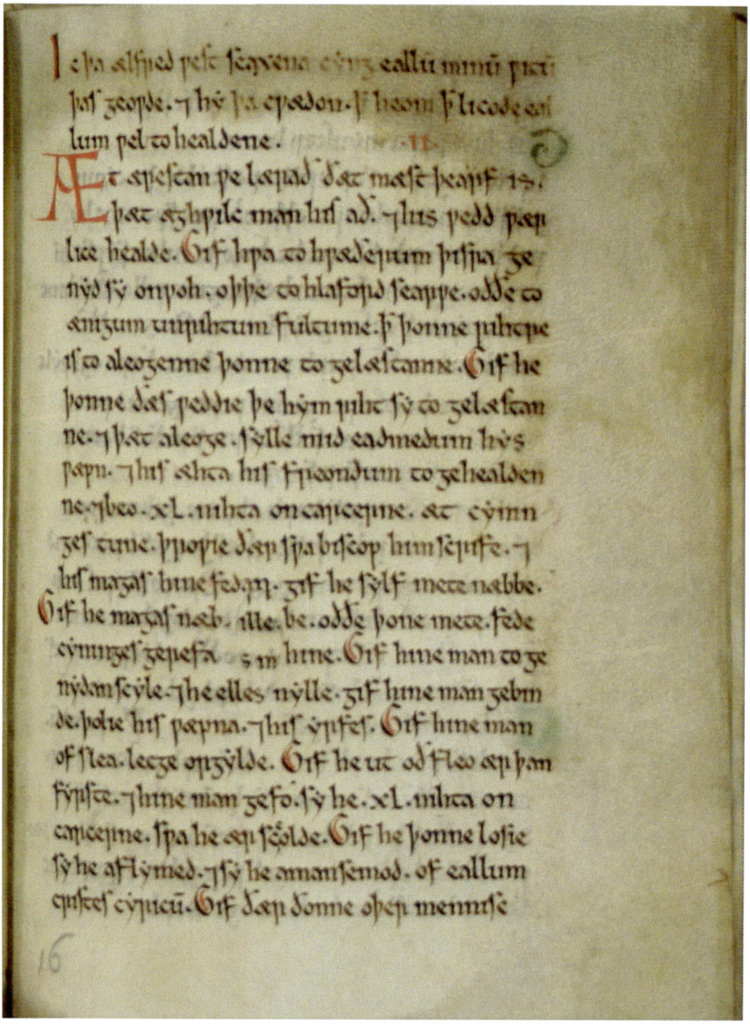

Plate 13.4 – Medway Archive and Local Studies Centre, MS DRc/R1, fol. 16r. The laws of Alfred.

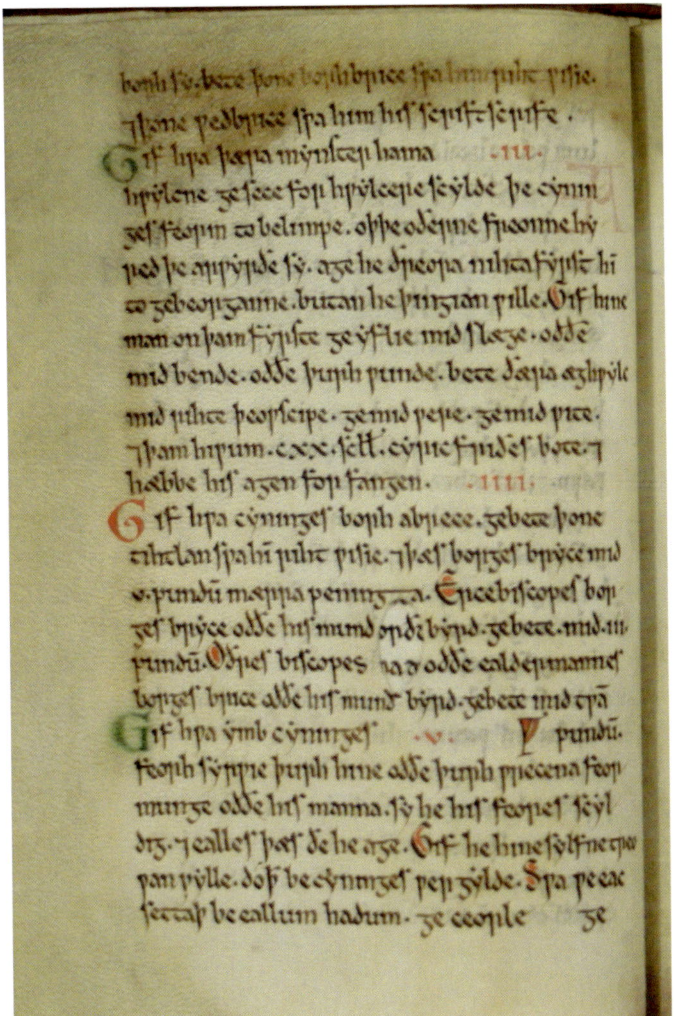

Plate 13.5 – Medway Archive and Local Studies Centre, MS DRc/R1, fol. 16v. The laws of Alfred.

13.

NUMBERS IN MANUSCRIPTS OF ANGLO-SAXON LAW

First published 2006: *Writing and Texts in Anglo-Saxon England*, ed. A. R. Rumble, Publications of the Manchester Centre for Anglo-Saxon Studies 5 (Woodbridge: D. S. Brewer), 114–136.

Our knowledge of Anglo-Saxon legislation depends substantially on a small number of extant manuscripts. The earliest is Cambridge, Corpus Christi College 173, fols. 33–52, a tenth-century copy of the *domboc* issued *c.* 887–893 by King Alfred the Great, combining his own laws with those of the seventh-century West Saxon King Ine, and prefaced by a list of rubrics and a translation of Mosaic law. Written mainly by a single scribe during the second quarter of the tenth century,[1] this copy of the *domboc* comprises the third booklet of the manuscript which also contains the earliest of the *Anglo-Saxon Chronicles*.[2] Following the Cottonian fire of 1731, little remains of an early eleventh-century witness to this and other legal texts in BL, Cotton Otho B.xi, but the readings of the burned leaves are recorded in a transcript made by Laurence Nowell in 1562 to which we shall return. Another copy of the rubric list and Preface survives in BL, Cotton Nero A.i, a composite manuscript of which Part A dates from the mid eleventh century and also contains laws of Cnut (*c.* 1020–1023) and Edgar (*c.* 959–963), together with two anonymous texts known as *Romscot* (or *Peter's Pence*) and *Iudex*. The collection was written by two scribes, one being responsible for Cnut's laws, and the other for the remaining texts. Part B is earlier, dating from the first half of the eleventh century, and was not only made for Archbishop Wulfstan but is annotated in his hand. As well as homilies by Wulfstan and extracts from his *Institutes of Polity*, it contains laws of

[1] Another scribe wrote the first page of the rubric list only.

[2] M. B. Parkes, 'The Palaeography of the Parker Manuscript of the *Chronicle*, Laws and Sedulius, and Historiography at Winchester in the Late Ninth and Tenth Centuries', *Anglo-Saxon England* 5 (1976), 149–71.

Æthelstan (*c.* 925–939), Edmund (*c.* 939–946), Edgar and Æthelred (*c.* 978–1014), and an anonymous text known as *Grið*. Also dating from the mid-eleventh century is CCCC 201, a more extensive collection of legal material including the *Law of the Northumbrian Priests*, *Geþyncðo*, *Norðleoda Laga*, *Mircna Laga*, *Að*, *Hadbot*, and laws of Æthelred, Edgar, Æthelstan, Edmund and Cnut.[3]

Much Anglo-Saxon legislation, however, survives only in manuscripts dating from after the Norman Conquest. The major collections are CCCC 383, mostly written by a single scribe during the late eleventh or early twelfth century, Medway Archive and Local Studies Centre, MS DRc/R1 (henceforth *Textus Roffensis*), copied by a single scribe and datable on internal evidence to 1122 x 1123, and *Quadripartitus*, an early twelfth-century Latin translation of Old English originals in several manuscripts. To these three we owe the seventh-century Kentish laws of Kings Æthelberht, Hlothhere and Eadric, and Wihtred, uniquely preserved on the first six folios of *Textus Roffensis*, the only surviving fragment of IV Æthelstan, also preserved in *Textus Roffensis*, *Gerefa*, uniquely preserved in CCCC 383, III Æthelstan, III Edmund, IV Æthelred and VII Æthelred, uniquely preserved in *Quadripartitus*; the treaty of Alfred and Guthrum, I Edgar, II Æthelred, *Dunsæte* and *Rectitudines*, recorded in CCCC 383 and *Quadripartitus*; V and VI Æthelstan, III Æthelred, *Ordal*, *Pax* and *Walreaf*, recorded in *Textus Roffensis* and *Quadripartitus*; *Hit Becwæð*, recorded in *Textus Roffensis* and CCCC 383, and I and II Edward, the so-called treaty of Edward and Guthrum,[4] I Æthelred, *Be Blaserum*, *Forfang*, *Wergeld*, *Swerian* and *Be Wifmannes Beweddunge*, recorded in all three twelfth-century collections together with additional copies of the Alfred/Ine *domboc* and other legal material. Also dating from the twelfth century is a copy of Cnut's laws preserved in Part B of BL, Harley 55, another composite manuscript of which Part A dates from the early eleventh century and includes II and III Edgar alongside non-legal texts. IV Edgar is preserved only in two Worcester manuscripts:

---

[3] P. Wormald, *The Making of English Law: King Alfred to the Twelfth Century*, vol. 1 *Legislation and its Limits* (Oxford, 1999), p. 208, demonstrates that the section of the manuscript containing the laws, together with Wulfstan homilies, *Institutes of Polity*, and *Apollonius*, originated as a self-contained unit, representing a 'larger-scale equivalent' of the corresponding section of BL, Cotton Nero A.i (B), and possibly deriving ultimately from '"a master-copy" kept in Wulfstan's cathedral libraries'.

[4] The authorship of the alleged treaty by the eleventh-century archbishop Wulfstan was demonstrated by D. Whitelock, 'Wulfstan and the So-Called Laws of Edward and Guthrum', *English Historical Review* 56 (1941), 1–21.

BL, Cotton Nero E.i, fols. 185–6, dating from the late tenth or early eleventh century, and CCCC 265, dating from the mid-eleventh. Neither manuscript contains other legislative material, and indeed the two folios of Cotton Nero E.i in question originally belonged to a different codex.

These legal manuscripts have been approached from many different angles in attempts to identify transmission patterns and manuscript stemmata. Textual variants have been quarried extensively. This approach is facilitated by Liebermann's turn-of-the-nineteenth-century edition of the Anglo-Saxon laws, which presents parallel texts from all extant witnesses with variant readings printed in bold,[5] and by the subsequent publication of facsimile editions of CCCC 173,[6] Cotton B.i[7] and *Textus Roffensis*,[8] the latter two within the Early English Manuscripts in Facsimile Series.[9] Codicological and palaeographical evidence has also been subjected to close scrutiny, both in the introductions to the latter two facsimiles and in separate studies.[10] Manuscript context and structure have likewise been investigated, with detailed comparison between the content and layout of the major collections;[11] and relationships between groups of texts have

[5] *Die Gesetze der Angelsachsen*, ed. F. Liebermann, 3 vols. (Halle, 1903–16).

[6] *The Parker Chronicle and Laws (Corpus Christi College, Cambridge, MS. 173): A Facsimile*, ed. Robin Flower and Hugh Smith, Early English Text Society os 208 (London, 1941).

[7] *A Wulfstan Manuscript: Containing Institutes, Laws and Homilies. British Museum Cotton Nero A.I*, ed. H. R. Loyn, Early English Manuscript in Facsimile 17 (Copenhagen, 1971).

[8] *Textus Roffensis: Rochester Cathedral Library Manuscript A.3.5. Part I*, ed. P. H. Sawyer, Early English Manuscripts in Facsimile 7 (Copenhagen, 1957).

[9] All have been extensively used during the preparation of this paper. I am grateful to the Librarian of the Parker Library, Corpus Christi College, Cambridge, for allowing generous access to legal and other manuscripts during seminars of the Research Group on Manuscript Evidence and visits by the Medieval Manuscripts class from the University of Glasgow, and for kindly providing me with a microfilm of MS 383. Warm thanks are also due to Mr Stephen Dixon, Borough Archivist, and the staff of the Medway Archives and Local Studies Centre for their unfailing helpfulness during my visits to Strood to work on the *Textus Roffensis* manuscript.

[10] D. N. Dumville, *Wessex and England from Alfred to Edgar: Six Essays on Political, Cultural, and Ecclesiastical Revival* (Woodbridge, 1992), pp. 135–9; P. Wormald, '*Laga Eadwardi*: The *Textus Roffensis* and its Context', *Anglo-Norman Studies* 17 (1995), 243–66; reprinted in P. Wormald, *Legal Culture in the Early Medieval West: Law as Text, Image and Experience* (London, 1999), pp. 115–38; C. Hough, 'Palaeographical Evidence for the Compilation of *Textus Roffensis*', *Scriptorium* 54 (2001), 57–79 and 10 plates, reprinted in this volume.

[11] M. P. Richards, 'The Manuscript Contexts of the Old English Laws: Tradition

been posited on the grounds of common idiosyncracies in the arrangement of material in different witnesses.[12] The purpose of this paper is to draw attention to another type of evidence which remains to be explored, and which may yield interesting results.

Legal texts by their nature contain a high incidence of numbers. Particularly common are references to the number of pennies, shillings or *sceattas* payable as fines or compensation, the number of days or months within which payment must be made, the number of witnesses or oath-helpers required under various circumstances, the number of pennies comprising the legal value of standard items, the number of shillings making up the *wergild* of people of different classes, and so on. These numbers can be represented graphically in one of two ways. They can either be written out in full as words, or they can be written as Roman numerals. **Plates 13.1–3** show the opening section of Ine's laws on CCCC 173, fol. 47r, CCCC 383, p. 27 and *Textus Roffensis*, fol. 24v. In the final chapter of Alfred's code in line 4 of each page, CCCC 383 writes out the word *hund*, while CCCC 173 and *Textus Roffensis* use the Roman numeral *C*. In Ine, ch. 2, on the other hand, CCCC 173 (line 18) writes out the word *ðritegum* while CCCC 383 and *Textus Roffensis* (both line 22) have Roman numerals, and all three manuscripts use numerals in the following line for the second occurrence of the same number within the same clause. Taken individually, these might appear to be minor variants: small matters of presentation and layout which could at first sight be attributed to scribal preference. Taken together, however, closer investigation reveals identifiable patterns which may throw light on the compilation of the extant manuscripts and the earlier transmission of the texts.

Tables 13.1–10 set out the proportions of numbers represented as numerals to numbers written out as words in the major legal manuscripts, both as actual figures for each text and as percentages rounded to one decimal place.[13] As chapter numbers are invariably represented as numerals, these have been ignored. So too have ordinal numbers written

---

and Innovation', *Studies in Early English Prose: Sixteen Original Contributions*, ed. P. E. Szarmach (Albany, N.Y., 1986), pp. 171–92; M. P. Richards, 'Texts and Their Traditions in the Medieval Library of Rochester Cathedral Priory', *Transactions of the American Philosophical Society* 78 (1988); Wormald, *The Making of English Law*, pp. 162–260.

[12] Wormald, '*Laga Eadwardi*'.

[13] Several occurrences of *þusend* in *Norðleoda Laga* have been ignored, as a numeral may not have been regarded as an obvious alternative.

as words,[14] and later additions of any kind.[15] Anglo-Saxon legislation is unusual among Germanic law in being written in the vernacular, and we are concerned here with the Old English material only, excluding the Latin translations of *Quadripartitus*, whose manuscript traditions are in any case too complex to be incorporated within the present study.[16] The order of texts is that in which they now appear, notwithstanding the fact that quires have been displaced both in CCCC 383, where the Alfred/Ine *domboc* should precede *Be Blaserum*, and in *Textus Roffensis*, where the contents of fols. 88–95, from VI Æthelstan through *Hit Becwæð*, should come between *Mircna Laga* and Edward–Guthrum.

Some texts contain too few numbers to be statistically significant. Nonetheless, it is immediately apparent that a range of practices is represented within individual manuscripts. In *Textus Roffensis* (**Table 13.8**), numerals account for a massive 94.5% of all numbers in Æthelberht's code and for 89.9% within the Kentish laws as a whole, whereas the figure goes down to 72.7% in III Æthelred and to 46.7% in *Wergeld*. The texts known as *Be Blaserum*, *Ordal* and *Walreaf*, which, as Wormald notes, were added by the scribe on 31v21–32v24 in larger lettering and darker ink,[17] use almost exclusively words, and so does I Æthelred. I have demonstrated elsewhere that the *Textus Roffensis* scribe was strongly influenced by the letter-forms of his exemplars, notably as regards the use of *þ* and *ð*, and of alternative graphs for *s* and *y*,[18] and it would therefore be surprising only if he departed from his sources with regard to the representation of numbers. However, similar inconsistencies are apparent in other manuscripts, and it seems reasonable to conclude that these too reflect the practice of different exemplars. CCCC 201 (**Table 13.4**) uses numerals for forty-six out of forty-nine numbers in the *Law of the Northumbrian Priests* and for twelve out of sixteen in *Norðleoda Laga*, but for only one out of six in II Edgar, one out of six in *Að*, five out of twelve in *Hadbot*, and six out of sixteen in VIII Æthelred;

---

[14] Exceptional instances of ordinal numbers written as numerals have, however, been included.

[15] This applies for instance to the rubrics to Cnut's laws in CCCC 383, which are unlikely to be by the original scribe (Wormald, *The Making of English Law*, p. 235). The rubrics to the Alfred/Ine *domboc* in the same manuscript, however, have been included within the tables.

[16] The several manuscripts comprising *Quadripartitus* are discussed in detail by Patrick Wormald, 'Quadripartitus', *Law and Government in Medieval England and Normandy: Essays in Honour of Sir James Holt*, ed. G. Garnett and J. Hudson (Cambridge, 1994), pp. 111–47.

[17] Wormald, '*Laga Eadwardi*', 253.

[18] Hough, 'Palaeographical Evidence'.

while CCCC 383 (**Table 13.7**) shows a strong preference for words in its incomplete texts of II Æthelstan, the Alfred/Ine *domboc* and the laws of Cnut, but an equally strong preference for numerals in II Æthelred, *Dunsæte* and *Rectitudines*. Words also predominate in the copy of Cnut's laws preserved in Harley 55 (B) (**Table 13.6**), but the reverse applies in the copy of the same text in Cotton Nero A.i (A) (**Table 13.3**). The rubric list and Preface to the Alfred/Ine *domboc* in the latter manuscript reflect a fairly even distribution of words and numerals, although comparison with CCCC 173 (**Table 13.1**) raises the possibility that this might not have been maintained throughout the laws themselves. A mixture of both practices appears in Cotton Nero A.i (B) (**Table 13.2**) and in Harley 55 (A) (**Table 13.5**), but none of their texts contains sufficient numbers to allow clear trends to be identified.

The rest of this paper will explore the implications of this range of evidence, beginning with the twelfth-century collections. On the basis of shared material, Liebermann suggested a lost Canterbury manuscript as the common source for CCCC 383, *Textus Roffensis* and *Quadripartitus*.[19] Although followed by Sawyer in the introduction to the facsimile edition of *Textus Roffensis*,[20] this view is no longer tenable, as more recent work has indicated that each of the three was assembled from a range of sources by its respective compiler.[21] Nonetheless, the degree of overlap is considerable, and there are grounds for believing that some of the texts may already have been circulating as self-contained collections. Wormald points out that II Æthelred is followed by *Dunsæte* in both CCCC 383 and *Quadripartitus*, with *Rectitudines* as the next item in CCCC 383, and suggests that all three may have been grouped together at an earlier stage of transmission on account of a Somerset connection.[22] As noted above, these texts are differentiated from others in CCCC 383 by a strong tendency to represent numbers as numerals rather than as words. Indeed, discounting those with less than half-a-dozen numbers in total, **Table 13.7** shows that II Æthelred, *Dunsæte* and *Rectitudines* are the only texts to show a weighting of 70% or more in favour of numerals, the next highest being *Wergeld* at a mere 53.3%. This is at least a remarkable coincidence. While it falls far short of proof of a common exemplar for the three texts, it does constitute a small piece of supporting evidence in favour of such a hypothesis.

---

[19] *Gesetze*, ed. Liebermann I, xxvii and III, 31.

[20] *Textus Roffensis*, ed. Sawyer, pp. 19–20.

[21] Wormald, '*Laga Eadwardi*'; Hough, 'Palaeographical Evidence'.

[22] Wormald, *The Making of English Law*, pp. 232–3.

Another 'mini-collection' posited by Wormald on the basis of comparison between the contents of the three twelfth-century collections,[23] and subsequently supported by palaeographical evidence from *Textus Roffensis*,[24] comprises I and II Edward, I and II Edmund, Alfred–Guthrum, Edward–Guthrum, *Swerian*, *Be Wifmannes Beweddunge*, *Wergeld*, a Charm for the Recovery of Cattle, and *Hit Becwæð*. The charm has not been included here as it is not strictly speaking a legal text and contains only three numbers, represented as words in both *Textus Roffensis* and CCCC 383; while I Edmund, *Swerian*, *Be Wifmannes Beweddunge* and *Hit Becwæð* are devoid of numbers. The remaining members of the group – I and II Edward, II Edmund, Alfred–Guthrum, Edward–Guthrum and *Wergeld* – contain too few numbers to be statistically significant, although it is worth noting that a preference for numerals over words in the CCCC 383 version runs counter to the preference for words in preceding texts.[25] What is striking, however, is how often within this group the distribution of numerals coincides in *Textus Roffensis* and CCCC 383. Of the seven numbers in I and II Edward, six are represented as numerals in both manuscripts (I Edward, chs. 1,4 and 2,1 (x2), II Edward, chs. 1,3 (x2) and 2), while both write out in full the word *feower* 'four' in II Edward, ch. 8. Of the four numbers in II Edmund, both scribes write out the word *twelf* 'twelve' in ch. 1, but use numerals for all three numbers in ch. 7,3. The treaty of Alfred and Guthrum is preserved (twice) in CCCC 383 only, but of the eight numbers in the purported treaty of Edward and Guthrum, seven are represented in the same way in the *Textus Roffensis* and CCCC 383 copies. Both scribes use numerals for the first number in ch. 3,1 and words for the second, both use words for the single number in ch. 3,2, for both numbers in ch. 4,1, and for the single number in ch. 10, and both use numerals for the second number in ch. 7, diverging only as regards the first number in the same chapter, written out as *twelf* by the *Textus Roffensis* scribe but represented as *XII* in CCCC 383. Of the fifteen numbers in *Wergeld*, seven are represented by numerals in *Textus Roffensis*, and eight in CCCC 383. With the single exception again of *twelf* / *XII* in ch. 3, they are a perfect match: both scribes use numerals for the third and fourth numbers in ch. 3, for the first two of the three numbers in ch. 4,1, and for all three numbers in ch. 6, but use words for both numbers in ch. 1, for both numbers in ch. 1,1, for the first number in ch. 3, for the third number in ch. 4,1, and for the single number in ch. 7. It is

[23] Wormald, '*Laga Eadwardi*', 256.

[24] Hough, 'Palaeographical Evidence', 66.

[25] The exception is Edward–Guthrum, with three numerals and five words, but this is scarcely significant.

difficult to account for this in terms of different scribes consistently making the same random choices. A single ancestor cannot be far away.

Turning to pre-Conquest manuscripts, it has been noted above that IV Edgar is preserved only in Cotton Nero E.i, fols. 185–6, and in CCCC 265, both apparently from Worcester. Wormald describes the latter as 'close kin and perhaps descendant' of the former;[26] and such a relationship is strongly supported by the presentation of numbers. Out of six numbers, equally distributed between numerals and words in CCCC 265, and at a ratio of 2:4 in Nero E.i, scribal choices coincide in five of the six instances.[27] Again, this seems unlikely to be coincidence.

Something similar happens with the twelve numbers in the Preface to Alfred's *domboc* in CCCC 173 and Cotton Nero A.i (A), where numerals are used in four and five instances respectively out of the twelve. Again, they occur in the same places. Both manuscripts use numerals for the two numbers in ch. 3, for the single number in ch. 11, and for the same one out of the three numbers in ch. 21, while words are used for the other two numbers in ch. 21, for the two in ch. 17, and for the singletons in chs. 25 and 28.[28] They are at variance only in ch. 24, where CCCC 173 has two numerals and Cotton Nero A.i has one numeral and one word. So too with the rubrics to the Alfred/Ine *domboc*: of the eight numbers that appear, both manuscripts use numerals for the rubrics to Alfred, ch. 31 and Ine, chs. 64, 65 and 66, but words for the rubrics to Alfred, chs. 29 and 30 and Ine, ch. 70. They diverge only for Alfred, ch. 10, where CCCC 173 has *twelfhyndes* and Cotton Nero A.i has *XIIhyndes*. The provenance of these manuscripts has been much discussed in recent years, and it is no longer possible to assign both to Canterbury, as Liebermann thought.[29] Nonetheless, the correspondence between the distribution of numerals suggests a close relationship between the two versions of the Alfred/Ine *domboc*.

In the *Textus Roffensis* copy, all twelve numbers in the Preface to the *domboc* are represented by words. At first sight, this looks very odd.

---

[26] Wormald, *The Making of English Law*, p. 184.

[27] Numerals appear in chs. 4 and 5, words in chs. 6,2 (x2) and 8,1. The exception is in ch. 9, where Nero E.i has *fif* and CCCC 265 has *V*.

[28] The numbering of chapters varies in different manuscripts, and is particularly problematic as regards the Alfred/Ine *domboc*. For the sake of consistency, I use the numbering system established by *Die Gesetze der Angelsachsen*, ed. Liebermann, , which is now widely accepted as standard.

[29] Current thinking is summed up by Wormald, who explains that CCCC 173 represents 'not a Canterbury but a Court-Winchester nexus in the relevant 940–1010 period', while Cotton Nero A.i 'may be from Canterbury but could just as well be from elsewhere' (*The Making of English Law*, p. 266).

The preceding rubrics use numerals in five out of nine instances, while the incidence of numerals in the laws themselves stands at around 84% in both the Alfred and Ine sections. But there is an explanation. Recent work on the manuscript has established that fols. 11–13 and 16 are not original. Orthographical corrections common throughout the first four quires of the manuscript are absent from these folios,[30] and the distribution of letter-forms also differs significantly from the rest of quire 2.[31] Alfred's Preface is copied on fols. 11r4–16r3, and the twelve numbers all occur on fols. 11–13.[32] Their anomalous presentation provides yet further evidence that this section of the manuscript has been rewritten. However, the implications go beyond this. It is now recognized that the *Textus Roffensis* scribe had access to two different sources for the Alfred/Ine *domboc*. The first was used for the main text, while the corrections, which are both textually and palaeographically distinct, were taken from a second.[33] Moreover, whereas Liebermann believed that the *domboc* exemplar used by the *Textus Roffensis* scribe was close to the version in CCCC 383, Wormald has demonstrated that the similarities apply to the second exemplar, not to the first.[34] Since the Preface itself is missing from CCCC 383, it is not possible to use textual evidence in order to establish which of the two exemplars lies behind the rewritten *Textus Roffensis* copy. The distribution of letter-forms, which agrees with the corrections rather than with the main text,[35] points to the second, and this is confirmed beyond reasonable doubt by the treatment of numbers. A feature of the extant *domboc* in CCCC 383 (**Table 13.7**) is the preponderance of words over numerals: an average of 88.7% across the combined laws of Alfred and Ine. With regard to the missing Preface, then, the likelihood is that most if not all of the twelve numbers would have been represented as words. This is exactly what happens in the *Textus Roffensis* Preface, and I therefore suggest that the version of the Preface preserved on the replacement fols. 11–13 and 16 of quire 2 does not belong with the main text of the *domboc* in this manuscript.[36]

---

[30] Wormald, '*Laga Eadwardi*', 250.

[31] Hough, 'Palaeographical Evidence', 71.

[32] Fols. 11r13, 11r14, 11v3, 12r16 (x2), 12v6, 12v7, 12v14, 13r1, 13r2, 13r9 and 13r15.

[33] Wormald, '*Laga Eadwardi*', 256–60; Hough, 'Palaeographical Evidence', 67.

[34] Wormald, '*Laga Eadwardi*', 259–60.

[35] Hough, 'Palaeographical Evidence', 71.

[36] One of the corrections to the rubric list in *Textus Roffensis* 9r22, where the rubric to Alfred, ch. 26 has *tyn* 'ten' written over an erasure, also suggests an exemplar with numbers written out. The reading in fact corresponds neither to the rubric in CCCC 383 (where rubrics are integrated with the laws rather than being set out at

Rather it represents a different recension of the *domboc*, of which an incomplete version of the laws only is preserved in CCCC 383.

One problem with this theory remains to be addressed. The rewritten folio 16 of *Textus Roffensis* contains the last three lines of Alfred's Preface and the first four chapters of his laws (**Plates 13.4– 5**). Since the scribe appears to be using the second exemplar at this point, the expectation is that numbers will be represented as words rather than as numerals. But this proves not to be the case. Of the six numbers on fol. 16, five are written as numerals (16r13 *xl*, 16r21 *xl*, 16v11 *cxx*, 16v15 *v*, 16v16 *iii*), and only one as a word (16v18 *twam*). Unfortunately this section of the laws is missing from CCCC 383, so that no direct comparison can be made. It is, however, notable that this folio contains an unusually high incidence of abbreviations, perhaps indicating that the scribe was aware of a need to save space. The last section of the Preface has been squashed into the first three lines of fol. 16r (**Plate 13.4**), with three abbreviations in line 1, two in line 2, and the short form *cyng* in line 1 rather than the form *cyning* which appears at the corresponding point in CCCC 173 and on the previous page of *Textus Roffensis* (15v11). On the verso of the leaf (**Plate 13.5**), the text of several lines encroaches further than usual into the right margin, while the number *twam* in line 18 is written out as a word but abbreviated, as is the following word *pundum*, which is also written below the line. In light of this, it seems possible that the use of numerals on fol. 16 is explicable as part of a deliberate attempt to economize on space in order to dovetail with the text already written on the next leaf.

As regards the source for the original version of the Alfred/Ine *domboc* in *Textus Roffensis*, Wormald suggests that both this and the unique text of the seventh-century Kentish laws on fols. 1–6 might derive from a single manuscript produced at Rochester.[37] Some though not all aspects of the palaeographical evidence support such a hypothesis,[38] and it may be significant that the two sets of laws are united in a strong preference for numerals, averaging over 79% in both instances even with the rewritten *domboc* Preface. This is certainly consistent with the theory of a common exemplar.

There may indeed be even closer links between particular sections of the Kentish and Alfredian legislation. In ch. 49,9 of his Preface, Alfred claims to have drawn on Æthelberht's laws as well as on those of Offa of Mercia and Ine of Wessex:

---

the beginning of the *domboc* as in other manuscripts) nor to the text of Alfred, ch. 26 in any extant manuscript.

[37] Wormald, '*Laga Eadwardi*', 262.

[38] Hough, 'Palaeographical Evidence', 63.

Ic ða Ælfred cyning þás togædere gegaderode 7 awritan het, monege þara þe ure foregengan heoldon, ða ðe me licodon; 7 manege þara þe me ne licodon ic áwearp mid minra witena geðeahte, 7 on oðre wisan bebead to healdanne. Forðam ic ne dorste geðristlæcan þara minra awuht fela on gewrit settan, forðam me wæs uncuð, hwæt þæs ðam lician wolde ðe æfter ús wæren. Ac ða ðe ic gemette awðer oððe on Ines dæge, mines mæges, oððe on Offan Mercna cyninges oððe on Æþelbryhtes, þe ærest fulluhte onfeng on Angelcynne, þa ðe me ryhtoste ðuhton, ic þa heron gegaderode, 7 þa oðre forlét.[39]	Then I, King Alfred, gathered these together and ordered to be written many of those which our forefathers kept, which pleased me; and with the advice of my councillors I rejected many of those which did not please me, and ordered them to be kept in a different way. Therefore I did not dare presume to set in writing many at all of my own, because I did not know what would please those who should come after us. But those that I found either from the time of my kinsman Ine, or of Offa, king of the Mercians, or of Æthelberht, who first received baptism among the English, which seemed to me most just, I collected here, and omitted the others.

The extent to which this genuinely reflects Alfred's methodology as opposed to the image he wished to present of himself as legislative heir to the three earlier law-givers is debatable, but it is generally considered likely that the personal injury tariff comprising chs. 44–77 of his laws was inspired by the corresponding section of Æthelberht's code (chs. 33–72). This may have a bearing on the representation of the numbers. As can be seen from **Tables 13.1–10**, the only extant copy of Æthelberht's laws contains a higher proportion of numerals to words than any other legal text containing enough data to be statistically significant. Both CCCC 173 and *Textus Roffensis* already show a marked preference for numerals over words throughout the Alfred/Ine *domboc*. CCCC 173 uses numerals for 72.8% of occurrences within Alfred's laws and for 73.6% within the composite *domboc*, while the corresponding figures for *Textus Roffensis* are 84% and 79.4%. But within this particular section, the figures rise to 93.4% and 96.7% respectively.[40] Even CCCC 383 has 14.8%, slightly higher than its average of 12.7% for Alfred's laws and of 11.3% for the composite *domboc*. In one manuscript, this might be coincidence. But for it to happen in three manuscripts, whose texts of the

[39] *Gesetze*, ed. Liebermann I, 46.

[40] These figures are not included within the tables, but have been calculated separately.

domboc are not closely related, may suggest an influence from the way Æthelberht's laws were represented graphically, strengthening the hypothesis that this section of Alfred's code was based on Æthelberht's.

This is of course to assume that the extant twelfth-century text of Æthelberht's code is close to the seventh-century original. Arguments to the contrary have been put forward;[41] but the retention of archaic graphs and spellings, combined with distinctively early Kentish forms, appears to offer reasonable support for such a view.[42] It remains unclear, however, whether the three Kentish codes were transmitted together from an early stage in their history, or separately up to the time when they were incorporated into *Textus Roffensis*. The weight of evidence suggests the former, but there are some contra-indications, raising the possibility that the second and third series may have been transmitted separately from the first.[43] It is therefore relevant to note that whereas the proportion of numerals to words is 94.5% in Æthelberht's code and 100% in that of Wihtred, the figure drops to 57.9% in the laws of Hlothhere and Eadric. This in itself suggests that at some point the second series was written down independently of the other two. Equally significant is the distribution of words and numerals within the second series itself. Written forms of numbers are not distributed evenly throughout the laws of Hlothhere and Eadric, but occur primarily within the first few clauses. Chs. 1–5 account for five of the eight written forms of numbers in this code, followed by eleven numerals in chs. 6–15, an isolated word in ch. 10 and two words in the final ch. 16. This may help to throw light on the circumstances under which the laws were promulgated. It is uncertain whether the legislation preserved in the joint names of Hlothhere and Eadric represents a collection of laws originally issued separately by each king, or a single code issued jointly. Evidence of a tradition of joint kingship in Kent has led to the latter being considered most likely.[44]

[41] Most recently by P. Lendinara, 'The Kentish Laws', *The Anglo-Saxons from the Migration Period to the Eighth Century: an Ethnographic Perspective*, ed. J. Hines (Woodbridge, 1997), pp. 211–30.

[42] This is briefly discussed in Hough, 'Palaeographical Evidence', 70–2, and will be demonstrated more fully in my forthcoming paper 'The Earliest English Texts? The Language of the Kentish Laws Reconsidered', *Textus Roffensis in Context. Law, Language, and Libraries in Early Medieval England*, ed. B. O'Brien and B. Bombi, Studies in the Early Middle Ages (York).

[43] Hough, 'Palaeographical Evidence', 72.

[44] C. Hough, 'Legal and Documentary Writings', *A Companion to Anglo-Saxon Literature*, ed. P. Pulsiano and E. Treharne (Oxford, 2001), pp. 170–87, at p. 173, reprinted in this volume.

The preamble is ambiguous on this point, but at least makes it clear that the aim was to supplement the existing laws of Æthelberht:

Hloþhære 7 Eadric Cantwara cyningas ecton þa ǽ, þa ðe heora aldoras ær geworhton, ðyssum domum þe hyr efter sægeþ.[45]	Hlothhere and Eadric, kings of the people of Kent, augmented the laws which their predecessors had made by these decrees, which are stated hereafter.

Unlike Æthelberht's legislation, then, the laws of Hlothhere and Eadric were not intended as a self-contained code. They may well have been issued piecemeal. The first four clauses have the closest link with the earlier laws, following on from where Æthelberht left off. As Wormald points out, chs. 1–4 not only take up the theme of the delinquent servant from the final section of Æthelberht's code, but also constitute balanced pairs which are differentiated syntactically from the following laws.[46] We can now see that they are also differentiated graphically, through the use of written forms of numbers rather than numerals. This may suggest that they originally circulated separately, only later being combined with other legislation to form what has become known as the second series of Kentish laws. It may even be possible to speculate that these were laws originally issued by Hlothhere, whether or not the remaining clauses were issued by Eadric alone or by the two kings together.[47]

We turn finally to the fire-damaged Cotton Otho B.xi, among whose contents are a version of the *Anglo-Saxon Chronicle* and the Alfred/Ine *domboc* copied by a single scribe during the early eleventh century. These are preceded by a copy of the Old English translation of Bede's *Historia ecclesiastica*, written in the mid tenth century by a scribe who also wrote part of the *Anglo-Saxon Chronicle* in CCCC 173. The Otho B.xi version of

[45] *Gesetze*, ed. Liebermann I, 9.
[46] P. Wormald, '"Inter cetera bona ... genti suae": Law-Making and Peace-Keeping in the Earliest English Kingdoms', *Settimana di Studio del Centro Italiano di Studi sull' alto Medioevo* 42 (1995), 963–96, at 975–6; reprinted in his *Legal Culture in the Early Medieval West*, pp. 179–99.
[47] By contrast, the first series of Kentish laws displays a strong uniformity of presentation, offering no support for perennial claims that the opening section of Æthelberht's laws represents a later addition. The so-called Æthelberht, ch. 1 is set out as seven separate clauses in the manuscript, and will be treated as such by L. Oliver, *The Beginnings of English Law* (Toronto, 2002), pp. 60–1. Each of the seven contains a single number written as a numeral, the standard mode of presentation throughout Æthelberht's code.

the *Chronicle* appears to have been copied directly from the Corpus manuscript,[48] but it is less certain whether the same applies to the *domboc*. In favour of such a hypothesis is the close similarity between the texts. Against it is the fact that a line omitted from the text of Alfred, ch. 1,2 in CCCC 173 is present in Otho B.xi. The matter has been much discussed. Dumville comments that 'On the evidence offered by Liebermann ... one would say firmly that the Alfredian lawcode in Otho B.xi could not be a copy of that in CCCC 173';[49] although Keynes and Lapidge offer the theory that 'the Otho scribe, or a later corrector, had access to another text of the code, now lost'.[50] Wormald considers it just possible that Otho B.xi 'descends from a very close relative of CCCC 173', but prefers the explanation that 'it was corrected to a limited extent after it was copied'.[51]

The readings of the *domboc* are in the main recoverable only from a transcript by Laurence Nowell preserved as BL, Additional MS 43703, fols. 236v–55, so that any palaeographical or codicological evidence has been lost. However, there is a reasonable possibility that the type of evidence discussed in this paper may have survived. Recent work on Nowell's transcription practice has established that although he does not always reproduce spellings or inflections accurately, and sometimes attempts to regularize the language, substantive changes are few. Through a comparison of the transcript of *Historia ecclesiastica* with the undamaged sections of Otho B.xi, Raymond Grant demonstrates that:

> Nowell's transcript of the Bede is of no use to the student of spellings, phonology or inflections and no dialect indications can be drawn from it. ... Yet we can reflect that very few words are omitted, homoeoteleuta are very rare and changes of word-order are few. The transcript can therefore be used as evidence for the contents and word-order of [Otho B.xi] ... It can

[48] Ker (*Catalogue*, p. 231) describes the Otho B.xi text with caution as 'a chronicle closely related to and probably copied directly from the Parker chronicle' More recently, however, Keynes and Lapidge comment that 'its [Otho B.xi] text of the *Anglo-Saxon Chronicle* was certainly derived ... directly from this manuscript [CCCC 173]' (S. Keynes and M. Lapidge, *Alfred the Great: Asser's* Life of King Alfred *and Other Contemporary Sources* (London, 1983), p. 306), and Dumville is able to refer to 'universal agreement that the G-text [Otho B.xi] is a copy of A [CCCC 173]' (*Wessex and England from Alfred to Edgar*, p. 57).

[49] Dumville, *Wessex and England from Alfred to Edgar*, p. 57.

[50] Keynes and Lapidge, *Alfred the Great*, p. 306.

[51] P. Wormald, 'BL, Cotton MS Otho B.xi: A Supplementary Note', *The Defence of Wessex: The Burghal Hidage and Anglo-Saxon Fortifications*, ed. D. Hill and A. R. Rumble (Manchester, 1996), pp. 59–68, at p. 60; reprinted in Wormald, *Legal Culture in the Early Medieval West*, pp. 71–80.

> be safely assumed that Nowell brought a similar attitude to bear on the other texts he copied.[52]

Of particular relevance to the present discussion is the fact that although Nowell does not always retain the same numbers as Otho B.xi, he seems not to change the actual form of presentation. Among instances of confusion cited by Grant are the substitution of *hundtweontig* for *hundteontig*, while deliberate changes include *hundtwentig* for *hundtwelftig* and *feower 7 twentig* for *feower 7 þritig*.[53] Crucially, the graphic representation is retained even where the numerical value has been altered, and it therefore seems likely that the distribution of numerals and written forms in Nowell's transcript will reflect that of Otho B.xi.

We can see from **Table 13.1** that the composite *domboc* contains 276 numbers, of which eight appear in the rubrics, twelve in the Preface, 147 in the laws of Alfred, and 109 in the laws of Ine. In CCCC 173, 203 of the total are represented as numerals, and seventy-three as words. The question is how closely these correlate with the distribution in Otho B.xi. Of the eight numbers in the Alfred/Ine rubrics, four are presented as numerals in CCCC 173 and four as words. Nowell makes the same choices in five out of the eight instances, retaining all the words and one of the numerals, but changing three numerals to words. Of the twelve numbers in Alfred's Preface, four are presented as numerals in CCCC 173 and eight as words. Nowell makes the same choices in every instance. Of the 147 numbers in the laws of Alfred, 107 are presented as numerals in CCCC 173 and 40 as words. Nowell makes the same choices in 139 out of the 147 instances, retaining all the words and ninety-nine of the numerals, but changing eight numerals to words. Of the 109 numbers in the laws of Ine, eighty-eight are presented as numerals in CCCC 173 and twenty-one as words. Nowell makes the same choices in 104 out of the 109 instances, retaining all the words and eighty-three of the numerals, but changing five numerals to words. A consistent pattern thus emerges, whereby either Nowell or the Otho B.xi scribe occasionally expands numerals to words, but never abbreviates words to numerals. Overall,

---

52 R. J. S. Grant, 'Laurence Nowell's Transcript of BM Cotton Otho B.xi', *Anglo-Saxon England* 3 (1974), 111–24, at 124.

53 Grant, 'Laurence Nowell's Transcript of BM Cotton Otho B.xi', 122–3. With regard to the substitution of *hundtweontig* for *hundteontig*, Grant comments: 'Obviously Nowell is unhappy about derivatives of *teon*, such as *hundteontig* used in C [Otho B.xi] to emphasize that 100 is meant and not the "long hundred" of 120 which Nowell substitutes'.

the correlation with CCCC 173 is strikingly close, with 260 out of 276 numbers being presented in the same way in both copies.

The significance of this should of course not be over-stated. It has long been recognized that if the exemplar of Otho B.xi was not CCCC 173, it was a close relative of it. But the evidence presented here is at least strongly consistent with the hypothesis that Otho B.xi was a copy of CCCC 173.

In conclusion, the graphic representation of numbers in both pre- and post-Conquest manuscripts preserves important evidence relating to the transmission and structure of the texts. Although most obviously applicable to the legal corpus because of the high incidence of numbers within this type of text, the methods of investigation outlined in this paper might usefully be extended to other manuscripts whose contents include numerical data.

Tables

Table 13.1 – Numbers in Cambridge, Corpus Christi College 173, fols. 33–52 (s. x med.)

Text	Numerals	Words	% Numerals	% Words
Alfred/Ine rubrics	4	4	50%	50%
Alfred Preface	4	8	33.3%	66.7%
Alfred laws	107	40	72.8%	27.2%
Ine laws	88	21	80.7%	19.3%
Alfred/Ine *domboc* total	203	73	73.6%	26.4%

Table 13.2 – Numbers in London, British Library, Cotton Nero A.i (B) (s. xi in.)

Text	Numerals	Words	% Numerals	% Words
I Æthelstan	0	0	—	—
I Edmund	0	0	—	—
III Edgar (incomplete)	1	2	33.3%	66.7%
V Æthelred	5	2	71.4%	28.6%
Grið	7	3	70%	30%
VIII Æthelred (incomplete)	3	1	75%	25%
V Æthelred	5	2	71.4%	28.6%

Table 13.3 – Numbers in London, British Library, Cotton Nero A.i (A) (s. xi med.)

Text	Numerals	Words	% Numerals	% Words
I Cnut	16	10	61.5%	38.5%
II Cnut	48	24	66.7%	33.3%
II Edgar	1	4	20%	80%
III Edgar	0	3	0%	100%
Alfred/Ine rubrics	5	3	62.5%	37.5%
Romscot	1	1	50%	50%
Iudex	0	0	—	—
Alfred Preface	5	7	41.7%	58.3%

Table 13.4 – Numbers in Cambridge, Corpus Christi College 201 (s. xi med.)

Text	Numerals	Words	% Numerals	% Words
VIIa Æthelred	2	4	33.3%	66.7%
Law Northumbrian Priests	46	3	93.9%	6.1%
II Edgar	1	5	16.7%	83.3%
III Edgar	3	2	60%	40%
V Æthelred	3	3	50%	50%
I Æthelstan	0	0	—	—
VIII Æthelred	6	10	37.5%	62.5%
I Edmund	0	0	—	—
Geþyncðo	2	0	100%	0%
Norðleoda Laga	12	4	75%	25%
Mircna Laga	3	3	50%	50%
Að	1	5	16.7%	83.3%
Hadbot	5	7	41.7%	58.3%
I Cnut (incomplete)	0	1	0%	100%
II Cnut (incomplete)	4	0	100%	0%
VI Æthelred (incomplete)	4	0	100%	0%

Table 13.5 – Numbers in London, British Library, Harley 55 (A) (s. xi[1])

Text	Numerals	Words	% Numerals	% Words
II Edgar	2	4	33.3%	66.7%
III Edgar	2	3	40%	60%

Table 13.6 – Numbers in London, British Library, Harley 55 (B) (s. xii med.)

Text	Numerals	Words	% Numerals	% Words
I Cnut	2	19	9.5%	90.5%
II Cnut	14	56	20%	80%

Table 13.7 – Numbers in Cambridge, Corpus Christi College 383 (s. xi/xii)

Text	Numerals	Words	% Numerals	% Words
Be Blaserum	0	2	0%	100%
Forfang	0	3	0%	100%
I Edgar	3	6	33.3%	66.7%
I Æthelred	0	10	0%	100%
Alfred and Guthrum	5	0	100%	0%
Edward and Guthrum	3	5	37.5%	62.5%
II Æthelstan (incomplete)	0	8	0%	100%
Alfred laws (incomplete)	18	124	12.7%	87.3%
Ine laws	11	104	9.6%	90.4%
Alfred/Ine *domboc* total	29	228	11.3%	88.7%
I Cnut (incomplete)	1	3	25%	75%
II Cnut	28	46	37.8%	62.2%
I Edward	3	0	100%	0%
II Edward	3	1	75%	25%
I Edmund	0	0	—	—
II Edmund	3	1	75%	25%
Swerian	0	0	—	—
Alfred and Guthrum	3	0	100%	0%
Be Wifmannes Beweddunge	0	0	—	—
Wergeld	8	7	53.3%	46.7%
Hit Becwæð	0	0	—	—
II Æthelred	7	3	70%	30%
Dunsæte	13	1	92.9%	7.1%
Rectitudines	38	11	77.6%	22.4%
Gerefa	0	0	—	—

Table 13.8 – Numbers in Medway Archive and Local Studies Centre, MS DRc/R1 (*Textus Roffensis*) (1123 x 1124)

Text	Numerals	Words	% Numerals	% Words
Æthelberht	104	6	94.5%	5.5%
Hlothhere/Eadric	11	8	57.9%	42.1%
Wihtred	9	0	100%	0%
Kentish laws total	124	14	89.9%	10.1%
Hadbot	9	2	81.8%	18.2%
Alfred/Ine rubrics	5	4	55.6%	44.4%
Alfred Preface	0	12	0%	100%
Alfred laws	126	24	84%	16%
Ine laws	92	18	83.6%	16.4%
Alfred/Ine *domboc* total	223	58	79.4%	20.6%
Be Blaserum	0	2	0%	100%
Forfang	0	1	0%	100%
Ordal	1	5	16.7%	83.3%
Walreaf	0	1	0%	100%
II Æthelstan	40	10	80%	20%
V Æthelstan	1	1	50%	50%
IV Æthelstan (fragment)	0	3	0%	100%
Pax	6	1	85.7%	14.3%
Swerian	0	0	—	—
Að	2	4	33.3%	66.7%
Mircna Laga	4	2	66.7%	33.3%
Edward & Guthrum	2	6	25%	75%
Wergeld	7	8	46.7%	53.3%
I Edward	3	0	100%	0%
II Edward	3	1	75%	25%
I Edmund	0	0	—	—
II Edmund	3	1	75%	25%
I Æthelred	1	9	10%	90%
William I, On Exculpation	1	1	50%	50%
III Æthelred	24	9	72.7%	27.3%
VI Æthelstan	26	7	78.8%	21.2%
Geþyncðo	0	2	0%	100%
Norðleoda Laga	13	2	86.7%	13.3%
Be Wifmannes Beweddunge	0	0	—	—
Becwæð	0	0	—	—

Table 13.9 – Numbers in London, British Library, Cotton Nero E.i, fols. 185–6 (s. x/xi)

Text	Numerals	Words	% Numerals	% Words
IV Edgar	2	4	33.3%	66.7%

Table 13.10 – Numbers in Cambridge, Corpus Christi College 265 (s. xi med.)

Text	Numerals	Words	% Numerals	% Words
IV Edgar	3	3	50%	50%

INDEX